ESSENTIALS OF SPANISH CONTIGO

INSTRUCTOR'S EDITION

OSCAR OZETE
University of Southern Indiana

SERGIO D. GUILLÉN
Anderson College

HOLT, RINEHART AND WINSTON

New York   Chicago   San Francisco   Philadelphia
Montreal   Toronto   London   Sydney
Tokyo   Mexico City   Rio de Janeiro   Madrid

Publisher Nedah Abbott
Executive Editor Marilyn Pérez-Abreu
Developmental Editor Irwin Stern
Project Editor Paula Kmetz
Production Manager Lula Als
Art Director Renée Davis
Text Design Gayle Jaeger
Drawings Tom O'Sullivan
Picture Research Rona Tuccillo

Photo credits appear on page 323.

Library of Congress Cataloging-in-Publication Data

Ozete, Oscar.
    Contigo, essentials of Spanish.

    Includes index.
    1. Spanish language—Text-books for foreign speakers—
English.   2. Spanish language—Grammar—1950—
I. Guillén, Sergio D.   II. Title.
PC4129.E5092   1987   468.2'421   86—25775

ISBN 0-03-001829-3   Instructor's Edition
                    Student's Edition: 0—03—001828-5

Address correspondence to:
383 Madison Avenue
New York, NY 10017

CBS COLLEGE PUBLISHING
Holt, Rinehart and Winston
The Dryden Press
Saunders College Publishing

Preface

Contigo is a first-year college text that focuses on comprehension, communication and cultural understanding. While stressing the essentials, *Contigo* nonetheless covers fully the fundamentals. The text is thoroughly integrated — teaching the four skills — through structures and situations that facilitate rapid understanding and communication. Maximum practice with common functions of language is possible since low-frequency constructions appear primarily as recognition items only. As such, *Contigo* responds to the current foreign language trend that calls for an oral proficiency-based curriculum. In addition, a strong reading strand runs through the book. Relying on illustrations, pre-reading activities and similarities across languages, students quickly read and understand extended prose passages that progress from simple to complex cultural topics.

Organization

The *Primera parte* of *Contigo* contains six *Conversaciones diarias* that provide basic hearing, reading and speaking practice for successful communication from the outset. *Notas culturales* sections provide relevant cultural information. Pronunciation exercises concentrate on distinctive Spanish sounds.

The *Segunda parte* and *Tercera parte* of *Contigo* consist of fourteen *Lecciones* which gradually develop proficiency in the language. The lessons begin with short, real-life dialogues that engage students and help them attain an oral command of the content. Subsequent questions and adaptations encourage creative recombinations of the material introduced. The vocabulary from the lessons centers around a thematic unit, e.g., the airport, the hotel reception desk, the market, and so forth. *Lecciones* 7 and 14 consist of extended readings that introduce geographic, historical, and artistic information. The final section, *Otras consideraciones,* includes grammatical explanations and practice for those classes wishing to go beyond the essentials covered in the core of the text.

Grammatical explanations are succinct and represent contemporary usage. Emphasis is on the communicative function of the grammatical items. Salient grammatical features and expressions are reintroduced systematically to sharpen accuracy while at the same time engendering creative use of the language. Command forms and the use of the subjunctive after verbs denoting *wish* or *emotion* are introduced in the first half of the text. This allows students greater flexibility in communication, since it does not unduly delay their ability to state what they want done or to express how they feel about situations affecting them.

A variety of exercises has been incorporated in the lessons to enhance student participation both in asking for and supplying information. The exercises stress the practical and communicative function of language within the appropriate social setting. Most of these activities are designed to encourage group interaction so that communication is more lifelike and learners feel more at ease. Students advance from single answer questions to original use of the language through role playing, interviews, problem-solving situations, and paragraph writing.

Observaciones sections present cultural readings of a more utilitarian nature, providing the student with important social, political, and economic information. The lessons end with *Actividades,* a brief exercise or exercises, generally adapted from Spanish-language periodicals or realia. Four *Exámenes,* self-tests, provide a comprehensive review of previous lessons through exercises that emphasize the re-entry of vocabulary and structures in a varied format.

Supplementary Materials

Manual de ejercicios y Manual de laboratorio complements the main text. It provides further practice in listening, pronunciation, standard and functional exercises, dramatic reading of dialogues, and dictations. This *Instructor's Edition* provides suggestions for introducing and enriching the text material. Detailed plans for each lesson offer helpful hints for a wide range of teaching and learning styles. A comprehensive *Testing Program* contains quizzes and examinations which can be administered after individual lessons or groups of lessons.

Contents —Instructor's Edition

I. PLANNING THE COURSE

Contigo has been designed to cover successfully the essentials of Spanish in a one-year college-level course. Your plans will naturally vary depending on the number of class hours per week and on student background and motivation. Keep in mind that a well-planned course also provides time for cultural enrichment in class or in the Spanish club, e.g., films, slides, songs, food preparation, and presentations. Below are scheduling suggestions for the semester and quarter systems. Modify these to suit the special needs of your class.

SEMESTER SYSTEM

Week	1st Semester		Week	2nd Semester
1	Conversaciones diarias		1	6, 7*
2	Examen I		2	
3	Lección 1		3	8
4	2		4	
5			5	9
6			6	Examen III
7	3		7	10
8			8	
9	4		9	11
10	Examen II		10	
11			11	12
12			12	
13	5		13	13, 14*
14			14	Examen IV

*Lessons 7 and 14 are cultural reading selections that may be assigned separately during the course.

QUARTER SYSTEM

Week	1st Quarter		Week	2nd Quarter		Week	3rd Quarter
1	Conv. diarias		1			1	
2	Examen I		2	5		2	10
3	Lección 1		3			3	
4	2		4			4	11
5			5	6, 7*		5	
6	3		6			6	12
7			7	8		7	
8	4		8			8	13, 14*
9	Examen II		9	9		9	Examen IV
10			10	Examen III		10	

*Lessons 7 and 14 are cultural readings.

II. *AIMS AND METHODS*

A Neither the instructor nor the student should realistically expect fluency to have developed after one year of instruction, but *Contigo* and its supplementary materials can help achieve these goals:

1. Listening comprehension

Both the teacher and the student must assume a great deal of responsibility in this area. The sound system of the language is gradually and systematically presented in the book, and ample opportunities for practice are available through the exercises and, in particular, in the *Manual de laboratorio*. If abundant practice is provided, the student should be able to:

a. understand Spanish spoken at moderate to normal conversation speed.
b. understand short narratives dealing with everyday topics and/or special topics that have been studied in the text.
c. control the sound system of Spanish so that a smooth transition into the speaking and writing skills will occur.

2. Speaking

Conversations with other fluent speakers based on everyday situations treated in the text should be possible. Many exercises in the text encourage the student to speak Spanish. Again, the teacher and the student must take much responsibility for formal and informal speaking practice.

3. Reading

The students should be able to read materials of moderate difficulty based on general aspects of Hispanic culture, especially those based on materials covered in the dialogues, exercises, and readings.

4. Writing

The student should be able to write simple sentences correctly based on the topics treated in the text. Written exercises should follow oral practice. Numerous exercises require a moderate level of controlled creativity.

5. Cultural awareness

The student should acquire basic knowledge about the customs and contributions of the different racial and national groups that form the Hispanic world.

B Some *dos* and *don'ts* for teaching with *Contigo*

- Use Spanish as much as possible, especially for basic constructions.
- Speak clearly and normally. Avoid unnecessary repetitions.
- Use words and constructions within the range of the students' experience, but do not hesitate to challenge them to "guess sensibly."
- Use a variety of activities, letting the student know when one activity ends and another one begins.

- Don't use English where Spanish could be used.
- Don't speak so slowly that speech becomes unnatural. The student needs to understand Spanish spoken at normal speed.
- Don't overwhelm the students with language they have never heard. Raising your voice or repeating an item several times will not provide meaning.
- Don't stay too long on the same activity, but avoid the confusion that results from jumping unexpectedly from one thing to another.

- Keep a lively pace, especially during choral work.

- Use your imagination while planning and conducting the class. Yours should not be a solo act. Let students participate.
- Prepare and plan well.

- Be honest concerning your knowledge (especially in matters related to cultural patterns).

- Reward good performance with varied expressions: *muy bien, qué bien, magnífico, estupendo,* etc.
- Learn to ignore minor mistakes and/or how to correct them without crushing good efforts.
- Be sensitive and tactful during practice time. Separate *practice time* from *testing time.*
- When asking a question, address it to the entire class, pause, and *then* call on a student. This will, at least for a few moments, make everyone responsible for the answer.
- Be clear and consistent in your assignments.
- Tell students to skip lines in all translation assignments and in any others they find difficult.
- Test the speaking skills through speaking; for example, information questions with *qué, quién, a quién, dónde, cuándo,* etc.
- Be sure that testing of all the skills takes place during the course. Be sure that the performance in the skills is reflected in the final grade. Use the lab materials in your tests.
- Be positive in your general attitude toward your students. Enthusiasm creates enthusiasm.

- Don't create a circus atmosphere by trying to speak (or having the students speak) faster than normal.
- Don't be inflexible. Deviating from your plan(s) for purposeful activities can lead to a good experience for the class.
- Don't waste time because of a lack of planned activities.
- Don't invent knowledge to avoid showing that you don't know. A good answer tomorrow is better than something wrong today.
- Don't delay praise until responses are perfect. Avoid the constant "okay" reward.
- Don't highlight minor mistakes. This will increase the student's reluctance to participate.
- Don't embarrass students anytime, especially in front of peers.

- Don't ask questions as a form of reprimand.

- Don't wait until the last minute to make assignments.
- Don't write all the corrections to the student's errors. Use symbols such as *n* for noun, *g* for gender, and so on.
- Don't confuse dictations and listening comprehension with speaking.

- Don't use solely pencil-and-paper tests.

- Don't forget the Spanish saying: *Se agarran más moscas con miel que con vinagre.*

III. *GENERAL SUGGESTIONS FOR THE INDIVIDUAL SECTIONS OF THE LESSONS*

A   Diálogos

Dramatization is a fun and effective way to learn practical expressions. The dialogues should be read and acted out with natural intonation, gestures, and props. Suggestions:

- Model the dialogue for the students using figure sticks, personal belongings, and objects in the classroom.
- Practice the dialogue until students can repeat it reasonably well, using choral, small-group, and individual practice. Walk around and listen in order to help students with pronunciation and intonation.
- Provide the first word or two of a line and then have students complete the line.
- Change the words and order of the lines and ask students to make the corrections.
- Be careful about dialogue memorization. The ability to adapt, personalize, and ask and answer questions about its content is far more valuable than literal repetition.

B   Pronunciación

- Let everything you do in class develop pronunciation: dialogues, questions and answers, vocabulary practice, and so on.
- Encourage students to read portions of the reading texts aloud to each other.
- Do not make a big issue about pronouncing certain sounds like the *rr*. Keep practicing them both as listening and speaking exercises through choral and individual repetition. Use minimal pairs and vary the order of presentation; for example,

pero − perro	vara − barra
carro − caro	cerro − cero

- Check for listening comprehension. Give students handouts with sets of contrasting words. As you say the word, have students circle the corresponding written form; for example, as you say *dos*, they choose from *doce, tos, dos*. Include vowel contrasts such as *peso, paso, puso* and *cero, serio, ciro*.
- Remember that cognates are great friends for the rapid learning of vocabulary but can be real enemies of pronunciation. Correct the transferring of the English neutral vowel sound *uh* to Spanish.

C   Estructura y práctica

Whether you first have students read the grammar explanation at home and then introduce it in class or vice versa depends on the complexity of the material, the background of the students, and your teaching style. In our opinion, the study of grammar boils down to its practical function. Can the students manipulate the structures for speaking and writing purposes or not? As a consequence, the instructor should try to minimize talking *about* language and promote talking *in* the language. Suggested strategies:

- Use the overhead projector to save time and to avoid writing on the board with your back to the class.
- Write with chalk or markers of different colors to highlight major features. This is particularly helpful when teaching verb endings, stem changes, and noun and adjective agreement.

- Pace the presentation of complex structures, e.g., the irregular preterites. Divide explanation and practice into segments.
- Supplement pattern practice with free speaking, role playing, reading aloud, and brief translation exercises from the text, the *Cuaderno*, or those you prepare. Have students write the translations on the board before class begins. Now and then assign translations with a topic, e.g., description of a person, a home, or daily chores.

D Situaciones

Use the adaptation and situation exercises to promote role-playing activities and enliven language practice. Additional suggestions:

Introductory Lessons

1. Prepare role-playing activity cards (3″ × 5″). Each card should contain an occupation from the list in *Conversación diaria 5* or others you add. Next to the occupation, note an adjective to describe how the student is to act, e.g., *el profesor (distraído), la modelo de ropa (esnob), el atleta (chauvinista)*, etc. Below, include these instructions.

   - Strike up a conversation with the people in your group. Act according to the occupation and description on your card.
   - Tell your name, where you are from and what you do.
   - Ask this same information from those in your group.
   - Use a few exclamations such as:

¡caray!	¡caramba!	*wow!*
¡ajá!		*aha!*
¡qué va!		*really now!*

   Divide the class into groups of four or five students. Distribute the cards at random, one per student. Tell the group that they are passengers on a cruise ship and must get to know each other at their dinner table. As they meet, they should remember as much information about their fellow passengers as possible, following the instructions on the cards. After about fifteen minutes of socialization, the instructor calls on the various groups to recall the information requested and asks them about the other passengers' personalities.

2. Make activity cards based on the material taught so far. Assign the same card (problem) to groups of two or three students, asking them to expand on the instructions and to come up with reasonable solutions. Allow the students a few minutes to prepare their lines as you walk around, helping out with vocabulary they need. Afterwards, let each group act out the situation for the class. Consider giving the students this activity:

You, the parent(s), are worried about your child's school work.
You talk to the principal and discuss the following:

1. Miguelito doesn't like school.
2. He doesn't want to attend classes.
3. He doesn't study at home.
4. He wants to read and watch television.
5. He spends too many hours with the computer.
6. Ask the principal what you should do.

Intermediate Lessons
Activity cards with the situation below could be passed out.

You are at the reception desk of a hotel:

1. Ask for a room with a bath and air conditioning.
2. Say you want a room with an ocean view.
3. Ask if breakfast is included and what time it is served.
4. Say you plan to be here a week.
5. Ask how much the room costs.

E   Simulaciones

In the advanced lessons try a simulation activity. Here the students maintain their own
identities as they interact in an imaginary situation. Act out the story below using
figure drawings on the board to represent the characters and places. After telling the
story for the second time, divide the class into three or four groups. Ask each group as
a whole to rank the characters accordingly: *de más humanitario a menos humanitario.*
This will allow students to persuade and influence each other, while revealing their
own value system. The instructor could prod now and then with questions, e.g., *¿Qué
culpa tenía Inocencia (don Juan . . .)?* After ten to fifteen minutes of discussion, ask
each group to write its ranking on the board.

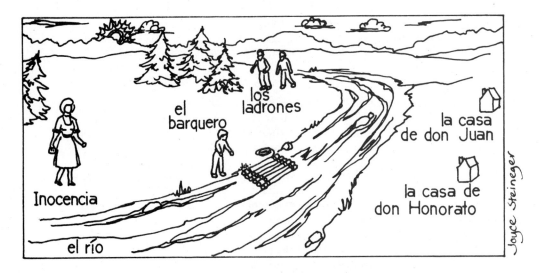

Inocencia quiere a don Juan. Está enamorada locamente de él. Don Honorato quiere
mucho a Inocencia. Un día Inocencia decide vivir con don Juan. Ella sale de casa, y
mientras camina por el bosque los ladrones le roban el dinero. Inocencia sigue cami-
nando hasta llegar al río. El barquero es un viejo *verde* y le dice a Inocencia: «Si
quieres cruzar el río en mi bote, tienes que darme la ropa pues tú no tienes dinero».
Inocencia quiere tanto a don Juan que ella le da la ropa al barquero. Por fin ella llega
a casa de don Juan. Ella vive con don Juan unos días. Él no desea casarse con ella. En
realidad don Juan nunca quería a Inocencia, y por eso le hace salir de su casa.
Inocencia no sabe qué hacer. Después de llorar mucho, recuerda que don Honorato la
quería a ella. Inocencia corre a la casa de don Honorato. Él ya no quiere a Inocencia
porque sabe que vivió con don Juan. El honor de don Honorato no permite aceptar a
Inocencia. Don Honorato le dice que se vaya, porque es mala mujer.

F   Lecturas

The text contains three types of reading selections: the *Notas culturales,* the *Observaciones*, and the longer, cultural passages that make up lessons 7 and 14. These two reading lessons need not be presented in the sequence of the book, but rather can be postponed or introduced earlier according to the objectives and background of the class. The instructor will have to determine, based on the time available and on personal discretion, how detailed the study of the various readings will be. Generally, the *Observaciones* have explicit suggestions at the beginning to help students interpret the content. You might also consider the following:

- Do the first few readings in class, assigning segments to be read aloud, checking for pronunciation and preliminary comprehension through yes/no and either/or questions.
- Anticipate difficult portions and provide cues to decipher them, e.g., synonyms, antonyms, and paraphrases.
- Recommend that students look up essential words only after the entire sentence or paragraph has been read once or twice.
- Ask brief *who, when,* and *where* questions when students read aloud, preferably excluding the person who just read the last segment.
- Use the readings to develop listening comprehension. Follow up with true/false statements, multiple-choice questions and short dictations.

G   Exámenes

The four *Exámenes* are intended to serve as reviews and self-evaluations of the material presented. Excluding the listening and speaking sections, students should take the *Exámenes* at home. Afterwards you may want to spot-check a few of the items in class. Depending on your class size, you may want to hold oral interviews in lieu of class time and office hours. Ask two or three advanced students from other classes to help with the interviews. Make sure the types of questions, activities, and grade-recording procedures are clearly understood. Let these two or three students observe you conduct the interview beforehand.

IV. *SPECIFIC PLANS FOR* CONVERSACIONES DIARIAS *1−6*

The purpose of the *Conversaciones diarias* is for students to gain control of the sound system of Spanish and to acquire confidence in speaking the language. After completing these introductory lessons, students will be able to speak, first, about themselves and their own immediate world (personal characteristics, likes, dislikes) and then about their families, friends, and other topics of personal interest. In addition, they will gain cultural insights related to the lessons presented.

Since most of the grammatical structures in these lessons will be covered later, the instructor should resist the temptation to teach more grammar than required. Moreover, these lessons need not be taught vertically nor page by page. The creative instructor should feel free to move across the lessons in a horizontal fashion. The days of the week can be taught earlier and one day at a time, e.g., *Hoy es lunes* on Monday, *Hoy es martes* on Tuesday, and so on. The same can be said about weather expressions, gestures, and other topics.

Conversación diaria 1 *LOS NOMBRES*

A   Presentación (approximately 10 minutes)

- Write on the board your name, office (building and room), telephone number, and office hours. Write elsewhere on the board: *¿Cómo se llama usted?* and *Me llamo . . .*
- Introduce yourself in Spanish. *Buenos días. Me llamo . . . y soy su profesor(a) de español.*
- Point to the question and answer on the board and pronounce these several times. Then start around the room asking each student's name. Try to provide Spanish names for the students and expand the practice to include *mucho gusto / el gusto es mío* as well as a firm handshake. Next, have students introduce each other.

B   Conversación (approximately 15 minutes)

- Write the five vowels on the board, giving students plenty of choral and individual practice. After a few repetitions, simply point to the vowels, asking for responses. You might try: *a, e, i, o, u el burro sabe más que tú.*
- Have students repeat in chorus a few of the cognates in the lesson. Go back and select adjectives for controlled conversation with *¿Es usted . . . ?* Start with two-form adjectives, then introduce gender agreement with the four-form adjectives.

C   Números (approximately 5 minutes)

Introduce the numbers 0−12. Use your thumb for *uno*, your thumb and index finger for *dos* and so on. Refer to your office and telephone numbers.

D   Acentuación (approximately 10 minutes)

Following the rules in the lesson, have these words on the board for choral and individual practice.

VOWELS (n, s)	CONSONANTS
ni-ño	es-pa-*ñol*
a-*mi*-gos	se-*ñor*

car-ta   pa-*pel*
es-*tu*-dian

Distribute a handout with familiar words and have students underline the stressed syllable as you pronounce each word. Pick two or three students to write their work on the board to serve for correction purposes.

E   Administrative Procedures (approximately 5 minutes)

Explain the ground rules such as attendance, grading system, homework, and so forth. Write assignments on a specific spot on the board each day, e.g.:

> *Para el miércoles ... de septiembre:*
> 1. Estudiar Conversación diaria 1.
>   (Tell them one of the objectives is for them to see what these new Spanish words look like.)
> 2. Escribir el diálogo con otros nombres.
> 3. Aprender de memoria tres de las expresiones útiles.
> 4. Practicar los números 0 − 12.

Teach students the expression *¿Cómo?* to indicate "I don't understand."

F   Repaso (approximately 5 minutes)

Try to end all lessons with a quick review of the key structures covered, e.g., *Buenos días* / *¿Cómo se llama?* / *¿Es Ud. ... ?* / *los números.*

Conversación diaria 2   LOS SALUDOS

A   Warm-up (approximately 5 minutes)
Review the patterns from the first lesson: *¿Cómo se llama ...? ¿Es usted* + adj.?
Introduce a few adjectives of nationality such as *inglés, norteamericano, español,* etc.
Amplify to include nouns: *estudiante, profesor, médico, secretaria, mecánico,* and so on.
Allow students to ask the questions.

B   Diálogo (approximately 10 minutes)

Use stick-figure drawings or your own hands (as puppets) to introduce the dialogue. Point to the figures and present them to the students; for example, *Se llama Yolanda. Yolanda es una señorita de Costa Rica.* Model the dialogue and follow up with choral and group practice. Vary the dialogue, using the *Expresiones* that appear below it. Next, personalize by asking students how they feel. Elicit brief adverb-adjective responses at this point for the question: *¿Cómo está Ud.?* — *Muy bien* / *Así, así* / *Regular* / *Más o menos* / *Un poco cansado(a),* etc.

C   La familia (approximately 15 minutes)

Draw and label a family tree on the board to represent Yolanda's immediate family. Play the role of Yolanda while you incorporate the narrative in the book, beginning with *Somos cuatro en mi familia ...* Personalize after each of the short paragraphs, e.g., *¿Cómo se llama Ud.?* Expand so students use their two surnames. Continue with *¿Cuántos son en su familia? ¿Cómo se llama su mamá? ¿Son Uds. de ... ?*

D   Pronunciación (approximately 5 minutes)

Provide choral and individual practice with *b/v, ll/y,* and *ñ.*

E   Números (approximately 5 minutes)

Introduce numbers 13–30, combining choral and individual recitation. Refer to *Situaciones* in this lesson.

F   Repaso (approximately 5 minutes)

Review quickly today's lesson and incorporate portions of yesterday's too, especially the *Expresiones útiles* assigned as homework. With the *Expresiones* use gestures to present and elicit responses.

G   Tarea

1. Estudiar Conversación diaria 2.
2. Preparar dos árboles genealógicos:
   a. el árbol de Yolanda
   b. el árbol de Ud. Incluir una descripción de los miembros de su familia: *Mi abuela es Anita. Es de Los Ángeles. Es magnífica.*
3. Practicar Conversaciones 1–3: *Manual de laboratorio.*

Conversación diaria 3   EL TIEMPO

A   Warm-up (approximately 5 minutes)

Let students talk to each other about their families, referring to the family tree prepared for today.

B   El tiempo (approximately 15 minutes)

Use drawings or transparencies of different weather scenes, including the months associated with each scene or season. Provide plenty of question/answer practice, teacher to student and later on students to students: *¿Hace calor? ¿Hace calor aquí en diciembre? ¿Hace frío aquí en febrero? ¿Llueve mucho en abril?* Introduce the dialogue for this lesson, allowing students to act it out. Afterwards personalize: *¿Hace mal tiempo hoy? ¿Llueve? ¿Nieva? ¿Tiene Ud. paraguas?*

C   La hora (approximately 15 minutes)

Use flash cards to review the numbers 0–30. Write on the board *¿Qué hora es? Es/Son . . .* To cue a wide variety of time combinations, you might draw a clock on the board, drawing in the minute hand (pointing at 12, then 6, then 3 and 9) and pointing or using your pencil to indicate the hour.

You may wish to read and interpret the *Nota cultural.* Remember that some people are very punctual regardless of their nationality. Point out that the Spanish clock *anda* (walks), while the American clock "runs."

D   Pronunciación (approximately 5 minutes)

Give special attention to *g* before *e/i.* Contrast: *gente/gu*erra   *Gilberto/Gu*illermo.

E   Números (approximately 10 minutes)

After introducing the numbers 31–99, have students give their own (or fictitious) telephone and room numbers, their social security and license plate (*la placa*) numbers. Include other situations such as temperature, distances, price tags, and so on.

F   Repaso (approximately 5 minutes)

G Tarea

Distribute a review sheet. Tell students that the format—not the content—will be the same for the quiz. Possible format for 100 points:

    I. Preguntas orales (5 × 5 = 25 points)
    (Students write out the answers after the instructor reads each question twice.)
       1. ¿Es usted estudiante?
       2. ¿Cuántos son en su familia?
       3. ¿Qué tiempo hace?
       4. ¿Qué hora es?
       5. ¿ ?

    II. Complete el diálogo (10 × 2 = 20 points)
    (Administer as a dictation or have students fill in the blanks from memory.)
    Clara: Buenas _____, Sr. Álvarez.
              ¿_____ _____ usted?
    Sr. A: Muy _____, _____. ¿Y _____?
    Clara: Un poco _____. ¿Y _____ familia?
    Sr. A: Todos _____, gracias. Adiós.
    Clara: Hasta _____, Sr. Álvarez.

    III. Las letras (10 × 1 = 10 points)
    Listen to the following words and fill in the blank space with the letter that represents the sound you hear.
       1. pe___o   5. a___o   8. fa___orito
       2. el ___anco   6. ca___es   9. ¿ ?
       3. pa___ión   7. ma___o   10. ¿ ?
       4. die___
    (peso, el banco, pasión, diez, año, calles, mayo, favorito)

    IV. Números (5 × 3 = 15 points)
    Write out the numbers in the price tags.
       1. $15 _____ dólares
       2. $129.99 _____ dólares y _____ centavos.

    V. La familia (20 points)
    Describe a male and female member of your family in three sentences.
    Modelo:
       1. Mi mamá es Laura Jones de Price.
       2. Es de . . .
       3. Es muy . . .

    VI. Traduzca Ud. (10 points)
       1. Open the door.
       2. Is it raining?
       3. It's five-thirty.

Conversación diaria 4 LOS MESES Y LAS ESTACIONES

A Warm-up (5 minutes)

Ask questions based on the review sheet. Let students ask each other questions as well.

B Repaso (5 minutes)

Spot check for problems with the review sheet.

C   El calendario (approximately 15 minutes)

Draw a calendar on the board for *se(p)tiembre* and write out the days of the week, starting with *lunes*. Fill in the first few numerals only. After providing choral practice with the day, ask *¿Qué día es hoy?* Have students reply in a sentence: *Hoy es viernes.* Expand to *¿Qué día es mañana? ¿Qué día es el 15?*, etc. Next, introduce the months and seasons. Ask *¿Cuáles son los meses de invierno?*, etc. Have students read aloud portions of the *Nota cultural.* Point out on a map the areas mentioned. Finally, write on the board: *Mi cumpleaños es el 5 de octubre* and then go on to individual practice of the expression.

D   Pronunciación (approximately 5 minutes)

E   Prueba (approximately 15 minutes)

F   Tarea
1. Estudiar Conversación diaria 4.
2. Escribir las respuestas para las prácticas:
   ¿A qué hora es . . . ? / ¿Hay . . . ?

Conversación diaria 5   *EL HORARIO*

A   Warm-up Review (approximately 10 minutes)

Return graded quizzes before class begins. Have students write on the board those items missed most frequently. Proceed to go over the quiz.

B   Horario (approximately 15 minutes)

Do choral and individual practice with the names of the subjects commonly taught in college. Refer to Antonio Rivera's schedule to provide questions and answers. Personalize the questions too: *¿Qué clases tiene Ud. los lunes?* and so on. *¿A qué hora es su clase de . . . ?* After asking a few students the same basic questions, allow them to ask each other the same information.

C   Me gusta(n) (approximately 10 minutes)

Start with singular nouns and verbs, e.g., *¿Le gusta la biología?* (*la historia, escribir, leer, hablar español*), etc. Next, bring in plural nouns: *¿Le gustan las matemáticas?* (*las lenguas, los deportes*).

D   Linking (approximately 5 minutes)

E   Spot-check (approximately 5 minutes)

Review orally and on the board selected items from today's assignment.

F   Tarea

1. Estudiar Conversación diaria 5 y preparar (escribir) las prácticas: fechas, alfabeto, los números 100−1000.
2. Practicar Conversaciones 4−6 en el *Manual de laboratorio.*

Conversación diaria 6   EN LA CLASE

A   Warm-up (approximately 5 minutes)

Review questions with time, calendar, and schedules.

B   Alfabeto (approximately 10 minutes)

Introduce and drill the alphabet with flash cards. Have students spell their last names.
Go over today's assignment.

C   En la clase (approximately 10 minutes)

Present the vocabulary, pointing to the various items in the classroom. After choral and
individual practice, point to items at random and ask *¿Qué es?* Now and then give the
wrong name to an item and have students correct you.

D   Colores (approximately 10 minutes)

Teach the colors by using construction paper of different colors, crayons, or even a
serape. Introduce: *Tengo el pelo . . . y los ojos . . .*

E   Números (approximately 10 minutes)

Review numbers 0–100, then introduce 100–1000. Bring currencies from different
Spanish-speaking countries to class. Tell students that an item may sell for several
hundred pesos in one country and for several thousand in another, depending on the
country's inflation.

Go over the *práctica* that deals with dates.

F   Tarea

    1. Estudiar Vocabulario: Conversaciones diarias 1–6.
    2. Tomar: Examen I

Administer a quiz on the material covered.

V. SPECIFIC SUGGESTIONS FOR LESSONS 1—14

The suggestions below, covering selected portions of the text, are merely guidelines for presenting and practicing the material. The instructor must decide, at times on a daily basis, on the teaching strategies that will work best with each class. We recommend an eclectic approach that will benefit the learning styles of as many students as possible. Good classes seldom happen by themselves. Consider these tips as you prepare your lessons:

- Plan a warm-up for each class.
- Prepare activities that provide maximum practice for the students.
- Arrange the activities so they flow from one to another, e.g., first review or present vocabulary you'll need for subsequent practice.
- Review previously taught material that relates to material about to be presented, e.g., go over subject pronouns prior to the introduction of object pronouns.
- Use realia and pictures to help avoid using English.
- Conduct good choral practices. Watch for "mumblers" who are really faking or not saying the proper sounds.
- Move from choral to individual responses.
- Provide listening practice through true/false statements, short dictations, and acting out commands.
- Avoid saying everything twice.

Lección 1: LAS OCUPACIONES

This section should serve as both review and introduction to -ar verbs. Encourage students to prepare brief narratives on people's occupations. Provide students with an information grid to guide them; for example,

Nombre	Estado civil	Ocupación	Lugar
Adela Campos	soltera	secretaria bilingüe	Laboratorios Balboa
Rubén Ortiz	casado	analista programador	Mexicana de Aviación
Gustavo Ponce	divorciado	cocinero	Restaurante Internacional

Narrative:
Adela Campos es soltera. Es secretaria bilingüe. Trabaja en los Laboratorios Balboa.

As additional practice, prepare a ditto or transparency that resembles a sample job application. Let students fill out the information and subsequently say the information without looking at the application.

Sustantivos y artículos

Some students will wonder why inanimate objects such as *silla* and *cuaderno* are feminine and masculine, respectively. Don't go into a lengthy explanation, but simply say this is a classification procedure many languages use. Proceed to write a few nouns on the board and elicit their corresponding definite article. Be sure to review nouns without obvious clues to their gender: *llave, clase, día, estudiante*, etc. You might compare: *el papá, la papa, el Papa.*

Dos Contracciones

Before practicing *¿Adónde va?* / *Voy . . .* teach several nouns of places. For example, put flash cards with pictures of a post office, restaurant, church, beach, and so forth, on the ledge of the board. Provide choral and individual repetition, then move on to the question/answer practice. Some commercially available flash cards may be useful. Expand the exercises to include days, time, months, and seasons. Time permitting, introduce *van* and *vamos*.

EXAMPLE: ¿Adónde va(n)?
                Student A: **Voy (vamos) al banco.**
                Student B: **Voy al banco el viernes.**
                Student C: **Voy al banco el viernes a las diez.**

To practice *del,* try: *Vengo del banco (la biblioteca, el correo,* etc.).

Subject Pronouns (*Yo, usted . . .*)

Many students need to be persuaded that subject pronouns need not be used in every sentence. *Yo* comes from the Greek *ego*. Excessive use of *yo* could give the impression of "egoism." Use subject pronouns for emphasis or contrast:

¡Yo necesito el dinero hoy!
Ella va al cine, yo no.

If you assigned Section III, *yo, usted* beforehand, have students summarize briefly in English the linguistic and social differences between *tú* and *usted* with corresponding plurals. Lay down ground rules for use in class. For a bit of historical trivia: *Usted* comes from *vuestra merced* "Your Grace". Nobility was not to be addressed directly, but rather indirectly through the third person form comparable to "Your Highness wishes, prefers . . . "

El presente de los verbos regulares -ar

Introduce analytically the present forms of -ar verbs, relying on what students already know and drawing comparisons with English. Use three columns to segment a verb on the board; for example, *trabaj-a-s* and *trabaj-a-mos*. Use pronouns and nouns as subjects of verbs at first.

      yo   trabaj o
      tú   trabaj a s
      él   trabaj a
  Irene   trabaj a

- Provide practice with other verbs as soon as possible, but be sure that students know the meaning of the verbs and of the sentences.
- Begin using negative forms and questions.
- Watch for excessive stress on verb endings, e.g., *llegó* instead of *llego*.
- Remember that "conjugating" a verb from *yo* to *ellos* is a grammatical accomplishment but not an end in itself. The real test of conjugating verbs comes when students can actually use the verb for communicating their ideas and understanding those of others.
- Allow students to ask each other questions as you lead them, e.g., *Pregúntele a _____ si trabaja los sábados. Contéstele que no trabaja . . .* Include information questions: *¿Dónde trabaja? ¿Qué días trabajas? ¿Cuántas horas . . . ? ¿Con quién . . .? ¿Dónde deseas trabajar?* In turn, let students ask you questions: *¿Qué día trabaja Ud?* Once in a while ask with the *yo* form: *¿Hablo rápido? ¿Necesito regresar mañana?*

Observaciones

This reading could also be used to promote the study of foreign languages as an adjunct skill to other fields of study. Newspapers from metropolitan areas often advertise for individuals with second-language skills.

Assign one or two paragraphs for oral practice at home. The next day, in groups of two or three, have students read the paragraphs aloud to each other while you go around checking pronunciation, linking, and intonation.

To enhance listening practice, have a native speaker record the passage in a cassette for students to duplicate and use at home.

Lección 2   EN EL AEROPUERTO

As an introduction to the dialogue, prepare flash cards to depict signs a traveler would encounter at the airport, e.g., *llegada, salida, cambio, equipaje,* etc. To supplement the dialogue, have students act out situations where they describe a missing item to an airline employee. Provide an information grid on a ditto as reference:

Objeto perdido	Tamaño	Color	Material	Nombre
una maleta	grande	azul	plástico	su nombre
una bolsa	pequeño(a)	marrón	cuero	sus iniciales
una cartera	mediano(a)	rojo(a)	tela	
un paquete			cartón	
una caja				

> EXAMPLE: Me falta una maleta pequeña. Es roja. Es de cuero. Lleva las iniciales J.M.

Las preguntas

Try a visual approach. Write the words of the question on separate strips of plastic and project them on the overhead projector. As you ask a question, arrange the words to reflect the structure and then do likewise when you answer the question. Proceed from the visual presentation to oral and then written practice.

Saber *y* conocer

These two verbs, in addition to their own communication value, offer excellent opportunities to use the personal *a (conocer)* and to review many other infinitives with *saber* in expressing the notion "to know how to" do something.

> EXAMPLES: Conozco a Cecilia.
> Ella sabe usar la computadora.

Observaciones

The setting for Julie Miller's letter is Bogotá, Colombia. This would be a good opportunity to show a film on Colombia and/or to acquaint the students with the country through maps and pictures. Consider inviting a guest speaker from that country. Students could prepare questions for the speaker in advance; for example: *¿De dónde es Ud? ¿Cuántas personas viven en Colombia? ¿Qué tiempo hace en . . . ? ¿Qué comen los colombianos? ¿Cuáles son los productos principales? ¿Juegan al béisbol? ¿Qué estudian en las escuelas?,* etc.

Lección 3   EN LA CLÍNICA

Before introducing the dialogue, teach the parts of the body. One day, draw a funny face on the board and label its parts. Students should repeat the labels in choral and individual practice. Afterwards, erase the labels and elicit the names as you point to various parts. The next day, follow the same procedure to present the other parts.

For fun, make big flash cards with Spanish words on one side and English on the other. Hold up one card at a time, varying the sides so that some words appear in Spanish and others in English. Form two or three teams of students. Each team takes a turn giving the correct translation (Spanish or English) for the word shown. If the answer is correct, the same student may try for a second point by using the word correctly in a sentence. The instructor should write a few appropriate verbs on the board beforehand, e.g., *ver, respirar, escribir,* etc. to cue answers such as *Veo con los ojos,* and so forth. On another occasion play a Spanish version of "Simple Simon says, touch . . . " / *Tonto Tony dice que se toque . . .*

To supplement the dialogue, have students name several ailments and the remedies they associate with them. Provide an information grid:

Enfermedad	Remedio
fiebre	vitamina C
catarro	té
dolor de cabeza	jugo
dolor de estómago	un refresco
gases	aspirinas
tos	Alka-Seltzer
. . .	. . .

EXAMPLE: Cuando tengo dolor de cabeza tomo dos aspirinas.

Los adjetivos

Introduce formally the concept of two-form (grande) and four-form (nuevo) adjectives. Write a list of adjectives (masculine, singular) on the board. Include adjectives of nationality. Drill with adjectives in predicate position after *ser.* That is, you provide a series of noun subjects (*el periódico, la revista, Cristina,* etc.) and students create the sentences, e.g., *La revista es vieja (francesa . . .).* Next, introduce the concept of n + adj, showing how adjectives follow when they distinguish or have contrasting functions. You can repeat the preceding exercise with the constructions *Tengo un(a) . . ., Necesito . . . , Me gusta el(la) . . .*

Ser y estar

Review *ser* expressions, expanding to include *eres/son: ¿De dónde eres (son)? ¿Eres norteamericano(a)? ¿Son Uds. estudiantes, turistas, vendedores . . . ? ¿De qué color es (son) . . . ? ¿De quién es . . . ? ¿Qué día es hoy?* Next, ask *¿Cómo está(s)?* and proceed to write the replies on the board: *Estoy bien, mal, cansado(a),* etc. Expand the questions to include *¿Cómo está ella (Rosa)? ¿Cómo están Uds.?*
Write two pairs of sentences on the board and contrast *ser* and *estar* with regard to adjectives (adverbs).

| Luis es amable. | (What he is *like)* |
| Luis está bien. | (How he *feels*) |

Mercedes está cansada.
Mercedes es morena.   (Ask student to explain the difference.)

Practice by pointing to one student and then asking another the pair of questions: *¿Cómo está Pablo, bien o mal?* / *¿Cómo es Pablo, simpático or antipático?* Repeat the procedure with other students, changing the adjectives now and then. Point out other sentences which are useful for teaching the *ser/estar* contrasts; for example,

Pedro es gordo. / Pedro está gordo.
Los gauchos son de la Argentina. / Están en Nueva York.

Lección 4   DE COMPRAS

This dialogue has several new vocabulary items. Use transparencies, visuals, props, native dolls, and advertisements to present the vocabulary. Experiment a little: have a fashion show and encourage students to wear Hispanic clothes. Four or five students could serve as masters of ceremonies. They should mention the garment, the color, the material, and two appropriate adjectives.

Verbos con el cambio radical: e → ie, o → ue
Taking *cerrar* or *empezar* as the point of departure, begin writing the conjugation on the board. Elicit student participation for the person/number endings: *-s, -mos, -n.* Point out that in certain verb stems the vowel *e* alternates with *ie.* The *ie* occurs when the stem is stressed, the *e* when it is not.

Follow up with drills and questions, gradually introducing other stem-changing verbs. Since students need to memorize which verbs are stem-changing, a recommended practice is to have them memorize the infinitive plus the first person, e.g., *cerrar/cierro.*

Los pronombres reflexivos
Begin with the pattern students know already: *¿Cómo se llama Ud. (él, ella)? ¿Cómo te llamas?* Introduce new reflexive verbs in personalized contexts: *¿A qué hora te levantas? ¿Dónde te sientas, aquí o allí?* . . . Have students prepare ten sentences for extended discourse where they describe their daily routine, beginning with *Me levanto a las . . .* and ending with *Me acuesto a las . . .*

Lección 5   EN EL HOTEL

There are clean and efficient hotels all over Spain, rated by stars. A four-star hotel is generally luxurious but expensive; two-star is generally comfortable but without frills, that is, neither soap nor washcloths are provided, and rooms probably don't have private baths. Also, the room key must be left at the front desk. Many hotels include a continental breakfast (rolls and hot chocolate or coffee) in the price of the room.

Notice in the dialogue that Armando and Ernesto say to the clerk, *Quisiéramos una habitación . . .* The form *queremos* may convey the notion of command and even arrogance, when requesting a service. Conversely, *(yo) quisiera* and *quisiéramos* denote courtesy and are standard forms for requesting services. Review such expressions as: *por favor, muchas gracias, con mucho gusto,* and *con permiso.*

Los adjetivos posesivos
Begin by pointing to one student, then asking another, *¿Es su hermano?* Try to elicit the reply, *No, no es mi hermano.* Call for multiple choral repetitions of the answer. Now ask individual students, changing the nouns, e.g., *tía, papá, amigo, prima,* etc. Point to two students and ask a third *¿Son sus padres?* Elicit *No, no son mis padres* and

follow up with practice using other plural nouns. Introduce the models *¿Es tu papá?
No, no es mi papá.* Compare the *Ud./su papá* and *tú/tu papá* pattern. Provide multiple choral repetitions with the *tu(s)/mi(s)* pattern. Supply a series of nouns and let students ask and answer the questions.

Mention that possession is never expressed with *'s* in Spanish. Note the patterns:

1. n + *de* + n (proper) el amigo de Julia (Julia's friend)
2. n + *de* + def art + n el libro del profesor (the professor's book)

Practice intensively the exchange *¿De quién es (el libro)? (El libro) es de ...* Have several nouns (of persons) on the board: *Roberto, la profesora, los estudiantes,* etc.; then provide students with a noun like *libro* and have them form sentences such as *El libro es de ...,* choosing one of the nouns on the board. Later, personalize with items belonging to the students, e.g., *¿De quién es el lápiz?* Do not accept *Es de mí,* but rather reinforce *Es mío* or *Es mi lápiz.*

Try the exercise below to avoid the transfer of the *'s* (possession) to Spanish. Use familiar vocabulary.

INSTRUCTOR	STUDENT A	STUDENT B
Gloria's paper	su papel	el papel de Gloria
Gloria's papers	sus papeles	los papeles de Gloria
the professor's books	sus libros	los libros del profesor

Expresiones con tener
Point out that English uses adjectives with such expressions as *I'm hungry/thirsty/ sleepy.* By contrast, Spanish and several other languages use nouns. Write this comparison on the board.

I'm very sleepy. Tengo much*o* sueñ*o*.
  adv → adj   adj → n

Use gestures and visuals to add realism to the exercises.

Actividades
1. Present a slide show that depicts architecture in Spain throughout the ages.
2. Distribute ditto copies of the Iberian peninsula. Have students fill in the main cities, rivers, and mountains.

Lección 6 EN LA AGENCIA DE TURISMO
You or your students should bring to class pictures of the famous landmarks of Mexico City. Note that Mexico City is 7,240 feet above sea level and that 18 million people live there. Chapultepec is a Nahuatl word meaning "grasshopper hill."

Los mandatos formales
After explaining how commands are formed, lead the students to practice them. Begin with very familiar verbs and when possible, have students perform the actions: *Abra la puerta/Cierren el libro/Salude a Ramona/Déme el papel/Levántese/Venga acá/Siéntense,* etc.

El subjuntivo

You may want to write these two sentences on the board to contrast the indicative and subjunctive modes:

> Mother insists that he sleeps 8 hours. Indicative (facts/reporting)
> Mother insists that he sleep 8 hours. Subjunctive (indirect command)

Cite other examples of the subjunctive in English; for example, "God bless America," "God save the Queen," "It's important that he go," "We demand that she pay." During the practice sessions, contrast the use of the infinitive with the subjunctive; for example, *¿Qué quieres leer? / ¿Qué quieres que él lea? ¿Es preciso pagar ahora? / ¿Es preciso que (yo) pague ahora?* Translation exercises like these are helpful:

I. Escoja la repuesta que mejor traduzca la oración.
  1. I prefer to rest a little.
      a. Prefiero que descanse un poco.
      b. Prefiero descansar un poco.
  2. They want me to clean the room.
      a. Quieren limpiarme la habitación.
      b. Quieren que yo limpie la habitación.
  3. He hopes she has a good time.
      a. Espera que se divierta.
      b. Espera divertirse.
II. Traduzca al español.
  1. a. I want to eat here.
      b. I want them to eat here.
  2. a. We prefer to sit there.
      b. We prefer that you sit there.

Observaciones

When speaking about the major cities of the Hispanic world, point out both their advantages and disadvantages. Explain the term *herencia cultural indoespañola.* Remember that it will be difficult for the students to speak about cities they have never seen. Try to present pictures, slides, or films in which cities are highlighted.

Assign one of the *Temas* under section *C* as homework over the next two class periods. This should allow time for you to help students with their writing. If you choose to work with *Mi ciudad,* have students describe their hometown:

- In the first paragraph they could begin by writing:
  Soy de ... Es muy bonita y ...
  En la calle (plaza) mayor hay ... El correo está en la calle ...
  La tienda ... Tenemos ... Tambien tenemos ...
- In the second paragraph they could describe the town's main festivals:
  En julio celebramos ... Hay carreras (*races*), regatas ... La gente ...
- In the third paragraph students could invite the reader to visit the town and give directions on how to get there from the university.

On the following days, have one or two students write their composition on the blackboard before class begins. In lieu of this, the instructor may want to put a couple of the compositions on a ditto or overhead projector for correction and amplification of sentences. Let students make the corrections wherever feasible. Also, as warm-ups, let different pairs of students talk to each other about their town as you walk from group to group to help out with vocabulary, grammar, and pronunciation. Finally, you may want to incorporate the composition topic as a section of a quiz taken in class or request that the final, typed version be turned in for a separate grade.

Actividades

Point out, if need be, that *ojalá* means "I hope" (may Allah grant) and that the expression is not conjugated, as is the verb *esperar*. *Ojalá* always takes the subjunctive.

Espero que ellos vayan. ⎫
Ojalá que ellos vayan. ⎬ Comparable

Espero ir. *but not* Ojalá ir.

You may want to mention other words of Arabic origin, e.g., *cero, álgebra, algodón, alcohol, almohada, alcázar.*

Lección 7 PANORAMA HISTÓRICO DE LATINOAMÉRICA

You may want to introduce this reading in the order of the lessons, postpone it until after formal presentation of the past tenses, or simply make it optional. If you choose the first option, you might consider the following:

1. Give a *brief* overview of the preterite and imperfect. At this point you simply want students to recognize the verb forms. Go over *¿Comprende Ud?* (part a) before starting the reading.
2. Ask a few general questions to ascertain how much students know about Latin American history as well as to arouse curiosity.
3. Read aloud the first couple of paragraphs, listing on the board historically related information; for example, *en 1519, los aztecas, la región central de México,* etc.
4. Assign the remaining paragraphs to groups of students. For example, they should prepare a list of terms they consider important and then summarize the main ideas.
5. Have students point out on a wall map the location of the regions studied.

Lección 8 LAS VENTAS INTERNACIONALES

You may want to mention a few cultural aspects in connection with the dialogue; namely:

1. American salesmen generally would not be as well versed in Spanish as David Johnson.
2. Salespersons are used to waiting, but more so in Latin America.
3. Early-morning business calls and meetings are discouraged.
4. Dinner engagements may be best suited for social amenities and not explicit business discussions.
5. Completion of a big sale may hinge upon special discounts or favors bestowed directly on the purchasing agent. These favors (bribes, in the United States) are expected and not considered offensive.

El pretérito de los verbos regulares y de cambios radicales

Tell students that in the next few days they'll be practicing verb forms that will enable them to talk about the past, to recall things that happened earlier. In essence, they'll be answering questions such as: "What did you do yesterday (last night, last Saturday, last month)?" "What happened this morning?" In your presentation use three columns to segment the verbs. Indicate that there are no stem-changing -*ar* and -*er* verbs in the preterite. Point out that the third column has not changed, except for the second person. What students need to focus their attention on is the middle column. Provide choral and individual practice to distinguish between preterite and subjunctive, that is, *Estudié / ¡Estudie Ud.! Pagué / ¡Pague Ud.!*

Review the spelling changes reflected earlier in the present subjunctive:

1. Verbs whose stems end in the letter *g* need the letter *u* before the first person preterite ending in order to keep the sound [g]: *jugué, llegué.*
2. Verbs whose stems end in the letter *c* replace the *c* with *qu* before the first person preterite ending in order to retain the sound [k]: *busqué, practiqué.*
3. Verbs whose stem ends in *z* replace *z* with *c* before the first person preterite ending: *empecé, crucé.*

regres	é	
pens	a	ste
1. jug	ó	
2. busc	a	mos
3. empez	a	steis
	aro	n

Segment *-er/-ir* verbs similarly: *com-i-ste, com-i-mos, com-iero-n.*

Dictation exercises help reinforce these changes. For example,

1. No jugué al básquetbol.	*5.* Llegué temprano.
2. Sí, pagué la cuenta.	*6.* Empecé a jugar.
3. Toqué la guitarra.	*7.* No crucen la calle.
4. Llegaron tarde del parque.	*8.* Quiero que Ud. juegue.

To facilitate manipulation with the preterite in normal context, include adverbial phrases of time in the practice, e.g.,

ayer, anteayer, anoche, esta mañana
el mes (año, domingo, etc.) pasado
la semana pasada

In connection with *comer* you may want to teach the names of a few foods to elicit answers besides *tacos* and *hamburguesas.* Look ahead to Lessons 9 and 10 for food vocabulary. With *leer* have several props to refer to, such as *el periódico, la revista, la carta, la tarjeta, el libro de ...* As for *divertirse*, ask students for places where a person can have fun, and then have them ask you: *¿Se divirtió Ud. en el cine, la fiesta, la reunión, la playa, en la clase de ... ?*

As warm-ups for the next couple of days, have a list of infinitives on the board, beginning with *-ar* the first day and *-er/-ir* the next. Group students in threes. Have student 1 in each group tell what he/she did yesterday, referring to the list on the board. In turn, let number 2 paraphrase what he/she heard to number 3. Students should rotate in telling what they did and paraphrasing what they heard. You might include transitional words on the board for students to incorporate in their talk, e.g.; *primero, luego, después, más tarde, entonces,* etc.

Los adjetivos y pronombres demostrativos

Place several familiar props on your desk. Ask a student to stand next to the desk and another a couple of steps away. Start with masculine singular nouns (props) and have student pick up the prop and say: *¿Quieres este bolígrafo?* Student 2 then answers, *Sí, (No, no) quiero ese bolígrafo.* Proceed in the same fashion as you introduce the other demonstratives.

Comparaciones

Comparisons can be taught without much need for translation. Refer to pictures or stick figures and say:

> Elena es más alta que Luisa.
> Aquí hay menos hombres que mujeres.

Consult a wall map and say:

> Ecuador es menos grande que Perú.
> Perú es más montañoso que Uruguay.
> El río Amazonas es más largo que el Orinoco.
> El río Amazonas es el río más largo de Sudamérica.

For comparisons with numbers requiring *de,* ask students to count the money they have on them and round off the amount to the nearest dollar. Then try to guess the amount for a couple of students following this pattern:

> Instructor: ¿Tienes dos dólares?
> Student: Tengo más de dos dólares.
> Instructor: ¿Tienes cinco dólares?
> Student: Tengo menos de cinco.

Continue until you guess the amount. Next, have students in groups of two practice the same pattern with each other.

Observaciones

This short essay has a triple purpose. The first one is to give the instructor and the class an opportunity to discuss the value and validity of language study. The concept of *value* is practical and useful and will appeal to those students who see education in terms of its almost immediate value. *Validity* is a more idealistic concept and is more related to the ideal of *liberal arts* and to the future than to immediate usefulness. The instructor should be ready to explain (and sometimes defend) both aspects of language study.

The second purpose of the essay is to increase recognition of the imperfect tense. More in-depth study of this tense will take place in Lesson 9. For now, let's give students the chance to observe how this tense is used. At this point, simply note the *continued* or *unfinished* nature of these events or situations mentioned in the essay:

> Los japoneses creían ...
> ... los productos ... eran ...
> ... nosotros insistíamos ...
> ... no vivían pendientes ...
> ... las personas conversaban más ...

A third purpose of this essay could be to point out to students the importance of cultural patterns or habits and how intimately they are related to the language. Highly recommended for background purposes are *Culture Capsules — Mexico* and *Culture Capsules — USA — Hispanic South America* by J. Dale Miller et al., Newbury House, Rowley, Mass.

Lección 9   EN EL MERCADO

The fact that Margarita Núñez is from Illinois should not surprise the students. A large Puerto Rican colony lives in Chicago and some of them return to Puerto Rico for various reasons. Preparing for a hurricane is a serious matter in the Caribbean and Gulf regions. A hurricane (from the Indian word *huracán*, "a storm") is the tropical equivalent of a blizzard.

The use of *chinas* for *naranjas* is typically Puerto Rican, although in certain countries there is a type of orange called *naranja china*. Our tangerines are called *mandarinas*, thus revealing the Asian origin of these citric fruits.

Displaying food advertisements and weather report sections in Spanish newspapers will enhance the presentation of the dialogue.

El pretérito de verbos irregulares

Students may ask how *ir* and *ser* can be distinguished. Show them that *ir* is frequently followed by the preposition *a; ser,* by either nouns or adjectives. As for *hacer,* once students learn that *hice, hiciste,* etc., mean "did," warn them that it is not an auxiliary verb; for example, the erroneous translation ¿*Hizo trabajó?* for "Did you work?"

El imperfecto

You may want to refer to the *Observaciones* (Lesson 8) to point out how the imperfect was used. Elsewhere, you could go back to previous *Prácticas* to create transformation exercises, contrasting the forms and meanings of the present with the imperfect. See, for example, the *Práctica* that follows the introduction of the verbs *tener, venir,* and *decir* in Lesson 5.

1. *Uds.* tienen   Uds. tenían   (yo) tenía
2. *Mis padres* no tienen   no tenían   (nosotros) teníamos
3. *Carlos* dice   decía   (tú) decías

At least three advantages for this type of practice are obvious: (1) students work with familiar vocabulary; (2) they review stem-changing verbs and see how the imperfect tense has no stem changes; and (3) they become aware of shades of meaning that the imperfect brings about. The instructor should not hesitate to help students translate this new tense.

Contrastes entre el pretérito y el imperfecto

Although the English "was . . . ing", "used to", and "would" are reliable cues for the imperfect, their use is limited. Consequently, students need to learn to associate the imperfect tense with a grammatical concept and not with English equivalents. Write on the board:

used to talk was (were) talking would talk	Imperfect — ongoing event
talked	Imperfect — ongoing Preterite — completed

Have students summarize orally the rules of thumb in Lesson 9, that is, the use of the imperfect for: (1) telling time: *Eran las 10 de la mañana*. (2) depicting background description: *Hacía frío, llovía* . . . or physical (emotional) conditions: *Estaban muy cansados (tristes)*.

Draw a wavy line to illustrate the imperfect and an X on a wavy line to show the preterite at a specific point in time.

Work with the *Práctica* in Lesson 9 that starts with *Fueron/Eran . . . las tres de la tarde cuando Carmen . . .* Let students read the paragraph silently for a couple of minutes, then begin eliciting the answers P/I and asking for an explanation. For additional practice, duplicate or place on the overhead projector the following narrative:

(Era, Fue) __1__ una mañana bonita cuando Luis (llegaba, llegó) __2__ a su casa. Como de costumbre (buscaba, buscó) __3__ la llave para entrar, pero de pronto (empezaba, empezó) __4__ a llover. Por fin (encontraba, encontró) __5__ la llave, e (iba, fue) __6__ a entrar cuando la puerta se (cerraba, cerró) __7__ .

Respuestas: 1. I   2. P   3. I   4. P   5. P   6. I   7. P

Observaciones

Be sure to emphasize that there has been considerable industrial development in Latin America (Mexico, Argentina, and Chile are among the leaders in this area) but that agriculture is still extremely important. Since agricultural products have not increased in price as dramatically as manufactured goods, Latin America has been placed at a great disadvantage in comparison with the industrialized nations. As a supplement, have a map of Latin America showing the principal products of the countries.

Lección 10   EN EL RESTAURANTE

Bring visuals and realia to class for this dialogue. Some teachers bring a table, dishes, menus, and utensils to create a restaurant atmosphere. This dialogue lends itself for acting out a number of scenes. It is advisable to study and practice the vocabulary related to foods before performing dialogue adaptations or skits.

To heighten interest prepare *churros y chocolate* in class or in the Spanish club meetings. Another time, make guacamole dip or imitation sangría. Teach the vocabulary associated with the preparation of these foods.

RECETA PARA 30 CHURROS

2 tazas de agua
una cuchara de aceite (de ensalada)
1/4 cucharita de sal

2 tazas de harina
aceite para freír
azúcar para espolvorear (*sprinkle*) los churros

Ponga al fuego el agua, el aceite y la sal. Cuando rompa el hervor (*boils*), añada la harina, retire del fuego y bata fuertemente hasta que la masa quede suave. Ponga la masa en la churrera* y haga churros de cuatro pulgadas. Use tijeras para cortar. Fría los churros en aceite bien caliente (390°) hasta que empiecen a dorarse *un poquito*. Ponga los churros en una toalla de papel y espolvoréelos con azúcar. No deje enfriarse los churros.

*A pastry bag or cake decorator fitted with a 3/8″ fluted tube (#105) would do as well.

SANGRÍA (imitación)

una botella (1 1/2 qt.) de Welch's (red) Sparkling Grape Juice
una botella (1 qt.) de 7Up
una naranja, un limón y un limón verde en tajadas
hielo

El futuro

The instructor may choose to review the preterite and present tenses before introducing the future. The students ought to know that Spanish speakers often use the present tense to express immediate future actions: *Te veo mañana.* (I'll see you tomorrow.) *Ellos llegan a las tres.* (They'll arrive at three.)

For review, divide the class into three teams: *Presente, Pretérito,* and *Futuro.* The instructor says an infinitival phrase plus a subject. Each team takes turns saying the answer (or writing it on the board).

Instructor:	Limpiar la casa (nosotros).
Present team:	Nosotros limpiamos la casa.
Preterite team:	Nosotros limpiamos la casa.
Future team:	Nosotros limpiaremos la casa.

After three players from each team have had a chance to answer, rotate the tense for each team.

The future is also used to express probability as well as a sense of curiosity or wondering in the present. If a student is absent, ask the class: *¿Dónde estará Alberto? ¿Estará enfermo?* Also ask the class questions such as *¿Quién tendrá más dinero en su cartera? ¿Cuándo habrá un examen aquí?*

As for the conditional, stress that it is used to make requests sound softer or more polite: *Me gustaría ver eso.* (I would like to see that.)

Los pronombres de complemento directo

Since students are already acquainted with reflexive pronouns and their position in relation to conjugated verbs and infinitives, it would be wise to begin the explanation with a brief review of the topic.

Use the overhead projector for variety. Cut small squares from a plastic transparency and write a direct object pronoun in each, preferably in a color other than black. Next cut out strips of plastic to write the other words of a sentence, preferably in black. Now you or your students demonstrate the possible word-order combinations. For example:

	trae	la mercancía
	la	trae
El vendedor	va a traer	los productos
	los	va a traer
	va a traerlos	

After the class knows how to manipulate these structures, bring in the other tenses studied. Also include affirmative and negative commands.

Los pronombres con preposiciones

The position of these prepositional phrases may vary within the sentence, but at this elementary level it would be best to keep them at the end.

(Yo) la quiero a ella.   (I love her.)
Cuento contigo.   (I count on you.)

Observaciones

Students enjoy a tasting party and quite often are willing to prepare a dish to share with the class. If this is not possible, bring spices frequently used in Spanish cuisine: *comino* (cumin), *laurel* (bay leaves), *azafrán* (saffron), *orégano, ajo,* and so on.

When reading the *Observaciones,* remind the class that the economic status and customs of each family will determine *what* and *how often* they eat. However, one thing can be said with considerable certainty: mealtime is an occasion for conversation while eating and after eating, i.e., *la sobremesa.*

Lección 11 POR TELÉFONO

It is not necessary to memorize the long lines of dialogue, but do lead the students in communicating the main points, e.g.,

Sr. Vega, ¿me ha enviado los tejidos?
Sr. Vega, necesito saber cuándo llega el pedido ...

In other words, instill in the students that what really matters is to express a message that can be understood. This should be kept in mind while acting out the accompanying three *Situaciones.* Encourage accuracy, but not to such a point that students become intimidated.

Use a phone book from a foreign or U.S. city and point out how easy it is to dial direct to and from most of the Latin American and Spanish cities. If the students have a printed list, a good review of numbers could take place.

¿Cuál es el área de Caracas?
Es el ...

Pronombres de complemento indirecto

Review reflexive and direct object pronouns. List these pronouns on the board as students say them to you. Next, list the indirect object pronouns, drawing comparisons with the others. For practice in complete sentences, refer to the transparency squares and strips you prepared for the previous lesson. In addition, have students in pairs show, lend, give, and pass items between each other as they ask and answer questions; for example,

Informal
Student A: ¿Me prestas el periódico (la revista)?
Student B: Sí, te lo (la) presto en seguida.

Have a list of verbs on the board that students could refer to for variety: enseñar, dar, pasar, traer, devolver, leer, comprar, regalar.

Formal
Student B: ¿Me presta Ud. el periódico?
Student A: Sí, se lo presto en seguida.

Los tiempos compuestos (Compound or Perfect Tenses)

Remember that the tense generally called "present perfect" in English is called *pretérito perfecto* in traditional Spanish grammars. This tense actually is used by many people (in Madrid, for example) as a substitute for the preterite. At the elementary level of Spanish, it is not necessary to lecture the students on these fine points. It would suffice to say that the "present perfect" refers generally to a recently completed past action. Point out that "perfect" in grammatical terms means "completed."

At the time of teaching the irregular past participles, the instructor may want to refer to others with similar irregularities:

abierto: descubierto, cubierto
dicho: predicho, contradicho
escrito: descrito, inscrito, prescrito
hecho: deshecho, satisfecho
puesto: dispuesto, compuesto, impuesto
vuelto: devuelto, envuelto, revuelto

El pluscuamperfecto

In order to help students visualize the function of the past perfect (*pluscuamperfecto* in Spanish, i.e. more than finished), draw a line on the board to represent time and label it accordingly:

	pasado		*presente*
X		X	
6:15 A.M.		7:00 A.M.	
(ellos)		(yo)	

Cuando yo desayuné a las siete,   When I ate breakfast at seven, they
    ellos ya habían desayunado.   had already eaten (breakfast).

Observaciones

A physical map of Latin America will help to explain the difficulties involved in developing land transportation in that area. Moreover, students who have crossed the Rocky Mountains or other mountainous regions will be able to relate to those difficulties. This information could be elicited in Spanish:

¿Ha(n) cruzado Ud.(Uds.) las montañas Rocosas?
¿Vive(n) cerca de las montañas Smoky?

Similar questions about rivers could be asked. All this should lead the students to understand the transportation problems in South America. You might point out that in South America:

- Bridges and railroads have been built at a higher altitude than some of the highest mountains in North America.
- The Amazon River has a volume of water twenty times greater than the Mississippi, and at times the opposite shore is not visible. Try building a bridge across that!
- Tremors along the Pacific Coast can destroy or block a road in a matter of seconds.
- Railroads in some countries were not built to join cities but rather to transport minerals and other products to shipping or production sites. This was the case in Bolivia and Argentina. The latter, however, now has an excellent railroad system.

Lección 12   LAS FIESTAS

Although the degree of protection that Hispanic parents feel toward their children may vary according to such factors as social status, church influence, age of the children, urban vs. rural or semirural areas, it is a generally accepted fact that the Hispanic home is sheltered. The women, in general, are more sheltered than their American counterparts, although this situation has changed dramatically in the last few years. The children of the elite families appear to be pampered as well as sheltered and protected.

Los pronombres indirectos con los verbos gustar, parecer y faltar

A chart or transparency can be very helpful for sight-oriented learners. Write *gusta* on one strip of plastic and *gustan* on another. Place the appropriate strip on the transparency, depending on the subject chosen; for example,

Me		la clase.
Te		los deportes.
Le		mi trabajo.
Nos	(gusta or gustan)	estudiar.
(Os)		viajar.
Les		esas canciones.

Remind students that *parecer* is used to ask for or express an opinion.

¿Qué te pareció la película?
Me gustó muchísimo.

Watch for the incorrect use of *¿Cómo le gusta ... ?* for *¿Qué le parece el libro, la clase ... ?,* (What do you think of ... ?) Compare: *¿Cómo le gusta el café, con leche y azúcar?* (How do you like your coffee, with milk and sugar?)

El subjuntivo

Review previous use of the subjunctive; for example,

¿Quieres que yo (ella, ellos) ... ?
¿Temen Uds. que él (Panchita, yo) ... ?

Introduce the adverbial conjunctions that always require the subjunctive and have students memorize them and their meaning. Provide practice with questions such as:

¿Irás al cine (concierto, partido ...) con tal que yo vaya?
¿Hablarás con Lupe antes de que ella salga (se marche, se acueste ...)?
¿Sales sin que lo sepa (tu papá, tu mamá, tu novio/a ...)?

Present the adverbial conjunctions that take either the indicative or subjunctive. Emphasize that if the intention of the speakers is to express pending or future actions, they will choose the subjunctive. Conversely, if their intention is to refer to actions that already occurred or generally do occur, they will use the indicative. Write on the board:

Estudio cuando puedo. (habitual, generally occurs)
Estudi*aré* cuando pued*a*. (pending, future action)
    (future)

Hablan hasta que se cansan.
Van a hablar hasta que se cans*en*.
    (future)

Try a few transformation exercises; for example,

INSTRUCTOR: *Trabajo* cuando puedo. (Trabajaré)
STUDENT: *Trabajaré* cuando pueda.

1. *Voy* cuando tengo tiempo. (Iré)
   Iré cuando . . .
2. Llaman cuando llegan. (Llamarán)
   Llamarán cuando . . .
3. Descansas cuando estás allí. (Descansarás)
   Descansarás . . .
4. Paramos cuando pasamos por ese pueblo. (Pararemos)
   . . .
5. Se lo digo a Ciro cuando lo veo. (Se lo diré)
   . . .
6. Firmo los cheques cuando los recibo. (Firmaré)
   . . .
7. Me baño cuando hay agua caliente. (Me bañaré)
   . . .
8. Sueño contigo cuando duermo. (Soñaré)
   . . .

Palabras afirmativas y negativas

Use the overhead projector and plastic strips to demonstrate the use of more than one negative word within a sentence. As for the students, it must be made clear to them that in order to handle these structures well they must know the affirmative words and their negative counterparts *al pie de la letra.*

Observaciones

To supplement the reading, you may want to share these points with the students:

- Hispanic children participate more than their U.S. counterparts in social occasions such as parties, baptisms, weddings, and funerals.
- Due to the above practice, the need for baby-sitters is minimal. Members of the family usually fulfill this role.
- Family-oriented fiestas are more common than parties for certain age groups.
- Movies are a favorite form of entertainment. Spain, Argentina, Mexico, and Brazil produce many films each year. American films are shown, but in many countries the voices must be dubbed in Spanish. This provides work for Hispanic actors and actresses.
- Social events in the newspapers are described with particular flair and style. The instructor may wish to duplicate segments from the society page of a newspaper to illustrate.

Lección 13 *LOS PROBLEMAS SOCIO-POLÍTICOS*

It would be easy to turn this section into a political discussion in English. If this begins to happen, lead the discussion back to Spanish. With suitable questions and preparation, the students will surprise you with their ability to express their opinions.

The instructor may also set up a press conference in which students question recently arrived persons from Latin America. In addition, the instructor could record television newscasts from SIN, the Spanish International Network, to have available for students.

El subjuntivo después de los antecedentes indefinidos y negativos

Write examples on the board that illustrate definite/indefinite and existent/nonexistent antecedents:

Busco *al joven* que repara bicicletas.	(definite, specific)
Busco *un joven* que repare bicicletas.	(indefinite; is there such a person here?)
¿Hay *alguien* que vaya al centro hoy?	(indefinite; you don't know)
No, no hay *nadie* que vaya.	(nonexistent, negative)
Sí, hay *alguien* que va.	(existent; yes you know who)

Provide plenty of practice with questions that students answer both affirmatively and negatively; for example,

¿Hay alguien (alguno, alguna) que lo sepa todo?
¿Conoces a alguien que trabaje en ... ?
¿Buscas un profesor que enseñe (explique, hable, cante ...) mejor?
¿Necesitas una persona que te (comprenda, ayude, quiera ...)?
¿Tienes un bolígrafo (lápiz, diccionario, engrapador ...) que sirva?

Elsewhere, let students describe the person they would like to marry. Have the first student in each row write one sentence describing that ideal person. The student folds the answer so that the next student doesn't see it. The second student follows the same procedure, and so on, until the end of the row. The last student in each row then reads all the descriptions for his/her row.

To make the exercise move quickly, the instructor should have the following on the board:

Quiero casarme con una persona que ...
ser/inteligente, astuta, cariñosa ...
tener/los ojos ... el pelo ...
hablar/ ...
gustarle/ ...
saber/cocinar, reparar ...

El subjuntivo con expresiones de duda y negación

Explain this use of the subjunctive, drawing the students' attention to similarities with patterns in previous lessons: there is a subordinate (dependent) clause introduced by *que* and the cue for the choice of mode is in the main clause. The cue may be a verb of doubt (*dudar*) or a negation. Compare:

Creo que son ellos.
No creo que sean ellos.
Dudo que sean ellos.

For practice, place several classroom items on the desk. Hold up a pen and ask *¿Es un bolígrafo?* Have students reply, *Sí, creo que es un bolígrafo.* Next, hold up a notebook and ask *¿Es un lápiz?* and have students answer *No creo que sea un lápiz.* Vary the cues to elicit positive and negative responses.

El imperfecto (pasado) del subjuntivo

Review the subjunctive in Lesson 6 and use the exercises to transform present to past subjunctive. Add translation exercises such as these:

1. a. I don't believe they'll stay.
      No creo que (quedarse) _____.
   b. I didn't believe they'd stay.
      No creía que _____.
2. a. They want us to be here at ten.
      Quieren que (estar) _____.
   b. They wanted us to be here at ten.
      Querían que _____.
   c. They wanted to be here at ten.
      _____.
3. a. I'll bring Miriam so that you'll meet her.
      Traeré a Miriam para que (conocer) _____.
   b. I brought Miriam so that you'd meet her.
      Traje a Miriam _____.
4. a. We don't see anything we like.
      No vemos nada que (gustar) _____.
   b. We didn't see anything we liked.
      No vimos nada que _____.
   c. We saw something we liked.
      _____.

Cláusulas con si (If-clauses)

Briefly review the forms and functions of the conditional in Lesson 10. Then illustrate the contrary-to-fact function on the board:

Si tenemos dinero, iremos.	If we have money, we'll go. (It's likely we have the money.)
Si tuviéramos dinero, iríamos.	If we *had* the money, we'd go. (It's unlikely we have the money. In fact, we don't.)

For practice, say a few negative statements and have students convert them to hypothetical (contrary-to-fact) questions.

No soy rico(a). ⟶   ¿Qué haría si fuera rico(a)?
No soy mecánico. ⟶   ¿Qué haría si ... ?
No estoy en México. ⟶   ¿Qué haría ... ?
No estoy cansado(a). ⟶
No salgo con ellos. ⟶
No voy a la fiesta (al cine ...) ⟶

Observaciones

Use this essay for reading aloud, and for dictations and other classroom exercises. The first full paragraph lends itself very well for a composition exercise. Ask students to rewrite the paragraph, referring instead to the United States.

Lección 14   LAS OBRAS MAESTRAS

Enrich this lesson through pictures, slides, records, visits to the museum, guest artists, and the like. Elsewhere assign, or let students choose, a famous Hispanic personality to research. Group students in threes, having each group investigate a different person. Each group should consult the library and prepare a joint one-and-a-half page report in Spanish. The report, checked by the instructor beforehand, could be presented to the class with appropriate visuals or music.

If you do the *Interpretación* (e 1-6) for Velázquez's *Las meninas,* consider the differences in opinion regarding whom Velázquez was painting. One theory holds that he was painting the monarchs as reflected in the mirror in the background. Another states that the canvas in front of Velázquez was too big for a single portrait and, as a consequence, he was painting the scene we now observe.

OTRAS CONSIDERACIONES

This section covers those grammatical items we deemed not crucial for a first-year text. The items, however, appear throughout the book for recognition purposes. They appear also under separate headings after Lesson 14 to serve as a bridge to second-year Spanish, where their functions could be more readily understood and practiced.

SOURCES OF CULTURAL INFORMATION

Argentina

Dirección Nacional de Turismo
Subsecretaría de Turismo
Suipacha 1111
Buenos Aires, Argentina
Tel: 31-4412

Bolivia

Instituto Boliviano de Turismo
Plaza Venezuela, Edificio Herrmán
4° Piso, Casilla 1868
La Paz, Bolivia
Tel: 35-8213, 32-7135

Embassy of Bolivia
3014 Massachusetts Avenue, N.W.
Washington, D.C. 20008
Tel: (202) 483-4410/11/12

Chile

Servicio Nacional de Turismo
(SERNATUR)
Catedral 1165, 3er Piso
Santiago, Chile

Embassy of Chile
1732 Massachusetts Avenue, N.W.
Washington, D.C. 20036
Tel: (202) 785-1746

Colombia

Corporación Nacional de Turismo
(CNT)
Calle 28, No. 13A-15, Piso 16
Apartado Aéreo 8400
Bogotá, D.E., Colombia
Tel: (212) 688-0151

Costa Rica

Instituto Costarricense de Tiros (ICT)
Calle Alfredo Volio
(entre Av. 4 y 6)
San José, Costa Rica
Tel: 23-1733

Costa Rica Institute of Tourism
200 S.E. First St., Suite 606
Miami, Florida 33131
Tel: (800) 327-7033
(305) 358-2150

Cuba

Instituto de Turismo Nacional e
Internacional (CUBATUR)
Calle 23, No. 156, Vedado
La Habana, Cuba

Cuban Interest Section
Embassy of Czechoslovakia
2639 16th Street, N.W.
Washington, D.C. 20009
Tel: (202) 797-8518

Ecuador

Dirección Nacional de Turismo
(DITURIS)
Reina Victoria 514
Quito, Ecuador
Tel: 23-9044

Embassy of Ecuador
2535 15th Street, N.W.
Washington, D.C. 20009
Tel: (202) 234-1494/1692

El Salvador

Instituto Salvadoreño de Turismo
(ISTU)
Calle Rubén Darío 619
San Salvador, El Salvador
Tel: 22-8000, 26-6666

Embassy of El Salvador
2308 California Street, N.W.
Washington, D.C. 20008
Tel: (202) 265-3480/3482

Guatemala

Instituto Guatemalteco de Turismo
(INGUAT)
7a Avenida 1—17, Centro Civic
Ciudad de Guatemala, Guatemala
Tel: 51-5311, 31-8203, 31-1333/1347

Guatemala Tourist Commission
2220 R Street, N.W.
Washington, D.C. 20008
Tel: (202) 745-4852/53

Honduras

Instituto Hondureño de Turismo
(IHT)
Apartado 154-C
Tegucigalpa, Honduras
Tel: 22-8934/7752/1183/9544

Honduras Tourist Bureau
530 West 6th Street, Room 401
Los Angeles, California 90014
Tel: (213) 485-0285

México

Secretaría de Turismo (SECTUR)
Avenida Presidente Mazaryk N 172
Colonia Polanco
México, D.F. 11587, México
Tel: (905) 250-8228
        250-8558

Mexican Government Tourist Office
405 Park Avenue, Suite 102
New York, New York 10022
Tel: (212) 755-7261

Nicaragua

Dirección Nacional de Turismo
Avenida Bolívar 808
Apartado Postal 122
Managua, Nicaragua
Tel: 25-436, 22-498/962

Embassy of Nicaragua
1627 New Hampshire Avenue, N.W.
Washington, D.C. 20009
Tel: (202) 387-4371/4374

Panamá

Instituto Panameño de Turismo
(IPAT)
Vía España 124
Apartado Postal 4421
Panamá 5, Panamá
Tel: 23-8067/64-3935

Embassy of Panama
2862 McGill Terrace, N.W.
Washington, D.C. 20008
Tel: (202) 483-1407/13

Paraguay

Dirección General de Turismo
Olivia y Alberdi
Asunción, Paraguay
Tel: 4-1530, 4-5306

Embassy of Paraguay
2400 Massachusetts Avenue, N.W.
Washington, D.C. 20008
Tel: (202) 483-6960/6962

Perú

Ministerio de Industria,
  Turismo e Integración
Calle 1, Oeste, CORPAC
Lima, Perú
Tel: 40-4032/7120

Fondo de Promoción Turística
(FOPTUR)
1450 Coral Way, Suite 2
Miami, Florida 33145
Tel: (305) 856-1498

República Dominicana

Dirección Nacional de Turismo
Calle César Nicolás Pensón N° 59
Apartado 497
Santo Domingo, República Dominicana
Tel: 688-5537
        682-1317

Dominican Republic Tourist
  Information Center
485 Madison Avenue
New York, New York 10022
Tel: (212) 826-0750
        (800) 221-4677

Uruguay

Dirección Nacional de Turismo
Avenida Agraciada 1409, Piso 7
Montevideo, Uruguay
Tel: 90-6201

Embassy of Uruguay
1981 F Street, N.W.
Washington, D.C. 20006
Tel: (202) 331-1313/1316

Venezuela

Corporación de Turismo de Venezuela
Centro Capriles, Plaza Venezuela
Apartado 50200
Caracas, Venezuela
Tel: 781-3834
      782-5911

Venezuelan Government Tourist Office
450 Park Avenue
New York, New York 10022
Tel: (212) 355-1101

REFERENCES

Morgenstern, Douglas. *Manual del instructor, ¿Habla español?*
New York: Holt, Rinehart and Winston, 1982.

Quilter, Daniel. *Lesson Plans for First-Year College Spanish,* Indiana University,
Bloomington, IN. (ditto copies, n.d.)

Sevin, Dieter, et al., *Tips für den Unterricht, Wie Geht's?*
New York: Holt, Rinehart and Winston, 1984.

ANSWER KEY — *MANUAL DE EJERCICIOS*

CONVERSACIÓN DIARIA 1: **A.** 1. Answers vary. **B.** 1. once 2. nueve 3. siete 4. tres 5. un 6. una
C. 1. Buenos días. Buenas tardes. Buenas noches. 2. ¿Cómo se llama usted? 3. ¿Es usted estudiosa? 4. No soy muy tímido/a. 5. ¡Escuche! ¡Repita!

CONVERSACIÓN DIARIA 2: **A.** 1. C 2. F 3. C 4. F 5. F 6. C 7. C **B.** 1. veinticinco y cinco son treinta
2. catorce y trece son veintisiete 3. dieciocho menos nueve son nueve 4. diecisiete y seis menos dos son veintiuno 5. tres menos dos y quince son dieciséis **C.** es; un; estudiante; simpática; primos; profesora; estudiante. **D.** Answers vary. **E.** 1. veinticinco centavos 2. diez centavos 3. treinta centavos
4. veinticuatro centavos 5. treinta y ocho centavos **F.** ¿Cómo está usted? 2. ¿Qué tal? 3. ¿Cómo está la familia? 4. Muy bien. 5. Un poco cansado/a. 6. Somos cinco en mi familia: mi madre, mi padre, mi hermano, mi hermana y yo. 7. Soy de (state).

CONVERSACIÓN DIARIA 3: **A.** 1. ganar 2. cada 3. tela 4. cena 5. exacto **B.** 1. Hace mucho calor; noventa y ocho grados. 2. Nieva; treinta y dos grados. 3. Hace fresco; sesenta grados. 4. Hace viento; veintitrés grados. **C.** Answers vary. **D.** 1. Son las tres. 2. Son las doce y veinticinco. 3. Son las ocho menos diez.
4. Son las nueve y quince. 5. Son las once y veinticinco. **E.** 1. México 2. Puerto Rico 3. Nicaragua
4. Colombia 5. Perú 6. Argentina 7. España **F.** 1. noventa y nueve dólares 2. ochenta y siete dólares
3. setenta y ocho dólares 4. ciento dos dólares 5. ciento cincuenta y seis dólares **G.** 1. ¿Qué tiempo hace?
2. Llueve. 3. No hace calor. 4. ¿Qué hora es? 5. ¿Cuál es su número de teléfono? 6. Tengo cincuenta pesos.

CONVERSACIÓN DIARIA 4: **A.** 1. el primero de enero 2. el veinticuatro de junio 3. el dieciséis de septiembre 4. el veinticinco de diciembre **B.** el lunes, el miércoles, el jueves **C.** 1. Hay cinco trenes en total a Sevilla el lunes. 2. El viernes por la tarde hay trenes a las doce y doce, a las seis de la tarde y a las once de la noche. 3. El último tren el jueves es a las once. 4. No, no hay tren a las tres y cuarto el sábado. 5. El primer tren el domingo es a las seis y media de la mañana. **D.** 1. ¿Qué fecha es hoy? 2. ¿Cuándo es su cumpleaños? 3. ¿A qué hora es el desayuno? 4. Es a las siete y media de la mañana. 5. ¿Hay un banco en la plaza?

CONVERSACIÓN DIARIA 5: **A.** 1. Mi primera clase no es a la una. 2. ¿Hay una fiesta en casa de Alicia? 3. El almuerzo es a las dos y media. 4. ¿No está aquí el primo Antonio? 5. ¿A qué hora es la exhibitión?
B. 1. My first class is not at one o'clock. 2. Is there a party at Alice's house? 3. Lunch is at two-thirty.
4. Isn't cousin Anthony here? 5. At what time is the exhibition? **C.** 1. che; efe; ge; hache; jota; elle; cu; erre; equis; zeta. **D.** 1. la economía 2. la ingeniería 3. la literatura francesa 4. la biología 5. la medicina 6. la computación 7. la contabilidad 8. el español **E.** Answers vary. **F.** 1. doscientos sesenta 2. cien 3. ciento ochenta 4. seiscientos 5. nueve mil **G.** Answers vary. **H.** 1. ¿Le gusta bailar? 2. Me gustan los deportes.
3. No me gusta la música. 4. ¿Cuánto cuesta? 5. Es fácil; no es difícil. 6. primero, ultimo

CONVERSACIÓN DIARIA 6: **A.** Answers vary. **B.** 1. La camisa es roja y los pantalones son negros. 2. La camisa es gris y los pantalones son azules. 3. La camisa es anaranjada y los pantalones son verdes. 4. La camisa es parda y los pantalones son amarillos. **C.** Answers vary. 1. Por favor. 2. Perdón. 3. Perdón. 4. De nada.
5. Con permiso. **D.** 1. ¡Ojo! 2. un poquito 3. más o menos 4. Es tacaño. **E.** Dialogue.

LECCIÓN 1: **A.** 1. banquera 2. obrero 3. comerciante internacional 4. estudiante 5. profesora 6. ingeniero
B. 1. el 2. los 3. las 4. el 5. la 6. los **C.** 1. al 2. de la 3. del 4. del 5. de la 6. a las 7. de la
8. a la 9. a **D.** 1. un papel 2. una aspirina 3. unas lecciones 4. unos días 5. un programa **E.** 1. Uds.
2. tú 3. Ud. 4. nosotros 5. Uds. 6. Uds. **F.** 1. toma 2. trabajan 3. caminamos 4. enseña 5. compras
G. Answers vary. **H.** 1. Hablo inglés y español. 2. Alonso necesita unos dólares. 3. Estudian la contabilidad, las matemáticas y la computación. 4. Buscamos una farmacia. 5. ¿Adónde vas hoy? 6. ¿Qué es la dirección del restaurante?

LECCIÓN 2: **A.** llego; está; debe; deseo; toma; creo; conozco; necesita **B.** 1. venden 2. lees 3. comen
4. vivo 5. escribimos 6. deben 7. comprende 8. saben 9. correr 10. abren **C.** Answers vary, but all verb forms are in the first person. **D.** Answers vary, but all verb forms are in the first person. **E.** 1. ¿Comen los Durán en casa? 2. ¿Escribes el problema correctamente? 3. ¿Acepta el restaurante cheques de viajeros?
4. ¿Damos un paseo hoy? 5. ¿Es mecánico Rogelio? **F.** 1. ¿Cómo se llama Ud.? 2. ¿Dónde vive Ud.?
3. ¿Cuál es su teléfono? 4. ¿Qué estudia Ud.? 5. ¿Cuándo asistes a clases? 6. ¿A quién desea conocer?
G. 1. a 2. no change 3. a 4. a 5. a **H.** 1. saber 2. saber 3. conocer 4. saber 5. conocer 6. saber

I. Composition **J. 1.** Bienvenido a los Estados Unidos, Señor Flores. ¿Cómo está usted? **2.** Primero pase Ud. por la Inmigración y después por la Aduana. Allí, necesita abrir las maletas. **3.** Julie Fulton es norteamericana. Tiene el cabello marrón and los ojos azules. Sabe hablar español. Es amable pero muy exigente. **4.** Debemos esperar en la entrada a la hotel hasta las nueve y media, ¿de acuerdo? **5.** En las clases de español escuchamos, hablamos, leemos y escribimos todos los días. Aprendemos mucho.

LECCIÓN 3: **A. 1.** la espalda **2.** la mano **3.** el ojo **4.** la garganta **5.** los labios **6.** el cuello **7.** los dedos del pie **8.** el pecho **9.** la pierna **10.** el brazo **B.** Answers vary. **C. 1.** Cecilia es otra estudiante española. **2.** Ella lee tres artículos aburridos. **3.** Conrado es mi buen amigo salvadoreño. **4.** Hay varias mesas desocupadas aquí. **5.** Construyen pocas casas de ladrillo en el campo. **D. 1.** estar **2.** ser **3.** estar **4.** ser **5.** estar **6.** ser **7.** estar **E. 1.** es **2.** está **3.** está **4.** Es **5.** es **6.** es **7.** es **F. 1.** ¿De dónde es Clementina? **2.** ¿De qué son las flores? **3.** ¿De quién son los quince mil pesetas? **4.** ¿Dónde está el señor Río? **G.** Dialogue

H. 1. Juliana y Emiliano están enfermos, ¿verdad? **2.** ¿A qué hora es su cita con el médico? **3.** Perdon, ¿dónde está la embajada chilena? **4.** Miriam es alta y bonita. **5.** El señor Quirantes es de Nicaragua, pero está ahora en Miami. Es profesor. **6.** ¡Salud! **7.** La iglesia está cerca, a la izquierda.

LECCIÓN 4: **A.** los pantalones, el traje de baño, los zapatos, la cartera, el vestido **B.** Answers vary. **C. 1.** Él siempre lo entiende todo. **2.** Los chicos quieren irse. **3.** La mujer prefiere llamar a su esposo. **4.** Duermo en casa. **5.** Los señores Mora almuerzan con nosotros. **D. 1.** Brenda recuerda la dirección de los Ferrer, ¿no? **2.** ¿Prefieres ir al cine? **3.** Queremos conocer al Sr. Estrada. **4.** ¿Cuánto cuestan las camisetas de algodón? **5.** Diana y Sonya juegan al sófbol los sábados. **E. 1.** se prueba **2.** lavamos **3.** se despiertan **4.** pones **5.** se casa **F. 1.** me levanto **2.** me lavo **3.** me pongo **4.** me siento **5.** me voy **6.** estoy **7.** almuerzo **8.** juego **9.** me divierto **10.** regreso **G. 1.** se levanta **2.** se lava **3.** se pone **4.** se sienta **6.** se va **6.** está **7.** almuerza **8.** juega **9.** se divierte **10.** regresa **H. 1.** People don't work much here in the winter. **2.** A lot is said about television actors. **3.** No eating allowed in the library. **4.** Do you enter through here or (through) there? **5.** No passing. **I. 1.** Alejo y yo le damos una camisa amarilla a Porfirio. **2.** Tú le das un cinturón de cuero a Porfirio. **3.** Martina y Juliana le dan una chaqueta marrón a Porfirio. **4.** Francisca le da una camiseta de la universidad a Porfirio. **5.** Yo le doy ... a Porfirio. **J. 1.** Andrés y Joselín van con él al frontón de jai-alai. **2.** Lourdes va con él a la discoteca. **3.** Tú vas con él a un restaurante italiano. **4.** Yo voy con él a las tiendas. **K.** Answers vary. **L. 1.** Quiero probarme los pantalones blancos y la camisa azul. **2.** ¿Cuánto cuesta la gorra roja?—Es muy barata. **3.** Siempre nos levantamos a las seis y media de la mañana, nos desayunamos y vamos al trabajo. **4.** ¿A qué hora comienzan a llegar los invitados? **5.** Buenas tardes, ¿en qué puedo servirle? **6.** ¿Prefieres el algodón, la lana o la seda? **7.** Ellos piensan ir al cine, y después al club. **8.** Llueve mucho. Voy a ponerme el impermeable.

LECCIÓN 5: **A. 1.** cara **2.** baño **3.** precio **4.** pedir **5.** llenar **B. 1.** Mi madre quiere ir al teatro. **2.** Tus primos se divierten mucho. **3.** Lo siento, per no tengo su visa. **4.** Nuestro hijo se casa en junio. **5.** Nuestras clases comienzan a fines de agosto. **C. 1.** Son sus pantalones. Son los pantalones de él. **2.** Es su bolsa. Es la bolsa de ella. **3.** Es su cartera. Es la cartera de él. **4.** Son sus maletas. Son las maletas de ellos. **D.** Possible answers: **1.** Sí, quiero ver sus fotos. **2.** Sí, tengo mis llaves. **3.** Sí, esperamos a nuestros amigos. **4.** Sí, doy un paseo con mi perrito. **5.** Sí, buscamos nuestro coche. **E.** Part of answers varies. **1.** pides, pido **2.** piden, piden **3.** piden, piden **4.** I ask for a soft drink. **5.** I am asking what drinks you have. **F. 1.** siguen; Seguimos **2.** siguen; Siguen **3.** sigues; Sigo **4.** sigue; Sigue **5.** sigue; Sigo. **G. 1.** salen, salgo **2.** te pones, me pongo **3.** traen, traigo **4.** hacen, hago **5.** dice, digo **6.** vienen, venimos

H. 1. Tengo calor. **2.** Tenemos frío. **3.** tiene sed **4.** tienen que estudiar el vocabulario **5.** tienen sueño **6.** tienes razón **7.** tengo diecinueve años **8.** tenemos miedo **9.** tienen mucha hambre **10.** Tengo prisa.

I. Answers vary. **J. 1.** Dígame el precio del vino. **2.** ¿Dónde están las maletas de Sr. Ponce? **3.** ¡Dios mio! El agua está caliente hoy. **4.** Me gustaría ver el cuarto primero. **5.** El estudiante escucha y luego repite las palabras. **6.** Digo que ellos no tienen razón. **7.** Uds. no tienen que preocuparse. Tengo mucho cuidado cuando manejo. **8.** Todo el mundo pide una habitación con aire. **K.** Dear Sirs: Please reserve a double room at a moderate price from the first to the fifth of June. Cordially, Elba Rojas.

LECCIÓN 6: **A.** Entre, vaya; Pague; Dígame; Pase, siga; Suba, pida **B. 1.** Cierren bien la puerta. **2.** No pongan el radio muy alto. **3.** Apaguen la luz de la cocina. **4.** No peleen. **5.** No se sienten cerca de la televisión. **6.** Den de comer al gato. **7.** No toquen las cosas en la sala. **8.** Báñense bien. **9.** No se acuesten tarde. **10.** No permitan entrar a nadie. **C. 1.** pueda **2.** llames **3.** hacemos **4.** escriban **5.** regrese **6.** están

D. trabaje; lea; conteste; prepare; haga; vaya; busque; comprenda; acepte   **E. 1.** Sí, él quiere que ella trabaje más.   **2.** El Sr. León quiere que ella lea y conteste su correspondencia.   **3.** Prefiere que Librada prepare el almuerzo al mediodía.   **4.** Por la tarde, le pide que haga café.   **5.** Tiene que ir a hacer compras para el Sr. León.   **6.** Ella cree que es sirvienta.   **7.** No quiere seguir trabajando para el Sr. León.   **8.** Es necesario que ella busque otro trabajo.   **9.** Librada espera que él comprenda y acepte su renuncia.   **10.** Yo creo que el Sr. León es injusto con Librada.   **11.** No siento que Librada se vaya.   **12.** No deseo trabajar para el Sr. León. El Sr. León es muy exigente.   **F. 1a.** Quiero abrir la carta.   **b.** Quiero que abras la carta.   **2a.** Lila prefiere caminar.   **b.** Lila prefiere que caminemos.   **3a.** ¿Prefieres que yo sirva?   **b.** ¿Prefieres servir?   **4a.** Esperamos que descansen un poco.   **b.** Esperamos descansar un poco.   **5a.** Siento llegar tarde.   **b.** Siento que lleguen tarde.   **6a.** Quieren comer más.   **b.** Quieren que comamos más.   **7a.** Prefiero que vayas a la tienda.   **b.** Prefiero ir a la tienda.   **8a.** Manolo quiere esperar aquí.   **b.** Manolo quiere que esperen aquí.   **G.** Answers vary.   **H. 1.** ¡Busque la carta y mire lo que dice Benito!   **2.** ¡Por favor, levántense! ¡No se sienten!   **3.** Quiero que rebajen los precios.   **4.** Esperamos que ellos visiten Chapultepec.   **5.** Ellos tienen miedo de que ella no llegue a tiempo.   **6.** Siento que Ada esté enferma. Espero que se mejore pronto.   **7.** ¡Claro yo puedo ayudar! Dígame lo que quiere que yo haga.

LECCIÓN 7:   **A. 1.** ella: entró, miró, compró, descansó, ayudó, se levantó, se sentó   **2.** ellos: bajaron, jugaron, limpiaron, encontraron, empezaron, se bañaron, se acostaron   **3.** usted: comió, perdió, decidió, abrió, salió, permitió, entendió   **4.** ustedes: corrieron, movieron, prometieron, recibieron, vendieron, vivieron, escribieron   **B. 1.** llegaron   **2.** desarrollaron   **3.** dejó   **4.** se unieron   **5.** estableció   **C.** The Spaniards arrived in Mexico in 1519.   **2.** The Aztecs developed agriculture.   **3.** Nicarago left his name to his country.   **4.** The tribes joined the Spaniards.   **5.** Spain established an empire in America.   **D. 1.** Several indigenous tribes used to inhabit the Antilles.   **2.** The Aztecs used to dominate the central valley of Mexico.   **3.** Mayan civilization was in complete decadence when the Spaniards arrived in the New World.   **4.** The Incas were excellent artisans and architects.   **5.** They knew a lot about medicine and used anesthesia in delicate operations.   **E. 1.** Los mayas vivían en el Yucatán y en América Central.   **2.** Eran arquitectos excelentes. Sus templos en Chichén-Itza y Uxmal servían de centros religiosos.   **3.** Desarrollaron un calendario muy exacto.   **4.** Comían mucho maíz.   **5.** Estudiaban los cursos del sol y la luna.

LECCIÓN 8:   **A. 1.** desperté   **2.** levanté   **3.** bañé; lavé   **4.** puse   **5.** bajé; desayuné   **6.** repasé   **7.** leí   **8.** estudié; escribí   **9.** salí   **10.** llegué   **11.** estacioné; caminé   **12.** entré; senté   **13.** hablé   **14.** esperé   **15.** aprendí; divertí   **B. 1.** despertó   **2.** bañó; puso   **3.** desayunó   **4.** salió   **5.** revisó; escribió; llamó   **6.** caminó   **7.** sentó; pidió   **8.** regresó   **C. 1.** cenaron   **2.** comieron   **3.** hablaron; pasaron   **4.** tomaron; siguieron   **5.** levantaron; leyeron   **6.** ayudaron; jugaron   **7.** vieron; acostaron   **D. 1.** Él piensa hacer este trabajo.   **2.** Nunca pensé comprar esas chaquetas.   **3.** Vamos a viajar a aquellos lugares interesantes.   **4.** El señor llegó a este hotel ayer.   **5.** ¿Con quiénes van a esa exposición?   **E. 1.** éstas y no ésas   **2.** éste y no aquél   **3.** éstos y no ésos   **4.** ésta y no ésa   **5.** esto   **F. 1.** Tú eres menos prudente que yo.   **2.** Ellos son más prácticos que nosotros.   **3.** ¿Quiénes tienen más experiencia que Hortensia?   **4.** Ella son las más simpáticas.   **5.** Él asiste a tantas clases como Norma.   **G.** Answers vary.   **H.** Composition   **I. 1.** A propósito, ¿hablaste con los dueños de la fábrica?   **2.** Me acosté a la medianoche anoche y me levanté a las siete esta mañana.   **3.** Quisiéramos ver este anillo de plata, esa cadena de oro y aquellos pendientes de oro allí.   **4.** Yo busqué la cartera de mi hijo toda la mañana. ¿Quién sabe dónde estará?   **5.** Paco durmió más que nosotros porque trabajó todo el día ayer.   **6.** Queremos que conozcas a Mercedita. Ella es la más joven de la familia.   **7.** Yo comencé a verificar la mercancía que llegó ayer.   **8.** ¡Felicitaciones! Ud. ganó más de un millón de pesos.   **J.** boca, rodillas, abrigo, zapatos, ojos, sangre, brazos

LECCIÓN 9:   **A. 1.** dimos   **2.** hizo   **3.** fueron   **4.** diste   **5.** hicieron   **B.** Answers vary.   **C. 1.** di de comer   **2.** dieron un paseo   **3.** dio las gracias   **4.** dimos prisa   **D. 1.** tuve   **2.** quise, pude   **3.** estuve, dormí   **4.** supe, vino   **5.** trajo   **6.** di   **7.** dije   **E.** Answers vary.   **F. 1.** era   **2.** vivíamos   **3.** había   **4.** asistía   **5.** aprendía   **6.** caminaba   **7.** iba   **8.** pescaban   **9.** traían   **10.** estábamos   **G. 1.** Huberto nació en el pueblo de Santa Bárbara.   **2.** De niño era astuto y sociable.   **3.** Mientras Huberto asistía al instituto, él conoció a Corina un día en la clase.   **4.** Se enamoró de Corina y se casó con ella.   **5.** Poco después se mudaron a la capital porque ...   **6.** allí ellos conocían a unos viejos amigos del instituto.   **7.** Huberto y Corina abrieron una tienda de ropa fina.   **8.** Los domingos generalmente daban un paseo o veían una comedia.   **9.** Un año después ellos tuvieron una hija preciosa ...   **10.** y le pusieron el nombre de Barbarita.   **H. 1.** nos divertimos

2. Alquilamos 3. salimos 4. Tomamos 5. comenzamos 6. iba 7. rompió 8. tuvimos 9. esperábamos
10. decidimos 11. podíamos 12. era 13. llegó 14. cambió 15. seguimos 16. llegamos 17. fuimos
18. hablaba 19. visitaba 20. asistimos 21. comimos 22. bailamos 23. se ganó **I.** Composition. **J. 1.** Por
favor, quiero que me traigas estas cosas del supermercado: tres libras de jamón, dos libras de arroz, una docena
de naranjas, una libra de frijoles negros y cinco libras de patatas. **2.** Mis padres se mudaron de su
apartamento y compraron una casa nueva. Tiene tres dormitorios, un baño y medio, una cocina, un comedor,
una sala, un salón de estar, un garaje y . . . una hipoteca grande. **3.** Nos quedamos dos días en el Hotel Caribe
mientras estábamos en San Juan. El sábado nuestros amigos nos buscaron en el hotel y nos enseñaron la
ciudad. **4.** Se nos acabó el dinero y tuvimos que llamar el banco en seguida. **5.** Carmencita dijo que tenía
mucha sed y que bebió todo el jugo de toronja. **6.** Yo trabajaba en el supermercado, pero la semana pasada yo
comencé a trabajar en la farmacia de mi tío.

LECCIÓN 10: **A.** *carnes:* el jamón, el tocino, el cerdo; *vegetales:* el maíz, los frijoles, la cebolla, el arroz; *bebidas:*
el vino, la cerveza, la leche; *frutas:* la manzana, la naranja, la toronja, las uvas, el melocotón **B. 1.** está
crudo **2.** está muy dulce . **3.** no pedí eso **4.** dije revueltos y no fritos **5.** está fría **6.** esto está sucio
C. conocerás, conocerá, conoceremos, conocerán; tomaré, tomarás, tomará, tomaremos, tomarán; tendré, tendrás,
tendrá, tendremos, tendrán; veré, verás, verá, veremos, verán; almorzaré, almorzarás, almorzará, almorzaremos,
almorzarán; sabré, sabrás, sabrá, sabremos, sabrán; asistiré, asistirás, asistirá, asistiremos, asistirán; iré, irás, irá,
iremos, irán; saldré, saldrás, saldrá, saldremos, saldrán. **D. 1.** Te cansarás de esperar. **2.** Hará fresco en el
campo. **3.** Te dirán que pagues más. **4.** Querrán que salgamos por aquí. **5.** No nos entenderán bien.
E. Composition. **F. 1.** Los niños tendrían hambre. **2.** Me gustaría el bistec medio. **3.** Estefanía dice que
vendría a los Estados Unidos en el verano. **4.** ¿Me podría Ud. ver por la mañana? **G.** Answers vary. **1.** No, no
la conozco. **2.** Sí, lo conozco. **3.** Sí las conozco. **4.** No, no los conozco. **5.** Sí, te conozco bien a ti.
H. 1. podré ayudarte **2.** voy a seguirlo **3.** los recogeré temprano **4.** llámame por teléfono más tarde
5. espéranos en el café **I. 1.** Cópielo. No lo copie. **2.** Escríbalos. No los escriba. **3.** Póngala. No la ponga.
4. Menciónelas. No las mencione. **5.** Tráigalo. No lo traiga. **J.** Composition. **K.** ¡Caray! ¿dónde pusiste las
cucharitas, los cuchillos y los tenedores? **2.** ¿Comerán comidas picantes? **3.** ¿No se cansa de trabajar todo el
día? **4.** Me gustaría probar el vino tinto. **5.** ¿Estos platos? Los traje de Mexico. ¿Esas tazas? Las compré aquí.
6. El jefe está pensando en Ud, no en mí. **7.** ¿Quieren Uds. ir de compras conmigo esta tarde?
8. Marilú y Estela te esperarían a ti a la entrada del teatro.

LECCIÓN 11: **A. 1.** Armando le mandó una invitación al dueño. Armando sent an invitation to the owner.
2. ¿Me quieres traducir la carta? Do you want to translate the letter for me? **3.** Te regalamos las entradas. We
are giving you the tickets as a gift. **4.** Les presté los discos de música española a los profesores. I loaned the
Spanish music records to the teachers. **5.** Les trataré de escribir más frecuentemente. I will try to write to you
more frequently. **B. 1.** te **2.** le **3.** le **4.** le **5.** le **6.** nos **7.** le **8.** le **9.** te **C. 1.** Yo les enseñé la casa a los
compradores. Yo se la enseñé a ellos. **2.** ¿Quiénes darán donaciones a ti? ¿Quiénes te las darán?
3. Consuelo nos envió los paquetes a nosotros. Consuelo nos los envió. **4.** Mañana les devolveré las cosas a
ellos. Mañana se los devolveré. **5.** ¿Le trajiste el informe al profesor? ¿Se lo trajiste al profesor? **D. 1.** Sí, se las
envié. **2.** Sí, se las pedí. **3.** Sí, se las compramos. **4.** Sí, te las lavé. **5.** Sí, te la limpiamos. **E.** Answers
vary: **1.** ¿Cuántos años trabaja Ud. en ese lugar? Trabajo . . . **2.** ¿A qué universidad asiste Ud.? Asisto a . . .
3. ¿En qué se especializa Ud.? Me especializo en . . . **4.** ¿Cuántos días perdió Ud. de trabajo este año? Perdí . . .
5. ¿A quiénes les pidió Ud. cartas de recomendación? Pedí cartas de recomendación a . . . **6.** ¿Qué innovación
significativa hizo Ud. en su último empleo? En mi último empleo yo . . . **F. 1.** Tito había llegado antes a la
clase. **2.** Rita y Bruno habían escrito en la pizarra antes. **3.** Nadie había visto la película «Don Quijote»
anteriormente. **4.** Alejo y yo habíamos dicho el diálogo ya. **5.** Yo había terminado el examen más
temprano. **G.** Dialogue. **H. 1.** ¿En qué puedo servirle? **2.** Déme el paquete a mí no a él. **3.** ¿Quiere mandar
la mercancía a ellos? **4.** ¿El dinero? Él se lo pedirá a ellos. **5.** ¿Las tijeras? ¿A quién las prestaste? **6.** ¿Has
ido al oeste recientemente? **7.** El mecánico no había revisto las ruedas ni los frenos. **8.** Su auto no era
confortable. Era muy estrecho y ruidoso. **9.** Prefiero que la llames a cobrar. **10.** Mis abuelos me regalaron un
suéter bonito de lana, pero tuve que devolverlo a la tienda esta mañana porque era demasiado pequeño.

LECCIÓN 12: **A.** mundo; Aunque; sin; gran; casarse; atrae; gustan; escritores; Algunas; mejores. **B. 1.** Nos gusta
el fútbol, pero no nos gustan las carreras de auto. **2.** Te faltan las entradas, pero no te falta el recibo. **3.** Les
parecen caros las sandalias, pero no les parecen caros los zapatos. **4.** Le gusta viajar, pero no le gustan los

hoteles. **C.** Composition. **D. 1.** Possible answers include: compres algo, pagues la cuenta, hagas las compras, vayas a . . ., traigas . . . **2.** Possible answers include: salgan de casa, contesten la carta, se acuesten, se muden, vendan . . . **3.** Possible answers include: explique, diga, repita, mencione . . . **4.** Possible answers include: lleve, acompañe, recoja, traiga, ayude **E.** Answer vary, but all are in the subjunctive. **F.** Answers vary.

G. 1. juegues. We will pay for your studies provided (that) you play basketball. **2.** aprendas. We will help you with English so (that) you will learn more quickly. **3.** comience. We will present you to the instructors in your major area before the school year begins. **4.** vengas. We will give you a private room when you come. **5.** estorbe. You will be able to study without anyone bothering you. **H. 1.** Nadie te resolverá el problema. **2.** Nada bueno nos pasará. **3.** Nunca celebro mi cumpleaños. **4.** Tampoco me pareció divertido el paseo. **5.** Ninguna de las jóvenes bailará conmigo. **I. 1.** No te resolverá el problema nadie. **2.** No nos pasará nada bueno. **3.** No celebro nunca mi cumpleaños. **4.** No me pareció divertido el paseo tampoco. **5.** No bailará conmigo ninguna de las jóvenes. **J. 1.** Salimos también. **2.** Alguien llegó tarde. **3.** Siempre me gano algo. **4.** Falta alguno de ellos. **5.** Siempre diríamos eso. **K.** Composition. **L. 1.** A ellos les gusta ir a los mejores restaurantes extranjeros de la ciudad. **2.** Nos parece que faltan algunos ingredientes. **3.** Quiero que comas algo antes de que te vayas al trabajo. **4.** Siéntense Uds. para que la gente atrás puedan ver mejor. **5.** No me dormiré con tal que me lave la cara y tome una taza de café. **6.** Bruno conducirá un poco más aunque está cansado. **7.** Vimos a Loreta cuando fuimos a la boda de su hermano. **8.** Los Fernández no tendrá ninguna otra celebración grande hasta que su hija tenga quince años.

LECCIÓN 13: **A. 1.** ¿Necesitan Uds. un empleado que escriba a máquina bien? **2.** Ellos buscan un restaurante que sirva comida criolla. **3.** No hay nadie que sepa la respuesta. **4.** Conozco personalmente al candidato que ganó las elecciones pasadas. **5.** ¿Hay algo que les guste a Uds. aquí? **6.** ¡Lo sentimos, pero no hay nada que nos guste! **7.** Necesito una loción que me proteja del sol. **8.** ¡Caramba! No conozco a nadie que olvide tantas cosas como tú! **B. 1.** ¿Crees que la profesora esté preocupada? Sí, creo que está preocupada. No, no creo que esté preocupada. **2.** ¿Duda que la profesora esté de mal humor? Sí, dudo que esté de mal humor. No, no dudo que la profesora está de mal humor. **3.** Están seguros que la profesora está enferma hoy? Sí estamos seguros que la profesora está enferma hoy. No, no estamos seguros que la profesora esté enferma hoy. **4.** ¿Es cierto que la profesora está harta de revisar tantos papeles? Sí, es cierto que la profesora está harta de revisar tantos papeles. No, no está cierto que la profesora esté harta de revisar tantos papeles. **5.** ¿Es posible que la profesora esté enamorada de alguien? Sí, es posible que esté enamorada de alguien. No, no es posible que esté enamorada de alguien. **C.** Answers vary. **D. 1.** Nuestro candidato buscaba soluciones que fueran justas y imparciales. **2.** Era posible que él mejorara la economía. **3.** No conocía a nadie que tuviera más experiencia. **4.** Les pedía que protegieran su voto contra el fraude. **5.** Les llamaba para que Uds. apoyaran a nuestro candidato. **E.** Answers vary. **F.** Composition. **G.** Answers vary. **H. 1.** Esperamos que el nivel de vida en América Latina mejore. **2.** No hay nadie que te ofrezca más dinero que yo. **3.** Conozco a un amigo que puede reparar tu auto. **4.** Dudamos que el gobierno reduzca los impuestos este año. **5.** Te digo que estoy harto de tanto papeleo. **6.** Nuestro profesor de español quería que leyéramos la biografía de la reina Isabel. **7.** Si yo fuera Ud., no discutiría este problema con nadie ahora.

LECCIÓN 14: **A.** Answers vary. **B.** "Simple Verses": I am a sincere man / from where the palm tree grows, / And before I die, I want / to pour forth my verses from my soul. / Everything is beautiful and constant, / everything is music and reason, / And everything, like the diamond / before being light is coal. "Song of the Horseman" Cordoba / Distant and lonely. / Black pony, large moon / and olives in my saddlebag. / Although I know the roads / I will never arrive in Cordoba. Through the plains, through the wind, / Black pony, red moon. / Death is looking at me / from the towers of Cordoba. Oh, what a long road! / Oh, my valiant pony! / Oh, death awaits me / before arriving in Cordoba. / Cordoba / Distant and lonely.

Essentials of Spanish CONTIGO

OSCAR OZETE
University of Southern Indiana

SERGIO D. GUILLÉN
Anderson College

HOLT, RINEHART AND WINSTON   New York   Chicago   San Francisco   Philadelphia

ESSENTIALS OF SPANISH **CONTIGO**

Montreal Toronto London Sydney Tokyo Mexico City Rio de Janeiro Madrid

*Con cariños a nuestras familias
por su paciencia y devoción.*

PUBLISHER *Nedah Abbott*
EXECUTIVE EDITOR Marilyn Pérez-Abreu
DEVELOPMENTAL EDITOR Irwin Stern
PROJECT EDITOR Paula Kmetz
PRODUCTION MANAGER Lula Als
ART DIRECTOR Renée Davis
TEXT DESIGN Gayle Jaeger
DRAWINGS Tom O'Sullivan
PICTURE RESEARCH Rona Tuccillo
COMPOSITION AND CAMERA WORK *Waldman Graphics, Inc.*

Photo credits appear on page 323.

Library of Congress Cataloging-in-Publication Data

Ozete, Oscar.
   Contigo, essentials of Spanish.

   Includes index.
   1. Spanish language—Text-books for foreign speakers—
English.   2. Spanish language—Grammar—1950–
I. Guillén, Sergio D.   II. Title.
PC4129.E509   1987   468.2'421   86–14945

ISBN 0-03-001828-5

Address correspondence to:
383 Madison Avenue
New York, NY 10017

CBS COLLEGE PUBLISHING
Holt, Rinehart and Winston
The Dryden Press
Saunders College Publishing

Prefacio

Overview

Contigo is a first-year college text that focuses on the practical, communicative function of language. While stressing the essentials, **Contigo** nonetheless covers fully the fundamentals. The text is thoroughly integrated — teaching the four skills — through structures and situations that facilitate rapid understanding and communication. Maximum practice with common spoken language is possible since more low-frequency constructions appear primarily as recognition items only. As such, **Contigo** responds to the current foreign language trend that calls for an oral proficiency-based curriculum. The Spanish in **Contigo** is simple but natural, with emphasis on language that best enables students to express their ideas, feelings, interests and experiences.

Organization

The *Primera parte* of **Contigo** contains 6 *Conversaciones diarias* that provide basic hearing and speaking practice for successful communication from the outset. *Notas culturales* sections provide relevant cultural information. Pronunciation exercises concentrate on distinctive Spanish sounds. The *Segunda parte* and *Tercera parte* of **Contigo** consist of 14 *Lecciones* which gradually develop proficiency in the language. The lessons begin with short, real-life dialogues that engage students in attaining an oral command of the content. Graded exercises are included to modify and expand the major structures presented in the dialogues. The vocabulary from the lessons centers around a thematic unit, e.g., the airport, the hotel reception desk, the market, and so forth.

Grammatical explanations are succinct and represent contemporary usage. Emphasis is on the communicative function of the grammatical items. Command forms and the subjunctive after verbs denoting wish or emotion are introduced in the first half of the text. This allows students greater flexibility in communication, since it does not unduly delay their ability to state what they want done or to express how they feel about situations affecting them.

A variety of exercises has been incorporated in the lessons to enhance student participation both in asking for and supplying information. The exercises stress the practical and communicative function of language within the appropriate social setting. Most of these activities are designed to encourage group interaction so that communication is more lifelike and learners can feel more at ease. Salient grammatical topics and expressions are systematically reintroduced to sharpen accuracy while at the same time engendering the creative use of language.

Observaciones sections present cultural readings of a more utilitarian nature, providing the student with important social, political and economic information. The lessons end with *Actividades*, a brief exercise or exercises generally adapted from Spanish language correspondence, realia, or periodicals. Four *Exámenes* provide a genuine review of previous lessons through exercises that emphasize the re-entry of vocabulary and structures in a varied format. *Lecciones* 7 and 14 consist of readings that introduce geographic, historical, and artistic information.

Supplementary Materials

The *Manual de ejercicios y Manual de laboratorio* serves primarily as a workbook and secondarily as a lab manual. Lessons from the main text have corresponding listening, speaking and writing exercises in the *Manual*. The cassettes that accompany the workbook have sufficient explanations and cues so that portions of the tapes could easily be used without referring to the printed page, e.g., while traveling in a car or working at home.

The front matter of the *Instructor's Edition* provides suggestions for introducing the text material, as well as helpful hints and techniques to enrich the communicative competence of the students. Sample lesson plans and a sample quiz are provided.

Acknowledgments

The authors would like to thank the following reviewers for their insightful and much appreciated comments: Emilie Cannon, Wright State University; Teresa Cook, Piedmont Virginia Community College; James Davis, Howard University; Frank A. Domínguez, University of North Carolina at Chapel Hill; James Ford, University of Arkansas; Richard Ford, University of Texas at El Paso; Alan Garfinkel, Purdue University; Barbara González-Pino, University of Texas at San Antonio; Donna J. Gustafson, San José State University; Kathleen Hennessey, Rock Valley College; Deane Hetric, Southern Connecticut State; Philip Johnson, Baylor University; Carol Klee, University of Illinois; Jaime Montesinos, Borough of Manhattan Community College; Thomas D. Morin, University of Rhode Island; Rosa Perelmutter-Pérez, University of North Carolina; Mildred Wilkinson, Southern Illinois University; Juan C. Zamora, University of Massachusetts at Amherst.

We would also like to express our sincere gratitude to Vince Duggan for his steadfast support in the launching of this project, Paula Kmetz for her painstaking efforts in leading the manuscript through production, and Mary Root Taucher for her thorough reading of the manuscript.

Finally, special thanks to Susan Kriege and Judy Zinszer for their help in preparing the manuscript.

O.O.—S.D.G.

Contenido

Primera parte
Conversaciones diarias

1 *Los nombres* (NAMES)

It is the first day of class, and two students are introducing themselves.
They smile and shake hands.

LUIS Buenos días. Me llamo° Luis Alonso. ¿Cómo se llama usted?°
IRENE Me llamo Irene Pérez.
LUIS Mucho gusto,° Irene.
IRENE El gusto es mío.°

My name is (lit. I call myself) / What is your name?

Glad to meet you

The pleasure is mine.

Expresiones

Buenos días   *Good morning*
Buenas tardes   *Good afternoon*
Buenas noches   *Good evening*

Listen carefully as your instructor pronounces the Spanish names below.
Learn to recognize these names in Spanish and be ready to assume a Spanish
name in class.

Adela	Elena	María	Andrés	Jaime (Diego)	Pedro
Ana, Anita	Inés	Patricia	Antonio	José (Pepe)	Ricardo
Bárbara	Isabel	Sara	Carlos	Juan	Roberto
Berta	Juana	Susana	Eduardo	Miguel	Tomás
Carmen	Margarita	Teresa	Francisco (Pancho)	Pablo	Vicente

ADAPTACIÓN
Act out the opening dialogue with a classmate. Try to use your Spanish
name and vary Buenos días to Buenas tardes or Buenas noches.

Los números 0–12

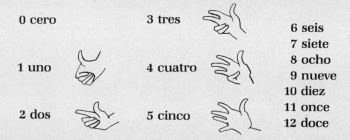

0 cero	3 tres	6 seis
1 uno	4 cuatro	7 siete
		8 ocho
		9 nueve
2 dos	5 cinco	10 diez
		11 once
		12 doce

Uno becomes **un** before a masculine noun: **un amigo**—*a (one) male friend.*
Una is used before a feminine noun: **una amiga**—*a (one) female friend.* The
same occurs with larger numbers ending in **uno** (21, 31, 101, etc.).

PRÁCTICA
a Lea *(Read)* en español.

3 amigos	12 pesos	1 secreto	6 estudiantes
1 maestro	10 minutos	5 días	1 maestra

b Below are signs you might see in a Spanish-speaking country. Rank
them from most important (1) to least important (5) according to your
opinion. Then compare your ranking with another student.

MODELO: **Número uno... Número dos es...**

ascensor   prohibido   caja   fuego   (push)
            fumar   (fire)

Pronunciación

Las vocales

Spanish vowels are more tense and shorter, and do not have the accompanying glide or diphthong that characterizes English vowels. Unlike English,
Spanish vowels maintain their basic sound and do not reduce to an *uh* sound
in unstressed positions.

Pronounce these words after your instructor.

a as in f*a*ther:

casa banana sala mala fama

e as in b*e*t:

mesa tenis peso de tela

i and **y** as in f*ee*t:

sí fin piso cinco minutos y

o as in h*o*me, but without the *u* glide:

como solo dos pico foto

u as in t*oo*l:

uno tú Cuba luna gusto

¡en acción!

Los diptongos

A diphthong is the combination of any two vowels that includes **i** (**y**) or **u**. The emphasis falls on the strong vowels **a**, **e**, and **o** and not on the weak vowels **i** (**y**) and **u**.

siete tiene seis gracias aire estudio soy
agua cuando auto bueno duermo Luis muy

In a diphthong with two weak vowels **i** (**y**) and **u**, the second vowel has the stronger stress:

Luis fui ciudad viuda

La acentuación

Words that end in a vowel, a diphthong, or the consonants **n** or **s** are stressed on the next to the last syllable. (Each syllable has one vowel or diphthong.)

pa-so a-**mi**-ga fa-**mi**-lia es-**tu**-dio es-**tu**-dian **tar**-des **fe**-o

Words that end in a consonant other than **n** or **s** are stressed on the last syllable.

se-**ñor** pa-**pel** es-tu-**diar** us-**ted**

Words that do not follow the above two patterns have a written accent to indicate the stressed syllable:

a-**diós** me-**cá**-ni-co te-**lé**-fo-no es-ta-**ción**

Accents are also used:

1. with interrogative words:

¿Cómo? *How?* ¿Cuándo? *When?* ¿Qué? *What?*

2. exclamations:

¡Qué gusto! *What a pleasure!*

3. to differentiate words identical in spelling but different in meaning:

tú *you* tu *your* sí *yes* si *if*
él *he* el *the* sólo *only* solo *alone*

Palabras familiares *(Familiar words)*

Many Spanish words will become familiar to you as you learn the sounds of your new language. Listen and repeat after your instructor.

importante	famoso	inteligente	interesante	tímido
sincero	moderno	estudioso	expresivo	serio
flexible	curioso	intenso	magnífico	sentimental
generoso	ambicioso	atractivo	afectuoso	fantástico
activo	cómico	dinámico	eficiente	impresionante

CONTESTE EN ESPAÑOL. *(Answer in Spanish.)*

MODELO: ¿Es usted tradicional? *(Are you . . . ?)* **Sí, soy tradicional.** *(Yes, I am . . .)*
No, no soy... *(No I am not . . .)*

1. ¿Es usted sentimental?
2. ¿Es usted tolerante?
3. ¿Es usted ambicioso (ambiciosa, *f.*)?
4. ¿Es usted modesto(a)? ¿sarcástico(a)?
5. ¿Es usted muy *(very)* sociable?
6. ¿Es usted curioso(a)? ¿famoso(a)?
7. ¿Es usted muy estudioso(a)?
8. ¿Es usted discreto(a) o *(or)* indiscreto(a)?
9. ¿Es usted muy paciente o muy impaciente?
10. ¿Es usted muy responsable o muy irresponsable?

PRIMERAS IMPRESIONES

a Use five of the adjectives above to describe your first impressions of your instructor; then compare your impressions with a classmate's.

MODELO: **Es inteligente.**
Es atractivo(a).

b Using five adjectives, describe your first impressions of a classmate. See if he or she agrees with you.

MODELO: *You:* **Usted es muy estudioso(a).**
Classmate: **Sí, soy muy estudioso(a).**
No, no soy...

¿Inglés o español?

English and Spanish share many words derived from Latin. Listen carefully as your instructor reads the Spanish words.

INGLÉS	ESPAÑOL	INGLÉS	ESPAÑOL
nation	**nación**	*history*	**historia**
society	**sociedad**	*fantastic*	**fantástico**
curious	**curioso**	*student*	**estudiante**

¿CÓMO SE DICE EN ESPAÑOL?   *(How do you say . . . ?)*
tradition, civilization, university, public (**púb...**), family, delicious, studious, direction, variety

Expresiones para la clase

Escuche usted.	*Listen.*
Repita.	*Repeat.*
Pregúntele.	*Ask him (her).*
Contéstele.	*Answer him (her).*
Abra el libro.	*Open the book.*
Cierre la puerta.	*Close the door.*

The preceding commands can be made plural by adding **n** to the verb.
Usted(es) may be left out.

Escuchen (ustedes).	*Listen. (you, pl.)*
Pregúntenle.	

SITUACIÓN
Introduce two students to one another.

MODELO: Usted:.   **Juanita Mendoza, David Vega**
Juanita: **Mucho gusto.**
David: **El gusto...**

DOS **2** *Los saludos* (GREETINGS)

Yolanda and a family friend, Mrs. del Valle, run into each other. They stop and ask how each other is.

Señora del Valle, ¿Cómo está?

YOLANDA Buenas tardes, señora del Valle. ¿Cómo está usted?°	*How are you?*
LA SEÑORA Muy bien, gracias. ¿Y usted?°	*Very well, thank you. And you?*
YOLANDA Así, así... un poco cansada.° ¿Cómo está la familia°?	*So so . . . a little tired. / family*
LA SEÑORA Todos bien, gracias. Adiós.°	*All fine, thank you. Good-bye.*
YOLANDA *Hasta luego.°	*See you later.*

Expresiones

¡Hola!	*Hello! Hi!*
¿Qué tal?	*How are things?* (less formal than **¿Cómo está usted?**)
Hasta* mañana.	*Until tomorrow.*
señor (Sr.)	*sir, Mr.*
señora (Sra.)	*madam, ma'am, Mrs.*
señorita (Srta.)	*miss*

*The **h** is not pronounced in Spanish except in the consonant group **ch** (**mucho**).

9

ADAPTACIÓN

Complete the following dialogue with a classmate. Use the person's first name.

A: ¡Hola, _____! ¿Qué tal?

B: Así, _____, gracias. ¿Cómo está la familia?

A: Todos _____, _____. Adiós.

B: Hasta _____.

La familia Ochoa

Julio Ochoa
el padre *(the father)*

Marta García de Ochoa
la madre *(the mother)*

Diego
el hijo *(the son)*

Yolanda
la hija *(the daughter)*

NOTA CULTURAL

In Spanish-speaking countries married women retain their maiden names. The husband's surname, prefaced by **de** (of), is added to the wife's name. Thus, Marta García adds **de Ochoa** to her name. The children, in turn, have the surname of each parent. For example, for official purposes Yolanda is referred to as Yolanda Ochoa García.

Masculino y femenino

Nouns and adjectives in Spanish are either masculine or feminine. However, in a group of both males and females, Spanish uses the masculine plural form. For example, **hermanos** can refer to a group of both brothers and sisters (siblings) as well as to a group of brothers only; likewise, **padres** can refer to both parents or to fathers. The feminine plural refers only to females: **hermanas** means sisters; **amigas** means female friends.

Yolanda y su° familia
her

Somos° cuatro en mi familia: mi mamá, mi papá, mi hermano y yo.° Todos somos de° San José, Costa Rica.

We are / I from

Mis abuelos° Carmen y Jesús Ochoa son muy simpáticos.° Son° de España.

grandparents / nice / They are

Tío° Pedro es agricultor° y tía Gloria es ama de casa.° Mi prima° Conchita es profesora de biología y su esposo,° Fermín, es administrador. Mi primo° Juanito es estudiante. Es muy alegre° y simpático.

Uncle / farmer / housewife / cousin (f.)

spouse / cousin (m.) happy

PRÁCTICA

Describe Yolanda's family indicating the relationship of each member to her.

MODELO: **Juanito es su primo.**

El árbol genealógico

ADAPTACIÓN

Using Yolanda's description of her family as a guide, describe your family. Use your family tree or a family photo to illustrate.

MODELO: **Mi abuela es Anita. Es de Los Ángeles. Es magnífica.**

La familia hispana es muy unida.° El divorcio es raro. Tradicionalmente° el padre es el jefe° absoluto de la familia. La señora atiende° a los hijos y la casa.

Los abuelos ocupan una posición importante en la familia. Frecuentemente tres generaciones viven° en una casa: los abuelos, los padres y los niños.°

Los niños tienen° padrinos.° Generalmente son un tío o una tía o unos buenos amigos de la familia. Los padrinos tienen la responsabilidad de ayudar° a los niños.

united / Traditionally
chief, head / takes care of

live / children
have / godparents
of helping

Pronunciación

H is not pronounced in Spanish.

Escuche y repita. (*Listen and repeat.*)

hasta hermana hombre hoy ahora ahí

B and **v** are pronounced alike in Spanish. At the beginning of a word group or after an **m** sound, **b** (**v**) is made with both lips close together like the English *b* in *boat*. Elsewhere, **b** (**v**) is made with the lips barely touching.

LIPS CLOSED		LIPS BARELY TOUCHING	
va	también	no va	nueve
bueno	nombre	el banco	deben
ve		muy bien	favorito

Ll and **y** at the beginning of a syllable, as in **mayo** (ma-yo), are pronounced like the English *y* in *yes* by most Spanish speakers. **Ll** forms one consonant in Spanish.

llamo calle callo llueve mayo Yucatán vaya ayer

Ñ is pronounced approximately like the English *ni* in *onion*. (The wavy line above the letter is called **la tilde**.)

español mañana señor año niña otoño montaña

S, z, and **c** (before **e** or **i**) in Latin America are pronounced like *s* in *sit*.*

sí solo San Francisco diez Venezuela cero cinco

Unlike English, the **s** between vowels is *not* voiced (the z sound of English). This also applies to **z**.

casa	peso	presidente	música
lazo	cerveza (*beer*)	razón (*reason*)	rosa

*In Spain **z** and **c** before **e** or **i** are pronounced like *th* in *then*.

Make sure you maintain the **s** sound in the endings **-sión** and **-ción** and avoid the English *-shun*.

mi**sión** pa**sión** confu**sión** na**ción** esta**ción**

C before **a**, **o**, and **u** has a hard **k** sound like *c* in *Coca-Cola*.

California ¿**c**ómo? **c**urva

División en sílabas

1. The most common syllable pattern is a single consonant (including **ch**, **ll**, and **rr**) plus a vowel or diphthong.

se-ñor bue-no sie-te mu-cho gui-ta-rra va-lle fa-mi-lia a-mi-go

2. When there are two consonants together, the syllable is divided between the two, except in most words where **l** or **r** is the second consonant.

gus-to es-pa-ñol can-sa-do lec-ción ar-te
BUT cua-tro pa-dre blan-co ha-bla

3. Three consonants are divided between the second and the third, unless the third is **l** or **r**.

ins-tan-te trans-mi-tir
BUT nom-bre com-pren-der

4. A written accent over the **i** or **u** breaks the diphthong:

dí-a, Ra-úl

The strong vowels (**a**, **e**, and **o**) are separated:

i-de-a le-o

PRÁCTICA
Pronounce the following words then write each word and divide it into syllables. Underline the stressed syllable.

MODELO: gracias gra-cias

niña	muy	calle
madre	carro	ahora
América	particular	escribir
adiós	fácil	transporte
muchacho	mío	apartamento
treinta	estudio	
inglés	Puerto Rico	
acción	teatro	

Los números 13–30

13	trece	22	veinte y dos (veintidós)
14	catorce	23	veinte y tres (veintitrés)
15	quince	24	veinte y cuatro (veinticuatro)
16	diez y seis (dieciséis)	25	veinte y cinco (veinticinco)
17	diez y siete (diecisiete)	26	veinte y seis (veintiséis)
18	diez y ocho (dieciocho)	27	veinte y siete (veintisiete)
19	diez y nueve (diecinueve)	28	veinte y ocho (veintiocho)
20	veinte	29	veinte y nueve (veintinueve)
21	veinte y uno (veintiuno)	30	treinta

Note that the numbers 16–29 may be written as one word. Recall that numbers formed with *uno* have masculine and feminine forms: veinti*ún* muchachos; veinti*una* muchachas.

La aritmética

$$+ \text{ y} \qquad - \text{ menos} \qquad = \text{ son}$$
$$6 + 6 = 12 \qquad \text{Seis y seis son doce.}$$
$$10 - 5 = 5 \qquad \text{Diez menos cinco son cinco.}$$

LEA Y COMPLETE.

1. $15 + 5 =$	4. $7 + 7 =$	7. $25 - 5 =$	
2. $8 + 5 =$	5. $10 + 11 =$	8. $16 - 8 =$	10. $24 - 12 =$
3. $9 + 6 =$	6. $30 - 2 =$	9. $21 - 10 =$	

SITUACIONES

a Several students are telling how far they live from the center of campus. What do they say?

MODELO: 30 km   **treinta kilómetros**

1. 25 km	3. 12 km	5. 27 km	7. 11 km	9. 26 km
2. 18 km	4. 15 km	6. 30 km	8. 14 km	

b Marisa is buying stamps of different denominations at a Mexican post office. What does she say?

MODELO: 10/\$4   **diez sellos de cuatro pesos**

1. 15/\$4   2. 13/\$10   3. 8/\$15   4. 12/\$20   5. 4/\$25   6. 2/\$30

Mexico uses the \$ sign for **peso.** You can check with banks or newspapers to get current exchange rates.

TRES **3** *El tiempo* (THE WEATHER)

Hace (mucho) sol.

It's (very) sunny.

Hace (mucho) calor.

It's (very) hot.

Hace fresco.

It's cool.

Hace buen tiempo.

The weather is fine.

Hace (mucho) frío.

It's (very) _____ .

Hace (mucho) viento.

It's (very) _____ .

Llueve.

It's _____ .

Nieva.

It's _____ .

Two friends are talking about the weather. They're in Central America, where the rainy season lasts from May until November and showers are common around midday.

GILDA ¿Qué tiempo hace,° José?

JOSÉ Hace mal tiempo.°

GILDA ¿Llueve?

JOSÉ Sí, mucho.

GILDA ¡Caramba, y no tengo paraguas!°

How's the weather?

The weather is bad.

Golly, and I don't have an umbrella!

ADAPTACIÓN

Have a classmate play the role of a foreign student who asks about the weather in your city during February, April, July, and October. Supply the appropriate information in the blanks.

1. a. ¿Hace frío en febrero?
   b. _____
   a. ¿Nieva mucho?
   b. _____

2. a. ¿Qué tiempo _____ en abril?
   b. Hace _____
   a. ¿Llueve?
   b. _____

3. a. ¿ _____ en julio?
   b. _____
   a. ¿Hace calor?
   b. _____
   a. ¿Hace sol?
   b. _____

4. a. ¿Hace fresco en octubre?
   b. _____
   a. ¿Hace viento?
   b. _____

PRÁCTICA

a Pregúntele a otro(a) estudiante. (*Ask another student.*)

1. ¿Llueve?
2. ¿Tienes (*Do you have*) paraguas?
3. ¿Qué tiempo hace?
4. ¿Hace frío en la clase? ¿en la cafetería?

b Can you match the weather forecaster's words with the symbols?
soleado lluvia nieve nublado

1. ◯

2. ◔

3. ❈

4. ▨

¿Qué hora es? *(WHAT TIME IS IT?)*

Son las nueve.

Son las once.

Son las doce y cuarto (y quince).

Es la una y media (y treinta).

Son las diez menos cuarto (menos quince).

Son las ocho menos cinco.

Son las is used from two to twelve o'clock, and **es la** is used for one o'clock. Minutes are added to the hour up to and including the half hour (+ **y**). Between the half hour and the next hour, minutes are subtracted from the next hour (− **menos**).

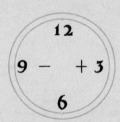

El reloj *(watch, clock)*

ADAPTACIÓN
¿Qué hora es?

1. Son las _____ .

2. Son las _____ .

3. Son las _____ .

4. Son las _____ .

5. Son las _____ .

6. Es la _____ .

7. _____ .

8. _____ .

9. _____ .

Pregúntele a otro(a) estudiante: ¿Qué hora es?

NOTA CULTURAL

El concepto de la hora es diferente en Hispanoamérica y España, especialmente en los círculos° sociales. Las personas normalmente llegan° a una fiesta
treinta minutos o una hora tarde°. Esto° permite terminar los preparativos
para° la fiesta. Las conversaciones son largas° y animadas.

circles / arrive
late / This
for / long

Los países

PRÁCTICA
Choose the correct answer.
¿Qué país... *(What country...)*

1. forma parte de la América Central?
   a. Chile   *b.* Honduras   *c.* Paraguay
2. es una isla *(island)* en el Mar Caribe?
   a. Cuba   *b.* Islas Canarias   *c.* Venezuela
3. es una república grande en Sudamérica?
   a. España   *b.* Argentina   *c.* México
4. fue *(was)* colonia de Portugal? El portugués es la lengua oficial.
   a. Guatemala   *b.* Perú   *c.* Brasil
5. es un estado libre *(free)* y asociado con los Estados Unidos? La capital es San Juan.
   a. Ecuador   *b.* República Dominicana   *c.* Puerto Rico

Pronunciación

J is pronounced approximately like the English *h* in *hat*.

bajo	Jiménez	junio
jefe	mujer	José

J has a more guttural sound in Spain than it does in Spanish America. The **x** in the words **México** and **Texas** is also pronounced like the Spanish **j**. **G** before **e** or **i** is also pronounced like the Spanish **j**.

gente	generoso	agente	agencia
gigante	gimnasio	página	general

In all other positions **g** has a hard sound like *g* in *go*.

negocio	supongo	golfo	garaje
gigante	programa	gusto	gato

Note that **u** is not pronounced in the letter groups **gue** and **gui**.

guitarra (gui-ta-rra)	**guí**a (guí-a)	**Gui**llermo (Gui-ller-mo)
si**gue** (si-gue)	pa**gue** (pa-gue)	**gue**rra (gue-rra)

P is said without the puff of air that accompanies the English *p*.

pan peso prensa por piso puro papá

Qu is pronounced like *k* and appears before **e** or **i**.

que quince quien porque yanqui

But notice the **k** sound for **c** with other vowels.

café cosa cuánto Caracas

X before a consonant is pronounced like English *ss* in *miss*.

extra expreso explicar extremo

Between vowels, **x** is pronounced like the English *ks* or *gs*, but never as *gz*.

exacto sexo examen máximo

Los números 31–99

31	treinta y uno*	50	cincuenta	80	ochenta
32	treinta y dos	60	sesenta	90	noventa...
40	cuarenta	70	setenta	99	noventa y nueve

Los hispanos expresan la temperatura en centígrados y no en grados Fahrenheit.

C	0°	5°	10°	15°	20°	25°	30°	35°
F	32°	41°	50°	59°	68°	77°	86°	95°

*But: treinta y *un* kilómetros; treinta y una personas

The average high temperatures and number of rainy days in July appear below for three capital cities: México D.F. (Distrito Federal); Madrid, España; Buenos Aires, Argentina.

JULIO			
	México, D.F.	Madrid	Buenos Aires
TEMPERATURA (centígrados)	16°	30°	14°
DÍAS LLUVIOSOS	27	3	8

CONTESTE, POR FAVOR
En julio...

1. ¿hace fresco en México?
2. ¿hace frío o calor en Madrid?
3. ¿hace calor en Buenos Aires?
4. ¿dónde *(where)* llueve mucho?
5. ¿dónde llueve poco?
6. ¿hace calor aquí?

Spanish speakers frequently express telephone numbers in tens. For example:

20–31–45	veinte–treinta y uno–cuarenta y cinco
6–53–97–80	seis–cincuenta y tres–noventa y siete–ochenta
17–05–10	diez y siete–cero, cinco–diez

PRÁCTICA
a   Lea los números.

Hotel Presidente: 30–14–20
Restaurante Toledo: 16–50–72
Policía: 10–30–50
Taxi: 4–76–93–21
Banco Nacional: 7–80–65–90

b   ¿Cuál es su teléfono? *(What is your telephone number?)*

4 Los meses y las estaciones
(MONTHS AND SEASONS)

EL INVIERNO *winter*
- **diciembre** *December*
- **enero** *January*
- **febrero** *February*

LA PRIMAVERA *spring*
- **marzo** *March*
- **abril** *April*
- **mayo** *May*

EL VERANO *summer*
- **junio** *June*
- **julio** *July*
- **agosto** *August*

EL OTOÑO *fall*
- **septiembre** *September*
- **octubre** *October*
- **noviembre** *November*

La Paz

Madrid (izquierda); La Habana

23

En Norteamérica y España hace frío en diciembre, enero, febrero y marzo; pero en Sudamérica hace calor. Muchas de las capitales en la América Latina están en las montañas°: Bogotá, Colombia; La Paz, Bolivia; Quito, Ecuador; la ciudad° de México. Allí° hace fresco generalmente. El clima° de la América Latina varía mucho. Hace frío en los Andes y calor en el Mar Caribe,° donde llueve frecuentemente de mayo a noviembre.

are (located) in the mountains
city / There / climate
Carribbean

CONTESTE, POR FAVOR

a Las estaciones

1. ¿En qué meses hace calor aquí *(here)*?
2. ¿Cuándo hace fresco? ¿frío?
3. ¿Cuándo llueve?
4. ¿Cuándo nieva?
5. ¿Cuándo es la primavera en Norteamérica?
6. ¿Cuándo es el invierno en Sudamérica?

b Los deportes *(sports)*

1. ¿En qué estaciones jugamos *(we play)* al golf? En la primavera y...
2. ¿En qué estaciones jugamos al béisbol? ¿al tenis? ¿al fútbol? ¿al básquetbol?

¿Cuál es la fecha? *(WHAT IS THE DATE?)*

Spanish uses cardinal numbers to express dates except for the first (**primero**) of the month.

Hoy es el quince de septiembre.
Today is the fifteenth of September.

Mañana es el diez y seis.
Tomorrow is the sixteenth.

Mi cumpleaños es el primero de mayo.
My birthday is the first of May.

Invitación a una Fiesta

Fecha: el 12 de octubre
Hora: 8:30 de la noche
Lugar: San Martín #365
Firma: Pilar González

place
signature

¡feliz cumpleaños!

PREGÚNTELE A OTRO(A) ESTUDIANTE

1. ¿Cuál es la fecha de hoy?
2. ¿Cuándo es su cumpleaños?
3. ¿Cuándo es el cumpleaños de su mamá? ¿de su papá?
4. ¿Cuándo es el cumpleaños de Jorge Wáshington?
5. ¿Cuándo es el día de la independencia?
6. ¿Cuándo es la fiesta de Pilar González?

Los días de la semana (DAYS OF THE WEEK)

The days of the week in Spanish are masculine and are not capitalized.

el lunes	*Monday*
el martes	*Tuesday*
el miércoles	*Wednesday*
el jueves	*Thursday*
el viernes	*Friday*
el sábado	*Saturday*
el domingo	*Sunday*

NOTA CULTURAL

Para los hispanos el lunes es el primer° día de la la semana. Cada° día del° calendario tiene el nombre de un santo.° Es costumbre ponerle° a un niño o una niña el nombre de un santo o una santa.

first (primer [o]) / Each / of the / saint / to put (give)

El día de la Raza, o *Columbus Day* en Norteamérica, conmemora la herencia° española en todo el mundo° hispánico.

heritage
world

OCTUBRE

LUNES	MARTES	MIÉRCOLES	JUEVES	VIERNES	SÁBADO	DOMINGO
			1	2	3	4
5	6	7	8	9	10	11
12	13	14	15	16	17	18
19	20	21	22	23	24	25
26	27	28	29	30	31	

PRÁCTICA

a Refiérase a la página 25 para contestar estas (*these*) preguntas.

1. ¿Qué día es el 7 de octubre? (**Es...**) ¿Qué día es el 10? ¿el 15? ¿el 28? ¿el 30? ¿el primero?
2. ¿Cuántos (*How many*) lunes hay (*are there*) en octubre? (**Hay...**)
3. ¿Cuántos sábados hay?
4. ¿Cuántos días hay en octubre, treinta o treinta y uno?
5. ¿Cuándo es el Día de la Raza?
6. De verdad (*Really,*) ¿qué día es hoy? (**Hoy es...**)
7. ¿Qué día es mañana?
8. ¿Qué día fue ayer (*was yesterday*)?

b Lea en español.

MODELO: Monday, July 10   **el* lunes, 10 de julio**

1. Tuesday, July 4	*4.* Sunday, March 3
2. Saturday, May 30	*5.* Friday, November 22
3. Wednesday, February 1	

Pronunciación

D in Spanish is dental; that is, the tongue tip presses against the upper front teeth to produce the sound. At the beginning of a word or word group, or after **n** or **l**, the **d** has a hard sound (the flow of air in the mouth is stopped). Elsewhere the **d** is soft (the air is allowed to escape) and is pronounced similarly to the English *th* in *these*.

Escuche y repita.

HARD D		SOFT D	
de	¿**D**ón**d**e?	to**d**o	cinco **d**ólares
diez	un **d**ólar	na**d**a	ca**d**a **d**ía
dos	el **d**octor	na**d**ie	la fiesta **d**e Pilar
¿Cuán**d**o?	Gil**d**a		

At the end of a word, **d** is so soft that at times it disappears completely:

uste**d**   verda**d**   ciuda**d**   universida**d**

T in Spanish is also dental. While **d** is voiced (vocal chords vibrate), **t** is unvoiced (unaspirated).

tú	tiempo
tonto	tomate
tostada	tres
treinta	turista

---

*Use the masculine definite article **el** with the days of the week, except when answering variations of the question **¿Qué día es hoy?** — **Hoy es lunes; ayer fue domingo.**

R is similar to the English intervocalic *t (tt)* or *dd: water, butter, ladder.*

cara	para	tren	metro	grande	aprende	perdón
duro	pero	barco	febrero	cuarto	permiso	abril

RR is made exactly like **r**, but with the tongue vibrating several times. At the beginning of a word, **r** is always pronounced like **rr**.

rojo	carro	recibo	rápido
rico	perro	tierra	cierra
Roberto	carrera	párrafo	correo

REPASO (REVIEW)
¿Qué hora es?

1.   2.   3.

¿Qué hora es?

5:18   3:26   11:45   8:40

1.   2.   3.   4.

Expressing A.M. and P.M.

> **Ballet Folklórico de México**
>
> miércoles y domingos
> a las 21 horas

The phrases **de la mañana, de la tarde**, and **de la noche** help to distinguish between A.M. and P.M.

Son las ocho **de la mañana.**   *It's 8 A.M.*
Son las ocho **de la noche.**   *It's 8 P.M.*

De la tarde is used for the afternoon until around 7:30 P.M. Business hours and time schedules (planes, trains, and programs) are frequently expressed by using the twenty-four hour-clock system. The hours one to twelve refer to A.M. and the hours twelve to twenty-four refer to P.M.

El programa es a las 21 (veintiuna) horas.   *The program is at 9:00 P.M.*

¿A qué hora es? *(AT WHAT TIME IS IT?)*

A la(s) + *time* corresponds to the English *at* + time.

¿A qué hora es la fiesta? — A las
  nueve de la noche.
La reunión es a la una.

At what time is the party? — At
  9 P.M.
The meeting is at one.

PREGÚNTELE A OTRO(A) ESTUDIANTE
1. ¿A qué hora es su clase de español? (**Es a la(s)...**)
2. ¿A qué hora es su clase de inglés? ¿de matemáticas?
3. ¿A qué hora es su programa favorito de televisión?*
4. ¿A qué hora es la cena *(dinner)* en su casa? ¿el almuerzo *(lunch)*? ¿y el desayuno *(breakfast)*?

*Use el sistema de doce horas y de veinticuatro.

Hay / No hay

The word **hay** means both *there is* and *there are.*

Hay un banco en la plaza.   There's a bank in the plaza.
Hay varios edificios.   There are several buildings.
No hay un hospital.   There isn't a hospital.

PRÁCTICA

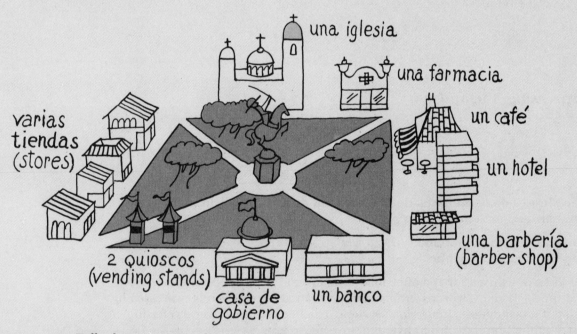

una iglesia
una farmacia
un café
un hotel
una barbería (barber shop)
varias tiendas (stores)
2 quioscos (vending stands)
casa de gobierno
un banco

a Tell what structures there are in the plaza.
Hay...

b   Conteste Ud.

1. ¿Hay árboles *(trees)* en la plaza?
2. ¿Hay animales?
3. ¿Hay un teatro?

c   Mention at least five things that are on Main Street or in the town square where you live.

d   Un anuncio (an advertisement). Conteste, por favor.

1. ¿De qué marca *(brand)* es el reloj?
2. ¿Qué por ciento (%) de descuento hay? (Hay...)
3. ¿Hay mucha selección?

5 El horario (THE SCHEDULE)

	lunes	martes	miércoles	jueves	viernes
9:00	matemáticas		matemáticas		matemáticas
10:00	inglés	historia	inglés	historia	inglés
11:00	educación física				
12:00		biología		biología	
1:00					
2:00	almuerzo				
3:00		literatura		literatura	
4:00	biblioteca*				

*library

CONTESTE, POR FAVOR
1. ¿Qué días tiene Antonio historia? ¿matemáticas?
2. ¿A qué hora es la clase de literatura? ¿la clase de inglés?
3. ¿A qué hora es el almuerzo?
4. ¿Tiene Antonio clases a la una?
5. ¿Hay biblioteca en la escuela (school)?

Las materias (SCHOOL SUBJECTS)

Catálogo

Editorial° Castilla

publishing house

Chemistry

Accounting
Computer Science

German

PREGÚNTELE A OTRO(A) ESTUDIANTE

1. ¿Qué clases tiene los lunes, miércoles y viernes? (Tengo...)
2. ¿Qué clases tiene los martes y jueves?
3. ¿Cuál es su clase favorita?
4. ¿Es fácil *(easy)* la clase de química? ¿la clase de sociología?
5. ¿Es difícil *(difficult)* la clase de geología? ¿la clase de oratoria *(speech)*?
6. ¿A qué hora es su primera *(first)* clase? ¿y su última *(last)* clase?
7. ¿Cómo se llama su profesor(a) de matemáticas?
8. ¿Tiene usted clases de noche *(at night)*?
9. ¿Hay clases de fotografía en la universidad? ¿de enfermería *(nursing)*?
10. ¿Hay clases de radio y televisión? ¿de periodismo *(journalism)*?

La Universidad de México (UNAM) es un importante centro de estudios. Tiene 400.000 estudiantes. No tiene residencias°. Los enormes murales en los edificios° representan la historia mexicana.

student dormitories
buildings

La Universidad Nacional Autónoma de México (UNAM)

¿Le gusta... ? *(Do you like . . . ?)*

¿Le gusta la música?
Sí, me gusta la música.   *Yes, I like . . .*
No, no me gusta la música. *No, I don't like . . .*

PREGÚNTELE A OTRO(A) ESTUDIANTE
1. ¿Le gusta la música popular?
2. ¿Le gusta la música clásica?
3. ¿Le gusta la guitarra?
4. ¿Le gusta la biología? ¿la química? ¿la psicología?
5. ¿Le gusta más *(more)* la literatura moderna o la literatura clásica?
6. ¿Le gusta más el comercio o la medicina?
7. ¿Le gusta correr *(to run)*?
8. ¿Le gusta esquiar *(to ski)*?
9. ¿Le gusta nadar *(to swim)*?
10. ¿Le gusta más nadar o correr?
11. ¿Le gusta bailar *(to dance)*?
12. ¿Le gusta cocinar *(to cook)*?
13. ¿Le gusta leer *(to read)*?
14. ¿Le gusta más leer o escribir *(to write)*?

¿Le gustan las lenguas? (Do you like languages?)

Sí, me gustan las lenguas.
No, no me gustan las lenguas.

Gustan is used when what you like is *plural.*

PREGÚNTELE A OTRO(A) ESTUDIANTE
1. ¿Le gustan las matemáticas? ¿las ciencias políticas? ¿las bellas artes?
2. ¿Qué clases le gustan más?
3. ¿Le gustan las clases a las ocho de la mañana?
4. ¿Qué deportes le gustan más?
5. ¿Le gustan más los deportes de verano o de invierno?

¿Qué deportes le gustan al hispano?

   Al hispano le gusta mucho el fútbol (sóquer), especialmente en España,
México y Sudamérica. Las escuelas y clubes deportivos de muchas ciudades
participan en el fútbol con gran entusiasmo. En el Caribe y en México, el

El fútbol

hispano juega° mucho al béisbol. Hay excelentes jugadores° hispanos de béisbol en los clubes norteamericanos. El jai-alai* es popular en varias regiones incluso° la Florida y Nueva York. Al hispano le gustan las carreras de caballos,° de bicicletas y de carros. Le gustan el tenis, el boxeo, la pesca° y la natación.°

    La corrida de toros es un espectáculo y no un deporte. No todas las naciones hispanas celebran la corrida. Las fechas del espectáculo varían de región a región según° el clima. Las corridas profesionales son en el otoño y en la primavera cuando hace menos calor.

plays / players

including

horse races / fishing

swimming

according to

*Jai-alai is a game like handball, played with a basketlike racket fastened to the arm.

El jai-alai

el golf
Lee Treviño

el béisbol
Fernando Valenzuela

La corrida de toros

Los números 100–1000

100	cien (ciento)	400	cuatrocientos	800	ochocientos
101	ciento uno	500	quinientos	900	novecientos
200	doscientos	600	seiscientos	1000	mil
300	trescientos	700	setecientos	10.000	diez mil

Cien becomes **ciento** when other numbers are added to it. However, with **mil** (1000), **millón, billón**, etc., Spanish uses **cien**:

$125 = **ciento** veinte y cinco dólares
BUT $100.000 = **cien** mil dólares/pesos

Spanish does not have the option of counting by hundreds after a thousand; for example, 1980 is **mil novecientos ochenta.**

1012	mil doce
1492	mil cuatrocientos noventa y dos
1776	mil setecientos setenta y seis
50.321	cincuenta mil trescientos veintiuno

The **y** appears only between sixteen and ninety-nine:

diez **y** seis, diez **y** siete, etc.
noventa **y** nueve

Note that Spanish uses a decimal point where English uses a comma.

PRÁCTICA
Escriba en español.

MODELO: February 12, 1865
el doce de febrero de mil ochocientos sesenta y cinco

1. October 7, 1940
2. December 25, 1965
3. September 16, 1810
4. March 10, 1615
5. April 1, 1779
6. su fecha de nacimiento (*your date of birth*)

Los gestos (GESTURES)

Los gestos son una parte intrínseca de la lengua española. Las personas expresan su personalidad y herencia cultural con los gestos. Observe unos gestos de un hispano:

1. No
2. Un momentito, un poquito (*a little bit*)
3. Es tacaño. (*stingy*)
4. Dinero

¿CUÁNTO CUESTA?   (How much does it cost?)

Pregúntele a otro(a) estudiante cuánto cuesta cada artículo en dólares. Use el gesto 4 con las preguntas.

¿Cuánto cuesta...

1. un televisor a colores?
2. una computadora pequeña (small)?
3. un carro pequeño? ¿grande?
4. un carro de sport?
5. una motocicleta?
6. un reloj de oro (gold)?
7. una cámara buena?
8. una casa modesta?

Pronunciación

El enlace (Linking)

In all speech, the pronunciation of words may change slightly as they blend with other words. In Spanish the final vowel of a word is joined with the first vowel in the next word. If the two vowels are the same, they are pronounced as a single vowel.

la_amiga (pronounced: « lamiga »)
su_hijo
¿Cómo_está_usted?
de_España

The final consonant of a word is joined with the initial vowel of the following word.

¿Quién_es?   el_abuelo   los dos_estudiantes

Repita, por favor.

una_amiga   mi tía   su_hijo_Orlando   su_última clase
veinte_y dos   treinta_y_uno   cincuenta_y seis
nueve_estudiantes   la clase de_español   Felipe_es_hermano de_Elena
¿Qué_es?   ¿Qué_hora_es?   ¿Cuál_es la fecha?   ¿Son_amigos?

El alfabeto

LA LETRA *(letter)*	EL NOMBRE *(name)*	EL EJEMPLO *(example)*
a	a	el, la artista
b	be	banquero(a) *(banker)*
c	ce	el, la computista *(computer operator)*
ch	che	el, la chófer *(chauffeur, driver)*
d	de	doctor(a)
e	e	el, la estudiante
f	efe	el, la fabricante *(manufacturer)*
g	ge	el, la gerente *(manager)*
h	hache	hostelero(a) *(innkeeper)*
i	i	ingeniero(a) *(engineer)*
j	jota	el, la juez *(judge)*
l	ele	lector(a) *(reader)*
ll	elle	el, la deta<u>ll</u>ista *(retailer)*
m	eme	maestro(a) *(teacher)*
n	ene	el, la naturalista
ñ	eñe	la ni<u>ñ</u>era *(babysitter)*
o	o	obrero(a) *(worker)*
p	pe	el policía, la mujer policía *(police woman)*
q	cu	químico(a) *(chemist)*
r	ere	redactor(a) *(editor)*
rr	erre	co<u>rr</u>edor(a) *(broker, runner)*
s	ese	secretario(a)
t	te	traductor(a) *(translator)*
u	u	universitario(a) *(university student)*
v	ve*	vendedor(a) *(salesperson)*
x	equis	el bo<u>x</u>eador *(boxer)*
y	i griega	el, la a<u>y</u>udante *(helper)*
z	zeta	el zapatero *(shoemaker, shoe dealer)*

*To distinguish between the names of the letters **be** and **ve**, speakers say **be grande** or **be de burro** and **ve chica** *(small)* or **ve de vaca** *(cow)*. **K** (**ka**) and **w** (**double ve**) appear only in foreign words or names.

PRÁCTICA

a Combine la pronunciación con la letra.

1. v _____   a. like the English *e* in p*e*t
2. ll _____   b. not pronounced
3. a _____   c. similar to the English *g* in *go*
4. ñ _____   d. Like the English *y* in *yes*
5. e _____   e. same as **b** in Spanish
6. z _____   f. multiple *r* sounds
7. g before **a, o,** or **u** _____   g. comparable to the English *h* in
8. j and g before **e** or **i** _____   *his*
9. h _____   h. similar to the English *a* in *car*
10. **r** in the beginning of a word; **rr**   i. comparable to the *ni* sound in
   within a word _____   *onion*
                                      j. in Spanish America
                                         pronounced like the English *s*
                                         in *sit*

b ¿Cómo se escribe su apellido?   *(How do you write your surname?)*

MODELO: Taylor   te-a-i griega-ele-o-ere

Doctor, ¿tiene usted sus anteojos? *(your eyeglasses)*

Las ocupaciones

Spanish omits the article when expressing a person's occupation.

¿Es usted artista?   — Sí, soy artista. No, no soy artista.

Compare: I'm *an* artist; she's *a* student.

CONTESTE
1. ¿Es usted estudiante? ¿mecánico? ¿secretaria? ¿maestra?
2. ¿Es profesora su madre? (Sí, mi madre es... No, mi madre no...) ¿Es
   doctora? ¿ama de casa? ¿administradora?
3. ¿Es vendedor su padre? ¿ingeniero? ¿fabricante? ¿agricultor?

6 En la clase

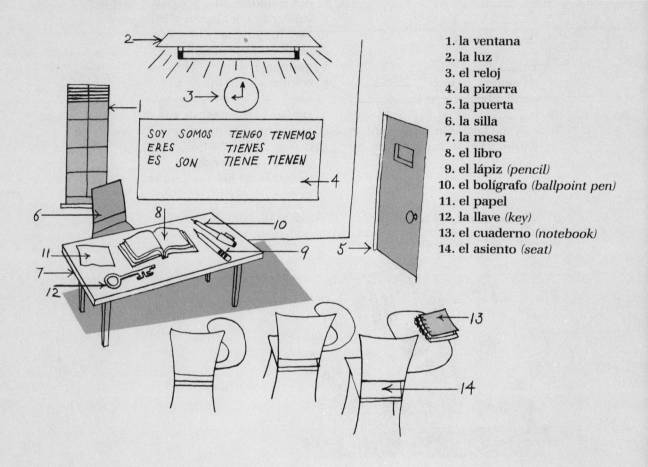

1. la ventana
2. la luz
3. el reloj
4. la pizarra
5. la puerta
6. la silla
7. la mesa
8. el libro
9. el lápiz *(pencil)*
10. el bolígrafo *(ballpoint pen)*
11. el papel
12. la llave *(key)*
13. el cuaderno *(notebook)*
14. el asiento *(seat)*

SOY SOMOS TENGO TENEMOS
ERES TIENES
ES SON TIENE TIENEN

REFRÁN

Libros y amigos, pocos y buenos.°   *With books, as with friends, it is quality, not quantity, that counts.*

PRÁCTICA
Practice saying the vocabulary items with your teacher. Then cover up
the list and try to name as many of these items as you can.

MODELO: **Cinco es la puerta.**

Los colores

azul *blue*	**negro** *black*	**amarillo** *yellow*
verde *green*	**pardo*** *brown*	**blanco** *white*
gris *gray*	**rojo** *red*	**anaranjado** *orange*

Adjectives of color ending in **-o** change their ending to **-a** when modifying a feminine noun.

Mi carro es amarillo.   *My car is yellow.*
Mi casa es blanca y azul.   *My house is white and blue.*

¿DE QUÉ COLOR ES...?   *(What's the color of...?)*
1. ¿De qué color es su casa? (**Mi casa...**)
2. ¿De qué color es su carro?

ASK A CLASSMATE THE COLORS OF THE CLASSROOM ITEMS BELOW

MODELO: (La mesa) ¿De qué color es la mesa?
       Es parda.

1. la silla	*3.* la pizarra	*5.* el lápiz	*7.* el cuaderno
2. la puerta	*4.* el asiento	*6.* el bolígrafo	*8.* el papel

La descripción

Gloria tiene el pelo negro.
Tiene los ojos castaños.†

Jorge tiene el pelo rubio *(blonde)*.
Tiene los ojos verdes.

Rosita tiene el pelo rojo.
Tiene los ojos negros.

PRÁCTICA
a   Conteste, por favor.

1. ¿Tiene usted el pelo rubio? ¿castaño? ¿blanco? ¿negro?
2. ¿Tiene usted los ojos azules? ¿grises? ¿castaños?

b   Pick two or three classmates and describe their hair and eyes to another student. See if this student can guess which ones you picked.

*Café and **marrón** (both invariable in form) also mean *brown*.

†**Castaño** *(brown)* generally refers to the color of eyes and hair; otherwise, **pardo** is used:
los zapatos pardos *(the brown shoes)*. Note that the plural form of the adjective modifies a plural noun.

La cortesía

Por favor.   *Please. (also used to get a person's attention)*
Perdón.   *Excuse me (for my mistake, for interrupting).*
Con permiso.   *Excuse me. (I'm leaving. I'd like to pass by.)*
Muchas gracias.   *Thank you very much.*
De nada.   *You're welcome.*
Lo siento.   *I'm sorry.*

PRÁCTICA
What would you say in these situations?

1. You're trying to get the clerk's attention in a store.

2. You've stepped on someone's foot by mistake.

3. You're in a theater and are trying to get to a seat in the middle of the row.

4. Your friends surprised you with a birthday party.

5.

Los gestos

¡Ojo! *(Watch out!)*

Mas o menos.

¡Delicioso!

Vocabulario: Conversaciones diarias 1–6

Hints for learning vocabulary

1. Study the vocabulary that appears at the end of every lesson carefully. Then cover the English translation and read the words aloud in Spanish, checking to see if you recall the meanings. For future study, mark those words whose meanings you are unsure of. If a word is a cognate or has a similar root in English, beware of differences in spelling and pronunciation. For example, **familia** ends in -*ia*, not -*y*; and **clase** and **profesor** have only one **s**.

2. To avoid errors in communication, do not reduce the vowels to an *uh* sound: **niño** *(boy)* but **niña** *(girl)*; **hombre** *(man)* but **hambre** *(hunger)*.

3. To strengthen your command of the vocabulary even more, prepare flashcards for each succeeding **Vocabulario.** Review these cards periodically, double-checking your pronunciation and spelling.

4. Try to use expressions and words in different situations and with different people. Practice with your classmates. The more associations you make with your new vocabulary words, the more easily you will remember them.

5. Each day while you wait for class to begin, try different Spanish expressions with your classmates.

EXPRESIONES

Buenos días. *Good morning.*
Buenas tardes. *Good afternoon.*
Buenas noches. *Good evening.*
¿Es usted... ? *Are you . . . ?*
Sí, soy... *Yes I am . . .*
¿Cómo se llama usted? *What's your name?* *(lit., What do you call yourself?)*
Me llamo... *My name is . . .*
¿Cómo está usted? *How are you?*
Muy bien, gracias. *Very well, thank you.*
¿Tiene usted... ? *Do you have . . . ?*
Sí, tengo... *Yes, I have . . .*
De nada. *You're welcome.*
¡Hola! *Hi! Hello!*
Hasta luego. *See you later. (Until later.)*
Adiós. *Good-bye.*
¡Feliz cumpleaños! *Happy Birthday!*

y *and*
o *or*
de *of, from*
poco *a little*
mucho *much, a lot*
¿Le gusta(n)? *Do you like? (lit., Is it (are they) pleasing to you?)*
Me gusta(n)... *I like . . .*
hay *there is, there are*
¿Qué? *What?*
¿Cuándo? *When?*
¿Cuántos? *How many?*
¿Cuál? *Which one? What?*
¿Cómo? *How?*
señor *sir, Mr.*
señora *madam, ma'am, Mrs.*
señorita *miss*

LA FAMILIA

el **abuelo**, la **abuela** *grandfather, grandmother*
los **abuelos** *grandparents; grandfathers*
el **padre** *father*
la **madre** *mother*
los **padres** *parents; fathers*
el **hijo**, la **hija** *son, daughter*
los **hijos** *sons; children*
el **niño**, la **niña** *child; boy, girl*
los **niños** *boys; children*

el **hermano**, la **hermana** *brother, sister*
los **hermanos** *brothers; brothers and sisters*
el **tío**, la **tía** *uncle, aunt*
los **tíos** *uncles; aunts and uncles*
el **primo**, la **prima** *cousin (m., f.)*
los **primos** *cousins*
el **esposo** (el **marido**), la **esposa** (la **mujer**)
    husband, wife (woman)
los **esposos** *spouses*

LOS MESES DEL AÑO *The months of the year*

enero *January*	**mayo** *May*	**septiembre** *September*
febrero *February*	**junio** *June*	**octubre** *October*
marzo *March*	**julio** *July*	**noviembre** *November*
abril *April*	**agosto** *August*	**diciembre** *December*

LOS DÍAS DE LA SEMANA Y OTRAS EXPRESIONES

lunes *Monday*	**sábado** *Saturday*	**mañana** *tomorrow*
martes *Tuesday*	**domingo** *Sunday*	**la mañana** *morning*
miércoles *Wednesday*	**hoy** *today*	**la tarde** *afternoon*
jueves *Thursday*	**ayer** *yesterday*	**la noche** *evening, night*
viernes *Friday*		

LAS ESTACIONES *The seasons*

la **primavera** *spring*
el **verano** *summer*

el **otoño** *autumn*
el **invierno** *winter*

¿QUÉ TIEMPO HACE? *How's the weather?*

Hace buen (mal) tiempo. *The weather is fine (bad).*
Hace (mucho) calor. *It's (very) hot.*
Hace (mucho) frío. *It's (very) cold.*
Hace (mucho) viento. *It's (very) windy.*

Hace (mucho) sol. *It's (very) sunny.*
Llueve (mucho). *It's raining (a lot).*
Nieva (mucho). *It's snowing (a lot).*

¿QUÉ HORA ES? *What time is it?*

Es la una. *It's one o'clock.*
Son las tres y media. *It's three-thirty.*
¿A qué hora es? *At what time is it?*

La fiesta es a las nueve de la noche. *The party is at nine in the evening.*

LOS NÚMEROS

0	cero	16	diez y seis	200	doscientos(as)
1	uno	17	diez y siete	300	trescientos(as)
2	dos	18	diez y ocho	400	cuatrocientos(as)
3	tres	19	diez y nueve	500	quinientos(as)
4	cuatro	20	veinte	600	seiscientos(as)
5	cinco	30	treinta	700	setecientos(as)
6	seis	40	cuarenta	800	ochocientos(as)
7	siete	50	cincuenta	900	novecientos(as)
8	ocho	60	sesenta	1000	mil
9	nueve	70	setenta		
10	diez	80	ochenta		
11	once	90	noventa		
12	doce	100	cien (ciento)		
13	trece				
14	catorce				
15	quince				

EN LA CLASE
el **asiento** *seat*
el **bolígrafo** *ballpoint pen*
el **cuaderno** *notebook*
el **lápiz** *pencil*
el **libro** *book*
la **luz** *light*
la **llave** *key*

la **mesa** *table*
el **papel** *paper*
la **puerta** *door*
el **reloj** *watch, clock*
la **silla** *chair*
la **ventana** *window*

LOS COLORES
amarillo *yellow*
azul *blue*
blanco *white*
negro *black*

pardo, café *brown*
rojo *red*
verde *green*

LA CORTESÍA
Por favor. *Please.*
(Muchas) gracias. *Thank you (very much).*

Perdón. *Excuse me.*
Lo siento. *I'm sorry.*

SUSTANTIVOS *(Nouns)*
el **amigo**, la **amiga** *friend*
el **apellido** *surname*
la **ciudad** *city*
el **dinero** *money*
el **dólar** *dollar*

el, la **estudiante** *student*
el **lugar** *place*
la **montaña** *mountain*
el **sello** *stamp*
la **tienda** *store*

ADJETIVOS
alegre *happy*
cansado(a) *tired*
difícil *difficult*
fácil *easy*
grande *big*

mexicano(a) *Mexican*
pequeño(a) *small*
primer(o)(a) *first*
simpático(a) *nice*
último(a) *last*

VERBOS
cocinar *to cook*
contestar *to answer*
correr *to run*
escribir *to write*

escuchar *to listen (to)*
leer *to read*
nadar *to swim*
preguntar *to ask*

Examen (Self-test)

Take the Listening and Speaking sections of the *Examen* with a classmate, who will supply phrases, numbers, and questions as needed. Do *not* look at what your classmate has chosen or written; rely instead on *your* listening and speaking skills.

Listening

I   Dictado. For the passage below your classmate will select answers from the choices offered in parentheses and then dictate that version of the passage two times to you. The first time listen for meaning; the second, write down what you hear during the pauses (indicated by two slashes).

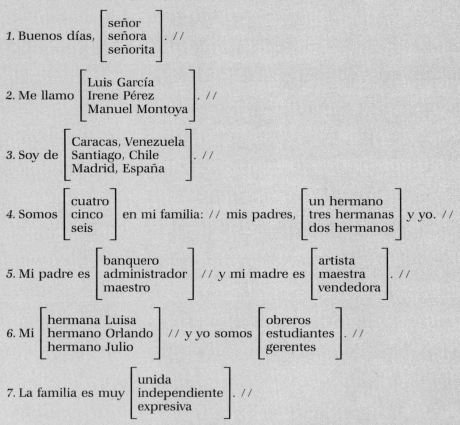

1. Buenos días, [señor / señora / señorita]. //

2. Me llamo [Luis García / Irene Pérez / Manuel Montoya]. //

3. Soy de [Caracas, Venezuela / Santiago, Chile / Madrid, España]. //

4. Somos [cuatro / cinco / seis] en mi familia: // mis padres, [un hermano / tres hermanas / dos hermanos] y yo. //

5. Mi padre es [banquero / administrador / maestro] // y mi madre es [artista / maestra / vendedora]. //

6. Mi [hermana Luisa / hermano Orlando / hermano Julio] // y yo somos [obreros / estudiantes / gerentes]. //

7. La familia es muy [unida / independiente / expresiva]. //

After completing the dictation, check your work with your classmate. Then, prepare a new version of the dictation to read to him or her.

II   Números. You will hear a series of telephone numbers. Write them down. (Do not spell them.)

1. El Restaurante Granada 46-74-07
2. El Museo de Historia ¿?-¿?-¿?
3. Galerías San Francisco ¿?-¿?-¿?

III   You are bargaining at an outdoor market. Offer two hundred pesos less than the merchant wants.

MODELO: *You hear:* cuatrocientos pesos
　　　　 You say: **doscientos pesos**

1. 850 pesos _____　　*4.* ¿? pesos _____
2. ¿? pesos _____　　*5.* ¿? pesos _____
3. ¿? pesos _____

IV   Alphabet. You'll hear four family names and their spelling. Write out the names correctly.

MODELO: *You hear:* Villar   ve chica-i-elle-a-ere
　　　　 You write: **Villar**

1. Herrera   *2.* ¿?   *3.* ¿?   *4.* ¿?

Possible names: Navarro, Portilla, Camacho, Reyes, Yáñez, Ortiz...

Speaking

I   Listen to each question and answer orally. Your classmate can change the order of the sample questions below, and create new questions, as well.

1. ¿Cómo está Ud.?　　　　　*6.* ¿Cuántos hermanos tiene Ud?
2. ¿Qué tiempo hace?　　　　*7.* ¿De qué color es su carro?
3. ¿Qué hora es?　　　　　　*8.* ¿A qué hora es el almuerzo?
4. ¿Cuándo es su cumpleaños?　*9.* ¿Qué deportes le gustan?
5. ¿Es Ud. estudiante?

II   Your classmate will give you a series of answers. You will then ask the question cued by the answer.

MODELO: *You hear:* Así, así,... un poco cansado.
　　　　 You say: **¿Cómo está usted? or ¿Qué tal?**

POSSIBLE ANSWERS

1. No, no me gusta cocinar.
　 Sí, me gusta leer.
　 Sí, me gustan las clases.

2. Sí, soy de los Estados Unidos.
　 Sí, soy de aquí.
　 No, no soy de la Argentina.

POSSIBLE QUESTIONS

　¿Le gusta cocinar?
　¿Le gusta leer?
　¿Le gustan las clases?

　¿Es usted de los Estados Unidos?
　¿Es usted de aquí?
　¿Es usted de la Argentina?

3. La clase es a las nueve.   ⎡ ¿A qué hora es la clase? ⎤
   El almuerzo es a la una.   ⎢ ¿A qué hora es el almuerzo? ⎢
   La fiesta es a las...   ⎣ ¿A qué hora es la fiesta? ⎦

4. El bolígrafo es negro.   ⎡ ¿De qué color es el bolígrafo? ⎤
   La mesa es...   ⎢ ¿De qué color es la mesa? ⎢
   ¿?   ⎣ ¿? ⎦

III   Tell a few things about yourself, including:

1. what your name is
2. where you are from
3. what you are like (Use at least two adjectives; for example, ...muy
   responsable y discreto,-a.)
4. what classes you have each day of the week and at what time they are
   scheduled
5. what things you like and don't like (Give two sentences in the affirmative
   and two in the negative.)

Writing

For the remaining sections of the *Examen*, write your answers on a separate
sheet of paper.

I   Tell what time it is by writing out the numbers and the appropriate
phrases for morning, afternoon, and evening.

1.   *2.*   *3.*

 p.m.    p.m.    a.m.

II   Write out the dates below.

1. November 8, 1519
2. July 14, 1789
3. January 20, 1991

III   Translate.

1. Good morning, Mrs. Gómez.
2. Thank you very much.
3. It's hot here in the summer.
4. There are twenty-four students here.
5. My cousin Marta is very nice.

6. Until tomorrow.
7. I have brown hair and green eyes.
8. Excuse me. (I'd like to pass by.)
9. How much is it?

Cultura

Write **sí** if the statement is correct, and **no** if it is not. Rewrite the statements you marked *no* in order to make them true.

1. El lunes es el primer día de la semana para *(for)* los hispanos.
2. El diez de mayo es el Día de la Raza.
3. El jai-alai es un deporte popular.
4. Los padrinos son generalmente el padre y la madre.

Reading

I   Match the English translation with the information on the signs.

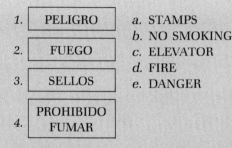

1. PELIGRO
2. FUEGO
3. SELLOS
4. PROHIBIDO FUMAR

a. STAMPS
b. NO SMOKING
c. ELEVATOR
d. FIRE
e. DANGER

II   Rolando writes about Independence Day in his country. Where you're given a choice, write the word that best completes each portion of the passage.

1. Me (llama, llamo) Rolando Morales.   *2.* (Soy, Se) de la República Dominicana.   *3.* Hoy es (la, el) 27 de febrero.   *4.* Es el (hora, día) de la Independencia. *5.* No (luego, tengo) clases hoy.   *6.* Es una (fecha, tienda) muy importante. Visito la plaza.   *7.* Escucho música (patriótica, pequeña). Participo en el desfile *(parade).*   *8.* Me (gusta, gustan) mucho los desfiles.

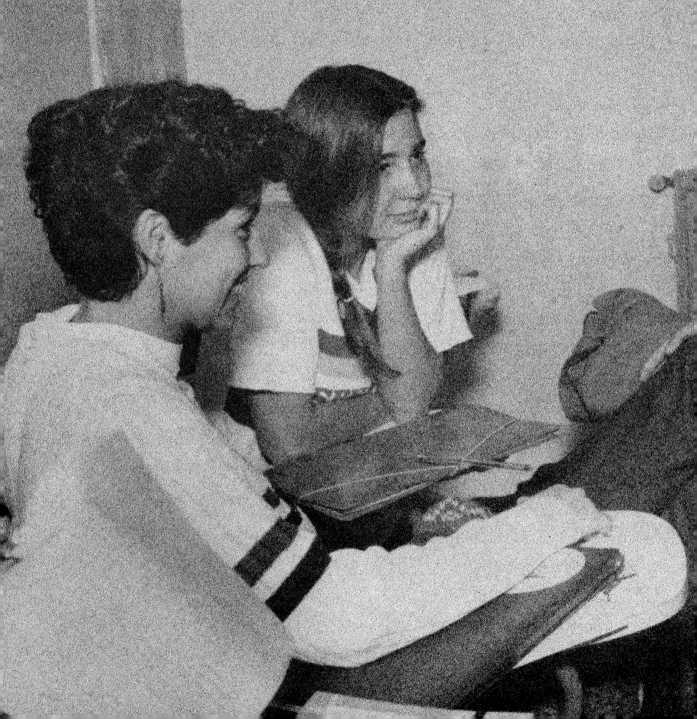

Lección **1** *Las ocupaciones*

Tres hispanos con ocupaciones diferentes hablan° de su vida.°   *speak / their lives*

Me llamo María Ruiz. Soy de España. Estudio arte comercial. Soy soltera.°   *single*

Me llamo Ramiro Delgado. Soy obrero.° Trabajo° en la compañía° Petróleos Nacionales de Venezuela. Hablo° inglés y español.   *worker / I work / company / I speak*

Me llamo Francisco López. Enseño° medicina en la Universidad Nacional de México. Soy casado.°   *I teach / married*

¿RECUERDA UD.?   *(Do you remember?)*

1. a. ¿Qué estudia María Ruiz? (**María Ruiz estudia...**)
   b. ¿Es soltera María Ruiz?
   c. ¿Es María Ruiz de Venezuela?
2. a. ¿Habla inglés Ramiro? ¿español?
   b. ¿Dónde *(Where)* trabaja Ramiro?
   c. ¿Es obrero o profesor Ramiro?
3. a. ¿Qué enseña el profesor López?
   b. ¿Dónde enseña el profesor?
   c. ¿Es soltero o casado?

ADAPTACIÓN

Hable usted un poco de su vida.

1. Me llamo...   4. Estudio...
2. Soy de...   5. Trabajo en...
3. Soy casado(a), soltero(a), etc.

PREGÚNTELE A OTRO(A) ESTUDIANTE

1. ¿Habla usted español? (**Sí, hablo... No, no hablo...**)
2. ¿Estudia usted inglés? ¿historia?
3. ¿Es usted de la América Latina? ¿de los Estados Unidos?
4. ¿Es usted soltero(a)?
5. ¿Enseña usted tenis? ¿golf?
6. ¿Trabaja usted mucho o poco?
7. ¿Qué días trabaja usted?

Estructura

I **Sustantivos y artículos**   *(Nouns and articles)*

A   Nouns referring to males, and for the most part those ending in **-o**, are labeled masculine. Those referring to females or those generally ending in **-a**, **-ción**, **-dad**, and **-tad** are called feminine.

el señor   el profesor   el cuaderno
la educación   la sociedad   la libertad

To make a noun plural add **-s** if it ends in a vowel and **-es** if it ends in a consonant. A final **-z** becomes **-ces** in the plural.

la amiga	las amigas	una lección	unas lecciones
el español	los españoles	un lápiz	unos lápices
el francés *(French)*	los franceses		

Note that nouns ending with a written accent drop the accent in the plural.

lección   lecciones (lec - **cio** - nes)

B   El artículo definido *(the)*.   The articles in Spanish are also either masculine or feminine. Spanish has four definite articles.

	SINGULAR	PLURAL
MASCULINO	**el** peso *(the peso)* **el** señor*	**los** pesos *(the pesos)* **los** señores
FEMENINO	**la** fiesta **la** amiga	**las** fiestas **las** amigas

It is helpful to learn the article with nouns that do not end in **-o** or **-a** as well as those that are exceptions to the rule.

el dólar   la clase   el día (Buenos días)
la mano *(the hand)*   el problema   el mapa

C   El artículo indefinido *(a, an)*.   Spanish also has four indefinite articles.

un amigo   *a male friend*   **unos** amigos   *some male friends*
una amiga   *a female friend*   **unas** amigas   *some female friends*

The plural **unos**, **unas** means *some* or *a few*.

PRÁCTICA

a   Use the singular definite article with the nouns below; then do the items again in the plural.

MODELO: señora   **la señora**, **las señoras**
          papel   **el papel**, **los papeles**

hermana, padre, amiga, casa, mano, nación, dólar, lección, sociedad, español, inglés, universidad, francés, mesa, luz, bolígrafo, llave, profesor, día, semana, asiento

b   Mention that you need the following items, using the indefinite article in your statement.

MODELO: pesos   **Necesito unos pesos.** *(I need some pesos.)*

libros	lección más fácil
aspirinas	vacaciones
teléfono	diccionario
papel	dólares
clase de inglés	bolígrafo
libro de español	sillas

*The definite article is used with titles except when addressing the person directly. **El Sr. Ruiz es mi profesor,** but, **Doctora Sánchez, ¿cómo está usted?**

II Dos contracciones

Spanish has only two contractions:

> a + el = **al**
> de + el = **del**

A The preposition **a** *(to)* plus the definite article **el** contract to **al**.

el parque: Voy **al** parque.   *I am going to the park.*
BUT las tiendas: Vamos **a las** tiendas.   *We're going to the stores.*

B The preposition **de** *(of, from)* plus the article **el** becomes **del**.

el título **del** libro   *the title of the book*
BUT el presidente **de la** república

PRÁCTICA
a   You've been asked ¿Adónde va usted? *(Where are you going?)* Answer the questions with the cues provided.

MODELO: el cine   **Voy al cine.** *(I am going to the show.)*

el teatro, el banco, las tiendas, el hotel, el parque, las clases, la fiesta, el auto, el restaurante, el médico, el trabajo, Los Ángeles

b   Study the vocabulary below, then alternate with another student asking each other where you are going. Try to expand your answers.

MODELO: ¿Adónde va?   **Voy al aeropuerto el viernes a las dos.**
Voy al centro en autobús.
Voy a casa con *(with)* **Conchita y Manuel.**

el aeropuerto

el correo

la estación

la farmacia

la iglesia   el templo

la casa*

la playa

el centro *(downtown)*

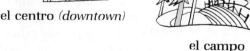
el campo

el museo

*To express *I'm going home*, Spanish speakers say **Voy a casa.**

c   Mention at least three places you're going to today. Tell with whom you are going and include the time you are going.

d   Complete con la forma correcta: del, de los, de la, de las.

1. El lunes es el primer día _____ semana.
2. Ch es una letra _____ alfabeto.
3. Son las diez y cuarto _____ mañana.
4. David es _____ Estados Unidos.
5. Soy amigo _____ Sr. López.
6. Raúl es el tío _____ niñas.
7. Yolanda es la hermana _____ niño.
8. Hablo _____ padres.

e   You need the addresses of several places and people. Form questions from the cues.

MODELO: **¿Cuál es la dirección del hotel?**

el museo, la farmacia, el correo, el restaurante, la universidad, la iglesia, el banco, el Sr. Pérez, los estudiantes

III *Yo, usted...*

Subject pronouns

PERSON	SINGULAR		PLURAL	
1	**yo**	*I*	**nosotros, nosotras**	*we*
2	**tú**	*you (familiar)*	**vosotros, vosotras**	*you (familiar)*
3	**él, ella**	*he, she**	**ellos, ellas**	*they*
	usted (Ud.)	*you (formal)*	**ustedes (Uds.)**	*you (formal)*

*The English subject pronoun *it* has no equivalent in Spanish: **Es Ricardo.** *It's Ricardo.*

Except for emphasis or clarification, Spanish speakers normally omit the subject pronouns since the verb endings indicate the subject.

Estudio inglés.   *I study English.*
Trabajan mucho.   *They work a lot.*

Spanish has two words for *you* (singular): **tú** and **usted. Tú** is informal and is used when addressing people with whom you are on a first-name basis. **Usted,** abbreviated **Ud.,** is formal and used with people you would address by their last name or with people you don't know very well. **Nosotros, vosotros,** and **ellos** refer either to groups of all males or to males and females combined. In Spain, **vosotros(as)** is used in place of **ustedes** (**Uds.**) among relatives and close friends. In Latin America, **ustedes** is the plural of both **tú** and **usted** and is the form practiced in this book.

PRÁCTICA

a   Which form of *you* (tú, Ud., Uds.) would you use to address these people in Latin America?

1. a teacher
2. a long-time friend
3. a stranger
4. Mr. and Mrs. Martínez
5. your cousins
6. your sister

b   Replace the noun subject with the appropriate pronoun: él, ella, nosotros, nosotras, ellos, ellas.

1. Ramiro habla español.
2. María es de España.
3. Olga y yo *(m.)* estudiamos arte.
4. La Sra. del Valle y su hija son muy bonitas.
5. Los padres necesitan unas vacaciones.

IV *El presente de los verbos regulares -ar*

The basic form (infinitive) of many Spanish verbs ends in **-ar;** for example, **hablar** *(to speak)*. To form the present tense of regular **-ar** verbs, we drop the infinitive marker **-ar** and add a set of endings to the remaining stem.

trabajar *to work*		
yo	traba**jo**	**Trabajo** el viernes.
tú	traba**jas**	**Trabajas** mañana.
él, ella, Ud.	traba**ja***	Ramiro **trabaja** aquí.
nosotros(as)	traba**jamos**	**Trabajamos** ocho horas.
vosotros(as)	traba**jáis**	**Trabajáis** mucho.
ellos, ellas, Uds.	traba**jan***	Ellos **trabajan** en la tienda.

*The **-a** ending is changed to **-e** when expressing a command: **¡Trabaje Ud.!** **¡Trabajen Uds.!** *Work!*

The Spanish present tense can have more than one meaning in English.

Trabajo mucho.   *I work, I do work, I am working a lot.*

The present tense can be used in place of the future tense to indicate immediate future action.

Hablamos mañana.   *We will talk tomorrow.*

Unlike English, Spanish does not use a helping verb *(do)* to form questions and negative statements. **No** is put before the verb to make a negative statement.

¿Trabajas hoy? — No, **no** trabajo hoy.   *Do you work today? — No, I don't work today.*

Ellos **no** hablan inglés.   *They **do not** speak English.*
No estamos cansados.   *We aren't tired.*

*Common **-ar** verbs*

bailar	*to dance*	**esperar**	*to wait for*
buscar	*to look for*	**estudiar**	*to study*
caminar	*to walk*	**llegar**	*to arrive*
cocinar	*to cook*	**necesitar**	*to need*
comprar	*to buy*	**regresar**	*to return*
enseñar	*to teach*	**tomar**	*to take, drink*

PRÁCTICA

a   Entrevista *(Interview)*. Ask your teacher questions using the verbs and additional words provided. Note that the subject follows the verb in forming questions.

MODELO: trabajar mucho   **¿Trabaja Ud. mucho?**

1. estudiar arte
2. hablar rápido
3. tomar café
4. esperar el autobús
5. comprar en Sears o Penney
6. caminar al centro
7. regresar el sábado
8. cocinar bien
9. buscar el libro de español
10. llegar a las ocho de la mañana
11. bailar mucho
12. visitar el museo

b   This time you and a classmate alternate asking and answering questions using the same words above.

MODELO: ¿Trabajas mucho? **Sí, trabajo mucho.**
                              No, no trabajo mucho.

Afterwards, be ready to present to the class as much information as you can about the person you questioned.

MODELO: **Betty estudia comercio y español. Trabaja en una oficina. No cocina mucho.**

c   Using the cues, tell what the following people are studying.

MODELO: yo... español   **Estudio español.**

1. tú... música
2. nosotros... lenguas
3. el Sr. López... medicina
4. Uds.... comercio
5. ellos... inglés
6. Clara y yo... literatura
7. yo... matemáticas
8. los señores... computación

d   Do the previous exercise again using the verb **enseñar**.

e   ¿Cómo se dice en español?

1. I speak Spanish.
2. Roberto works tomorrow.
3. They *(f.)* need five hundred pesos.
4. You (**tú**) buy a lot.
5. She doesn't drink coffee.
6. Do you (**Ud.**) teach English?
7. We *(m.)* are waiting for a taxi.
8. You (**Uds.**) arrive June 10 at 3:30 P.M.

f   Make original sentences with the subjects below, using a different verb each time.

MODELO: **Ellos buscan la llave del carro.**

1. Uds.	4. Diego y yo	7. Ellos
2. La Sra. García	5. Yo no	8. Mi amiga
3. Tú no	6. Él	9. ¿?

OBSERVACIONES

Reading in Spanish will be easier if you try to grasp the general ideas of the passage. Although you will recognize many cognates in Spanish and English, it will be necessary to make intelligent guesses about the meanings of words you don't know. Rely on the surrounding words to decipher the meaning of an unknown word. For example, can you guess the meaning of the glossed word in this series:

La manufactura, la minería° y la agricultura   mining

To help you with your reading, new words not readily discernible from the context are defined in the right margin.

La selección de una carrera

El estudiante de hoy debe pensar° mucho en su futuro y en su preparación académica. Un elemento muy importante de la preparación académica es el estudio de las lenguas extranjeras.° La persona que° habla español, portugués, francés o alemán no tiene garantías de un empleo°
importante con una agencia o con una compañía. Pero el individuo que
habla dos o más lenguas tiene una ventaja° muy grande.

La selección de una profesión es una decisión muy importante en la vida
del estudiante. La satisfacción personal del individuo depende en gran°
parte de la satisfacción en el trabajo.

La abundancia de trabajo en la manufactura, la minería y la agricultura
ya no° existe en los Estados Unidos. Hoy, los servicios técnicos y sociales y
el comercio internacional ofrecen excelentes oportunidades, específicamente:

Agencias de servicios sociales
Profesiones relacionadas° con la medicina
Ingeniería eléctrica, petrolífera, etc...
Comercio internacional
Agencias de publicidad
Comunicaciones
Contabilidad
Computación
Bancos
Compañías de seguros.°

should think

foreign / who

employment

advantage

great

no longer

related

insurance

¿COMPRENDE UD.?
Read the passage again without consulting the translations in the margin, if at all possible. Then tell whether the statements below are true
(**cierto**) or false (**falso**). Indicate the sentence in the reading that sup-
ports your answer.

1. La idea principal del artículo es la selección de una buena
   universidad.
2. La preparación académica del estudiante de hoy es muy importante.
3. El estudio de las lenguas extranjeras garantiza *(guarantees)* un
   empleo importante.
4. El portugués es una lengua extranjera.
5. El individuo que habla dos o tres lenguas tiene una ventaja.
6. La satisfacción personal no tiene relación con la satisfacción en el
   empleo.
7. En la minería y la manufactura existen abundantes oportunidades de
   trabajo.
8. Las agencias de publicidad y las compañías de seguros ofrecen
   buenas posibilidades de empleo.

Actividades: Los anuncios de empleo

1.

¡OPORTUNIDAD!

PART TIME $150

FULL TIME $360

Semanales

P E R S O N A S

Con auto, mayores de 21 años° que lean y escriban español bien. Que les guste el comercio. Pida° entrevista.

724-0545
991-8295

2.

DISTRIBUIDORA — Nacional de Cosméticos necesita vendedores y vendedoras, sueldo° básico $5.700 más comisiones de 10%, 15%, 20%. Presentarse° Av. 68 N°12-38 Sur. Entrevista de 2:00 a 4:30 pm.

salary

(to) present oneself

4.

Se necesitan administradores hotel restaurante categoría, experiencia mínima diez años. Entrevistas tres a cinco, Carrera Novena No. 22-87, oficina 202.

years

ask for

3.

¡FÁBRICA° BLUE JEANS NECESITA OBREROS(AS) EXPERTOS(AS)! ENVIAR° SOLICITUD,° No 68-48. AVENIDA 68.

factory

send / application

a   Conteste, por favor.

1. ¿Qué palabras *(words)* en inglés hay en los anuncios?

2. ¿Qué palabras son similares en inglés y español?

3. En el anuncio 2:

    a. ¿Cuál es la dirección? *Avenida...*

    b. ¿Cuánto *(How much)* es el sueldo?

    c. ¿A qué hora es la entrevista?

4. En el anuncio 3:

    a. ¿Qué necesita la fábrica?

    b. ¿Es necesaria una solicitud?

5. ¿Cuál de los cuatro trabajos le gusta más a Ud.? ¿Cuál menos?

b   Prepare usted un anuncio de trabajo. Use los modelos 1–4 y su imaginación.

Vocabulario

SUSTANTIVOS
el **aeropuerto** *airport*
el **alemán** *German*
el **arte** *art*
el **campo** *countryside*
la **casa** *house*
el **centro** *center; downtown*
la **compañía** *company*
el **correo** *post office*
el **empleo** *employment*
  España *Spain*
el **español** *Spanish*
la **estación** *station*
los **Estados Unidos** *United States*
la **farmacia** *pharmacy*
la **iglesia** *church*
el **inglés** *English*
el **museo** *museum*
el **obrero,** la **obrera** *worker*
la **playa** *beach*
el **sueldo** *salary*
el **templo** *temple*
la **universidad** *university*

ADJETIVOS
casado(a) *married*
extranjero(a) *foreign*
soltero(a) *single, unmarried*

VERBOS
bailar *to dance*
buscar *to look for*
caminar *to walk*
comprar *to buy*
enseñar *to teach, show*
esperar *to wait for*
estudiar *to study*
hablar *to speak, talk*
llegar *to arrive*
necesitar *to need*
regresar *to return*
tomar *to take; to drink*
trabajar *to work*

EXPRESIONES
a *to*
con *with*
de *of; from*
pero *but*

2 En el aeropuerto

Julie Miller, estudiante de intercambio,° llega al aeropuerto de Bogotá. Ella se especializa° en español, y desea vivir° y estudiar unos meses en Colombia.

exchange student
is majoring / wishes to live

ENTRADA (entrance) · Inmigración · Aduana (customs) · SALIDA (exit)

INSPECTOR DE INMIGRACIÓN Bienvenida° a Colombia.

JULIE Muchas gracias. Aquí tiene mi pasaporte y visa de estudiante.

INSPECTOR DE INMIGRACIÓN Muy bien... ¿Cuánto tiempo piensa estar?°

JULIE No sé° exactamente. Deseo estudiar unos meses en la universidad y después° viajar° y conocer° el país.°

INSPECTOR DE INMIGRACIÓN ¡Qué bueno!... Todo está en orden.° Pase° Ud. a la aduana.

INSPECTOR DE ADUANA Muy buenas tardes. ¿Tiene algo que declarar?°

JULIE Creo que no.° La cámara y la grabadora° son de uso personal.

INSPECTOR DE ADUANA Está bien. No necesita abrir° las maletas.°* La salida está a la izquierda.° Adiós.

JULIE Muy amable.° Adiós.

Welcome

How long do you plan to be (here)?

I don't know

afterwards / travel / get acquainted with / the country. / order / Pass (Go) on

Do you have anything to declare? / I believe not / tape recorder
to open / suitcases

is to the left

Very kind (of you)

Pase Para Abordar (boarding pass)
Vuelo 750 (flight)
16E Asiento (seat)
Fecha 9 de nov. (date)

*En muchos de los aeropuertos de la América Latina no inspeccionan las maletas si (*if*) la persona no tiene nada (*nothing*) que declarar cuando pasa por la aduana.

¿RECUERDA UD.?

1. ¿Cómo se llama la estudiante de intercambio?
2. ¿Dónde desea vivir ella?
3. ¿Qué documentos tiene?
4. ¿Cuánto tiempo piensa estudiar?
5. ¿Qué desea conocer?
6. ¿Qué objetos son de uso personal?
7. ¿Dónde está la salida?
8. ¿Es amable el inspector?

ADAPTACIÓN

Make up a conversation (eight to ten lines) with another student that takes place at the airport. One of you could be el **inspector** (**la inspectora**) and the other el (la) **turista**. The inspector may have questions about the items the tourist has not declared. Perhaps the tourist needs to pay duty (**pagar derechos de aduana**). Use any part of the previous dialogue you want along with any expressions you already know. Try to be imaginative, and don't hesitate to add a bit of humor. ¡**Magnífico**!

Estructura

I *El presente de los verbos regulares -er, -ir*

In addition to **-ar** verbs, Spanish has two other smaller groups of infinitives ending in **-er** and **-ir**. To form the present tense of regular **-er** and **-ir** verbs, we drop the infinitive markers and add a set of endings to the stem. Note that the endings are the same for the two types of verbs except for the **nosotros** and **vosotros** forms.

	comer *to eat*	**escribir** *to write*
yo	com**o**	escrib**o**
tú	com**es**	escrib**es**
él, ella, Ud.	com**e***	escrib**e***
nosotros(as)	com**emos**	escrib**imos**
vosotros(as)	com**éis**	escrib**ís**
ellos, ellas, Uds.	com**en***	escrib**en***

*The **-e** ending changes to **-a** to express a command: ¡**Coma Ud.**! ¡**Escriban**!

Common *-er* and *-ir* verbs

aprender	*to learn*	**Aprendemos** la lección.
comprender	*to understand*	No **comprendo** las instrucciones.
creer	*to believe, think*	**Creo** que Carlos regresa mañana.
deber + *infinitive*	*should, ought to*	Uds. **deben** estudiar más.
leer	*to read*	¿**Lees** el libro de español?
vender	*to sell*	Mi padre **vende** automóviles.
abrir	*to open*	¿A qué hora **abren** Uds.?
asistir a	*to attend*	**Asistimos** a clases.
recibir	*to receive*	**Recibes** muchas invitaciones.
vivir	*to live*	**Vivo** en la Avenida Constitución.

PRÁCTICA

a   Entrevista. Imagine that you are interviewing a student from Latin America. Ask him or her questions based on the information below. Afterwards, switch roles and have your classmate ask the questions with the cues in parentheses.

> MODELO: vivir / en la América Latina   **¿Vive Ud. en la América Latina?**
> CLASSMATE: **Sí, vivo...**
> **No, no vivo...**

1. vivir / en México (con su familia)
2. comer / un sándwich (tacos)
3. leer / *Selecciones del Reader's Digest (Time)*
4. comprender / el fútbol norteamericano (el sóquer)
5. vender / cosméticos (seguros de vida)
6. recibir / mucho dinero (muchas invitaciones)
7. escribir / mucho (poco)
8. asistir / al club de español (a la clase de inglés)

b   You believe the following people *should or should not* do certain things. Use items from columns A and B to state your opinion. Include other expressions familiar to you.

MODELO: **Papá debe regresar pronto.**
Ustedes no deben vender la casa.

A			B
1. Papá	6. Irene y Pepe	aprender español	vender la casa
2. Tú	7. Mi hermano	trabajar el domingo	viajar en avión
3. Ellos	8. Ustedes	regresar pronto	cocinar todos los días
4. Nosotros	9. ¿?	hablar rápido	abrir los ojos
5. Julia	10. ¿?	asistir a la reunión	¿?

c Learn the vocabulary and then tell what the people below are reading.

MODELO: Nilda... **Nilda lee la carta.**

el libro   la revista   el periódico

la carta   la tarjeta postal

1. Jorge

2. Ellos

3. Nosotros

4. Usted

5. Mis padres

6. (tú)¿?

7. (yo)¿?

d Entrevista. Prepare five questions to ask your instructor and then be ready to pose the same ones to a classmate. Use -er and -ir verbs.

MODELO: Para el instructor: **¿Come Ud. en la cafetería de la universidad?**
Para el estudiante: **¿Comes en...?**

II *Las preguntas* (Questions)

A Yes/No questions. The most common way of asking a question is to put the subject after the verb. If the subject is a noun, it often appears at the end of the question. In yes/no questions the voice rises slightly toward the end of the question.

¿Habla Ud. español?   *Do you speak Spanish?*
¿Comprende él la carta?   *Does he understand the letter?*
¿Es abogado su padre? *or* ¿Es su padre   *Is your father a lawyer?*
   abogado?

Sometimes the normal word order for a statement is used in a question. The voice rises toward the end to indicate a question.

¿Ud. habla español?   *Do you speak Spanish?*

B   Tag questions.   A statement can be turned into a question by adding the tags **¿no?, ¿verdad?,** or **¿de acuerdo?. ¿No?** appears after positive statements.

Ellos trabajan hoy, ¿no?	*They work today, don't they (right)?*
No comes carne, ¿verdad?	*You don't eat meat, do you?*
Esperamos aquí, ¿de acuerdo?	*We'll wait here, agreed (okay)?*

C   Information questions.   Questions asking for specific information begin with interrogative words such as **¿cómo?, ¿qué?,** and **¿cuándo?** followed by the verb.

Interrogative Words

¿Cómo?*	*How?*	**¿Cómo** está usted?
¿Qué?	*What?*	**¿Qué** venden ellos?
¿Cuándo?	*When?*	**¿Cuándo** es su cumpleaños?
¿Dónde?	*Where?*	**¿Dónde** vives?
¿Adónde?	*Where (to)?*	**¿Adónde** va usted?
¿Quién?	*Who?*	**¿Quién** habla? *Who (sing.) is talking?*
¿Quiénes?		**¿Quiénes** hablan? *Who (pl.) is talking?*
¿Con quién(es)?	*With whom?*	**¿Con quién** estudias? *With whom (sing.) are you studying?*
¿A quién(es)?	*Whom?*	**¿A quiénes** espera Ud.? *Whom (pl.) are you waiting for?*

*Spanish speakers also say **¿Cómo?** (comparable to *What did you say?*) when they don't hear or understand what has been said.

PRÁCTICA

a   Make yes/no questions of the statements below. First use normal word order for the statements, then use the more common inverted order.

MODELOS: Ellos viven aquí.   **¿Ellos viven aquí?**
¿Viven ellos aquí?

1. Uds. abren hoy.
2. Él busca los papeles.
3. Miguel es estudiante.
4. Ellas aprenden comercio.
5. Usted lee la carta.

b ¿Cómo se dice en español?

1. Carlos returns the fifteenth of July, doesn't he?
2. We'll eat at nine, agreed?
3. They don't understand, do they?
4. You (**Ud.**) read Spanish, don't you?

c Complete en español.

1. *(what)* ¿ _____ crees tú?
2. *(how)* ¿ _____ se llama?
3. *(who)* ¿ _____ es ella?
4. *(whom)* ¿ _____ busca Ud.?

5. *(when)* ¿ _____ llegan sus padres?
6. *(where)* ¿ _____ trabajas?
7. *(what)* ¿ _____ ? No comprendo bien.

III *La a personal*

> The personal **a** is used to introduce a direct object that represents a specific person or persons.

Conozco a la familia.   *I know the family.*
Buscamos a Ana.   *We're looking for Ana.*
BUT ¿Esperan Uds. el autobús?   *Are you waiting for the bus?*

PRÁCTICA

a ¿Dónde escribimos una a?

1. Esperamos _____ Teresa.
2. Leo _____ el periódico.
3. No conocen _____ la Sra. Delgado.
4. ¿Invitas _____ el profesor?
5. ¿ _____ quién busca Ud.?

b ¿Cómo se dice en español?

1. I know the grandparents.
2. We need twenty-five seats.
3. They're waiting for Diego.
4. Whom are you looking for?

IV *Saber y Conocer*

Saber and **conocer** both mean *to know*. However, each verb has specific definitions.

1. **Saber** indicates knowledge of facts or information (names, numbers, school subjects, etc.). Used with an infinitive, **saber** means *to know how to do something*.
2. **Conocer** means to be acquainted with a person, place, or thing. Both verbs are irregular in the first person singular.

saber		conocer	
(yo) **sé**	sabemos	(yo) **conozco**	conocemos
sabes	sabéis	conoces	conocéis
sabe	saben	conoce	conocen

No **sé** la dirección.
I don't know the address.
¿**Sabes** usar la computadora?
*Do you know how to use
the computer?*

Ellos **conocen** al Sr. Ruiz.
They know (are acquainted with) Mr. Ruiz.
¿**Conoces** el Canadá?
*Are you familiar (acquainted)
with Canada?*

PRÁCTICA

a   Pregúntele a otro(a) estudiante.

1. ¿Conoce Ud. al presidente de la universidad? ¿a la esposa? ¿a los hijos?
2. ¿A quién conoce Ud. en la clase de español?
3. ¿Conoce Ud. la ciudad de México? ¿San Juan? ¿Caracas?
4. ¿Qué ciudades grandes conoce? ¿Qué playas famosas conoce?
5. ¿Sabe Ud. qué día es hoy? ¿qué hora es?
6. ¿Sabe la lección de hoy?
7. ¿Sabe Ud. bailar? ¿nadar? ¿esquiar?
8. ¿Sabe jugar *(play)* al tenis? ¿al pin-pon? ¿a los bolos *(bowling)*?

b   Ricardo Vallejo, estudiante de intercambio, visita la ciudad donde usted vive. ¿Qué parques, edificios *(buildings)*, etc. debe conocer él? ¿A quién debe conocer? Prepare Ud. una lista de cinco o seis cosas *(things)*.

MODELOS: **Ricardo debe conocer el Parque Central.**
Debe conocer a la profesora.

c   Complete con la forma correcta de **saber** o **conocer**. Después traduzca *(translate)* al inglés las oraciones *(sentences)* 2, 4, 6 y 8.

1. Yo _____ al administrador.
2. Papá _____ cocinar muy bien.
3. Nosotros _____ la capital del país.
4. Tú _____ el número de mi teléfono, ¿no?
5. Yo _____ que estudias mucho.
6. Uds. no _____ el Museo de Historia, ¿verdad?
7. ¿Quién _____ la respuesta *(answer)*?
8. Ellos _____ álgebra.

d   Escriba Ud. seis oraciones originales donde compara **saber** y **conocer**.

MODELOS: **Sé inglés y español.**
No conocemos al Sr. Ortega.

OBSERVACIONES

Besides guessing the meaning of Spanish words through context and cognates, you will also understand many words that share common roots. From the verb **trabajar**, *for example, you could understand the noun* **el trabajo** (work). *Likewise, from the noun* **día**, *you could guess the meaning of the phrase* **todos los días** (every day). *Now read the letter below.*

Julie Miller escribe una carta a su profesora de español en los Estados Unidos.

ORQUÍDEA COLOMBIANA   25 de junio

Estimada° Sra. Wilson: *Dear*

    ¡Qué alegría! Por fin° estoy° en Colombia. Me gusta mucho Bogotá. Es *Finally / I am*
una ciudad de muchos contrastes — enormes edificios modernos y pequeñas casas coloniales. Poco a poco me adapto° a la altitud y a la comida° *adapt myself / food*
colombiana.

    Mi familia es muy amable. Salimos frecuentemente a las tiendas, al cine, a los museos y a las casas de los amigos. Los fines de semana damos un paseo por° la plaza o el campo. Las flores, especialmente las orquídeas, *take a walk (drive) along*
son preciosas.

    Vivimos cerca del° centro. El papá, el Sr. Quesada, trabaja en un banco. *near*
La señora es ama de casa. Son estrictos, pues° no me permiten° salir sola *since / they don't allow*
de noche con un amigo. La abuelita, la mamá de la señora, vive con la fa- *me*
milia. Es muy alegre y simpática. Los hijos estudian en la universidad.
Alicia (19 años) se especializa en medicina y Eduardo (20 años) en arquitectura. Los tres somos buenos amigos.

    El sistema académico aquí es diferente. No escogen° las materias. Toman *choose*
sólo las materias en su especialización. La asistencia no es obligatoria. Hay
estudiantes que sólo asisten a clases los días de examen. También creo que
los estudiantes participan más activamente en la política del país. Escriben
sus protestas en las paredes°. *walls*

    Todos los días aprendo algo nuevo y fascinante de Colombia y hasta° de *even*
los Estados Unidos. Tomo español para extranjeros, cultura y civilización y
literatura hispanoamericana. Me gustan todas mis clases, pero el profesor
de literatura es muy exigente°. Estudio horas y horas para esa° clase. *demanding / that*

    Bueno, hasta° otro día. Necesito preparar el trabajo de mañana. *until*

                                          Afectuosamente,

                                        Julie Miller Fulton

¿COMPRENDE UD.?

a   **Vocabulario.** Usted sabe los verbos **asistir a** y **especializar**. Busque (*Look for*) en la carta de Julie las palabras que significan *attendance* y *major field*.

Usted también sabe las palabras **alegre, la semana** y **poco**. Busque las frases que significan *What joy, happiness!; weekends; little by little*.

b   Imagínese que usted tiene carta de Julie. Dígale (*Tell*) a otro(a) estudiante la información más importante. Por ejemplo:

1. Tengo carta de...
2. Le gusta* mucho...
3. Su familia colombiana...
4. Vive cerca de...
5. El papá, el Sr. Quesada, trabaja..., etc.

Actividades

You wish to inquire about studies at the university in Colombia. What words should you choose in writing your letter?

MODELO: Me llamo Julie Miller y (voy, tengo, <u>soy</u>) estudiante.

Sr. Secretario de la
Universidad Nacional
Bogotá, Colombia

Muy estimado señor:
En junio pienso (deber, viajar, saber) a Colombia para estudiar español y (conocer, saber, creer) los lugares históricos (mes, más, mis) importantes (de la, de las, del) país. Soy Bachiller en Arte y (recibo, deseo, aprendo) tomar clases de historia y cultura (del, de la, de las) América Latina.

(Con permiso, De nada, Por favor), envíeme[1] todo informe referente al plan de estudios, costo de matrícula,[2] (cumpleaños, puertas, horarios) y días de clase.

Muy atentamente.[3]

Julie Miller

1. send me   **2.** registration fees   **3.** sincerely

*Also means He or She likes

Vocabulario

SUSTANTIVOS
la **carta** *letter*
la **comida** *food*
la **entrada** *entrance*
la **flor** *flower*
la **maleta** *suitcase*
el **país** *country, nation*
la **pared** *wall*
el **periódico** *newspaper*
la **revista** *magazine*
la **salida** *exit*
la **tarjeta postal** *postcard*
el **vuelo** *flight*

ADJETIVOS
amable *kind*
bienvenido(a) *welcome*
exigente *demanding*
norteamericano(a) *North American*

INTERROGATIVES
¿Dónde? *Where?*
¿Adónde? *Where (to)?*
¿Quién(es)? *Who?*
¿A quién(es)? *Whom?*

VERBOS
abrir *to open*
aprender *to learn*
asistir a *to attend*
comer *to eat*
comprender *to understand*
*****conocer (conozco)** *to know a person, be acquainted with*
creer *to believe*
deber + *infinitive should, ought to*
desear *to wish*
escribir *to write*
leer *to read*
pasar *to pass; to spend (time)*
pensar (pienso) + *infinitive to plan to*
recibir *to receive*
*****saber (sé)** *to know facts; to know how to*
*****salir (salgo)** *to go out*
viajar *to travel*
vender *to sell*
vivir *to live*

EXPRESIONES
¿Cuánto tiempo? *How long?*
*****dar (doy) un paseo (por)** *to take a walk, ride (along)*
después *afterwards*
hasta *until, even*
por fin *finally*
también *also*

*Verbs marked with an asterisk have an irregular first person singular. This form is given in parentheses following the infinitive.

3 En la clínica

La señora Leonor Aguirre de Reyes es doctora. Su clínica está situada° en el centro de la ciudad° de Panamá. Cristina Santos y Ana Sánchez están enfermas° y necesitan ver° a la doctora.

is located
city
are ill / to see

Dra. Leonor Aguirre de Reyes
oídos, nariz y garganta°

Clínica Las Américas
Av. Presidente No. 15

Horario: 2 pm a 7 pm
Telf. 46.31.50

ears, nose, throat

DRA. AGUIRRE Buenas tardes, señorita. ¿Qué le pasa?°

CRISTINA No estoy muy bien,° doctora. Tengo fiebre° y dolor de cabeza.° Mi amiga Ana también está enferma.

DRA. AGUIRRE ¿Está ella aquí con usted?

CRISTINA Sí, tiene cita° a las tres.

DRA. AGUIRRE Ud. está muy pálida,° y la fiebre indica que tiene gripe.° Con permiso, vamos a examinarle la garganta y los oídos.

CRISTINA ¡Ay, sí!... Perdone°... ¡Ah... chú!

DRA. AGUIRRE ¡Salud!*

What's wrong with you?
I don't feel very well / fever / headache

appointment

pale / indicates you have the flu

Pardon me

¿RECUERDA UD.?

a Complete con la palabra apropiada.

MODELO: La señora Aguirre de Reyes ____es____ doctora.

1. Su clínica _____ situada en el centro.
2. Cristina y Ana necesitan _____ a la doctora.
3. ¿Qué le _____ ?
4. (Yo) no _____ muy bien, doctora.
5. Tengo _____ y dolor de _____ .
6. Mi amiga Ana también está _____ .
7. Con permiso, vamos a examinarle la garganta y _____ .

*En español decimos (we say) **¡Salud!** o **¡Jesús!** cuando una persona estornuda (sneezes). También decimos **¡Salud!** cuando ofrecemos un brindis (toast). **La salud** significa health.

73

b Conteste, por favor.

1. ¿Es casada o soltera la doctora?
2. ¿Dónde está situada su clínica?
3. ¿Está Cristina bien o mal?
4. ¿Qué tiene Cristina?
5. ¿Cómo está su amiga?
6. ¿A qué hora es la cita de Ana?
7. ¿Quién está pálida?
8. ¿Qué indica la fiebre de Cristina?

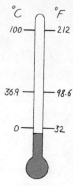

el termómetro

El cuerpo humano (The Human Body)

la cabeza *head*
la cara *face*
los labios *lips*
los dientes *teeth*
la oreja *(outer) ear*
el oído *(inner) ear*
la piel *skin*
el hueso *bone*
la sangre *blood*

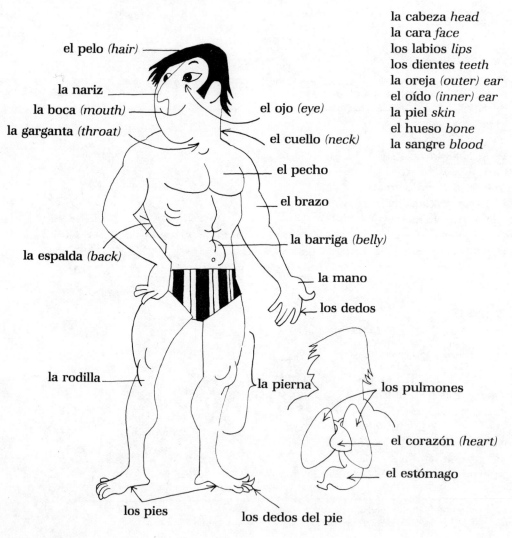

el pelo *(hair)*
la nariz
la boca *(mouth)*
la garganta *(throat)*
el ojo *(eye)*
el cuello *(neck)*
el pecho
el brazo
la barriga *(belly)*
la espalda *(back)*
la mano
los dedos
la rodilla
la pierna
los pulmones
el corazón *(heart)*
el estómago
los pies
los dedos del pie

PRÁCTICA

a Imagine you are sick. Explain your symptoms as described in the pictures.

MODELO: **Tengo dolor de cabeza.** *(I have a headache.)*

1.   2.   3.

4.   5.   6.

b ¿Qué partes del cuerpo asocia Ud. con estos verbos?

MODELO: leer   **los ojos**
        nadar   **los brazos y las piernas**

1. ver
2. escuchar
3. correr
4. respirar *(to breathe)*
5. hablar

6. bailar
7. reír *(to laugh)*
8. pensar
9. escribir
10. besar *(to kiss)*

ADAPTACIÓN

Usted y otro estudiante preparan una conversación que tiene lugar *(takes place)* en una clínica. Usen parte del diálogo anterior *(previous)* y la imaginación. Por ejemplo, Ud. es hipocondríaco y el otro estudiante es médico. Mencione todos sus dolores. Después del examen físico, el médico cree que Ud. debe tomar aspirinas, vitaminas, un laxante, un antibiótico, un tranquilizante...

Expresiones figuradas

En inglés se dice...,   pero en español se dice...

Don't pull my leg!

¡No me tomes el pelo!

It costs an arm and a leg.

Cuesta un ojo de la cara.

He's all thumbs.

No da pie con bola.

I Los adjetivos

Adjectives in Spanish are masculine or feminine, singular or plural, depending on the noun or pronoun they modify.

bonitas, lindas (pretty)   fea (ugly)

triste   alegres

alto   baja

rubio
(blonde)

morena
(brunette)

guapo
(handsome)

joven
(young)

viejos
(old)

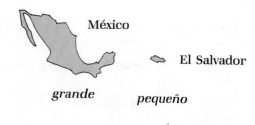

México

El Salvador

grande   pequeño

Nuevo México

Nueva York

Otros adjetivos:

rico   *rich*
pobre *poor*
trabajador   *hardworking*
perezoso   *lazy*
tonto   *silly*

mejor   *better*
peor   *worse*
fácil   *easy*
difícil   *difficult*

A   Singular adjectives.   Adjectives ending in **-o** change **-o** to **-a** to modify feminine nouns.

Roberto es alto.   Cristina es alta.

Adjectives of nationality ending in a consonant and those ending in **-dor** add **-a** to form the feminine.

Walter es inglés.   Betty es inglesa.
El carro es japonés.   La motocicleta es japonesa.
Abuelo es hablador.   Abuela es habladora *(talkative)*.

Most other adjectives in the singular do not change masculine and feminine.*

El patio es grande.   La casa es grande.
El vocabulario no es fácil.   La lección es fácil.

*****Los adverbios:** To form adverbs we change the **-o** ending of the adjective to **-a** and add **-mente** *(-ly in English)*. Adjectives with other endings simply add **-mente:** exacto   exacta**mente;** frecuente   frecuente**mente;** general   general**mente.**

PRÁCTICA

a   Replace the adjectives in each sentence with the adjectives in parentheses, making the necessary changes in the adjectives.

MODELO: (alto)   Gabriel es **alto** y su hermana es **alta** también.

1. El Sr. Durán es **espléndido** y su esposa es **espléndida** también.
   (generoso, rico, inteligente, guapo, alegre, moreno, viejo)
2. Mi tía es **baja** y su esposo es **bajo** también.
   (rubia, joven, triste, simpática, seria, pobre, trabajador, estricto)
3. El reloj es **japonés** y la cámara es **japonesa** también.
   (inglés, francés, alemán, mexicano, grande, pequeño, nuevo, bonito)

b   Situaciones. Descríbase Ud. mismo(a) *(yourself)* cuando habla con estas personas. Use un mínimo de tres adjetivos en cada situación.

MODELO: Generalmente soy **alegre, afectuoso** y **cordial** cuando hablo con mi
            novia.

1. el administrador, la administradora
2. mi novio(a) *(fiancé -e)*
3. el profesor, la profesora
4. un policía
5. mis rivales en fútbol
6. ¿?

B   **Plural Adjectives.**   As with nouns, the plural of adjectives is made by adding **-s** to adjectives ending in a vowel and **-es** to those ending in a consonant. A masculine plural adjective is used to modify two or more nouns different in gender.

Alicia y Ramón son mexicanos.   Ellos son jóvenes.

PRÁCTICA
Use los adjetivos para describir los sujetos.

MODELO: Uds.   (joven, activo)

          Uds. son jóvenes y activos.

1. Uds.   (alto, joven)

2. Uds.   (inteligente, bonito)

3. Nosotros   (curioso, estudioso)

4. Ellas   (bajo, moreno)

5. Ellos   (casado, alegre)

6. Las sillas  (grande, confortable)

7. Los carros (italiano, español)

8. Las flores (rojo, blanco)

9. Los árboles (¿?)
(¿?)

10. Las montañas

11. ¿?

12. ¿?

C **Placement of adjectives.** Most adjectives are *descriptive* (that is, they indicate type, size, color, nationality, etc.) and usually *follow* the noun they describe.

Jorge es un muchacho alto y rubio.   *Jorge is a tall and blonde boy.*

By contrast, adjectives that specify quantity normally precede the noun.

Hay muchos papeles aquí.   *There are a lot of papers here.*
Necesitamos otra mesa.   *We need another table.*

Bueno and **malo** *(bad)* may go before or after the noun. These two adjectives drop the **-o** before a masculine singular noun.

un buen (mal) ejemplo
un ejemplo bueno (malo)   *a good (bad) example*

una buena (mala) idea
una idea buena (mala)   *a good (bad) idea*

Descriptive adjectives may precede the noun for emphasis or dramatic effect.

¡Qué bonitos ojos tienes!   *What beautiful eyes you have!*

PRÁCTICA

a Describa a un(a) buen(a) amigo(a) en la clase de español. Use un mínimo de ocho adjetivos. Después pregúntele a él (ella) si la descripción es exacta o no.

MODELO: **Mi buen amigo es simpático, hablador,...**
Mi buena amiga es simpática, habladora,...

b Entrevista. Pregúntele a otro(a) estudiante.

1. ¿Tiene Ud. un buen trabajo?
2. ¿Come Ud. en los restaurantes mexicanos?
3. ¿Le gusta la comida china?
4. ¿Le gustan los carros grandes o pequeños?
5. ¿Vive Ud. en una casa nueva o vieja?
6. ¿Vive confortablemente?
7. ¿Es Ud. una famosa figura internacional?

II *Ser y Estar*

Both **ser** and **estar** mean *to be,* but they cannot be used interchangeably in Spanish without affecting the meaning.

ser	estar	
soy	estoy	*I am*
eres	estás	*you* (tú) *are*
es	está	*he, she, it is; you* (Ud.) *are*
somos	estamos	*we are*
sois	estáis	*you* (vosotros) *are*
son	están	*they, you* (Uds.) *are*

A   **Ser** is used:

1. To connect the subject with a noun or pronoun. It tells *who* or *what* the subject is.

Ellos son turistas.	*They are tourists.*
¿Es Cristina? — Sí, es ella.	*Is it Cristina? —Yes, it's she.*
Acapulco es una ciudad bonita.	*Acapulco is a pretty city.*

2. To indicate where the subject is from *(origin);* the *material* something is made of; *possession.*

¿De dónde es Ud.? — Soy de Honduras.	*Where are you from? —I'm from Honduras.*
La casa es de madera.	*The house is (made of) wood.*
¿De quién es el dinero? — Es de Mario.	*Whose money is it? —It's Mario's.*

PRÁCTICA

a Connect the subject with the noun by inserting a form of **ser.**

MODELO: Gabriel _____ mecánico.   Gabriel **es** mecánico.

1. Ellos _____ vendedores.
2. (yo) _____ la hermana de Luis.
3. (tú) _____ una persona práctica.
4. (nosotros) _____ buenos amigos.
5. La Sra. de Reyes _____ una doctora excelente.
6. Hoy _____ lunes, ¿no?

b ¿Cómo se dice? Use a form of **ser** plus **de** to indicate origin, material, or possession.

1. I'm from the United States.
2. The watch is Leonor's.
3. My house is made of brick. *(ladrillo)*
4. They are from Puerto Rico.
5. The door is made of wood.

B **Estar** is used to give the location of the subject.

¿Dónde están los Gómez?	*Where are the Gomezes?*
Están en el piso doce.	*They are on the twelfth floor.*
Estamos cerca del parque.	*We're near the park.*

Common adverbs and adverbial phrases indicating location

aquí *here*
allí *there*
arriba *up*
abajo *down*
derecho *straight ahead*
a la derecha *to the right*
a la izquierda *to the left*
cerca *nearby;* **cerca de** *near (to)*
lejos *far;* **lejos de** *far from*

PRÁCTICA

a Use the appropriate form of **estar** to indicate the location of the subject.

MODELO: Raquel _____ en Panamá.   Raquel **está** en Panamá.

1. (yo) _____ en la universidad.
2. Uds. _____ en su casa.
3. Los niños _____ cerca del patio.
4. (nosotros) _____ lejos del centro.
5. Los Pérez _____ aquí.
6. La oficina _____ a la derecha.
7. Lima _____ en el Perú.
8. Tú _____ arriba en el piso quince y yo _____ abajo en el once.

b Situación. Usted está en la recepción (X) de un hospital. Diga dónde están los diferentes departamentos.

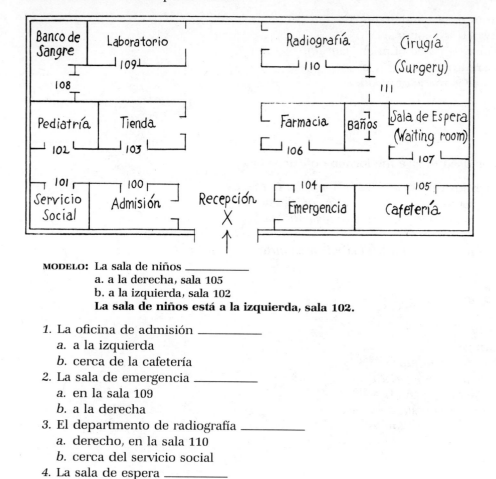

MODELO: La sala de niños _____
         a. a la derecha, sala 105
         b. a la izquierda, sala 102
         La sala de niños está a la izquierda, sala 102.

1. La oficina de admisión _____
     a. a la izquierda
     b. cerca de la cafetería
2. La sala de emergencia _____
     a. en la sala 109
     b. a la derecha
3. El departmento de radiografía _____
     a. derecho, en la sala 110
     b. cerca del servicio social
4. La sala de espera _____
     a. a la derecha
     b. arriba
5. El banco de sangre _____
     a. aquí, a la derecha
     b. a la izquierda, sala 108
6. La farmacia _____ ¿?
7. ¿?

IV *Ser y estar con adjetivos*

A When **ser** connects the subject with an adjective, the intention is to describe what is *typical* or *characteristic* of the subject.

Irene es alta y morena.   *Irene is tall and dark (brunette).*
Ustedes son muy amables.   *You're very kind.*

B   With **estar** plus an adjective (sometimes an adverb), the intention is to describe appearances or conditions (what the subject *looks like, feels like,* or *appears to be* at a certain time). Compare:

Eduardo está nervioso.	*Eduardo is (looks) nervous.*
Eduardo es nervioso.	*Eduardo is nervous. (He is a nervous person by nature.)*
Cristina está enferma.	*Cristina is (feels) sick.*
Yo estoy bien.	*I am fine.*
Los zapatos están nuevos.	*The shoes are new. (They look new despite wear.)*
Los zapatos son nuevos.	*The shoes are (brand) new.*
Estamos perdidos.	*We're lost.*

These adjectives frequently appear with **estar**:

cansado	*tired*	aburrido	*bored*	sucio	*dirty*
ocupado	*busy*	contento	*happy*	limpio	*clean*
preocupado	*worried*	abierto	*open*	roto	*broken*
		cerrado	*closed*		

PRÁCTICA

a   You haven't seen one of your girlfriends for a while, and she looks different to you. Describe how you see her now, using the contrasting words provided.

MODELO: linda / fea   **Alicia está (muy) linda hoy.** (or)
Alicia está (muy) fea hoy.

1. guapa / fea
2. bien / mal
3. ocupada / perezosa
4. pálida / quemada del sol *(sunburned)*
5. habladora / callada *(quiet)*
6. mejor / peor
7. contenta / triste
8. aburrida / animada

b   Repeat exercise **a** using a masculine subject.

c   Tell how you feel in the following situations. Make up at least a couple of situations, too. Refer to the columns on the right to express how you feel.

MODELO: **Cuando estoy en el cine, estoy contento(a).**

1. la playa	contento	quemado del sol
2. la universidad	triste	bien
3. el trabajo	excitado	mal
4. en casa	nervioso	perezoso
5. un baile	cansado	ocupado
6. una fiesta	elegante	callado
7. un banquete formal	aburrido	confortable
8. un partido *(match)* de básquetbol		

Resumen (Summary)

ser	estar
+ noun	
+ adjective (typical)	+ adjective (looks or feels like)
+ de + origin, possession, material	+ location

PRÁCTICA

a Complete las oraciones con la forma correcta de **ser** o **estar**.

1. La Dra. Aguirre _____ de Panamá.
2. Ellos _____ en el Hotel Presidente.
3. Tú no _____ cansada, ¿verdad?
4. Papá siempre _____ alérgico a la penicilina.
5. Los Ochoa _____ muy preocupados.
6. Los papeles _____ de la profesora.
7. Nosotros _____ norteamericanos.
8. La torta _____ de chocolate.
9. Las maletas _____ abajo en el carro.
10. Yo _____ perdido.
11. La cámara _____ rota.
12. Las tiendas _____ cerradas ahora.
13. ¿De quién _____ la llave?
14. La mesa _____ sucia.
15. Tú _____ una persona muy simpática.

b ¿Cómo se dice en español?

1. My friend Ana is sick.
2. Sergio is married.
3. The car is broken.
4. Julia Miller is young and single.
5. Gladys is my cousin.
6. Are you busy? (**Uds.**)
7. They're not bored.
8. I'm very happy here.

c ¿Quién soy yo? The class divides itself into groups of five or six students. In each group one student assumes the identity of a famous celebrity. The other students then ask "the celebrity" in their group questions to be answered with **sí** or **no** only. Possible questions to pose:

1. ¿Es Ud. de los Estados Unidos? ¿de la América Latina?
2. ¿Es Ud. hombre? ¿mujer (woman)?
3. ¿Es Ud. político? ¿actor? ¿actriz? ¿músico? ¿deportista?

4. ¿Es joven? ¿viejo? ¿guapo(a)? ¿moreno(a)? ¿rubio(a)? ¿alto(a)?
5. ¿Es soltero(a)?
6. ¿Está Ud. en California? ¿en México?
7. ¿Está Ud. contento(a)? ¿triste?

OBSERVACIONES

As you read the passage below keep in mind that in Spanish descriptive adjectives generally follow the nouns they modify. Jot down the nouns and their modifiers along the way; for example,

<u>instituciones</u> públicas o particulares

Afterwards, do the vocabulary section of ¿Comprende Ud.? When you have finished, reread the passage and seek out the one or two principal thoughts in each paragraph. Since the reading contrasts hospitals and clinics, look for words that highlight the comparisons.

Los hospitales y las clínicas

Los hospitales en los Estados Unidos son instituciones públicas o particulares.° En casos de enfermedades° o accidentes serios casi° todo el mundo° va a un hospital. Los individuos que están en una clínica casi siempre necesitan tratamiento° médico especial para° una enfermedad muy seria (cáncer, leucemia, etc.). La Clínica Mayo, por ejemplo, tiene fama universal. Pero en casi todos los hospitales es posible obtener el tratamiento especializado y personal que el individuo necesita. *private / illness / almost* *everybody* *treatment / for*

En Hispanoamérica (y también en Europa) la situación es muy diferente. El hospital, en general, es la institución de la gente pobre o de recursos° limitados. Los hospitales ofrecen tratamiento médico adecuado, pero si° es posible la gente° con suficientes recursos económicos prefiere ir° a una clínica particular. *resources* *if* *people / to go*

La clínica particular es mucho más pequeña que° el hospital y puede° ofrecer un tratamiento más íntimo y personal. Algunos° médicos trabajan en un hospital y también en una clínica. Otros tienen sus propias° clínicas y trabajan allí exclusivamente. *than / can* *Some* *their own*

Las clínicas pueden ser pequeñas, de veinte o treinta camas,° o pueden ser más grandes y estar equipadas para tratar° las enfermedades más serias y raras. *beds* *for treating*

El apoyo° de la familia es indispensable para el paciente. Frecuentemente varios familiares acompañan al enfermo a la clínica o al hospital. En ambos° lugares el propósito° es ayudar° a los enfermos a recuperar° la salud. *support* *both / purpose / to help / recover*

¿COMPRENDE UD.?

a **Vocabulario.** Find the equivalent of the following phrases in the passage.

1. poor people
2. a private clinic
3. special medical treatment
4. limited resources
5. all the hospitals
6. a very serious illness
7. more intimate and personal treatment
8. sufficient economic resources

b **¿Comprensión.** ¿cierto o falso?

1. En los Estados Unidos todos los hospitales son instituciones particulares.
2. En la América Latina los hospitales son para la gente de mucho dinero.
3. Los hispanos de la clase media prefieren ir a una clínica.
4. Los médicos en Hispanoamérica trabajan exclusivamente en clínicas.
5. En las clínicas particulares los médicos pueden tratar enfermedades serias.
6. Las clínicas particulares son más grandes y su tratamiento es más impersonal.
7. El enfermo hispano generalmente va solo al hospital o a la clínica.

c Rewrite the statements you have marked false in **práctica b** in order to make them true.

Actividades

Lea bien el anuncio y después conteste las preguntas en la página 87.

GRATIS
EXAMEN FISICO PARA
NIÑOS(AS)
Que entran al kindergarten y a primer grado. Llamen al **483-1447** hablen con Rebecca.

• CIRUGIA MENOR
• CUIDADO DEL NIÑO
• VACUNAS E INMUNIZACIONES

CENTRO MEDICO
SE HABLA ESPAÑOL

a Combine el inglés (las letras) con el español (los números).

1. gratis _____
2. examen físico _____
3. entran _____
4. llamen _____
5. primer grado _____
6. cirugía menor _____
7. vacunas _____

a. *call*
b. *minor surgery*
c. *first grade*
d. *vaccines*
e. *free of charge*
f. *(they) enter*
g. *physical examination*

b Conteste según el anuncio.

1. ¿Es gratis el examen físico para los niños?
2. ¿Es doctora o enfermera *(nurse)* la mujer en el anuncio?
3. ¿Habla español Rebecca?
4. ¿Qué servicios ofrece el Centro Médico?

c Situación. Imagínese que Ud. trabaja en la oficina de admisión en un hospital. ¿Qué le pregunta Ud. al paciente nuevo (otro estudiante)? Prepare un mínimo de diez preguntas. El paciente debe contestar todas las preguntas. Posibilidades: ¿Cómo se llama Ud.? ¿Dónde vive? ¿Cuál es el número de su seguro social? ¿Tiene Ud. seguro de hospitalización? ¿Tiene *medicare*? ¿Quién es su médico? En caso de emergencia, ¿a quién notificamos? ¿Es alérgico(a) a...?, etc.

Vocabulario

SUSTANTIVOS
la **boca** mouth
el **brazo** arm
la **cabeza** head
la **cara** face
la **espalda** back
el **estómago** stomach
la **mano** hand
la **nariz** nose
el **ojo** eye
el **pelo** hair
el **pie** foot

ADJETIVOS
aburrido(a) bored
alemán, alemana German
alto(a) tall
bajo(a) short
bonito(a) pretty, beautiful

buen(o), buena good
enfermo(a) ill, sick
español Spanish
feo(a) ugly
francés, francesa French
guapo(a) handsome
inglés, inglesa English
joven young
mal(o), mala bad
moreno(a) dark-haired
nuevo(a) new
ocupado(a) busy
pobre poor
rico(a) rich
rubio(a) blonde
sucio(a) dirty
trabajador(a) hard-working
triste sad
viejo(a) old

VERBOS
*****estar (estoy)** to be *(in a place or condition)*
*****ser (soy)** to be *(typical)*
*****ver (veo)** to see

EXPRESIONES
abajo down
a la derecha to the right
a la izquierda to the left
allí there
aquí here
arriba up
cerca near; **cerca de** near (to)
¿De quién es? Whose is it?
lejos far; **lejos de** far from
¿Qué le pasa? What's wrong?
derecho straight ahead

Lección 4 *De compras* (Shopping)

Daniel y Olga Marrero, de Venezuela, están de vacaciones° en la Florida. Antes de regresar° a su país van de compras a una tienda.

are on vacation
Before returning

OLGA Perdone, ¿habla usted español?

LA DEPENDIENTE° Sí, cómo no°. ¿En qué puedo servirles?°

clerk / of course / What can I do for you?

OLGA Quiero probarme° unos vestidos de verano.

to try on

DANIEL La ropa° aquí está muy barata.° Mientras° te pruebas° los vestidos, yo me voy a comprar unas camisas y pantalones y tal vez° una chaqueta.

clothing / cheap / While / you try on / perhaps

LA DEPENDIENTE La ropa de caballeros° está en el segundo piso.° Esta° semana tenemos una fantástica liquidación° de trajes y chaquetas.

gentlemen / second floor / This / clearance sale

DANIEL (A Olga) Bueno, cariño,° se ve que° vamos a necesitar dos o tres maletas más.

sweetheart / you can see that

¿RECUERDA UD.?

1. ¿Dónde están de vacaciones Daniel y Olga?
2. ¿De dónde son los Marrero?
3. ¿Adónde van de compras?
4. ¿Habla español la dependiente?
5. ¿Qué quiere probarse Olga?
6. ¿Qué quiere comprarse Daniel?
7. ¿Está barata o cara *(expensive)* la ropa?
8. ¿Dónde está la ropa de caballeros?
9. ¿Qué tiene la tienda esta semana?
10. ¿Por qué *(Why)* van a necesitar más maletas? Porque *(Because)*...

ADAPTACIÓN

Dos de ustedes preparan una conversación que tiene lugar en una tienda. Uno puede ser cliente y el otro puede ser dependiente. El cliente tiene problemas con la ropa: es muy grande / pequeña; está rota; el color es muy oscuro (*dark*), etc. El dependiente puede preguntarle al cliente si (*if*) tiene el recibo (*receipt*), si desea cambiar (*exchange*) la ropa o si desea su dinero. Usen la información en la conversación **De compras** y su imaginación.

La ropa

blusa

falda

vestido

el cinturón

sandalias

botas

las pantimedias

chaqueta

abrigo

el impermeable

sombrero

bolsa

¿Quién es Olga?

Lleva (*she's wearing*) una blusa, una falda, un cinturón y una bolsa.

1.   2.   3.   4.

camisa   corbata   los pantalones   camiseta   los calcetines

los pantalones cortos   gorra   zapatos de tenis   el suéter

el traje   zapatos   el traje de baño   cartera

¿Quién es Daniel?

Tiene el pelo negro. Usa anteojos. Lleva una camisa, una corbata y unos pantalones grises. No lleva chaqueta.

1.   2.   3.   4.

PRÁCTICA

a   **Situación.** Usted es dependiente en una tienda. Dígales a los clientes hispanos cuánto cuesta cada cosa.

MODELO: $20   **El suéter cuesta veinte dólares.**

   $38   **Los pantalones cuestan treinta y ocho dólares.**

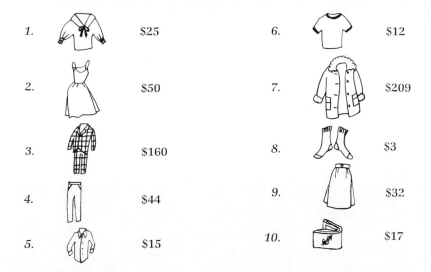

1. $25   6. $12

2. $50   7. $209

3. $160   8. $3

4. $44   9. $32

5. $15   10. $17

b   **¿Quién puede adivinar** (guess)? Describa Ud. la ropa que lleva una persona en la clase de español. No mencione el nombre. ¿Pueden adivinar los otros estudiantes quién es la persona?

MODELO: **Lleva unos zapatos** (¿color?), **un cinturón... , unos pantalones,** etc.

c   Conteste Ud.

1. ¿Qué ropa lleva Ud. cuando hace calor? ¿frío?
2. ¿Qué ropa lleva a un banquete formal? ¿a una fiesta de amigos?
3. ¿Qué lleva al campo? ¿a la playa?
4. ¿Qué lleva cuando llueve?
5. ¿Prefiere Ud. las camisas o las camisetas?

6. ¿Prefiere Ud. las rayas  ?   ¿los lunares ?   ¿los cuadros ?

7. ¿Le gustan las camisas de lana (wool)? ¿de poliéster?
8. ¿Le gustan las blusas de seda (silk)? ¿de algodón (cotton)?
9. ¿Le gusta más un color oscuro o un color claro (light)?
10. ¿Tiene Ud. un cinturón de cuero (leather)? ¿De qué color es?

d   **Situación.** El semestre nuevo empieza (begins) en la universidad y usted no tiene ropa nueva. Prepare una lista de la ropa que va a comprar. Debe incluir los colores y también el precio (price). El dinero no es un obstáculo pues usted tiene un cheque de quinientos dólares.

Estructura

I *Verbos con el cambio radical: e → ie, o → ue*

Stem-changing verbs change the **e** or **o** in their stem (**e** to **ie** and **o** to **ue**) when the stem is stressed. Throughout this book the type of stem change is indicated in parentheses, next to the infinitive. Since there isn't a systematic way to know which verbs do change stems, it's useful to learn the infinitive and the **yo** form of these verbs at the same time; for example, **cerrar, cierro**. To help you remember their pattern, these verbs are often referred to as **verbos de zapato**, as shown in the following illustration.

cerrar (ie) *to close*   **dormir (ue)** *to sleep*

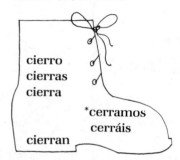

cierro
cierras
cierra
          *cerramos
           cerráis
cierran

duermo
duermes
duerme
          *dormimos
           dormís
duermen

¿A qué hora cierran Uds.?   — Cerramos a las doce.
¿Cuántas horas duermes?   — Duermo ocho horas.

A   Verbs with **e** to **ie** stem changes include:

empezar: **empiezo**   *to begin*
†entender: **entiendo**   *to understand*
nevar: **nieva**   *to snow (It's snowing.)*
pensar: **pienso**   *to think*
perder: **pierdo**   *to lose*
preferir: **prefiero**   *to prefer*
querer: **quiero**   *to want*

Pensar en means *to think of, about.*

Pienso en Uds.   *I think about you.*

Pensar + *infinitive* means *to plan to,* or *intend to.*

Ellos piensan ir de compras.   *They plan to go shopping.*

---

*There is no change because the stem vowels (**e, o**) are not stressed.
†¿Recuerda Ud. **comprender: comprendo** (to understand, comprehend)?

PRÁCTICA

a A classmate of yours has nothing to do. Ask if he or she wants to do the following activities.

MODELO: ir al cine **¿Quieres ir al cine?**
Sí, (No, no) quiero ir al cine.

1. ir de compras
2. jugar al tenis
3. dar un paseo
4. ver la televisión
5. escuchar música
6. nadar
7. pescar *(to fish)*
8. visitar a unos amigos
9. ¿?
10. ¿?

b This time ask two other students the same questions formed in exercise a. The two students should decide on an answer and reply accordingly.

MODELO: **¿Quieren Uds. ir al cine?**
— **Sí, (No, no) queremos ir al cine.**

c Several students are talking about their plans for today. Tell what they intend to do.

MODELO: Irene _____ estudiar en la biblioteca.
Irene piensa estudiar en la biblioteca.

1. Eduardo _____ salir con los amigos.
2. Tú _____ comer en un restaurante.
3. Rosa y María _____ regresar a casa.
4. Uds. _____ trabajar en el patio.
5. Marta y yo _____ tomar un refresco.
6. Ellos _____ ir al campo.
7. (yo) ¿?
8. ¿?

d Cambie Ud. el sujeto y el verbo del plural al singular y vice versa.

MODELO: Pensamos en Marco. **Pienso en Marco.**

1. Queremos regresar al hotel.
2. Cierro a las nueve de la noche.
3. Tú pierdes mucho dinero.
4. Ellos piensan en la familia.
5. Preferimos esperar unos minutos más.

e ¿Cómo se dice en español?

1. They prefer to go later.
2. Do you understand the professor? (tú)
3. Is it snowing?
4. My friends plan to travel to Latin America in the summer.
5. At what time does the program (el **programa**) begin?

B Verbs with **o** to **ue** stem changes include:

almorzar: **almuerzo**   *to have lunch*
costar: **cuesta**   *to cost* (**¿Cuánto cuesta?** *How much does it cost?*)
llover: **llueve**   *to rain (It's raining.)*
poder: **puedo**   *to be able (can)*
recordar: **recuerdo**   *to remember*
*volver: **vuelvo**   *to return, come back*

Jugar a *(to play)* changes its stem vowel **u** to **ue** in stressed position:

juego, **juegas**, **juega**, jugamos, jugáis, **juegan**

Jugar a means *to play a game or sport* and takes the preposition **a**.

Juego al dominó.   *I play dominos.*
Jugamos al sófbol.   *We play softball.*

If you want to say *to play* a musical instrument, use the verb **tocar**.

¿Tocas la guitarra?   *Do you play the guitar?*
No, pero toco la marimba.   *No, but I play the marimba.*

PRÁCTICA

a   El club de español va a tener una fiesta. Diga Ud. qué puede hacer *(do, make)* cada miembro para cooperar.

MODELO: la presidente _____ organizar la fiesta.
　　　　La presidente **puede** organizar la fiesta.

1. El vicepresidente _____ reservar la sala.
2. La secretaria _____ invitar a la gente.
3. Alicia y Gilberto _____ decorar la sala.
4. Uds. _____ ayudar a Alicia y Gilberto.
5. Tú _____ tocar la guitarra.
6. Margarita y Vicente _____ hacer el ponche.
7. Todos nosotros _____ preparar diferentes comidas.
8. Yo _____ sacar *(to take)* las fotos.

b   Aprenda Ud. el vocabulario y después diga a qué juega cada persona.

el dominó

las damas

las cartas

las damas chinas

el ajedrez

*¿Recuerda Ud. **regresar: regreso** *(to return)?*

MODELO: Ricardo y Julio

Ricardo y Julio **juegan a las cartas.**

1. Ellos

4. Uds.

2. Tú

5. Martín

3. Luisa y yo

6. (yo)¿?

c Complete con la forma apropiada del verbo.

1. La camisa (costar) _____ novecientos pesos.
2. Hace mal tiempo. (Llover) _____ mucho.
3. ¿A qué hora (almorzar) _____ (tú)?
4. Pepe y yo (volver) _____ mañana.
5. ¿(Recordar) _____ Uds. a Olga y Daniel Marrero?

d Entrevista. Formen Uds. grupos de tres estudiantes. El primer estudiante hace la pregunta, el segundo contesta, y el tercero *(third)* repite la respuesta.[1]

MODELO: (1) Pancho: **¿Qué quieres comprar?**
(2) Sara: **Quiero comprar un suéter beige.**
(3) Berta: **Sara quiere comprar un suéter beige.**[2]

1. ¿Dónde prefieres almorzar hoy?
2. ¿Adónde quieres ir el fin de semana?
3. ¿Qué piensas hacer luego?
4. ¿Cuándo vuelves?
5. ¿En quién piensas?
6. ¿Puedes jugar a...?
7. ¿Duermes en clase?

1. Switch roles after completing the series of questions so that all three of you have the opportunity to play each part. **2. Beige** is borrowed from French.

II *Los pronombres reflexivos*

A In a reflexive construction, the subject does the action to itself. The subject, the verb ending, and the reflexive pronoun all refer to the same person.

nonreflexive:	Llamo a Gloria.	*I call Gloria.*
reflexive:	(Yo) **Me llamo** Manuel.	*My name is Manuel. (I call myself Manuel.)*
nonreflexive:	El camarero sirve la comida.	*The waiter serves the food.*
reflexive:	**Ellos se** sirven.	*They serve themselves.*

Reflexive pronouns

SINGULAR	PLURAL
me *myself*	**nos** *ourselves*
te *yourself*	**os** *yourselves*
se } *himself, herself, itself, yourself* (Ud.)	**se** } *themselves, yourselves* (Uds.)

In vocabulary lists, the **se** attached to the infinitive indicates that reflexive pronouns accompany the verb forms.

B   Reflexive pronouns are placed *before* the conjugated verb form.

| Yo no **me levanto** temprano. | *I don't get up early.* |
| ¿Qué **te vas** a comprar? | *What are you going to buy for yourself?* |

They may also be attached to the end of the infinitive.

| Olga quiere probar**se** el vestido. | *Olga wants to try on the dress.* |
| Los Marrero van a sentar**se** allí. | *The Marreros are going to sit over there.* |

C   In Spanish verbs normally take reflexive pronouns:

1. When they denote physical or mental changes.

levantarse *to get up*	¿A qué hora te levantas?
sentarse (**ie**) *to sit down*	Lupe y Emilio se sientan a la mesa.
preocuparse *to worry*	La Sra. del Pino se preocupa mucho.

2. Or when they refer to personal care.

bañarse *to bathe*	Me baño pronto.
lavarse *to wash*	Nos lavamos las manos.[1]
ponerse[2] la ropa *to put on clothes*	¿Te pones el traje?[1]

1. Note that with parts of the body and clothing, Spanish generally uses the definite article. Compare the English: *We wash our hands.*   **2. me pongo, te pones, se pone, nos ponemos, os ponéis, se ponen.**

The following verbs are commonly used reflexively. The use of the reflexive may alter or intensify the meaning of the verb.

acostar (ue) *to put to bed*	Acuesto al niño.
acostarse *to go to bed*	Me acuesto tarde.
casar *to marry*	El pastor casa a Clara y Bruno.
casarse (con) *to get married (to)*	Clara se casa con Bruno.

despertar (ie) *to awaken*	El ruido *(noise)* despierta a la gente.
despertarse *to wake up*	¿Te despiertas temprano?
divertir (ie) *to amuse*	La televisión divierte a muchos.
divertirse *to have a good time*	Me divierto mucho en la playa.
ir *to go*	Humberto va al trabajo.
irse *to go away*	Nos vamos de vacaciones.

PRÁCTICA

a   Diga Ud. a qué hora se levantan estas *(these)* personas.

MODELO: Daniel / 6:30   **Daniel se levanta a las seis y media.**

1. su esposa / 6:15
2. sus hijos / 7:00
3. Uds. / 7:45
4. tú / 8:10
5. nosotros /¿?
6. yo /¿?

b   Use el sujeto entre paréntesis para hacer oraciones nuevas.

MODELO: Virginia se despierta temprano. (yo)   **(Yo) Me despierto temprano.**

1. Fernando se acuesta a las once. (yo)
2. Ellos se sientan a la mesa. (Cecilia)
3. ¿A qué hora se despierta Ud? (tú)
4. Rolando debe irse pronto. (nosotros)
5. Mis abuelos se divierten en las fiestas. (yo)
6. ¿Ud. se preocupa mucho, ¿no? (tú)
7. Ella no se llama Paquita. (yo)
8. ¿Quieres bañarte? (Uds.)
9. (Yo) me caso con Rosa. (él)
10. Me pongo los zapatos negros. (ellas)

c   Use el vocabulario para contestar las preguntas.

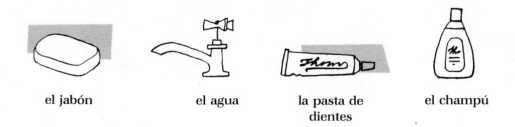

el jabón   el agua   la pasta de   el champú
                                   dientes

MODELO: ¿Con qué te lavas la cabeza?   **Me lavo la cabeza con champú.**

1. ¿Con qué te lavas las manos?
2. ¿Con qué te lavas los dientes?
3. ¿Con qué te bañas?

d Describa las actividades de Raquel.

MODELO: despertarse/temprano
Raquel se despierta temprano.

1. levantarse/a las 7:00

2. bañarse/pronto

3. ponerse la ropa

4. sentarse a la mesa

5. desayunarse

6. levantarse de la mesa

7. lavarse los dientes

8. irse al trabajo

e Repita la práctica *d* con los sujetos yo, **nosotros**, **ellos**, etc.

f ¿Cómo se dice?

1. I want to wash my hands.
2. Olga tries on the yellow blouse.
3. We can get up early.

4. At what time do you go to bed? (Uds.)
5. The students have a good time here.
6. Why don't you put on your coat? (tú)

III *El* **se** *impersonal*

When it is not important to identify the doer of the action, Spanish frequently uses **se** followed by a verb in the third person singular. This impersonal **se** may be translated as *one, people, they, you,* or a passive construction.

¿Cómo se dice?	*How does one say? How is it said?*
Se habla español.	*Spanish is spoken.*
Se cree que...	*It is believed (People believe) that* . . .
No se fuma aquí.	*You don't smoke here.*

PRÁCTICA

a Exprese Ud. con el **se** impersonal.

MODELO: Comen bien aquí. **Se come bien aquí.**

1. Aprenden mucho.
2. Regresan en taxi.
3. Dicen « coche »* en España.

4. Juegan al fútbol.
5. Ven perfectamente.
6. Hablan portugués en el Brasil.

*coche = **carro**

b ¿Cómo se dice? Use la forma impersonal se.

1. They eat at two.
2. One waits outside. (afuera)
3. It is said that Professor Casal's class is easy.

4. People work a lot here.
5. You don't pay now.

IV *Los verbos* **ir** *y* **dar**

ir *to go*	**dar** *to give*
voy*	**doy***
vas	**das**
va	**da**
vamos	**damos**
vais	**dais**
van	**dan**

*__Ir__ and **dar** are irregular in the first person singular.

A Verbs of motion like **ir, llegar, asistir**, and **venir** *(to come)*, require the preposition **a** when a destination is mentioned.

Vamos a la playa.   Llego a Caracas el viernes.

B Verbs of motion as well as **aprender, enseñar**, and **empezar** take the preposition **a** before an infinitive.

¿Aprendes a cocinar?	*Are you learning to cook?*
El dependiente empieza a contar el dinero.	*The clerk begins to count the money.*

C The construction **ir a** + *infinitive* is used to indicate future action.

Voy a estudiar luego.   *I'm going to study later.*

PRÁCTICA

a ¿Dónde necesitamos la preposición **a**?

1. Vamos _____ almorzar con los Martínez.
2. ¿Quieren _____ jugar Uds. al dominó?
3. ¿A qué hora empiezas _____ trabajar?
4. Aprendo _____ programar la computadora.
5. Uds. pueden venir _____ mi casa, ¿no?

b Situación. En el trabajo los empleados dan dinero a la beneficencia *(charity)*. Diga cuánto dinero cada empleado da. Recuerde Ud. que el cambio *(exchange)* de dinero varía de día a día y de país a país. En un país el cambio puede estar a 50 pesos por dólar y en otro a 200 pesos por dólar.

MODELO: El Sr. Castellanos / $4.000 **El Sr. Castellanos da cuatro mil pesos.**

1. La Sra. de Buendía / $7.500
2. Victoria y Ernesto / $6.000
3. Tú / $2.800
4. Ud. / $3.500
5. Nosotros / $8.900
6. Yo / ¿?

c Entrevista. Un(a) estudiante quiere saber qué va a hacer Ud. mañana. Usted también quiere saber qué va a hacer él (ella). Ustedes dos se turnan *(take turns)* en hacer y contestar las preguntas. Usen los infinitivos en la lista.

MODELO: levantarse temprano **¿Vas a levantarte temprano?**
Sí, (No, no) voy a levantarme temprano.

1. acostarse tarde	6. visitar a...
2. estar en casa	7. correr en el parque
3. divertirse mucho	8. jugar a...
4. estudiar...	9. ¿?
5. trabajar todo el día	10. ¿?

d Repitan la práctica **c** con tres estudiantes. Uno hace la pregunta con la forma verbal de **Uds.** y los otros dos contestan con la forma de **nosotros.**

MODELO: ¿Van a levantarse (Uds.) temprano?
Sí, vamos a levantarnos temprano.

e Escriba el párrafo pero cambie los verbos del presente al futuro idiomático, formado con **ir a** + infinitivo.

MODELO: Ellos toman el avión. Ellos **van a tomar** el avión *(airplane).*

Olga y Daniel llegan a Miami el viernes. Ellos visitan a sus amigos. El sábado Olga compra unos vestidos y zapatos mientras Daniel habla y juega al dominó con los amigos. Luego Olga y Daniel comen en un restaurante cubano. El domingo se bañan en la playa y asisten a un concierto. En total, están cinco o seis días en la Florida.

f Diga cinco cosas que Ud. va a hacer este *(this)* fin de semana.

MODELO: **Este fin de semana voy a...**

OBSERVACIONES

When reading a passage that contains new words, or familiar ones with apparently different meanings, you can rely on the general theme of the selection to help you understand the text. For example, you have studied the reflexives and the impersonal **se.** *Notice how context determines the meaning of* **se** *in these examples.*

1. *When talking about personal care, the reflexive is used:*
El niño se lava la cara y las manos.
2. *When referring to people in general, the impersonal* **se** *is used:*
Se vive bien aquí. *One lives well here. People live well here.*

In addition, note that the impersonal **se** *can also be used with a noun subject. The verb will be singular or plural depending on the noun. English resorts to the passive voice* (be + participle) *to translate these sentences.*

Se necesita cocinero.	*Cook (is) needed.*
Se usa el poncho en Sudamérica.	*The poncho is used in South America.*
Las camisas se hacen en México.	*The shirts are made in Mexico.*

First skim the reading below and jot down the various **se** *expressions you find; then proceed to do part* **a** *of ¿Comprende Ud.? Next, read the passage for main ideas; for example, note how people dress in different regions and how climate and customs affect what they wear. Refer to the translations in the margin only when necessary.*

La ropa

La ropa en las ciudades hispanas es generalmente formal. Las mujeres llevan vestidos o faldas, y los hombres se visten° de traje y corbata frecuentemente. Los pantalones, los trajes y las chaquetas son tradicionalmente de color azul, negro o gris. Entre° los jóvenes los blue jeans están de moda° en muchas partes. *get dressed / Among / in fashion*

Hoy se ven las tallas° S, M, L (*small, medium, large*) en varios almacenes° hispanos. Pero todavía se usan las tallas de Europa, especialmente en los zapatos. *clothing sizes / department stores*

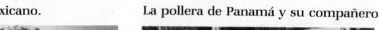

Números de zapatos

Damas (Ladies)						
Estados Unidos	4	5	6	7	8	9
España, Hispanoamérica	36	37	38	39	40	41
Caballeros						
Estados Unidos	8	8½	9	9½	10	10½	11
España, Hispanoamérica	41	42	43	44	45	46	47

La tradición y el clima influyen° en la manera de vestirse. Entre los grupos indígenas la ropa no cambia° mucho de generación a generación. Los campesinos° de México llevan ropa blanca de algodón° para protegerse del sol. Los campesinos de los Andes llevan ropa de colores vivos° de lana° que ofrece buena protección contra° el frío y la lluvia. *influence / change / peasants / cotton / colorful / wool / against*

El gusto° artístico de la región también contribuye° a la creación de trajes° típicos.° Hoy esos° trajes se llevan en fiestas especiales. *taste / contributes / clothes / typical / those*

Una joven con un vestido tradicional mexicano.

La pollera de Panamá y su compañero

A veces° la gente de las ciudades se enamora de° la ropa típica de las regiones rurales. Así es el caso de la guayabera, camisa elegante, que se usa mucho en partes del Caribe. También hoy el poncho, típico de los Andes, se usa en muchos países. La ropa de estilo° gaucho° también es popular en diferentes círculos sociales.

At times / falls in love with

style / herdsman from the pampas (plains)

Es verdad que la mayoría de hispanos se visten como° los norteamericanos, especialmente en las ciudades grandes como México, Lima y Santiago de Chile. Sin embargo,° muchos prefieren la moda europea, particularmente en España.

like

Nevertheless

guayabera

¿COMPRENDE UD.?

a Busque Ud. el equivalente de cada frase en la lectura *(reading).*

MODELO: Today one sees the sizes S, M, L. **Hoy se ven las tallas S, M, L.**

1. the sizes are still used
2. the men dress in suit(s)
3. the people . . . fall in love with
4. the guayabera, a fine shirt, is used . . .
5. those clothes are worn on special celebrations

b Busque en la columna B las traducciones *(translations)* de las palabras en la columna A.

A	B
1. talla _____	*a.* ladies
2. vestirse (me visto) _____	*b.* to influence
3. influir en _____	*c.* to dress oneself
4. estar de moda _____	*d.* gentlemen
5. damas _____	*e.* clothing size
6. caballeros _____	*f.* to be in fashion
7. lana _____	*g.* Argentinean herdsman
8. a veces _____	*h.* cotton
9. gaucho _____	*i.* to fall in love with
10. entre _____	*j.* at times
11. algodón _____	*k.* wool
12. enamorarse de _____	*l.* between, among

c Comprensión. ¿cierto o falso?

1. Las mujeres llevan pantalones cortos en las ciudades hispanas.
2. Los hombres llevan trajes de color gris o azul.
3. Una talla 8 en zapatos de mujeres en los Estados Unidos es una talla 36 en Hispanoamérica.
4. Los campesinos mexicanos llevan ropa de lana.
5. La guayabera es una camisa elegante.
6. El poncho es típico del Caribe.
7. Los gauchos son de las pampas.

d Cambie Ud. la información falsa (ejercicio ***c***) a la información cierta.

e Situaciones

1. Un amigo y una amiga van de vacaciones a México. ¿Qué ropa deben llevar en la ciudad de México? ¿en Cancún? Explique Ud. por qué.
2. Usted piensa pasar unos meses en Quito y quiere vestirse como los quiteños. ¿Qué ropa va a llevar?

Actividades

El anuncio de ropa

Ahorre 20% en blusa de mangas cortas, ¡aproveche!

Diseñadas en colores multicolores enteros como: amarillo, rojo, azul y beige para lucir en el verano. Tallas del 8 al 16. Precio regular $18 cada una.

14⁴⁰ cada una

20% de ahorro en pantalones cortos, pantalones deportivos, faldas casuales o faldas-pantalón

desde **17⁶⁰**

hasta **24⁶⁰**

a Interpretación del anuncio

1. Ahorrar quiere decir *to save*, y aprovechar *to take advantage of*.
   Escriba Ud. el imperativo *(command forms)* de los dos verbos.
2. Escriba las palabras que son similares en inglés y español.
3. Otra palabra que podemos usar para lucir es: a. perder b. llevar
   c. tocar

b Creación. Prepare Ud. un anuncio de ropa. Incluya palabras como:

¡Ahorre!
azul, rojo(a)
fantástico(a), estupendo(a), elegante
tremendos descuentos
los precios (prices)
las tallas

Vocabulario

SUSTANTIVOS
el **abrigo** *coat*
el **agua** *water*
la **blusa** *blouse*
la **bolsa** *purse; bag*
las **botas** *boots*
la **camisa** *shirt*
la **cartera** *wallet*
la **chaqueta** *jacket*
la **falda** *skirt*
el **jabón** *soap*
los **pantalones** *pants*
la **ropa** *clothing*
el **suéter** *sweater*
el **traje** *suit*
el **vestido** *dress*
los **zapatos** *shoes*

ADJETIVO
barato(a) *cheap*

VERBOS
acostarse (ue) *to go to bed*
bañarse *to bathe (oneself)*
casarse (con) *to get married (to)*
cerrar (ie) *to close*
*****dar (doy)** *to give*

divertirse (ie) *to have a good time*
dormir (ue) *to sleep*
empezar (ie) *to begin*
entender (ie) *to understand*
*****ir (voy)** *to go*
jugar (ue) a *to play (game, sport)*
lavarse *to wash (oneself)*
levantarse *to get up*
llevar *to wear, to take*
pensar (ie) en *to think of (about)*; **pensar +**
    infinitive / to plan to
perder (ie) *to lose*
poder (ue) *to be able (can)*
*****ponerse (me pongo)** *to put on (clothes)*
preferir (ie) *to prefer*
querer (ie) *to want*
sentarse (ie) *to sit down*
tocar *to play (an instrument); to touch*

EXPRESIONES
antes (de) *before*
entre *between, among*
¿En qué puedo servirle? *What can I do for you?*
mientras *while*
tal vez *perhaps*
todavía *still*

Examen II

Take the Listening and Speaking sections of the *Examen* with a classmate, who will supply phrases, numbers, and questions as needed. Do *not* look at what your classmate has chosen or written; rely instead on *your* listening and speaking skills.

Listening

Dictado. For the passage below your classmate will select answers from the choices offered in parentheses and then dictate that version of the passage two times to you. The first time listen for meaning; the second, write down what you hear during the pauses.

1. Daniel y Olga están de $\begin{bmatrix} \text{vacaciones} \\ \text{compras} \\ \text{visita} \end{bmatrix}$ en $\begin{bmatrix} \text{California} \\ \text{la Florida} \\ ¿? \end{bmatrix}$. //

2. Van de compras $\begin{bmatrix} \text{a una tienda} \\ \text{al centro} \\ \text{a la calle...} \end{bmatrix}$. //

3. Olga desea $\begin{bmatrix} \text{ver} \\ \text{comprar} \\ \text{probarse} \end{bmatrix}$ unos vestidos y $\begin{bmatrix} \text{unas faldas} \\ \text{unos zapatos} \\ ¿? \end{bmatrix}$. //

4. Daniel quiere $\begin{bmatrix} \text{comprar} \\ \text{probarse} \\ \text{ver} \end{bmatrix}$ unos pantalones y $\begin{bmatrix} \text{unos trajes} \\ \text{unas camisas} \\ ¿? \end{bmatrix}$. //

5. La ropa de $\begin{bmatrix} \text{verano} \\ \text{primavera} \\ ¿? \end{bmatrix}$ está muy $\begin{bmatrix} \text{cara} \\ \text{bonita} \\ \text{barata} \end{bmatrix}$. //

6. Daniel y Olga $\begin{bmatrix} \text{compran} \\ \text{ven} \\ \text{gastan} \end{bmatrix}$ mucho. //

7. Van a necesitar más $\begin{bmatrix} \text{tiempo} \\ \text{maletas} \\ \text{dinero} \end{bmatrix}$. //

After completing the dictation, check your work with your classmate. Then prepare a new version of the dictation to read to him or her.

Speaking

I Describe what these people are doing.

1. Carlos   2. Alicia y Diego   3. Tú   4. Nosotros   5. Yo

II Tell your classmate what you do on a typical day, including:

1. What time you get up.
2. Where you go. (Give three places.)
3. Where you have lunch.
4. With whom you talk.
5. What you read.
6. What you play.
7. What you do after dinner.
8. What time you go to bed.

III Listen to each question and answer it orally. Your classmate can change the order of the sample questions below and also create new questions.

1. ¿Dónde vives?
2. ¿Qué lees?
3. ¿Comen Uds. aquí o en casa?
4. ¿Cómo está Ud?
5. ¿Qué estudia Ud.?
6. ¿Es soltero(a)?
7. ¿Qué ropa te pones los domingos?
8. ¿Qué piensan hacer Uds. luego?
9. ¿A quiénes conoces en la clase?
10. ¿Adónde vas el sábado?

IV Referring to the drawings, tell what parts of your body ache.

1.   2.   3.   4.   5.

Writing

For the remaining sections of the *Examen,* write your answers on a separate sheet of paper.

I Draw and label at least eight parts of the body missing in this drawing.

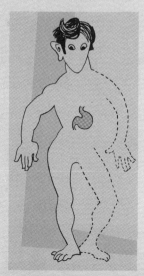

II Complete each sentence below with the present tense of the verb that best fits the context.

1. Daniel _____ un diccionario. (buscar, jugar, poder)
2. Tú _____ la lección, ¿no? (dormir, llegar, comprender)
3. Nosotros _____ contestar la carta. (perder, deber, llevar)
4. ¿Qué _____ usted del examen? (comer, vivir, creer)
5. Cristina y Ana _____ con la doctora. (hablar, desear, ser)
6. ¿Dónde _____ yo? ¿En el sofá? (bañarse, entender, sentarse)
7. Uds. _____ ir en taxi. (poder, abrir, caminar)
8. Mis amigos y yo _____ la televisión. (escribir, comer, ver)
9. Yo no _____ dónde viven ellos. (empezar, saber, esperar)
10. Ella _____ un paseo. (estar, dar, cerrar)

III Use the information provided to create questions and answers.

MODELO: a qué hora / comer (tú) **¿A qué hora comes?**
                                  Como a la una.

1. a qué hora / llegar (Ud.)
2. qué refresco / tomar (tú)
3. dónde / estar (la profesora)
4. a qué clases / asistir (tú)
5. a quién / esperar (Uds.)
6. a qué / jugar (tú)

IV Substitute the italicized portions of each sentence with the information in parentheses. Make whatever changes are needed.

MODELO: *Daniel* es venezolano. (ellos) **Ellos son venezolanos.**

1. Lupita tiene el *pelo* castaño. (ojos)
2. Vamos a *la cafetería*. (el parque)
3. *Federico* es español. (Josefina)
4. La carta es de *la Sra. Pérez*. (el esposo)
5. Tienes muchos *amigos* mexicanos. (dinero)
6. *Ellos* se ponen el abrigo. (yo)
7. *Pepita y yo* queremos ir de compras. (Berta y Mariana)
8. *Rosita* es una buena estudiante. (Arturo)
9. Buscamos *los papeles*. (el Sr. Ruiz)
10. *Pablo* es joven y guapo. (la hermana)
11. Viven en una casa *azul*. (madera)
12. Me gustan *las* fiestas. (la)

V Complete the following passage with the appropriate forms of **ser** or **estar**.

Teresa _____1_____ de Medellín, Colombia. Ella _____2_____ asistente de laboratorio. Ahora (Now) ella _____3_____ de vacaciones en Bogotá. Ella compra un poncho bonito. El poncho _____4_____ de lana (wool). Teresa y su amiga van a muchas tiendas y museos. Ellas ____5____ muy cansadas. Ellas regresan a casa. La casa ____6____ de los padres de la amiga. La casa ____7____ en un distrito nuevo de la capital.

VI   Look at the plan of a department store below. You are in the spot marked X. Indicate where the various places are as cued. Use these phrases in your replies: **arriba, abajo, a la derecha, a la izquierda, derecho.** Note that the ending -ría indicates *shop* or *store*. What would **zapatería** mean?

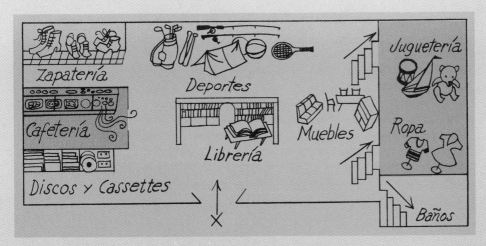

MODELO: **Los discos están a la izquierda, cerca de la cafetería.**

1. El departamento de muebles
2. La librería
3. El departamento de ropa
4. La zapatería
5. Los baños

VII   Write an original dialogue of at least eight lines. The situation could be either at an airport or at a doctor's office.

VIII   Translate the following.

1. How are you (**Uds.**)?
2. We're from the United States.
3. Do you (**Ud.**) speak English?
4. Where do you (**tú**) work?
5. Do you (**tú**) have a good time in Spanish class?
6. What can I do for you?
7. I want to try on the blue pants.
8. One eats early here. (Use an impersonal expression.)
9. For whom are you waiting?
10. You (**tú**) know how to play tennis, don't you?
11. Excuse me, I'm lost.
12. They should see Mrs. Flores today.

Reading

As you read the passage pick the most appropriate word in parentheses.

47 Millones de Hispanoamericanos

El gobierno federal (toma, cree, vende) que 47 millones de hispanos van a (vivir, enseñar, abrir) en los Estados Unidos en el año 2020. Debemos recordar que la influencia (español, latino, hispana) no es un fenómeno reciente. Los hispanos (bailan, tienen, leen) una larga historia en Norteamérica. Varios estados llevan nombres españoles: Nevada, tierra° de nieve;   *land* \
Colorado, rojo; Montana, montaña; Nuevo México; California, isla legendaria en una (periódico, novela, papel) española; y la Florida, tierra de las flores. Palabras como° plaza, chocolate, banana, patata, maíz y tomate forman   *like* \
parte (de la, de los, del) vocabulario inglés.

Los hispanos — 235 millones en el mundo° — son de diversos grupos ét-   *world* \
nicos y sociales. Además° de España, viven en México, la América Central,   *Besides* \
Cuba, la República Dominicana, Puerto Rico, en (toda, otra, una) Sudamérica menos el Brasil y las Guayanas. Las relaciones políticas, comerciales y culturales (hasta, depués, entre) los Estados Unidos y los hispanoamericanos son muy importantes.

Lección 5 En el hotel

Dos amigos, Armando y Ernesto, están de vacaciones en Madrid, España, y buscan habitación° en un hotel de precios° moderados. Van a la recepción y hablan con el empleado.°

    room / prices
    employee

EMPLEADO Muy buenas tardes señores. ¿En qué puedo servirles?
ARMANDO Quisiéramos° una habitación doble con baño particular.°
EMPLEADO Vale.° ¿Por° cuántos días?
ERNESTO Cinco. Dígame,° ¿está incluido° el desayuno en el precio de la habitación?

    We would like / private bath
    OK (in Spain) / For
    Tell me / included

EMPLEADO No señor, es aparte. La habitación cuesta 3.200 pesetas[1] por noche y el desayuno sólo 350 por persona.
ARMANDO Está bien. (A Ernesto) Llena°[2] el registro,° mientras yo traigo° las maletas del coche.°

    Fill out / registration / I bring / car

EMPLEADO Su habitación está en el quinto piso,° número 563. El desayuno se sirve de seis y media a nueve.

    fifth floor

ERNESTO Muchas gracias. Por favor, llámeme° a las seis. Tengo que° levantarme temprano.

    call me / I have to

EMPLEADO Con mucho gusto. A sus órdenes.°

    At your service.

1. La peseta es la moneda *(currency)* oficial de España. Note that the **empleado** would say **tres mil doscientas** (3.200) and **trescientas cincuenta** (350) to agree with **pesetas.** 2. Most affirmative **tú** commands are identical to the third person singular (**Ud., él, ella**) of the present tense: **¡Habla!** *Speak!*, **¡Come!** *Eat!*

quinto piso
cuarto piso
tercer piso
segundo piso
primer piso
planta baja

HOTEL PALACIO

NOTA CULTURAL

En Europa y la América Latina los pisos se dividen en planta baja *(ground floor)*, primer piso, segundo piso, etc.

1. ¿En qué ciudad están Armando y Ernesto?
2. ¿Qué buscan los dos?
3. ¿Adónde van ellos y con quién hablan?
4. ¿Qué clase de habitación quieren?
5. ¿Cuántos días piensan estar en el hotel?
6. ¿Cuánto cuesta la habitación? ¿el desayuno?
7. ¿Qué llena Ernesto?
8. ¿Qué trae Armando del coche?
9. ¿Dónde está la habitación de los dos? ¿Cuál es el número?
10. ¿A qué hora tiene que levantarse Ernesto?

ADAPTACIÓN

Imagínese que usted y otro(a) estudiante están de vacaciones y piensan pasar unos días en el Hotel Palacio. Ustedes entran al hotel y hablan con el empleado (la empleada) en la recepción. Preparen una conversación original; por ejemplo, ustedes creen tener una reservación, pero el empleado dice que no, y que hay un error.

Estructura

I Los adjetivos posesivos

Possessive adjectives in Spanish agree with the noun they modify and not with the possessor. The possessives **mi**, **tu**, and **su** have only two forms—singular and plural. **Nuestro** and **vuestro** have four forms: **-o**, **-a**, **-os**, and **-as**.

mi, mis *my*	**nuestro, nuestra** **nuestros, nuestras** } *our*
tu, tus *your (familiar)*	**vuestro, vuestra** **vuestros, vuestras** } *your*
su, sus *your (formal)* *his, her, its, their*	

mi padre, mi madre, mis padres	*my father, my mother, my parents*
tu hijo, tu hija, tus hijos	*your son, your daughter, your children*
nuestro primo, nuestra prima	*our cousin (m.), our cousin (f.)*
nuestros primos, nuestras primas	*our cousins*
su abuelo, sus abuelos	*your, his, her, their grandfather, grandparents*

For clarification or emphasis we can replace **su** or **sus** as follows:

su papel: el papel de él, de ella, de Ud., de ellos, de ellas, de Uds.
sus papeles: los papeles de él, de ella, etc.

Possession is never expressed with *'s* in Spanish. Instead, Spanish speakers use **de** + noun.

los anteojos **de** la muchacha   *the girl's glasses*
el amigo **del** Sr. Márquez   *Mr. Márquez' friend.*

Note the word order in Spanish: article + noun + **de** + owner

PRÁCTICA

a   Usted le enseña *(show)* varias fotos de su familia a un amigo (una amiga). Dígale quiénes son los miembros de su familia.

MODELO: La foto es de **mi hermana Irma.**

hermano, tíos, prima, abuelos, mamá, hijos, primos, familia

b   Ud. quiere ayudar a su compañero(a) de clase. Pregúntele si quiere las cosas en la siguiente *(following)* lista. Usen la forma familiar del verbo y de los adjetivos posesivos.

MODELO: **¿Quieres** *mi* **libro?**   — **Sí, quiero** *tu* **libro.**
         ¿Quieres *mis* **papeles?**   — **No, no quiero** *tus* **papeles.**

discos, cassettes, cuaderno, programa, libros, diccionario, revistas, periódico

c   Repitan Uds. la práctica b pero con la forma formal del verbo y los adjetivos posesivos. Cambien los verbos para tener un poco de variedad; por ejemplo, **necesita** o **prefiere.**

MODELO: **¿Necesita (Ud.)** *mi* **libro?**
         — **Sí, (No, no) necesito** *su* **libro.**

d   Las siguientes oraciones pueden ser ambiguas sin un contexto. Escriba las oraciones otra vez, pero use la frase de + la persona indicada entre paréntesis.

MODELO: Leo su carta. (él)   **Leo la carta de él.**

1. Quiero su dirección. (ellos)
2. Necesitamos sus papeles. (Ud.)
3. No comprendo sus preguntas. (ellas)
4. Hablo con su esposa. (él)
5. Están en su casa. (Uds.)
6. Conozco a sus hijos. (el Sr. Gómez)

e ¿Cómo se dice en español?

1. my books
2. her letter
3. Ricardo's key
4. our house
5. your (*fam. sing.*) room
6. their children
7. his suitcases
8. my mother's birthday

f Escriba Ud. un mínimo de cinco oraciones originales. Use diferentes adjetivos posesivos y describa a una persona o cosa.

MODELO: **Nuestro carro es rojo y pequeño.**
Tus padres están muy contentos.

II *Verbos con el cambio radical:* e → i

A few **-ir** verbs change the **e** of their stem to **i** when the stem is stressed.

pedir *to ask for, request*		
pido	Pido un refresco.	*I'm asking for a soft drink.*
pides		
pide		
pedimos	Pedimos agua fría.	*We're asking for cold water.*
pedís		
piden	¿Qué piden ellos?	*What are they asking for?*

Pedir means *to ask for, to request*. Remember, however, that **preguntar** means to ask a *question*. Compare:

Daniel pide un descuento.   *Daniel is asking for a discount.*
Tú siempre preguntas ¿por qué?   *You're always asking why?*

Stem-changing **-ir** verbs (**e → i**) include:

servir: **sirvo** *to serve*
repetir: **repito** *to repeat*
seguir*: **sigo**   *to follow, continue*

¿Recuerda Ud.? The **u** in **-gue** serves only to keep the hard **g** sound and is not needed in **-ga** or **-go: sigo.**

Sigo a Juanita   *I follow Juanita.*
Seguimos hablando.   *We continue talking.*

*sigo, sigues, sigue, seguimos, seguís, siguen

PRÁCTICA

a Cambie el sujeto y el verbo del plural al singular y vice versa.

1. Ellos siguen al señor.
2. Pides mucho dinero.
3. Los camareros sirven el almuerzo.
4. Uds. no repiten rumores, ¿verdad?
5. Pedimos una mesa para seis personas.

b Situación. Varias personas están en la recepción de un hotel y piden habitaciones según su preferencia. Use Ud. los sujetos (a la iz- quierda) y el verbo **pedir** para hacer oraciones originales. Puede referirse a la lista (a la derecha) para mencionar qué prefiere cada persona.

MODELO: **Pido una habitación con aire acondicionado.**

1. (tú)   aire acondicionado
2. Los Valdés   dos camas
3. Nicolás   cama de matrimonio (*double bed*)
4. (nosotros)   baño particular
5. Raquel y Josefina   televisión
6. (yo)   vista al mar (*ocean view*)
7. ¿?   vista al frente (*front view*)
8. ¿?   calefacción (*heating*)

c Entrevista. Pregúntele a otro(a) estudiante qué sirve con las diferen- tes comidas. Después de la entrevista, dígale Ud. a la clase qué sirve él o ella. Pueden usar la lista de bebidas (*beverages*) que sigue.

agua
café
té
refrescos
ponche

leche   vino   jugo

1. ¿Qué sirves con comida mexicana? ¿comida italiana?

2. ¿Qué sirves con pollo? ¿con pescado?
   ¿con biftec?

3. ¿Qué sirves con galleticas?

4. ¿Qué sirves con el desayuno? ¿con la cena?

5. ¿Qué sirves con un « dip »?

d ¿Cómo se dice?

1. Ernesto asks how much the room is.
2. Dad, I don't ask for a lot: a new suit, five shirts, six or seven trousers, and a jacket.

III *Verbos con la terminación -go*

A   The verbs below have the ending **-go** for the first person singular (**yo**) in the present tense.

hacer *to do, make*		**salir** *to leave, go out*	
hago	hacemos	**salgo**	salimos
haces	hacéis	sales	salís
hace	hacen	sale	salen
poner *to put*		**traer** *to bring*	
pongo	ponemos	**traigo****	traemos
pones	ponéis	traes	traéis
pone	ponen	trae	traen

*Note that **traer** adds **-igo.**

PRÁCTICA

a   Cambie los verbos del singular al plural y vice versa.

1. Salimos mañana.   4. Ellos ponen el carro en el garage.
2. Hago ropa de sport. 5. Traemos a los niños.
3. Ud. trae el almuerzo.

b   En español usamos el verbo **hacer** con varias expresiones diferentes. Use Ud. el verbo **hacer** para traducir los verbos en inglés.

1. *It's* sunny today.
2. I *exercise* (do exercises) (**ejercicios**).
3. They *pack* the suitcases.
4. I *play* the part of Don Juan (**el papel de don Juan**).

c   Conteste Ud.

1. ¿A qué hora sale Ud. de casa los lunes? ¿los sábados?
2. ¿Qué trae a clase?
3. ¿Qué pone en el banco? ¿en una biblioteca? ¿en una maleta? ¿en un refrigerador?

B   The **yo** form of **tener, venir,** and **decir** also ends in **-go.** These verbs also undergo stem changes.

tener *to have*	venir *to come*	decir *to say, tell*
tengo	**vengo**	**digo**
tienes	vienes	dices
tiene	viene	dice
tenemos	venimos	decimos
tenéis	venís	decís
tienen	vienen	dicen

PRÁCTICA

a Cambie los sujetos en cursiva *(italics)* por los sujetos entre paréntesis.

1. *Uds.* tienen mucho trabajo. (yo)
2. *Mis padres* no vienen al banquete. (nosotros)
3. *Carlos* dice el chiste *(joke)*. (tú)
4. *La Sra. Iglesias* viene a hablar con Ud. (yo)
5. *Ellas* dicen la verdad. (yo)
6. *Tú* no tienes dólares. (Luis y yo)

b Los chismes *(gossip)*. Hagan Uds. grupos de tres estudiantes. Número uno le dice un chisme al número dos en voz baja *(quietly)*, y el dos le repite el chisme al tres. Después el tres le dice otro chisme al número uno, etc.

MODELO: 1: **Margarita está enamorada de Tomás.**
2: **Él / Ella dice que Margarita está enamorada de Tomás.**

IV *Expresiones con* tener

Several common expressions are formed with **tener**. English translates these idioms with a form of the verb *to be*. Note that the adjective **mucho**—and *not* the adverb **muy**—is used to modify the noun.

Tengo (mucho) calor.	**Ellos tienen (mucho) miedo.**
I'm (very) warm.	*They're afraid. (They're very frightened.)*
¿Tienes (mucho) frío?	**Tenemos (mucha) prisa.**
Are you (very) cold?	*We're in a hurry.*
Tenemos (mucha) hambre.	**Ud. tiene (mucha) razón.**
We're (very) hungry.	*You're (so) right.*
Ricardo tiene (mucha) sed.	**Tengo... años.**
Ricardo is (very) thirsty.	*I am . . . years old.*
Tengo (mucho) sueño.	
I'm (very) sleepy.	
Tener que + *infinitive* means *to have to, must.*	
¿Tienes que pagar la cuenta?	*Do you have to pay the bill?*

PRÁCTICA

a   Use una expresión con **tener** para *(in order to)* describir cada situación.

1. Fernando   2. Julia y Arturo   3. Yo

4. Nosotros   5. Tú   6. Los muchachos

7. El profesor   8. Uds. no   9. Yo

b   Haga Ud. *(Make)* oraciones originales con las siguientes expresiones. Use diferentes sujetos en cada oración.

1. tener (mucha) sed
2. tener razón
3. tener... años
4. tener (mucho) sueño
5. tener (mucha) prisa
6. tener dolor de cabeza
7. no tener (mucha) hambre
8. tener que...

c Repaso de las expresiones *to be* en inglés. Traduzca Ud. las oraciones con el verbo apropiado *(appropriate):* **hacer, ser, estar, tener** o **llamarse.**

1. My name is . . .
2. I'm . . . years old.
3. I'm a student.
4. I am not tired.
5. It's hot today.
6. We're very warm.
7. We're thirsty.
8. We're very sleepy.
9. Diego is fine.
10. He has to be here at ten o'clock.

OBSERVACIONES

One quick way to expand your vocabulary is to recognize prefixes and suffixes attached to words you know already. The Spanish prefixes **des-, in-,** *and* **im-** *often reverse the meaning of a word:*

posible   **im**pos**ible**
suficiente   **in**suficiente
aparecer *(to appear)*   **des**aparecer

The suffixes **-ero(a), -dor(a),** *and* **-ista** *often indicate a person's occupation:*

rancho   ranch**ero(a)**
administración   administra**dor(a)**
periódico   periodi**sta**

Before reading the following selection, read exercise a *under* **¿Comprende Ud?** *Then read the selection, searching for the information asked for in the exercise. Read very carefully.*

Consejos para el viajero (Advice for the traveler)

Todos los años muchos vacacionistas hacen sus maletas y pasan sus vacaciones en el extranjero.° El viajero debe recordar que las costumbres° varían de país a país. — *abroad / customs*

El turista no tiene que ser experto en materias culturales para causar buena impresión. Es verdad que el dinero es necesario para conseguir° buena habitación, comida y diversión, pero hay ciertas° amenidades que el dinero no puede comprar. — *to get* / *certain*

Algunos° consejos prácticos para el viajero son: — *Some*

1. El concepto del tiempo, especialmente en los centros turísticos, es diferente en otras naciones. Si la persona siempre° tiene prisa va a sufrir muchas desilusiones. « El reloj no existe en las horas felices. » — *always*

2. El café en los países hispanos no se sirve hasta el final de la comida. Si insiste en tomarse cuatro o cinco tazas° de café con la comida, el cliente va a pagar° por cada una. Debe pedir la cuenta al terminar°[1] — *cups* / *to pay / when finishing*

---

1. A1 + infinitive means *upon* or *when;* for example, **al terminar** *when finishing.*

porque generalmente el camarero° no desea dar la impresión de
querer deshacerse° del cliente.

waiter
to get rid of

3. La cortesía es de gran importancia cuando se va de compras, hasta° en
el regateo.° Esta costumbre requiere humor y paciencia. El regateo se
practica en los mercados, pero en las tiendas normalmente los precios
son fijos.°

even
bartering

fixed

4. Si el turista visita lugares con tradiciones bien establecidas, debe respetar esas tradiciones. Por ejemplo, en algunas iglesias y templos las personas no pueden entrar si llevan pantalones cortos o camisetas sin
mangas.°

tank tops

5. Si quiere discutir la situación política nacional, la economía o la pobreza local, debe tener tacto y cuidado.° El nacionalismo es muy fuerte
en los países hispanos y la crítica de un extranjero° puede causar mo-
mentos desagradables.

care
foreigner

6. Si tiene cuidado puede evitar° engaños y desengaños.° Por ejemplo, es
mejor no comprar joyas° en las calles.°

avoid / deceit and
disappointments
jewelry / streets

7. El pasaporte es un documento importantísimo° que debe protegerse
contra la pérdida° y el robo.°

very important
loss / robbery

8. No todo el mundo° quiere ser modelo para las fotos del turista. Es
bueno pedir permiso antes de sacar la foto de una persona.

everybody

9. La energía eléctrica cuesta mucho en otros países y hay que°2 tener
consideración en el uso del agua caliente,° las secadoras° de pelo y
otros aparatos eléctricos. Además, el voltaje puede ser diferente de una
región a otra.

one must
hot / dryers

10. Cada turista es embajador de su país y su comportamiento° puede causar buenas o malas impresiones.

behavior

2. **Hay que** + *infinitive* means *one must;* for example, **hay que esperar** *one must wait.*

¿COMPRENDE UD.?

a Vocabulario. Añada Ud. *(Add)* el prefijo **des-** a las palabras y después seleccione el significado de las palabras nuevas.

MODELO: ventaja / **desventaja** *(disadvantage)*

<table>
<tr><td colspan="2" align="center">significados</td></tr>
<tr><td>1. ilusión / _____</td><td>a. to undo, get rid of</td></tr>
<tr><td>2. hacer / _____</td><td>b. disappointment</td></tr>
<tr><td>3. agradable / _____</td><td>c. disillusionment</td></tr>
<tr><td>4. engaño / _____</td><td>d. disagreeable</td></tr>
</table>

b Traducción. Busque las traducciones de las palabras en español
en la columna a la derecha.

<table>
<tr><td>1. turista _____</td><td>a. traveler</td></tr>
<tr><td>2. viajero _____</td><td>b. vacationist</td></tr>
<tr><td>3. extranjero _____</td><td>c. ambassador</td></tr>
<tr><td>4. vacacionista _____</td><td>d. tourist</td></tr>
<tr><td>5. embajador _____</td><td>e. foreigner</td></tr>
</table>

c   **Comprensión.**   Escoja *(Choose)* la letra o respuesta que mejor termine cada oración.

1. El turista que tiene prisa va a
   a. pasar unas vacaciones magníficas
   b. desilusionarse muchas veces
   c. conseguir buenas habitaciones y comida
2. El café en Hispanoamérica se sirve
   a. antes de la comida
   b. durante la cena
   d. después de comer
3. El regateo se practica en
   a. los mercados
   b. algunas iglesias y templos
   c. las tiendas con precios fijos
4. La energía eléctrica en el extranjero
   a. es generalmente barata
   b. consiste en 220 voltios en todas partes
   c. puede variar en voltaje
5. Para visitar una iglesia o templo el señor turista debe llevar
   a. traje de baño
   b. pantalones largos
   c. camiseta sin mangas

Actividades

Usted tiene que preparar una guía (guidebook) *de viajeros para los turistas que van a España. Combine las fotos con las descripciones en las páginas 122-123.*

Descripciones

1. Es la catedral más grande de España. La Giralda es un magnífico ejemplo de la arquitectura mora *(Moorish)*.

2. Contiene espléndidas pinturas *(paintings)* de Velázquez, El Greco y Goya.

3. Es una fabulosa residencia mora con bonitos jardines *(gardens)* fragantes.

4. Es un inmenso convento, palacio y mausoleo *(burial place)*.

5. Es una calle principal con tiendas y bancos.

6. Es excelente ejemplo de la arquitectura romana del siglo *(century)* primero. Se usaba *(It was used)* para traer agua a la ciudad.

a. Cibeles y calle de Alcalá, Madrid

c. El acueducto de Segovia

b. La Giralda, torre de la catedral de Sevilla

d. Monasterio de El Escorial

e. La Alhambra, Granada

f. Museo del Prado, Madrid

Vocabulario

SUSTANTIVOS
el **baño** bath
la **calle** street
el **cuidado** care
  tener cuidado to be careful
el **empleado**, la **empleada** employee
la **galletica** small cracker
la **galletica dulce** cookie
la **habitación** room
el **jardín** garden
el **jugo** juice
la **leche** milk
el **pescado** fish
el **pollo** chicken
el **precio** price
el **vino** wine

ADJETIVO
caliente hot

POSESIVOS
mi, mis my

tu, tus your (familiar)
nuestro(a),(os),(as) our
su, sus his, her, its, your (formal),
  their

VERBOS
*****decir (digo)** to tell, say
 ganar to earn, win
*****hacer (hago)** to do, make
 llenar to fill
 pagar to pay
 pedir (i) to ask for
*****poner (pongo)** to put, place
 repetir (i) to repeat
*****salir (salgo)** to go out, leave
 seguir (i) (sigo) to follow, continue
 servir (i) to serve
*****tener (tengo)** to have
  tener... años to be . . .
   years old
  tener calor to be hot
  tener frío to be cold

tener hambre to be hungry
tener miedo to be afraid
tener prisa to be in a hurry
tener razón to be right
tener sed to be thirsty
tener sueño to be sleepy
tener que + *infinitive* to
  have to (do something)
*****traer (traigo)** to bring
*****venir (vengo)** to come

EXPRESIONES
al + *infinitive* upon, when
Dígame. Tell me. (formal)
Llámeme. Call me. (formal)
para in order to, for
quisiera I would like
siempre always
todo el mundo everybody

6 En la agencia de turismo

Esperanza y su esposo Benito visitan la ciudad de México. Quieren conocer los lugares más interesantes y deciden ir a una agencia.

BENITO Querida,° quiero que decidas° entre° Chapultepec y las Pirámides.

AGENTE (Casi° interrumpiendo) ¡Oh no, señor! Uds. pueden ir a Chapultepec hoy y a las Pirámides mañana.

ESPERANZA ¡Ay, sí! Quisiera° ir a los dos lugares, pero también tenemos que comprar unos regalos.°

AGENTE Miren° Uds., en el paseo° a las Pirámides incluimos paradas° en las tiendas de artesanía.° ¿Desean que les haga las reservas?°

BENITO Bueno, Esperanza, di° tú, ¿vamos o no?

ESPERANZA ¡Claro que sí!... Pero, espero que tengamos tiempo° para el Ballet Folklórico esta noche.°

BENITO Y tiempo para descansar° un poco. Necesito acostumbrarme° a la altitud y al tráfico.

AGENTE ¡No se preocupen!° En nuestros paseos hay tiempo para todo.

Dear / I want you to decide / between
Almost

I'd like

gifts

Look / outing / stops
craft shops / Do you want me to make reservations for you?   say
I hope we have time

tonight

to rest / to get used to

Don't worry!

Cerca de la capital está la Zona Arquelógica de Teotihuacán. Aquí se encuentran (*are found*) las famosas Pirámides del Sol y de la Luna.

Chapultepec es un magnífico parque que tiene excelentes museos, jardines y monumentos.

¿RECUERDA UD?

1. ¿En qué ciudad están Esperanza y Benito?
2. ¿Qué quieren ver?
3. ¿Con quién hablan ellos?
4. ¿Cuándo pueden ir a Chapultepec? ¿y a las Pirámides?
5. ¿Qué tiene que comprar Esperanza?
6. ¿Dónde hacen paradas en los paseos?
7. ¿Adónde desea ir Esperanza esta noche?
8. ¿Por qué necesita descansar Benito?

ADAPTACIÓN

Imagínese que Ud. y un amigo hablan con una agente de turismo. Su amigo quiere pasar las vacaciones en la playa porque a él le gusta nadar y pescar. Usted prefiere la ciudad porque le gustan los museos y los teatros. La agente trata de *(tries to)* resolver el problema. Preparen una conversación original entre tres de ustedes.

Estructura

I Los mandatos formales *(Formal Commands)*

A A command is an order that one person gives directly to another: *Look! Listen!*

> Recall that the **Ud.** and **Uds.** affirmative and negative commands are formed by dropping the **-o** ending from the first person singular (present tense) and adding **-e / -en** to **-ar** verbs and **-a / -an** to **-er** and **-ir** verbs.

STATEMENTS	COMMANDS	
Hablo despacio.	¡**Hable** (**Ud.**) despacio!	*Speak slowly!*
	¡No **hablen** (**Uds.**)!	*Don't speak!*
Escribo más.	¡No **escriba** más!	*Don't write any more!*
	¡**Escriban**!	*Write!*

Ud. and **Uds.** may be included for emphasis or politeness.

These five verbs, whose **yo** form does not end in **-o**, have slightly different patterns.

INFINITIVE	Usted COMMAND	Ustedes COMMAND
dar	dé	den
estar	esté	estén
ir	vaya	vayan
saber	sepa	sepan
ser	sea	sean

PRÁCTICA

a   Dígale al profesor (a la profesora) que haga *(Tell the professor to do)* las siguientes cosas.

MODELO: esperar / un minuto   **Espere Ud. un minuto.**
        no leer / rápido   **No lea Ud. rápido.**

1. trabajar / menos
2. escribir / en la pizarra
3. abrir / la puerta
4. no regresar / mañana
5. no correr / mucho
6. comer / unas galleticas
7. vender / los libros viejos
8. pasar / unos días en el campo
9. escuchar / música clásica
10. permitir / uno o dos errores, ¿no?

b   Imagínese que usted trabaja en Latinoamérica. Dígales a sus compañeros de trabajo que hagan las siguientes cosas.

MODELO: estar / aquí temprano   **Estén aquí temprano.**

1. estar / aquí a las ocho
2. ir / a la oficina
3. ser / puntuales
4. dar / un descuento de diez por ciento
5. no discutir / la política ahora
6. no trabajar / los domingos
7. leer / las instrucciones bien
8. terminar / el trabajo pronto

B   Remember that some verbs have stem changes or irregular **yo** forms. The formal commands of these verbs reflect those changes.

pensar: pienso   **Piense** (Ud.).
dormir: duermo   **Duerma** (Ud.).
pedir: pido   **Pida** (Ud.).
hacer: hago   **Haga** (Ud.).
traer: traigo   **Traiga** (Ud.).
decir: digo   **Diga** (Ud.).
ver: veo   **Vea** (Ud.).

PRÁCTICA

El Sr. Suárez quiere saber si puede hacer las siguientes cosas o no. Contéstele Ud. afirmativa o negativamente.

MODELO: **¿Pedir unos refrescos o no?**
   Sí, pida unos refrescos. o **No, no pida unos refrescos.**

1. ¿Pedir vino o no?   4. ¿Ver la televisión o no?
2. ¿Traer a los niños o no?   5. ¿Cerrar las ventanas o no?
3. ¿Dormir la siesta o no?   6. ¿Decir un chiste o no?

C Verbs ending in **-car, -gar,** and **-zar** have spelling changes in the command forms in order to preserve the sound of the stem or for reasons of spelling conventions.

explicar buscar	$c \rightarrow qu$	¡Expli**qu**e Ud. el problema! ¡No bus**qu**en más!
pagar jugar	$g \rightarrow gu$	¡Pa**gu**e mil pesos! ¡No jue**gu**en en la calle!
empezar cruzar *(to cross)*	$z \rightarrow c$	¡Empie**c**en a comer! ¡**C**ru**c**e la Avenida Juárez!

PRÁCTICA

a Dé los dos mandatos Ud. y Uds. de los siguientes verbos.

MODELO: llegar temprano   **¡Llegue temprano!**
   ¡Lleguen temprano!

1. pagar la cuenta   4. no almorzar (ue) en el restaurante
2. empezar el trabajo   5. jugar al dominó
3. explicar el error   6. tocar un poco de música

b ¿Qué les recomienda *(recommend)* a las personas que hacen los siguientes comentarios? Usted puede usar la información a la derecha para expresar su opinión en forma de mandatos.

MODELO: Tengo hambre.   **¡Pues, almuerce ahora!**
   (Well then, have lunch now!)

COMENTARIOS

1. Tengo hambre.
2. Soy músico.
3. Paso muchas horas con el dominó, las cartas...
4. No sé donde están las llaves.
5. Quiero ir a México en carro.
6. Es tarde cuando entro por la puerta.
7. No hay suficiente luz para la cámara.

INFORMACIÓN

a. buscar en la casa / en el carro...
b. llegar a tiempo / más temprano...
c. almorzar ahora
d. tocar la guitarra / el piano...
e. cruzar la frontera *(border)* en El Paso / Laredo...
f. no jugar más a...
g. no sacar la foto ahora

D Reflexive pronouns as well as other object pronouns are attached to the affirmative commands. An accent mark is added to preserve the original stress of the verb.

¡Siéntense Uds.!	*Sit down!*
¡Pregúntele a ella!	*Ask her!*
¡Ayúdeme Ud., por favor!	*Please, help me!*

In negative commands these pronouns come *before* the verb.

¡No **se** sienten Uds.!	*Don't sit down!*
¡No **le** pregunte a ella!	*Don't ask her!*
¡No **me** ayude!	*Don't help me!*

PRÁCTICA

a Cambie a mandatos afirmativos.

MODELO: Ud. se sienta aquí.   **¡Siéntese aquí!**

1. Ud. se levanta a las siete.
2. Ud. se prueba la ropa.
3. Uds. se van el domingo.
4. Uds. se sientan en el sofá.
5. Uds. se divierten mucho.
6. Uds. se lavan las manos.
7. Ud. le pregunta a Esperanza.
8. Uds. se sirven la comida.
9. Uds. le pagan al vendedor.
10. Ud. me da mil pesos.

b Cambie los verbos en la práctica **a** a mandatos negativos.

MODELO: Ud. se sienta aquí.   **¡No se siente aquí!**

Lugares de interés en la ciudad de México

Plano del centro, ciudad de México

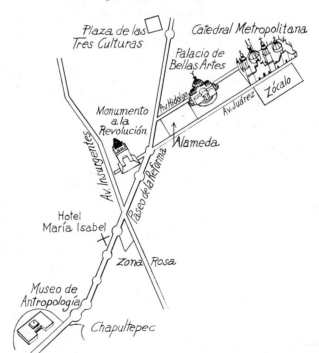

Monumento a la
Revolución

Alameda   (parque)

Catedral Metropolitana
y Plaza de la Constitución
El Zócalo

Paseo de la Reforma

Museo de Antropología

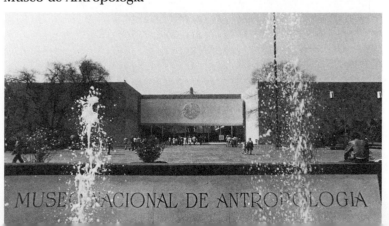

MUSEO NACIONAL DE ANTROPOLOGIA

Zona Rosa (comercios)

SITUACIONES

a   Ud. está en el Hotel María Isabel. (Vea el plano de la ciudad de México, página 128.) Varios turistas le preguntan cómo se va *(how one goes)* a diferentes lugares. Use el plano y las siguientes expresiones para ayudar a las personas.

vaya por   *go along*
vaya derecho   *go straight ahead*
doble a la derecha   *turn right*
doble a la izquierda   *turn left*
cruce la calle   *cross the street*
cruce la avenida   *cross the avenue*
hasta   *up to*

MODELO: ¿Cómo se va al Palacio de Bellas Artes?
Vaya derecho por la Reforma hasta la Avenida Hidalgo. Doble a la derecha.

1. ¿Cómo se va a la Catedral Metropolitana?
2. ¿Cómo se va al Zócalo (Plaza de la Constitución)?
3. ¿Cómo se va al Museo de Antropología?
4. ¿Cómo se va a la Zona Rosa (comercios)?
5. ¿Cómo se va al Monumento a la Revolución?
6. ¿Cómo se va a la Alameda (parque)?
7. ¿Cómo se va a la Plaza de las Tres Culturas?

b   Dos turistas hispanoamericanos están en la universidad donde usted estudia. Ellos quieren ir a diferentes lugares de la ciudad. Use la lista de lugares y el vocabulario adicional para ayudar a los dos turistas.

MODELO: el correo principal   **Vayan por la calle (avenida) hasta...**
Doblen a la...

Vocabulario adicional:

cuadra   *city block*
carretera   *highway*
semáforo   *traffic light*

1. el hotel
2. el banco
3. el museo
4. el teatro
5. el centro comercial
6. (otros lugares de interés)

II   *El subjuntivo*

A   The commands covered in the previous section are a *direct way* of asking someone to do something. By contrast, an indirect command tones down the order and is also applicable to other persons. Both types of commands are expressed by the subjunctive forms of the verb.[1]

DIRECT	INDIRECT
¡Regrese mañana!	Quiero que Ud. **regrese** mañana. *I want you to return tomorrow.*
	Queremos que **Benito regrese**. *We want Benito to return.*
¡Siéntense aquí!	Prefiero que **se**[2] **sienten** aquí. *I prefer that you sit here.*
	Abuela desea que **nos sentemos** juntos. *Grandmother wants us to sit together.*

1. The subjunctive is discussed further on in this lesson as well as in Lessons 12 and 13.
2. Object pronouns come before the verb in indirect commands.

¿Qué quieres que ponga — básquetbol, fútbol o boxeo?

Las formas del subjuntivo

	regresar	**leer**	**salir**
(yo)	regrese	lea	salga
(tú)	regreses	leas	salgas
(él, ella, Ud.)	regrese	lea	salga
(nosotros)	regres**emos**	lea**mos**	salg**amos**
(vosotros)	regres**éis**	le**áis**	salg**áis**
(ellas, ellos, Uds.)	regres**en**	le**an**	salg**an**

1. Notice that the subjunctive forms, which include the **Ud.** and **Uds.** commands, are the same as those of the present indicative, except that **-ar** verbs switch to **-e** endings and **-er** / **-ir** to **-a** endings. Irregular verbs to review are:

dar: **dé, des, dé demos, deis, den**
estar: **esté, estés, esté, estemos, estéis, estén**
ir: **vaya, vayas, vaya, vayamos, vayáis, vayan**

2. Stem-changing **-ar** and **-er** verbs maintain their same pattern of change:

cerrar: cierro → **cie**rre cerremos **cie**rren
poder: puedo → **pue**da podamos **pue**dan

3. The **-ir** stem-changing verbs keep their pattern except for the **nosotros** and **vosotros** forms in the following cases:

e → i verbs retain the **i**:

pedir: **pida, pidas, pida, pidamos, pidáis, pidan**

e → ie verbs reduce to **i**:

divertirse: **me divierta, te diviertas, se divierta, nos divirtamos, os divirtáis, se diviertan**

o → ue verbs reduce to **u**:

dormir: **duerma, duermas, duerma, durmamos, durmáis, duerman**

B Verbs have tenses and moods. A *tense* refers to the time of an action; a *mood* expresses the speaker's attitude toward that action. We use the *indicative* mood to report facts and events.

Ellos viven en España.
Irene va a estudiar literatura.

In contrast, we use the *subjunctive* mood to make requests or express our feelings concerning other persons or things. Typical expressions that convey desire or request include the various forms of:

desear que *to want, to desire*
preferir que
querer que

and the impersonal expression:

Es preciso que... *It is necessary that...*

Three common expressions that express feelings or emotions are the forms of:

esperar que	*to hope*
sentir(ie) que	*to be sorry*
temer que	*to fear*

If there is no change of subject after an expression of request or emotion, the infinitive is used—not **que** + *subjunctive*.

Quiero leer la carta.
I want to read the letter. (same subject)

Quiero que leas la carta.
I want you to read the letter. (I want/you read: change of subject)

Esperan llegar a tiempo.
They hope to arrive on time.

Esperan que Rubén llegue *a tiempo.*
They hope Rubén will arrive on time.

English has different ways of translating the Spanish subjunctive.

Quiero que Lola **vaya** con Uds.	*I want Lola to go with you.*
Prefieren que ella **vaya** con Uds.	*They prefer (that) she go with you.*
Esperamos que ella **vaya** con Uds.	*We hope (that) she will go with you.*

Remember:

> Expression of request or emotion + **que** + subjunctive

PRÁCTICA

a Usted quiere que las siguientes personas regresen a diferentes horas o días. Complete los oraciones con el subjuntivo.

MODELO: Quiero que Benito **regrese** a las tres.

Quiero que
{
Esperanza / el viernes
(tú) / el lunes
los niños / a las doce
Ud. / el sábado
él /¿?
}

Repita la práctica **a**, pero esta vez *(this time)* empiece con la expresión Prefiero que...

b Es preciso que varias personas hagan las reservas para diferentes eventos. Complete las oraciones.

MODELO: Es preciso que Uds. **hagan** las reservas para el teatro.

Es preciso que
{
(yo) / el restaurante
el agente / el paseo
(nosotros) / el concierto
(tú) / la corrida de toros
ellos /¿?
}

Repita la práctica b pero esta vez empiece con Es necesario que...

c El profesor de español espera que los estudiantes escriban varias cosas. Complete las oraciones.

MODELO: El profesor espera que Raquel escriba el vocabulario.

El profesor espera que
- (yo) / los verbos
- (nosotros) / las oraciones
- (tú) / el diálogo
- Uds. / una carta
- Diego /¿?

Repita la práctica c, pero use el modelo: El profesor **teme** que Raquel **no** escriba el vocabulario.

d Unas personas hablan con un agente de turismo y expresan sus preferencias o sentimientos en cuanto a *(as to)* varias opciones. Combine las expresiones de la columna A con las expresiones de la columna B para hacer un mínimo de doce oraciones originales.

MODELO: **Siento que ella no se divierta en la playa.**

A	B
Deseamos que	1. el agente / preparar el itinerario
Siento que	2. Uds. / reservar los asientos
Ella no quiere que	3. tú / no visitar los museos
Prefiero que	4. los niños / venir con nosotros
Temen que	5. Ud. / explicar las diferentes excursiones
Quiero que	6. ella / no divertirse en la playa
¿?	7. mis padres / ver los lugares más interesantes
¿?	8. tú / viajar solo(a)
	9. la secretaria / me dar unos folletos *(brochures)*
	10. él / pedir una habitación de lujo *(luxury)*
	11. ¿?
	12. ¿?

e Usted le pregunta a otro(a) estudiante si quiere que (prefiere que, etc.) usted haga varias cosas. Refiéranse a las siguientes preguntas y respuestas como modelo. Usen los infinitivos entre paréntesis como sugerencias *(suggestions)*.

USTED

1. ¿Qué quieres que (yo) *lea?*
   (escribir, estudiar, escuchar, aprender, ¿?)
2. ¿A quién deseas que *conozca?*
   (invitar, buscar, ver, llamar, ¿?)
3. ¿Dónde prefieres que *me siente?**
   (acostarse, descansar, comer, trabajar, ¿?)

OTRO(A) ESTUDIANTE

Quiero que (tú) leas...

Deseo que conozcas a...

Prefiero que...

*Compare **sentarse** *(to sit down)* y **sentir** *(to be sorry)*.

4. ¿Qué esperas que *haga?*
   (traer, decir, comprarse, probarse, ¿?)   ¿?

5. ¿Qué *temes* que?
   (¿?)   ¿?

f   Ahora su compañero(a) hace las preguntas y usted las contesta *(answer them)* según la práctica e. Para variar *(to vary)* un poco, cambien yo → nosotros y tú → ustedes.

MODELO: ¿Qué quieres que (nosotros) leamos?   **Quiero que (ustedes) lean...**

g   Un recado *(A message)*. Usted no puede terminar los quehaceres de la casa *(house chores)*, y antes de salir usted le escribe un recado a un miembro de su familia. En el recado le dice lo que él (ella) debe hacer. Use un mínimo de cinco oraciones con expresiones que requieren el subjuntivo; por ejemplo: **Quiero que... Deseo que... Es preciso que...**

MODELO: **Quiero que laves la ropa.**

Los quehaceres pueden incluir:

lavar los platos *to wash the dishes*	**limpiar** *to clean*
sacar la basura *to take out the garbage*	**guardar la ropa** *to put away the clothes*
cocinar *to cook*	**hacer las camas** *to make the beds*

h   ¿Cómo se dice?

1. Use el subjuntivo de **ser** (sea...) o **estar** (esté...) para traducir las oraciones.
   a. I'm sorry you're sick.
   b. I want you to be my friends.
   c. We fear that Benito won't be home.
   d. We hope the food is Mexican.
2. Use el subjuntivo, si es necesario.
   a. I want to rest a little, but my wife wants me to go shopping.
   b. María Carmen prefers that we spend a few days in her home.
   c. We hope to go to Spain in the summer.
   d. I'm afraid they go to bed early.

OBSERVACIONES

A local Spanish newspaper in the United States asked Tony Vázquez, a bilingual college student, to write his impressions of Latin American cities. Read his article below.

Centro Bolívar, Caracas

Las ciudades hispanoamericanas

He pasado° unas semanas en varias ciudades hispanoamericanas y quisiera compartir° mis impresiones con los lectores° de este periódico.

Estas° ciudades comparten ciertas semejanzas.° Tradicionalmente han crecido alrededor° de una plaza central donde se encuentran la catedral, la casa de gobierno° y los comercios. La plaza es un centro comercial y social. Allí se preservan los antiguos° edificios con sus portales° y tiendas pequeñas. Allí se reúnen° los amigos para charlar.° También es allí adonde los niños quieren que sus abuelos los lleven° a dar un paseo o a jugar.

Otra semejanza es el contraste entre el pasado y el presente. Junto a° los viejos edificios podemos ver modernos rascacielos.° No lejos de las calles estrechas° del centro podemos andar por anchos° bulevares que contienen glorietas° con monumentos o fuentes.° México, Quito y La Paz mantienen una herencia cultural indoespañola visible en su población, su arquitectura y en el ambiente° general de la ciudad. En cambio, Buenos Aires y Montevideo tienen un carácter más europeo. Caracas refleja° la influencia de los Estados Unidos.

I've spent
to share / readers
These / similarities
have grown around
government
ancient / porticos
get together / to chat
to take them
Next to
skyscrapers
narrow / go along the wide
contain traffic circles / fountains
environment
reflects

Una plaza colonial, Quito

Las capitales comparten el grave problema de la inmensa migración rural. Es lástima° que muchos campesinos abandonen el campo por la falsa ilusión de las ciudades. Al llegar a la capital los campesinos se dan cuenta° que hay pocas viviendas° y que los empleos son pocos y mal pagados.° Para vivir es preciso que muchos construyan casuchas° en las afueras.°

It's a pity / they realize / housing / paid / huts / outskirts

A pesar de° sus problemas, las ciudades tienen cierto encanto.° Allí es donde nos divertimos con gusto en los fabulosos parques, museos, teatros y otros lugares de recreo.° Espero que en un futuro cercano° ustedes también visiten las encantadoras ciudades hispanoamericanas.

In spite of / charm

recreation / near

¿COMPRENDE UD?

a Traducción. Busque el equivalente de las siguientes oraciones en la lectura. Después subraye *(underline)* el verbo en el subjuntivo en cada oración.

1. The children want their grandparents to take them for a walk.
2. It's a pity that the peasants abandon the country.
3. It's necessary for many to build huts in the outskirts.
4. I hope you'll visit the charming Spanish-American cities.

b Comprensión. Conteste las preguntas en oraciones completas.

1. ¿Cómo han crecido las ciudades hispanoamericanas?
2. ¿Qué se preservan en las plazas?
3. ¿Qué herencia cultural mantienen México y Quito?
4. ¿Cómo es el carácter de Buenos Aires?
5. ¿Qué grave problema comparten las ciudades?
6. ¿Cómo podemos divertirnos en las ciudades?

c Temas *(Themes)*. Escoja uno de estos temas para escribir una descripción de ocho a diez oraciones.

1. Mi ciudad. Empiece con la descripción de la calle mayor *(Main Street)* y sus edificios.
2. ¿Por qué (no) me gusta la ciudad? Sus razones *(reasons)* pueden ser negativas o positivas.

d Busque en la columna B las capitales de los países en la columna A.

A	B
1. Venezuela _____	a. Buenos Aires
2. El Perú _____	b. Managua
3. El Ecuador _____	c. Santiago
4. Nicaragua _____	d. Montevideo
5. Chile _____	e. Lima
6. La Argentina _____	f. Quito
7. Cuba _____	g. Caracas
8. El Uruguay _____	h. La Habana

Actividades

Las tarjetas de amistad *(friendship)*

Ojalá° que te mejores° pronto.

Deseamos que pasen muy felices la Navidad° y que el próximo año sea muy próspero para todos.

I hope / get better

Christmas

Usted escribe varias notas de amistad a sus amigos. Empiece cada nota con la frase **Ojalá que** que es otra manera de decir **Espero que** *(I hope that)*. En realidad, **Ojalá** significa *may Allah grant* en árabe, pero hoy día no tiene significado religioso.

MODELO: **Ojalá que tengas un buen viaje.**
Ojalá que tengan un próspero Año Nuevo.

Sugerencias: tener un feliz cumpleaños o aniversario, tener mucha suerte en..., mejorarse, ser feliz, regresar pronto, divertirse mucho... ¿?

Vocabulario

SUSTANTIVOS
el **Año Nuevo** *New Year*
la **basura** *garbage*
la **cama** *bed*
el **edificio** *building*
la **Navidad** *Christmas*
el **paseo** *outing, ride*
el **regalo** *gift*
el **tiempo** *time, weather*

ADJETIVOS
antiguo(a) *old, ancient*
encantador(a) *charming*
estrecho(a) *narrow*
inmenso(a) *immense*

VERBOS
ayudar *to help*
bajar *to lower, go (get) down*

cruzar *to cross*
descansar *to rest*
doblar *to turn*
esperar *to hope, wait for*
guardar *to put away*
limpiar *to clean*
mejorarse *to get better*
mirar *to look (at)*
mover (ue) *to move*
preocuparse (por) *to worry (about)*
sentir (ie) *to be or feel sorry*
temer *to fear*

EXPRESIONES
¡Claro! *Of course!*
es lástima *it's a pity*
es preciso *it's necessary*
esta noche *tonight*
ojalá *I hope*

Tercera parte

Panorama histórico de Latinoamérica

Until now you've been reading passages in the present tense. In this selection, depicting a historical panorama of Latin America, you'll find most of the text written in the past tense. For purposes of the reading, you need only be aware that Spanish has two simple past tenses: the *preterite* and the *imperfect*. (Lessons 8–9 treat these tenses in more detail.) Briefly stated, the preterite reports actions seen as having been begun or completed at a specific time in the past. By contrast, the imperfect describes actions or situations viewed as habitual or ongoing in the past, regardless of when they began or ended.

Many of the verb stems in the reading are already familiar to you. Note, however, that the endings are largely in the third person singular and plural of the past tense. These endings for regular verbs in the *preterite* are as follows:

	-ar verbs	-er / -ir verbs
él, ella, Ud.	**-ó**	**-ió**
ellos, ellas, Uds.	**-aron**	**-ieron**

Example: **ayudó**   *he, she, it helped*
        encontraron   *they found*

And for the same persons, the endings of regular verbs in the imperfect are:

	-ar verbs	-er / -ir verbs
él, ella, Ud.	**-aba**	**-ía**
ellos, ellas, Uds.	**-aban**	**-ían**

Example: **dominaban**   *they dominated (used to dominate)*
        tenía   *he, she, it had (used to have)*

Verbs in the preterite and imperfect appear in boldface in the following reading.

Mucho antes de la llegada° de los europeos, varias civilizaciones indígenas **habitaban** el Nuevo Mundo.° Los primeros indígenas que los españoles **encontraron**° en América **fueron**° los siboneyes, los taínos y los
caribes que **vivían** en las Antillas° y las costas° de Venezuela. Estos indígenas **tenían** su propia cultura, pero el nivel° de su civilización **era**° primi-
tivo. En el año 1519 los españoles **entraron** en pleno° contacto con los
aztecas en la región central de México, con las mayas en el sur° de México
y Centroamérica, y en 1531 con los incas de Sudamérica. Cada° uno de
estos grupos al fundir° su propia cultura con la de° los españoles **ayudó a**
crear° el carácter de muchas naciones hispanoamericanas.

    Los incas, mayas, y aztecas — a pesar de sus diferencias — **tenían** ras-
gos comunes° que los **identificaban** como pueblos civilizados. Estos rasgos
eran los siguientes:

- un sistema de gobierno dominado por el emperador y el clero°
- intenso desarrollo° de la agricultura, especialmente el maíz°
- excelentes conocimientos° de las industrias textiles y metalúrgicas y de
  la alfarería°
- gran habilidad matemática y astronómica[1]

Otro grupo con un notable grado de desarrollo **fueron** los chibchas, que
vivían en el norte de Colombia y partes de Centroamérica. Uno de sus
jefes, Bogotá, le **dio**° el nombre a la capital colombiana y otro, llamado Nicarago, **dejó**° su nombre a un país centroamericano. Las mejores mues-
tras° de la cultura chibcha son sus ornamentos de oro y plata y sus tejidos°
de algodón.

[1]R. R. Sardiña, *Breve historia de Hispanoamérica*, Cincinnati: South-western, 1982.

	arrival
	New World
	found / preterite of **ser**
	Antilles / coasts
	level / imperfect of **ser**
	came in full
	south
	Each
	upon fusing / that of
	to create
	common traits
	clergy
	development / corn
	knowledge
	pottery
	preterite of **dar**
	left
	samples / weavings

Templo maya de las mil columnas, Chichén-Itzá

Ruinas incaicas en Machu Picchu, Perú

Al llegar los españoles a México, la civilización maya **estaba** en plena decadencia con sus ciudades y centros religiosos abandonados y su pueblo disperso y desorganizado. Sin embargo,° sus contribuciones astronómicas, matemáticas, y literarias son extraordinarias. Porque su religión **estaba** relacionada con el tiempo, los mayas **tenían** un calendario sumamente° exacto y su escritura jeroglífica° **expresaba** más interés en el tiempo que° en la historia.

However

very
hieroglyphic / than

Los aztecas, que **dominaban** el valle central de México, **eran** conocidos por° su espíritu guerrero.° **Se distinguían** por° su capacidad para gobernar y construir bellos palacios, templos y pirámides.

were known for / warlike /
They distinguished
themselves by

El imperio precolombino más extenso y mejor organizado **era** el de los incas. Sus territorios **se extendían** desde° Colombia hasta Chile. Los incas **eran** excelentes artesanos° y arquitectos. **Construyeron** magníficas fortalezas,° caminos, y puentes.° **Sabían** mucho de medicina y hasta° **usaban** anestesia en operaciones delicadas.

from
artisans
fortresses / bridges / even

Los españoles **conquistaron** a los aztecas y a los incas con relativa facilidad a pesar de la enorme superioridad numérica de los indígenas. Entre los factores que ayudan a explicar las extraordinarias victorias de Cortés en México y Pizarro en el Perú se deben mencionar la mejor disciplina y armamentos de los españoles y la falta de° unidad entre los indígenas. En el Perú, Francisco Pizarro **encontró** a los incas en plena guerra civil. En México, los españoles **encontraron** fuertes aliados° entre las tribus que los aztecas **habían subyugado.**° Estas tribus se **unieron** a los españoles para vengarse de° los aztecas, a quienes **tenían** que pagar tributo y proporcionar° víctimas para los sacrificios humanos.

the lack of

allies
had subjugated
to take revenge on
provide

Después de la conquista, España **estableció** un imperio que se **extendía** desde partes de Norteamérica hasta el extremo sur del hemisferio. Cuando la labor de los indios y de los inmigrantes no **fue** suficiente para la explotación de la riqueza° de América, los ingleses, españoles y portugueses **comenzaron** a importar esclavos° africanos. Al principio° estos esclavos solo **parecían**° contribuir su labor, pero con el tiempo **dejaron** una rica herencia en su literatura, música y comida. **Fueron** el indio, el blanco, y el negro — y la mezcla° de estos grupos — quienes **crearon** el « latino » de hoy.

wealth
slaves / At first
seemed

mixture

Durante tres siglos, España **implantó** y **adaptó** sus instituciones y cultura al Nuevo Mundo, a veces haciendo° el bien y a veces el mal. Con los años, el imperio español **empezó a decaer.**° Los administradores ineptos, la discordia civil y la invasión de España por Napoleón Bonaparte en 1808 poco a poco **debilitaban**° el imperio.

doing
began to decline

weakened

Por su parte, los hispanoamericanos, cansados de las injusticias del sistema colonial, **deseaban** su libertad. Entre los héroes de las guerras de independencia **surgieron**° el padre Miguel Hidalgo (México), Simón Bolívar (Venezuela) y José de San Martín (la Argentina). Para° 1825 casi toda Hispanoamérica **tenía** su independencia. Las antiguas colonias en vez de° crear una sólida unión hispanoamericana, como **quería** Bolívar, **formaron** las repúblicas independientes de hoy día.

surged
Toward
instead of

¿COMPRENDE UD.?

a   Escriba el infinitivo de las siguientes formas verbales.

MODELO: deseaban   **desear**

1. usaban
2. tenían
3. quería
4. dejó
5. estaba
6. vivían
7. encontraron
8. ayudó
9. empezó
10. surgieron
11. crearon
12. formaron

b   Busque en la lectura *(reading)* el equivalente de cada una de estas oraciones.

1. The Caribes used to live in the Antilles.
2. The Mayas had an extremely accurate calendar.
3. The Aztecs distinguished themselves by their warlike spirit.
4. The Incas built marvelous fortresses, roads, and bridges.
5. Spain established an empire that extended from North America to South America.

c   Escoja la respuesta que mejor termine cada oración.

1. Los aztecas habitaban
   a. Centroamérica
   b. las Antillas y la costa de Venezuela
   c. la parte central de México
2. Los incas, mayas y aztecas desarrollaron
   a. la democracia
   b. la agricultura
   c. el alfabeto
3. El imperio precolombino más extenso y mejor organizado era
   a. el de los incas
   b. el de los siboneyes
   c. el de los mayas
4. Bogotá era el nombre de
   a. una federación
   b. una escritura jeroglífica
   c. un jefe chibcha
5. Dos héroes de las guerras de independencia son
   a. Cortés y Pizarro
   b. Moctezuma y el Padre Hidalgo
   c. Bolívar y San Martín

d   Resumen. Prepare un resumen de diez oraciones o más donde
menciona los rasgos y logros *(achievements)* de los incas, mayas y
aztecas.

MODELO: **El imperio de los incas se extendía desde Colombia hasta...**
Los incas eran excelentes...
**Los aztecas dominaban el valle central de México. Eran
conocidos...**
**Los mayas habitaban el sur de México y Centroamérica. Sus
contribuciones astronómicas,...**

Vocabulario

SUSTANTIVOS
  el **camino** *road*
  el **desarrollo** *development*
el, la **jefe** *chief*
  el **maíz** *corn*
  la **mezcla** *mixture*
  el **oro** *gold*
  la **plata** *silver*
  el **puente** *bridge*
  el **sur** *south*

ADJETIVO
cada *each*

VERBOS
comenzar (ie) *to commence*
crear *to create*
dejar *to leave behind*
dio *gave (preterite of* dar)
encontrar (ue) *to find*
era, eran *was, were (imperfect of* ser)
fue, fueron *was, were (preterite of* ser)

EXPRESIONES
a veces *at times*
al principio *at first*
desde... hasta *from . . . to*
en vez de *instead of*
la falta de *the lack of*

Las ventas internacionales

David Johnson, vendedor de productos farmacéuticos,° conversa con el   *pharmaceutical*
señor Gustavo Mendoza, director de una casa distribuidora. Los dos están
en la oficina del Sr. Mendoza en La Paz, Bolivia.

JOHNSON Buenas tardes, Sr. Mendoza. ¡Qué gusto verlo otra vez!°   *to see you again*

MENDOZA Gracias, igualmente.° Perdone la demora,° pero con tantas° in-   *likewise / delay / so many*
terrupciones...

JOHNSON ¡No se preocupe! A propósito,° ¡felicitaciones!° Anoche leí° que su   *By the way /*
firma° estableció otra sucursal° en Potosí.*   *congratulations / I read*
firm / branch (office)

MENDOZA Efectivamente.° Pasé unos días allí° el mes pasado para orientar   *That's right. / there*
al nuevo personal.°   *personnel*

JOHNSON A propósito, ¿Va a necesitar más mercancía° para esa sucursal?   *merchandise*

MENDOZA Sí, pero quiero que revisemos° la lista de precios.°   *we check / prices*

JOHNSON Exactamente. Ya° llamé a la oficina central y autorizaron des-   *Already*
cuentos° adicionales.   *discounts*

MENDOZA Muy agradecido,° pero vamos a ver si esos descuentos son me-   *grateful*
jores que los de° su competidor.   *better than those of*

¿RECUERDA UD.?
1. ¿Cuál es el oficio *(occupation)* de David Johnson?
2. ¿Quién es Gustavo Mendoza?
3. ¿Dónde están los dos señores?
4. ¿Está ocupado el Sr. Mendoza?
5. ¿Qué estableció la firma del Sr. Mendoza?
6. ¿Cuántos días pasó el Sr. Mendoza en Potosí?
7. ¿Qué quiere el Sr. Mendoza que ellos dos revisen?
8. ¿Qué autorizó la oficina de David Johnson?
9. ¿Qué va a ver el Sr. Mendoza?
10. ¿Usó el Sr. Johnson la forma formal o familiar de los verbos? ¿Por
    qué?
11. ¿Qué palabras lisonjeras *(flattering)* usó David?
12. ¿Es un buen vendedor David? ¿Por qué?

ADAPTACIÓN
Usted y otro(a) estudiante preparan un diálogo original basado *(based)*
en la conversación de los señores Johnson y Mendoza. Imagínese que
usted — el, la vendedor(a) — quiere venderle un producto nuevo al (a la)
otro(a) estudiante — el, la cliente. El problema es que el último pro-

---

*Potosí es una ciudad bien conocida por sus minas de oro *(gold)* y plata *(silver)*. Si una cosa
tiene gran valor *(value)* se dice que « vale *(it's worth)* un potosí ».

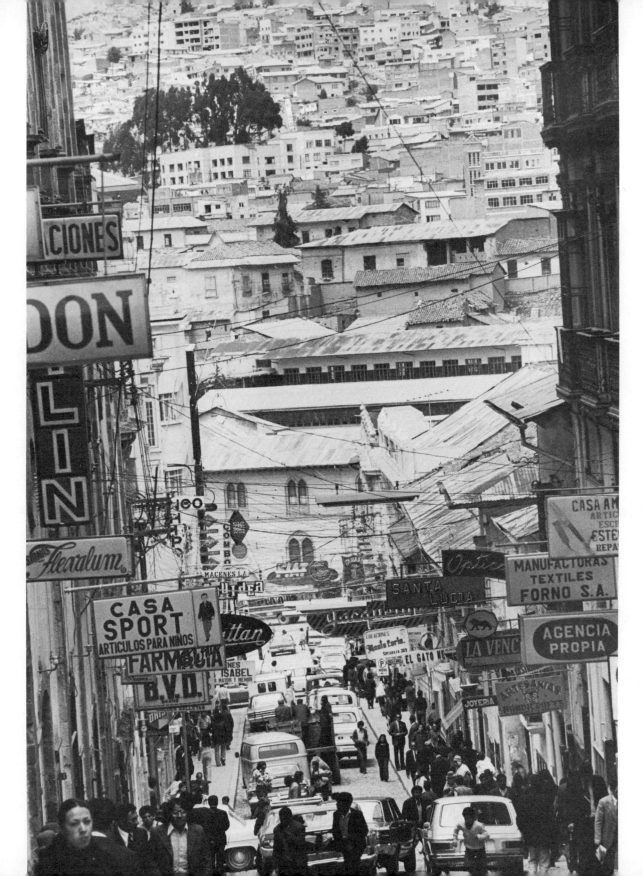

ducto que Ud. le vendió no fue *(was)* muy bueno y ahora él no desea comprar nada. Usted trata de convencer, de persuadir al cliente para ver si compra el producto. Por fin *(finally)* el cliente decide revisar la lista de precios y le pregunta qué descuentos da usted. Usen humor y persuasión y, si quieren, uno o más de estos productos:

Cosméticos: el perfume, el jabón, la colonia *(cologne)*, el talco, etc. Productos para la cocina: la sartén *(frying pan)* eléctrica, la tostadora, la cafetera, el horno de micro-ondas *(microwave oven)*, etc.

Estructura

I El pretérito de los verbos regulares y de cambios radicales

The preterite reports past actions that had a definite beginning and end. It focuses on the event as a completed unit. Adverbs such as **ayer** and **ano-che** often appear with the preterite.

¿Trabajaste anoche?	*Did* you work last night?*
No, no trabajé.	*No, I didn't* work.*
Ellos llegaron ya.	*They arrived already.*

	trabajar			
yo	trabaj**é** *I worked (did work)*		nosotros(as)	trabaj**amos**
tú	trabaj**aste**		vosotros(as)	trabaj**asteis**
él, ella, Ud.	trabaj**ó**		ellos, ellas, Uds.	trabaj**aron**

comer			salir		
com**í** *I ate (did eat)*		com**imos**	sal**í** *I went out (did go out)*		sal**imos**
com**iste**		com**isteis**	sal**iste**		sal**isteis**
com**ió**		com**ieron**	sal**ió**		sal**ieron**

A Regular **-er** and **-ir** verbs have the same endings in the preterite. The **nosotros(as)** forms for **-ar** and **-ir** verbs are the same as for the present. Context generally clarifies the meaning.

B Verbs that end in **-car, -gar** and **-zar** have these changes in the first person singular:

buscar	c → **qu**	bus**qué**
llegar	g → **gu**	lle**gué**
empezar	z → **c**	empe**cé**

*Note that the English auxiliary verb *did* in questions and negative statements is not translated.

C   When the stem of **-er** and **-ir** verbs ends in a vowel, the third person singular and plural endings become **-yo** and **-yeron**.

leer: le**yó**, le**yeron**
construir *(to build):* constru**yó**, constru**yeron**

D   Only **-ir** verbs have stem changes in the preterite, and these occur solely in the third person singular and plural. The stem vowel **e** changes to **i** and the stem vowel **o** to **u**.

pedir: pedí, pediste, p**i**dió, pedimos, pedisteis, p**i**dieron
divertirse: me divertí, divertiste, se div**i**rtió, nos divertimos, os divertisteis, se div**i**rtieron
dormir: dormí, dormiste, d**u**rmió, dormimos, dormisteis, d**u**rmieron

PRÁCTICA

a   Mencione sus actividades de ayer. Si es posible incluya información adicional.

MODELO: levantarse   **Ayer me levanté a las siete.**
        estudiar   **Estudié en la biblioteca.**

1. levantarse	4. caminar	7. cocinar	10. jugar
2. bañarse	5. estudiar	8. almorzar	11. comprar
3. desayunar(se)	6. hablar	9. trabajar	

También:

12. leer	15. salir	18. asistir a
13. aprender	16. correr	19. divertirse
14. escribir	17. comer	20. dormir

b   Use los verbos anteriores y diga cinco cosas que los miembros de su familia hicieron *(did)* ayer.

1. Mi hermano(a)...   2. Mis padres...   3. ¿?

c   Pregúntele a otro(a) estudiante si hizo *(did)* las siguientes cosas anoche. Él o ella debe contestarle a usted.

MODELO: hablar por teléfono   **¿Hablaste por teléfono anoche?**
                              Sí, (No, no) hablé por teléfono anoche.

1. hablar con la familia	9. ver* la televisión
2. preparar las lecciones	10. jugar con el perro
3. escribir una carta	11. salir con los amigos
4. cocinar una comida especial	12. regresar temprano
5. cenar en casa	13. divertirse mucho
6. tomar café	14. acostarse antes de las doce
7. descansar unos minutos	15. dormir bien
8. escuchar música latina	

*Ver *(to see)* has no accents in the preterite: **vi, viste, vio, vimos, visteis, vieron**.

d Esta vez hágale las preguntas a su profesor(a), usando las expresiones de la práctica anterior (***c***).

MODELO: **¿Habló Ud. por teléfono anoche?**

e Lea cada oración y después conteste las preguntas.

1. David comió en casa de los abuelos el domingo.
   ¿Dónde comió David?
   ¿Cuándo comió David con los abuelos?
   ¿Dónde comiste tú el domingo?
   ¿Comieron Uds. (tú y tus padres) juntos?
2. Catalina estudió álgebra con otra estudiante anoche.
   ¿Qué estudió Catalina?
   ¿Con quién estudió Catalina?
   ¿Qué estudiaste tú anoche?
   ¿Estudiaron Uds. (tú y tus amigos) mucho anoche?
3. Martín vivió dos años en México.
   ¿Dónde vivió Martín?
   ¿Cuánto tiempo vivió él en México?
   ¿Viviste tú en otro país?
   ¿Vivieron Uds. (tú y tu familia) en otra ciudad?
4. Los Mendoza se levantaron a las siete de la mañana y su hija se levantó a las siete y media.
   ¿A qué hora se levantaron los Mendoza?
   ¿A qué hora se levantó la hija?
   ¿A qué hora te levantaste?
   ¿A qué hora se levantaron tus hermanos?

f ¿Cómo se dice en español?

1. I arrived last Sunday (**el domingo pasado**).
2. Did you (**Ud.**) read today's newspaper?
3. He asked for milk and I asked for coffee.
4. I started to work at 8:45 this (**esta**) morning.
5. We went to bed early last night.
6. Did you (**tú**) look for the wallet?   —Yes, I looked everywhere (**por todas partes**).
7. I didn't go out last Saturday. I read a book and wrote three or four letters.
8. Last summer we spent two weeks in South America. We visited our friends in Caracas and La Paz and saw many interesting places: churches, museums, palaces, and universities. We ate in their homes and in various restaurants.
   After supper (**Después de la cena**) we spoke about (**de**) our families and our work.
   We had a good time and bought many beautiful things (**cosas**): shirts,

dresses, ponchos, wool sweaters, and souvenirs (**recuerdos**). We want to return soon.

g   Ahora escriba usted el número ocho de la práctica f en la primera persona singular (**yo**). Mencione otros lugares y cosas.

MODELO: **El verano pasado (yo)...**

II *Los adjetivos y pronombres demostrativos*

this	**este** abrigo	**esta** camisa
these	**estos** abrigos	**estas** camisas
that	**ese** vestido	**esa** chaqueta
those	**esos** vestidos	**esas** chaquetas
that (over there)	**aquel** traje	**aquella** falda
those (over there)	**aquellos** trajes	**aquellas** faldas

Demonstrative adjectives are used to point out a specific person or thing. They agree in gender and number with the nouns they introduce. Note carefully the endings for the masculine singular forms: **este, ese**, and **aquel**. Also note that Spanish distinguishes between *this, that (nearby)* and *that (over there)*.

Esta camisa es muy bonita.
This shirt is very pretty. (near the speaker)

Ese suéter cuesta cuatro mil pesos.
That sweater costs four thousand pesos. (near the listener or not far from the speaker)

Me gustan **aquellos** zapatos.
I like those shoes. (at a distance from both the speaker and listener)

Demonstrative adjectives can be used as pronouns; that is, in place of nouns. The accent mark distinguishes the pronoun (**éste, ése, ésa**) from the adjective.

Quiero este reloj, y no **ése**.   *I want this watch, and not that one.*
Esos pantalones son caros, pero   *Those pants are expensive, but these*
 éstos no.   *aren't.*

The neuter demonstratives **esto, eso**, and **aquello** refer to a statement, an idea, or something not yet identified.

¿Qué es **esto**? — No tengo la   *What's this? — I haven't the*
 menor idea.   *slightest idea.*
Eso es todo.   *That's all.*

PRÁCTICA

a Haga oraciones nuevas con las palabras indicadas.

MODELO: el libro **Necesito leer este libro.**

el periódico, la revista, las cartas, el anuncio, la novela, los artículos, las instrucciones, el programa

MODELO: la silla **Por favor, quiero que me traigas esa silla.**

la mesa, las flores, el bolígrafo, los lápices, el cuaderno, los papeles, la tarjeta, el regalo

b Imagínese que usted y su amiga están en una tienda de artesanía. Ud. necesita hacer unas compras. Su amiga le sugiere (*suggests to you*) varias cosas, pero Ud. prefiere otras.

MODELO: (un poncho) Usted: **Necesito comprar un poncho.**
Su amiga: **¿Por qué no compras éste?**
Usted: **¡Ése! ¡Ay, no! Prefiero aquél.**

1. un sarape
2. una cartera
3. unos platos
4. una muñeca (*doll*)
5. un sombrero
6. una camiseta
7. una guitarra
8. unas maracas
9. un ajedrez
10. un cinturón
11. unas sandalias
12. ¿?

c ¿Cómo se dice?

1. this morning, this month, this week, tonight
2. I like these pants, I don't like those.
3. By the way, we want you to check this list.
4. What's that? —Who knows?
5. I spoke with this clerk and not that one (over there).

d Hágale estas preguntas a otro estudiante.

1. ¿Qué vas a hacer esta tarde? ¿esta noche? ¿este fin de semana?
2. ¿Te* gusta esta clase? ¿este libro? ¿esta universidad? ¿?
3. ¿Quieres que (yo) mueva este asiento? ¿esa mesa? ¿aquellas sillas? ¿?
4. ¿Cómo se llama este estudiante? ¿y ése? ¿?

*Familiar form for **le**.

III *Comparaciones: ¿Más o menos?*

¿Quién es más alta — Ana o Berta?
¿Berta o Carolina?
¿Quién es la más alta?

Ana
(alta)

Berta
(más alta)

Carolina
(la más alta)

¿Quién es más fuerte — Diego o Ernesto?
¿Quién es el más fuerte?
¿Quién es el menos fuerte?

Diego
(fuerte)

Ernesto
(más fuerte)

Fermín
(el más fuerte)

In Spanish, unequal comparisons (*taller, stronger, less strong, more beautiful,* etc.) are made by putting **más** or **menos** before the word being compared. **Que** precedes the second item or person mentioned in the comparison.

Ana es más alta *que* tú.   *Ana is taller than you.*

De* replaces **que** when the comparison indicates the *most* or *least* in a group.

Ana es la más alta de la familia.   *Ana is the tallest in the family.*

The following comparatives are irregular and are *not* used with **más** or **menos**.

mejor	*better*	el / la mejor	*the best*	¿Cuál es **el mejor**?
peor	*worse*	el / la peor	*the worst*	Éstas son **peores** que ésas.
mayor	*older*	el / la mayor	*the oldest*	Papá es **mayor** que Mamá.
menor	*younger*	el / la menor	*the youngest*	Soy el **menor** de la familia.

***Más de** and **menos de** are also used when the comparison is followed by a number:
Tengo **menos de** cien dólares.

PRÁCTICA

a Su compañero(a) cree que « Patricio Perfecto » es mejor que Ud.
Claro, usted no está de acuerdo. Refiéranse al modelo para expresar sus
opiniones.

MODELO: generoso
        Compañero(a): **Patricio es más generoso que tú.**
             Usted: **¡Al contrario! ¡Es menos generoso!**

1. simpático	*5.* amable	*9.* sociable
2. guapo	*6.* inteligente	*10.* discreto
3. alegre	*7.* práctico	*11.* mejor
4. dinámico	*8.* trabajador	*12.* ¿?

b Repitan la práctica anterior, pero cambien el nombre a « Patricia
Perfecta ».

MODELO: generosa
        Compañero(a): **Patricia es más generosa que tú.**
             Usted: **¡Al contrario! ¡Es menos generosa!**

c Refiérase a estos dibujos (*drawings*) para contestar las preguntas.

Emilio
No estudia.

Lupe
Estudia unas horas.

Javier
Estudia frecuentemente.

1. ¿Quién estudia más, Emilio o Lupe? ¿Lupe o Javier?
2. ¿Quién es el (la) más estudioso(a)? ¿El (la) menos estudioso(a)?
3. ¿Quién tiene más libros? ¿Quién tiene menos?
4. ¿Quién es el (la) mejor estudiante? ¿el (la) peor?
5. ¿Quién lee más? ¿Quién lee menos?
6. ¿Quiénes están más contentos que Emilio? ¿Por qué?

d Use estos dibujos para hacerle no menos de cinco preguntas a su
compañero(a). Incluya preguntas como: ¿Quién es más rico(a)? ¿Quién
es mayor? ¿Quién tiene menos...?, etc.

Guillermo
Tiene 20 años.

Victoria
Tiene 30 años.

Silvia
Tiene 35 años.

IV Comparaciones de igualdad

In an equal comparison the persons or things compared are said to possess the same qualities or quantities as others. To express equal comparisons Spanish uses the following constructions:

tan + *adjective* or *adverb*... **como**
(*as . . . as*)

Es **tan** bonita **como** su hermana.
She's as pretty as her sister.
Hablas **tan** rápido **como** él.
You speak as rapidly as he.

tanto(a)(os)(as) + *noun*... **como** (*as many as*)

Tengo **tantas** responsabilidades
  como tú.
I have as many responsibilities as you.

tanto como (after a verb) (*as much as*)

Trabajamos **tanto como** ellos.
We work as much as they.

PRÁCTICA

a   Cambie las expresiones de desigualdad a expresiones de igualdad.

MODELO: Hace más frío que ayer.
       Hace **tanto** frío **como** ayer.

1. Hace menos calor que ayer.
2. Hay más muchachos que muchachas.
3. Tú tienes menos energía que yo.
4. Pasé más días en La Paz que en Sucre.
5. Exportamos menos petróleo que ellos.
6. Este cereal tiene más calorías que ése.
7. Tengo más hambre que tú.
8. Durmieron más que nosotros.
9. ¿Trabajaste más horas que yo?
10. Ofrecemos más descuentos que antes.

b   Compare estas personas o cosas según el modelo.

MODELO: Cecilia / expresivo / su mamá
       Cecilia es *tan* expresiva *como* su mamá.

1. Rolando / discreto / su hermano
2. Esta lección / fácil / ésa
3. Estos problemas / difícil / los otros
4. Julia y Tito / afectuoso / sus padres
5. Tú / sarcástico / él
6. Uds. / puntual / ellos
7. Yo / ¿?

c Combine las comparaciones con los dibujos.

a.

b.

c.

d.

Las comparaciones:

1. Tiene el pelo tan blanco como la nieve.
2. Es más alto que un pino.
3. Habla más que un loro *(parrot)*.
4. Más vale tarde que nunca. *(Better late than never.)*

d ¿Cómo se dice?

1. My brother Enrique is younger than my sister Clara. I'm the oldest of the three.
2. We didn't walk as many blocks (**cuadras**) as they did.
3. Mirta worries more than you.
4. You are less serious than he.
5. I don't see Mr. Mendoza as frequently as before (**antes**).

OBSERVACIONES

The passage below is written primarily in the two simple past tenses of Spanish. The preterite reports actions completed at a specific time in the past. The imperfect describes ongoing or habitual actions in the past, but the specific time they began or ended is not considered important. Since the regular preterite forms should be familiar to you by now, concentrate on recognizing the imperfect forms in the reading. You only need to recognize the third person forms of the imperfect at this point.

-ar verbs
  -aba   él **conversaba** *(he conversed, used to converse)*
  -aban   ellos **conversaban**
-er / -ir verbs
  -ía   ella **vivía** *(she lived, used to live)*
  -ían   ellas **vivían**

El comercio y el estudio de las lenguas

Hoy día el estudio de las lenguas va aumentando° en las escuelas y universidades norteamericanas. Las empresas° internacionales cada día reconocen° la importancia de las lenguas. John Naisbitt en su célebre° libro *Megatrends* declara que en los Estados Unidos las tres lenguas del futuro van a ser: el inglés, el español y « las computadoras ». *(is increasing / enterprises / recognize / celebrated)*

Otros países industrializados o semi-industrializados reconocieron mucho antes la verdadera° necesidad práctica e* intelectual de aprender lenguas extranjeras. En el Japón y en Alemania,° nuestros mayores° rivales en el comercio, las compañías exportadoras pronto comenzaron el estudio de las lenguas para el personal de ventas internacionales. Los japoneses **creían°** que la lengua de sus clientes **era°** la más importante. En cambio, algunas° empresas norteamericanas perdieron parte de (o todas) sus ventas° en Hispanoamérica porque los productos de otros países **eran°** de alta calidad° y porque nosotros **insistíamos** en hablar y vender en inglés. *(real / Germany / greatest / believed / was / some / sales / were / quality)*

Las empresas innovadoras adaptaron sus productos y su propaganda al gusto de los consumidores° extranjeros. Además de la lengua, los empleados se familiarizaron con las costumbres° del país. Pudieron° observar que los hispanos, entre otros grupos, no **vivían** pendiente del reloj° y **dedicaban** tiempo a la familia y los amigos. Los lazos familiares se **mantenían** más firmes en casa y en el trabajo. El protocolo y las reformas **llevaban°** más tiempo. También pudieron notar que las personas **conversaban** más cerca una a otra y que el abrazo° entre amigos y parientes **era** común. *(consumers / customs / preterite of poder / glued to the watch / took / embrace)*

*E *(and)* is used before words beginning with **i** (**hi**): **madre e hija**.

Efectivamente, el comercio hoy día requiere mejores comunicaciones entre países. Las fábricas° en manos de dueños° multinacionales van aumentando dramáticamente. Más y más empresas solicitan a las personas competentes que entienden la lengua y las costumbres de sus clientes.

factories / owners

¿COMPRENDE UD.?

a   Vocabulario. Complete las oraciones con la expresión verbal más adecuada a la derecha.

1. Otros países _____ la necesidad de aprender lenguas extranjeras.
2. Los japoneses _____ que la lengua de sus clientes era la más importante.
3. Algunas empresas _____ parte de sus ventas.
4. Las empresas innovadoras _____ sus productos al gusto de los consumidores.
5. El protocolo y las reformas _____ más tiempo.

perdieron
reconocieron
llevaban
adaptaron
creían

b   Comprensión. Escoja la respuesta que mejor termine cada oración.

1. Según John Naisbitt las tres lenguas del futuro en los Estados Unidos van a ser el inglés,
   a. el japonés y « el comercio »
   b. el alemán y « la lengua de la burocracia »
   c. el español y « las computadoras »
2. Los lazos familiares en Hispanoamérica son
   a. fuertes
   b. frágiles
   c. inconsistentes
3. Cuando los hispanos hablan, ellos
   a. usan pocos gestos
   b. mantienen poca distancia entre uno y otro
   c. están pendientes de la hora
4. Una buena compañía exportadora
   a. insiste en hablar y vender en inglés
   b. observa muy poco el protocolo
   c. se familiariza con las costumbres del país

c   Discusión. Según una encuesta *(survey)* los mexicanos creen que los norteamericanos son: reservados, serios, formales, cooperadores, insensibles, realistas, personas que se preocupan mucho por el tiempo y por la calidad.

1. ¿Está Ud. de acuerdo con la encuesta? ¿Por qué?
2. ¿Es Ud. serio(a)? ¿insensible? ¿Se preocupa mucho por el tiempo?
3. ¿Qué características asocia *(associate)* con los mexicanos? ¿con los ingleses? ¿con los franceses? ¿con otras nacionalidades?
4. ¿Prefiere usar estereotipos o conocer la persona? ¿Cuál es más fácil? ¿Cuál es más justo *(fair)*?

d Situación. Ud. trabaja para una empresa internacional y tiene que entrevistar a varios candidatos para un trabajo. ¿Qué preguntas puede hacerles? ¿Qué preguntas no debe hacerles?

HUMOR

Pero señor vendedor, ¿quién va a comprar un carro que no va?

NO VA

Actividades

Imagínese que su compañero de trabajo recibió esta carta y quiere que usted la traduzca *(translate it)* oralmente.

OLIVERO, MENDOZA Y CÍA
Productos Farmacéuticos

Casilla de Correo 8345   La Paz, Bolivia
                                                           12 de febrero de 19___

Sr. Michael Coy
31 Monument Circle
Indianápolis, IN 46815

Estimado Sr. Coy:

En respuesta a su oferta de fecha 6 del presente mes, nos es grato[1] notificarle nuestro interés en distribuir sus productos farmacéuticos en este país. Antes de hacer nuestros pedidos, deseamos que nos envíe[2] algunas muestras[3] por expreso aéreo.

En espera de sus noticias, le saludamos muy atentamente.

Gustavo Mendoza

Gustavo Mendoza
Jefe de Ventas

1. *it's a pleasure for us*   **2.** from **enviar,** *to send*   **3.** *samples*

Vocabulario

SUSTANTIVOS
el **abrazo** *embrace, hug*
la **calidad** *quality*
la **cosa** *thing*
el **descuento** *discount*
el **dueño,** la **dueña** *owner*
la **fábrica** *factory*
la **muñeca** *doll*
el **precio** *price*

ADJETIVOS
verdadero(a) *real, true*

DEMOSTRATIVOS
este, esta *this*
estos, estas *these*
ese, esa *that*
esos, esas *those*
aquel, aquella *that (over there)*
aquellos, aquellas *those (over there)*

COMPARATIVOS Y SUPERLATIVOS
tan... como *as ... as*
tanto(a)(os)(as)... como *as much (many) as*
el (la, los, las) más... *the most ...*

más (menos)... que *more (less) ... than*
mayor *older, oldest; greater, greatest*
mejor *better, best*
menor *younger, youngest; minor; lesser, least*
peor *worse, worst*

VERBOS
establecer (establezco) *to establish*
llevar *to take, wear*
pasar *to spend time, pass*
　¡Pase Ud.! *Come in!*
　¿Qué le pasa? *What's wrong with you?*
revisar *to check*

EXPRESIONES
anoche *last night*
allí *there*
a propósito *by the way*
ayer *yesterday*
e *and (replaces y before words beginning with i or hi)*
¡Felicitaciones! *Congratuations!*
igualmente *likewise*
muy agradecido(a) *very grateful*
otra vez *again*
ya *already*

9   En el mercado

Margarita Núñez, una joven de Illinois, se ha mudado° a San Juan, Puerto Rico. Su prima Adela la lleva° a un supermercado para hacer unas compras de emergencia.

has moved
takes her

MARGARITA Ojalá que este ciclón° no sea muy severo.

hurricane

ADELA ¡Que Dios no quiera!° El último ciclón hizo mucho daño.° No tuvimos electricidad, y en casa se nos acabó la comida.°

God forbid! / did a lot of damage / lit., food ran out on us

MARGARITA Allá° en Chicago cuando nevaba fuerte la ciudad casi se paralizaba.

Back there

ADELA ¿Y cómo se preparaban?

MARGARITA Pues la gente se volvía loca° comprando de todo.

went crazy

ADELA Igual que° aquí. Bueno, date prisa,° que van a cerrar la tienda. Mientras° tú buscas tomates, lechuga° y chinas,[1] yo voy a recoger pan,° queso,° jamón° y café.

*The same as / hurry up (**tú** command) / While / lettuce / to pick up bread / cheese / ham*

MARGARITA Espera° un momentito. ¿Qué son las « chinas »?

*Wait (**tú** command)*

ADELA Naranjas, mujer. Trae° dos docenas. Mamá me dio° suficiente dinero para comprar medio mundo.°

*Bring (**tú** command) / gave / half the world*

---

1. En Puerto Rico dicen **chinas** en vez de **naranjas** *(oranges)*.

1. ¿De dónde es Margarita Núñez?
2. ¿Adónde van Margarita y su prima?
3. ¿Cuál es un sinónimo de *huracán* en español?
4. ¿Qué hizo el último ciclón?
5. ¿Qué quiere Adela que Margarita busque?
6. ¿Qué va a recoger Adela?
7. ¿Cuánto dinero tiene Adela?
8. ¿Qué pasa en la ciudad de usted cuando nieva o llueve mucho?
9. ¿Cuáles de estos fenómenos ocurren en su área: ciclones, tornados, temblores *(tremors)*?
10. ¿Quiere Ud. mudarse? ¿Adónde?

ADAPTACIÓN

Imagínese que anunciaron una tormenta *(storm)*. Usted y su amigo(a) van al supermercado para hacer unas compras de emergencia. Uds. están enojados *(angry)* porque se acabaron varios productos. Además las colas (o líneas) para pagar son muy largas. Preparen una conversación que incluya esas ideas y otras que ustedes quieran.

Estructura

I **El pretérito de verbos irregulares** *(Primera parte)*

ser / ir		hacer		dar	
fui	fuimos	hice	hicimos	di	dimos
fuiste	fuisteis	hiciste	hicisteis	diste	disteis
fue	fueron	hizo	hicieron	dio	dieron

The verbs **ser** and **ir** have the same forms in the preterite. Context makes their meaning clear. The third person singular of **hacer** (**hizo**) is spelled with a **z** to keep the [s] sound of the infinitive. **Dar,** although an -ar verb, takes the -er / -ir endings of the preterite. Note that there are no accent marks on the **yo** and **usted** forms.

Fui secretaria del club.	*I was secretary of the club.*
Ud. me dio cinco mil pesos.	*You gave me five thousand pesos.*
Fui al mercado.	*I went to the market.*

PRÁCTICA

a Pregúntele a otro(a) estudiante si alguna vez *(ever)* fue vendedor(a), maestro(a), etc. Use las ocupaciones en la lista.

MODELO: ¿Alguna vez fuiste vendedor(a)?
—Sí, fui vendedor(a).
—No, nunca (never) fui vendedor(a).

secretario(a)	cocinero(a)	dependiente
supervisor(a)	jugador(a) de básquetbol	agricultor(a)
operador(a)	niño(a) explorador(a) (scout)	agente de turismo
camarero(a) (waiter, waitress)	carpintero(a)	vendedor(a) de periódicos

b   Imagínese que un amigo norteamericano quiere saber lo que dice este artículo del periódico. Traduzca el artículo oralmente:

La autora e intérprete Rosamaría Padilla Ibáñez fue elegida[1] presidente de la Sociedad Literaria Las Américas. Nació[2] en Río Piedras, donde realizó sus estudios superiores en la Universidad de Puerto Rico. Se diplomó en Literatura y Arte. Posteriormente hizo numerosos cursos y seminarios en temas relacionados con su profesión. En sus años de carrera ha sido[3] maestra, actriz y corresponsal de varios periódicos y revistas. Es una gran aficionada[4] a la pintura y al teatro.

1. *elected*   **2.** from **nacer,** *to be born*   **3.** *she has been*   **4.** *fan, follower*

c   Haga Ud. el papel de Rosamaría Padilla y escriba el artículo anterior en primera persona.

MODELO: **Me llamo Rosamaría Padilla Ibáñez. Fui elegida...**

d   La entrevista. Imagínese que usted es un(a) corresponsal de periódico y tiene que entrevistar a una persona famosa (otro,-a estudiante). Hágale las siguientes preguntas. Escuche Ud. bien pues es posible que tenga que relatar (relate) la información al resto de la clase.

1. ¿Dónde nació Ud.?
2. ¿Dónde hizo sus estudios superiores?
3. ¿Hizo otros estudios?
4. ¿En qué lugares trabajó?
5. ¿Es casado(a)? ¿Con quién se casó?
6. ¿Tiene hijos?
7. ¿Cuáles son sus pasatiempos (hobbies) favoritos?
8. ¿?

e   En español usamos el verbo **dar** con varias expresiones diferentes. Use Ud. el verbo **dar** para traducir los verbos en inglés.

1. *We went for a ride (walk) yesterday.* _____ un paseo ayer.
2. *Last night they showed an excellent film on television.* Anoche _____ un film excelente por la televisión.
3. *Did you (tú) feed the cat?* ¿Le _____ de comer al gato?
4. *Adela hurried up.* Adela se _____ prisa.
5. *You didn't realize the mistake.* Uds. no se _____ cuenta del error.
6. *I thanked them.* Les _____ las gracias.

f   Situación. Usted es el fantástico detective Pedro Pérez, y tiene que interrogar a una persona sospechosa *(suspicious)*. Ud. quiere saber adónde fue esa persona (otro,-a estudiante) el fin de semana pasado. Use las siguientes preguntas como modelo.

1. ¿Adónde fue Ud. el viernes por la tarde?
2. ¿A qué hora fue allí exactamente?
3. ¿Con quién fue allí? ¿Qué hicieron allí?
4. ¿Adónde fue el sábado por la mañana?
5. ¿?
6. ¿?

II *El pretérito de verbos irregulares*   *(Segunda parte)*

A   Most of the remaining irregular verbs in the preterite can be grouped according to their stem vowel.

INFINITIVES	STEMS WITH U	ENDINGS	
tener	tuv-	**-e** **-iste**	tuve, tuviste, tuvo, tuvimos, tuvisteis, tuvieron
estar	estuv-	**-o** **-imos** **-isteis**	estuve, estuviste, estuvo, estuvimos, estuvisteis, estuvieron
poner	pus-	**-ieron**	puse, pusiste, puso, pusimos, pusisteis, pusieron

Estuvieron en la oficina.   ¿Por qué no te pusiste el suéter?
They were in the office.   *Why didn't you put on your sweater?*

Other verbs with the **u** stem include: **poder** (**pude, pudiste,** etc.), and **saber** (**supe, supiste,** etc.).

Except for the **yo** and **usted** verb forms, the endings are the same as those of regular preterite -er/-ir verbs. Notice that the endings for the **yo** and **usted** verb forms are unstressed and do not have accent marks.

PRÁCTICA
a   Situación. Ricardo tuvo que preparar un informe *(report)* ayer. Note Ud. lo que él hizo.

1. Primero tuvo que ir a la biblioteca.
2. Allí tuvo que leer unos libros de historia.
3. Después tuvo que tomar unos apuntes *(notes)*.

4. Luego tuvo que organizar los apuntes.

5. Finalmente tuvo que escribir el informe.

Ahora repita Ud. las cinco oraciones anteriores, pero cambie el sujeto de **Ricardo** a **yo**. Luego haga lo mismo, usando los sujetos **nosotros** y **ellos**.

b Diga cinco cosas que Ud. tuvo que hacer esta mañana.

1. Esta mañana _____ que _____ .

2. Después _____ que _____ .

3. Luego _____ que _____ .

4. Más tarde _____ que _____ .

5. Finalmente _____ que _____ .

c Situación. Imagínese que el año pasado su familia visitó Puerto Rico. Mencione los lugares donde estuvieron Uds., según la siguiente información.

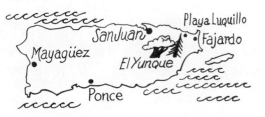

MODELO: **El año pasado estuvimos en San Juan.**

1. Mi papá _____ en Fajardo.

2. Mis hermanos _____ en Playa Luquillo.

3. Mi mamá _____ en El Yunque.

4. Yo _____ Mayagüez.

5. Todos nosotros _____ Ponce.

d Mencione tres lugares donde usted estuvo el domingo pasado.

MODELO: **Primero (yo)** _____ **en...**
Luego _____ **en...**
y más tarde _____ **en...**

e Situación. Imagínese que usted se mudó a un apartamento nuevo, y ahora usted le pregunta a su amigo dónde él puso varias cosas durante la mudada *(during the move)*. Estudien el dibujo a la continuación y después hagan y contesten las preguntas según el modelo.

MODELO: **¿Dónde pusiste el televisor?**
Puse el televisor en la sala.

1. ¿Dónde pusiste el sofá?

2. ¿el horno de micro-ondas?

3. ¿la cama?

4. ¿la mesa y las sillas?

5. ¿el jabón y las toallas *(towels)*?

6. ¿el escritorio *(desk)*?

7. ¿?

f   Diga qué ropa se pusieron las siguientes personas.

MODELO: Andrés fue a la playa.   **(Él) se puso unos pantalones cortos y una camiseta.**

1. Sara fue a la universidad. (Ella)...
2. Mis amigos y yo fuimos a un banquete. (Nosotros)...
3. Los niños fueron a una fiesta de cumpleaños. (Ellos)...
4. Fui al campo. (Yo)...
5. (Refiérase Ud. a otros sujetos y diga adónde fueron y qué ropa se pusieron.)

B   The following irregular preterite verbs can be grouped according to the **i** in their stems.

INFINITIVES	STEMS WITH I	
querer	quis-	quise, quisiste, quiso
		quisimos, quisisteis, quisieron
venir	vin-	vine, viniste, vino
		vinimos, vinisteis, vinieron
decir	dij-	dije, dijiste, dijo
		dijimos, dijisteis, dijeron*
Traer has the stem **traj.**		traje, trajiste, trajo
		trajimos, trajisteis, trajeron*

*Note that the **i** from the **-ieron** ending is omitted in **dijeron** and **trajeron.**

TRABALENGUAS
(TONGUE TWISTER)

No traje traje[1] no nado[2] nada.

1. traje de baño   **2. nadar** *(to swim)*

PRÁCTICA

a   **Situación.** Ayer hizo mal tiempo y varias personas no vinieron a la reunión del club español. Diga quién no vino.

MODELO: **Eva no vino a la reunión.**

1. Paco
2. yo
3. Ud.
4. Marta y Luis
5. el profesor / la profesora
6. tú
7. nosotros
8. ¿?

b **Situación.** Ustedes van a tener una fiesta y van a preparar un ponche. Diferentes miembros de la clase trajeron los ingredientes. Diga Ud. qué trajo cada uno.

MODELO: **Mercedes y Eduardo trajeron las naranjas.**

1. Nilda _____ jugo de naranja.
2. Tú _____ el hielo.
3. Nosotros _____ las manzanas.
4. Lisa y Cristina _____ Seven-Up.
5. Yo _____ una lata *(can)* de coctel de fruta.

Hielo
Ice

manzanas
(apples)

c **Substitución.** Use los verbos entre paréntesis para hacer oraciones nuevas en el pretérito.

1. No hicimos nada. (decir, traer, dar)
2. Decidió entrar. (querer, tener que, poder)
3. Esperé en el carro. (venir, estar, ir)
4. Compraron la ropa. (traer, ponerse, hacer)

d **Una charla** *(A talk).* Hable de un viaje *(trip)* que usted hizo. Use las siguientes preguntas para preparar su charla.

1. ¿A qué país o estado fue Ud.?
2. ¿Cuánto tiempo estuvo allí?
3. ¿Con quién fue?
4. ¿En qué viajó? (carro, avión, autobús)
5. ¿Cuánto tuvo que pagar por el viaje?
6. ¿Qué lugares interesantes vio?
7. ¿Qué le gustó más?
8. ¿Qué trajo de recuerdo?

III *El imperfecto*

A The imperfect tense is the other simple past tense in Spanish. It is used to describe habitual, continuous past actions or situations. Like the present tense, the imperfect focuses upon ongoing, evolving actions. It's as if the speaker were going back to the past to relive it.

—De niño° vivía
en una casa grande.
Era° blanca y tenía
techo° rojo...

As a child

It was

roof

The imperfect has several possible translations. For example, **yo trabajaba** can mean *I worked, I was working, I used to work, I would work* (when *would* implies habitual action). Except for *I worked*, which can correspond to either the preterite or imperfect, these translations indicate that the action was habitual, or that it was performed on a regular basis. Compare:

Trabajé esta mañana.
I worked this morning.

With the preterite the speaker stresses the *end* of the action.

Trabajaba todos los días.
I worked (used to work) every day.

With the imperfect the speaker stresses the *continuity* of the action.

Forms of the imperfect

trabajar	leer	dormir
trabajaba	leía	dormía
trabajabas	leías	dormías
trabajaba	leía	dormía
trabajábamos	leíamos	dormíamos
trabajabais	leíais	dormíais
trabajaban	leían	dormían

For clarity, subject pronouns often accompany the first and third person verb forms.

Stem-changing verbs do *not* change their stem in the imperfect since all the stems are unstressed: **pedía, jugaban.**

The imperfect of **hay** is **había** (*there was, there were, there used to be*).

Only **ser**, **ir**, and **ver** are irregular in the imperfect.

ser		ir		ver	
era	éramos	iba	íbamos	veía	veíamos
eras	erais	ibas	ibais	veías	veías
era	eran	iba	iban	veía	veían

PRÁCTICA

a   Diga quién hablaba con la profesora.

MODELO: **Rodrigo hablaba con la profesora.**

1. Lisa	*4.* yo
2. los estudiantes	*5.* Uds.
3. tú	*6.* Julio y yo

b Mencione qué fruta comían estas personas frecuentemente.

MODELO: nosotros / manzanas **Comíamos manzanas.**

1. ellos / piña
2. Laura / uvas
3. nosotras / toronja
4. Uds. / banana
5. tú / mango
6. yo / ¿?

melocotón (peach) mango toronja (grapefruit) uvas piña

c Mencione adónde iban estas personas todos los fines de semana.

MODELO: yo / la casa de mis amigos **Iba a la casa de mis amigos.**

1. Tina / la iglesia (el templo)
2. los Hernández / el parque
3. nosotros / el cine
4. tú / la casa de tus abuelos
5. yo / ¿?

HUMOR

Aclaración°
Una mujer, al dependiente en tono sarcástico:—¿Qué me dijo usted del
queso que me vendió ayer, que era importado o deportado de Suiza?°

Explanation

Switzerland

B Otros usos del imperfecto
The imperfect is used:

1. to describe *physical* or *emotional states* in the past.

Gustavo era alto y delgado.
Gustavo was (used to be) tall and thin.

¿Tenías miedo?
Were you afraid?

Estábamos muy cansados.
We were very tired.

2. to express *time* and *age* in the past.

Eran las diez de la noche.
It was eight o'clock at night.

Tenía dieciséis años en esta foto.
I was sixteen in this picture.

PRÁCTICA

a Cambie al imperfecto.

1. Uds. se preocupan mucho.
2. Papá se siente mal.
3. Juanita es baja y tiene el pelo negro.
4. Hace mucho frío.
5. Son las 6:30 de la mañana.
6. Ellos no están aburridos.
7. Hay más de quince personas aquí.

b Diga lo que usted hacía frecuentemente cuando era niño(a). Use las siguientes edades *(ages)* y actividades en su narración.

MODELO: 5 años / vivir en la ciudad
    Cuando tenía cinco años vivía en la ciudad.

1. 6 años / jugar en el parque
2. 7 años / asistir a la escuela primaria
3. 8 años / tocar un instrumento musical
4. 9 años / ser explorador(a)
5. 10 años / ir al cine los sábados
6. 11 años / ¿?

c Entrevista. Usted quiere conocer mejor a otro(a) estudiante. Hágale estas preguntas y después esté listo(a) *(be ready)* para decirle a la clase lo que dijo ese(a) estudiante.

1. ¿Dónde naciste?
2. ¿Dónde vivías?
3. ¿A qué escuela primaria asistías?
4. ¿En qué programas de la escuela participabas? ¿deportes? ¿música? ¿arte?
5. ¿Eras obediente? ¿estudioso(a)? ¿curioso(a)?
6. ¿Quiénes eran tus amigos?
7. ¿Dónde pasabas los veranos?
8. ¿A qué escuela secundaria asistías?
9. ¿En qué año te graduaste de la secundaria?
10. ¿Te gustaba la secundaria? ¿Por qué?
11. ¿Estudiaste español en la secundaria? ¿Cuántos años?
12. ¿Eras miembro(a) de un club? ¿Cuál?
13. ¿Trabajabas después de las clases? ¿Dónde?
14. ¿Adónde ibas los fines de semana?
15. ¿En qué año empezaste a estudiar en la universidad?

IV *Contrastes entre el pretérito y el imperfecto*

Both the preterite and the imperfect may occur in the same sentence, with the imperfect describing the *background* (what was going on) and the preterite reporting completed actions *within* that setting.

Llovía mucho cuando salí.   *It was raining a lot when I left.*

Speakers use the preterite to mark the *beginning* or *end* of an event as well as to refer to the event as a whole. With the imperfect, speakers focus on the *middle* of the event—what was going on—regardless of when it began or ended.

Empezamos a estudiar esta mañana.
We started to study this morning.

Beginning ⟶

Margarita rompió el plato.
Margarita broke the dish.

⟶*End*

Estuve en la Florida unos días.
I was in Florida a few days.

Whole

De repente oí un ruido.
Suddenly I heard a noise.

Instantaneous action; emphasis on completion

Oía un ruido.
I heard (was hearing) a noise.

Prolonged action; emphasis on continuity

The contrast between the preterite (beginning or end) and the imperfect (middle) requires particular attention when translating **conocer** and **saber.**

Conocí a Adela Núñez.
I met Adela Núñez. (I made her acquaintance.)

Conocía a Adela.
I knew Adela.
(I used to know her. I was acquainted with her.)

¿Supiste que Dolores se casa?
Did you learn (find out) that Dolores is getting married?

Creía que todo el mundo lo sabía.
I thought everybody knew it.

PRÁCTICA

a Describa lo que hacía Adela (sus actividades) cuando Margarita entró.

MODELO: **Adela *preparaba un informe* cuando Margarita entró.**

1. estudiar inglés
2. leer una revista
3. estar ocupada con los niños
4. conversar por teléfono
5. no hacer nada
6. dormir la siesta
7. pensar salir
8. escribir un informe
9. traducir unos papeles
10. ver unas fotos

b Describa lo que hacían tres o cuatro de sus amigos cuando usted llegó a clase. ¿Qué hacía la profesora?

MODELO: **Martín conversaba con Norma cuando (yo)...**

c ¿Pretérito o imperfecto? Lea el siguiente párrafo dos veces: la primera vez para saber qué ocurrió y la segunda para escoger entre el pretérito y el imperfecto. Después revise su trabajo con las respuestas abajo *(below)*.

(Fueron, Eran) ____**1**____ las tres de la tarde cuando Carmen y yo llegamos a casa. En seguida° (corrí, corría) ____**2**____ a poner la televisión. Queríamos ver nuestra novela favorita. Mientras (puse, ponía) ____**3**____ la televisión, el teléfono (sonó, sonaba°) ____**4**____ de pronto. Como siempre (fue, era) ____**5**____ Mamá que llamaba a esa hora. Inmediatamente le (dije, decía) ____**6**____ que yo iba a ver mi programa, pero ella poco a poco (insistió, insistía) ____**7**____ en hablarme y hablarme. Por fin, (recordó, recordaba) ____**8**____ que tenía que hacer la comida. Se despidió° y yo (regresé, regresaba) ____**9**____ a la sala.

—Ya (terminó, terminaba) ____**10**____ el programa—me dijo mi amiga.

At once

*from **sonar**: to ring*

She said good-bye

Respuestas:
1. **Eran** (time)   2. **corrí** (**En seguida** emphasizes instantaneous, unprolonged action.)
3. **ponía** (**Mientras,** *while,* stresses the act in progress and provides background for the next event—4—that suddenly intervened.)   4. **sonó**   5. **era** (**Como siempre,** *as usual*)
6. **dije** (**Inmediatamente,** same as 2)   7. **insistía** (**poco a poco,** ongoing action)
8. **recordó** (**por fin,** *finally,* same as 2 and 5)   9. **regresé** (emphasizes the end and not the duration of the action; the same applies to the previous verb, **se despidió**)
10. **terminó** (**ya,** *already,* stresses the end.)

d Complete las oraciones en español, escogiendo *(choosing)* entre el pretérito y el imperfecto.

1. *We were waiting outside.*
   (Esperamos, Esperábamos) afuera.
2. *I saw Mrs. del Monte yesterday.*
   (Vi, Veía) a la Sra. del Monte ayer.
3. *They often went to the park on Sundays.*
   A menudo (fueron, iban) al parque los domingos.
4. *Suddenly everybody got up and left.*
   De pronto todo el mundo se (levantó, levantaba) y se (fue, iba).
5. *It was raining a lot. The streets were full of water.*
   (Llovió, Llovía) mucho. Las calles (estuvieron, estaban) llenas de agua.
6. *It was twelve-thirty when René finally called.*
   (Fueron, Eran) las doce y media cuando René por fin (llamó, llamaba).

e ¿Pretérito o imperfecto? Dé la forma apropiada de los verbos entre paréntesis. La descripción (el imperfecto) debe predominar al principio *(at the beginning)* de este cuento *(story).*

Arturo Muñoz y su mujer, Clara, (vivir) ____**1**____ en San Juan. Arturo (ser) ____**2**____ vendedor para una fábrica de ropa. No (ser) ____**3**____ un señor rico, pero (ganar) ____**4**____ un sueldo° ade-

salary

cuado. Arturo y Clara (tener) _____5_____ dos hijos. Vicente (asistir

a) _____6_____ una escuela cerca de la casa. Rosita (quedarse°)

_____7_____ en casa porque sólo (tener) _____8_____ tres años. La casa

de la familia (estar) _____9_____ en un distrito viejo pero prestigioso.

to remain

Sin embargo,° ellos no (estar) _____10_____ contentos. Clara siempre

(echar) _____11_____ de menos° a la familia y los amigos de Ponce, el

pueblo donde ella (nacer) _____12_____. Arturo (estar) _____13_____ can-

sado de su rutina diaria. Además, el año pasado, el administrador no

le (aumentar°) _____14_____ el sueldo, pero sí° a algunos de los otros

vendedores.

Nevertheless

echar de menos: *to miss*

to increase / but did so

Un día (presentarse) _____15_____ la oportunidad de asistir a una

conferencia de vendedores. Allí, Arturo (conocer) _____16_____ al Sr.

Sierra, supervisor en una compañía próspera y bien administrada.

Los dos señores (hacerse°) _____17_____ amigos muy pronto, pues el

Sr. Sierra todavía° (trabajar) _____18_____ en Ponce, y él (conocer)

_____19_____ bien a los padres de Clara. También, el primer día de la

conferencia, Arturo (dar) _____20_____ una excelente presentación que

le (gustar) _____21_____ muchísimo al Sr. Sierra.

to become

still

Una semana más tarde, Arturo (recibir) _____22_____ una carta para

una entrevista en Ponce.

f Repita rápido los trabalenguas.

Paco Peco   Como³ poco coco⁴ como⁵
Chico rico   poco coco compro.
insultaba como¹ loco
a su tío Federico y éste
le dijo, « Poco a poco,
Paco Peco, poco pico. »²

1. *like*   **2.** *"a little less lip or back talk"*   **3.** *(inasmuch) as*   **4.** *coconut*   **5.** *comer*

OBSERVACIONES

You can extend your vocabulary by learning to identify words that have similar roots. Many verbs and nouns are closely related in meaning and form.

el verbo: **trabajar**   *el sustantivo:* **el trabajo**

As you read the passage below look for related words.

La agricultura

A pesar del formidable desarrollo° industrial en los centros urbanos, la
agricultura es todavía la base de la economía en Hispanoamérica. En el momento actual° la mayoría de los países más pequeños basan su economía
en uno o dos productos. Por ejemplo, en Centroamérica se cultivan el café

development

present

y los plátanos.° Las islas del Caribe producen azúcar, frutas y tabaco. Los   *bananas, plantains*
países más grandes cosechan° maíz° y trigo,° además de desarrollar la ga-   *harvest / corn / wheat*
nadería.° Para comerciar con otros países, Hispanoamérica exporta sus   *livestock*
productos agrícolas y especialmente sus minerales.

Desde los comienzos° del período colonial, la monoagricultura (el cultivo   *Since the beginnings*
intenso de un producto para la exportación) resultó en dos graves proble-
mas para la América Latina. Primero, una cosecha abundante del mismo°   *same*
producto en otras regiones o el cambio anormal del tiempo (una sequía,°   *drought*
un exceso de lluvia o una helada°) podían provocar serias crisis económi-   *frost*
cas. Segundo, las compañías exportadoras que controlaban las mejores
zonas agrícolas no estimulaban la producción de productos alimenticios° y   *nourishing*
los países tenían que importar más y más alimentos del extranjero.° En   *from abroad (foreign)*
realidad, muchos de estos alimentos podían cultivarse más económica-
mente localmente.

Los problemas mencionados todavía existen, pero los agrónomos han
ofrecido° estas soluciones: *have offered*
- mejor administración y más producción en los latifundios°   *large landholdings*
- mejores métodos para cultivar los alimentos básicos (maíz, arroz,° gra-   *rice*
  nos, papas,° frijoles,° etc.)   *potatos / beans*
- ayuda técnica y económica para los minifundios
- justo equilibrio° entre los precios de los productos agrícolas exporta-   *balance*
  bles y la maquinaria° importada   *machinery*

Es verdad que actualmente Hispanoamérica no produce lo suficiente
para alimentar a su población.° Sin embargo, ya que° Hispanoamérica   *populations / since*
cuenta con° el 16% (por ciento) de la tierra arable del mundo y con menos   *counts on*
del 10% de la población, el problema debe tener solución.

¿COMPRENDE UD.?

a   Vocabulario. Escriba el sustantivo que aparece en las **Observaciones**, para cada verbo en la lista.

MODELO: producir ⟶ **el producto**
        exportar ⟶ **la exportación**

1.	desarrollar	6.	poblar
2.	cosechar	7.	solucionar
3.	alimentar	8.	cambiar
4.	cultivar	9.	administrar
5.	ayudar	10.	llover

b   Comprensión. ¿Cierto o falso?

1. La economía de Hispanoamérica depende mayormente de la
   industria.
2. Centroamérica cultiva mucho café y plátanos.
3. Las islas del Caribe producen grandes cantidades de maíz y arroz.
4. Las compañías exportadoras controlan las mejores zonas agrícolas.
5. Los latifundios son muy pequeños.
6. México y la Argentina cosechan maíz y trigo.

Tres de las previas oraciones son falsas. Escriba las oraciones otra vez, cambiándolas (*changing them*) de falsas a ciertas.

c Opinión. Usted es agricultor(a) en Hispanoamérica. ¿Qué soluciones puede ofrecer para mejorar (*improve*) la agricultura?

***ADIVINANZA* (RIDDLE)**

Oro parece,° plata no es.   *looks like*
Quien no lo adivina° muy tonto es.   *guesses it*
(plá-ta-no)

Actividades

a Una biografía. Lea el informe biográfico.

El Cid

El Cid

> Rodrigo Díaz de Vivar (El Cid) nació en el año 1043.
> Era del norte de España.
> Luchó contra[1] los moros de África. A causa de sus victorias los moros lo[2] llamaron *Cid,* que significa « Mi Señor ».
> Murió[3] cuando tenía 56 años.
> El Cid se convirtió en el símbolo de todo lo grande[4] e ideal de España.
> Era fiel,[5] valiente y justo.

1. *He fought against*   **2.** *him*   **3. from morir:** *to die*   **4.** *all that's great*   **5.** *faithful*

b Use la actividad anterior de modelo para escribir un informe biográfico de Benito Juárez. Incluya esta información.

Benito Juárez

fecha de nacimiento: 1806
lugar: Oaxaca, México
lucha: contra la intervención francesa
   en México en 1863 y contra las injusticias sociales en su país.
vida: 66 años
símbolo: las ideas democráticas y la
   reforma social
características: reformista, patriótico,
   determinado

c Escoja otra famosa persona hispana y escriba un informe biográfico de no menos de seis oraciones. Por ejemplo: Simón Bolívar, José de San Martín, Isabel la Católica, Gabriela Mistral, Picasso...

Vocabulario

SUSTANTIVOS
el **arroz** *rice*
la **cosecha** *harvest*
el **daño** *damage, harm*
el **hielo** *ice*
el **jamón** *ham*
el **pan** *bread*
el **queso** *cheese*

LAS FRUTAS
la **banana**
la **manzana** *apple*
el **melocotón** *peach*
la **naranja** *orange*
la **piña** *pineapple*
el **plátano** *banana, plantain**
la **toronja** *grapefruit*
las **uvas** *grapes*

LAS LEGUMBRES
los **frijoles** *beans*
la **lechuga** *lettuce*
el **maíz** *corn*
la **papa** *potato*
el **tomate** *tomato*

LA CASA
el **baño** *bath*
la **cocina** *kitchen*
el **comedor** *dining room*
el **cuarto** *room*
la **sala** *living room*

ADJETIVO
igual *same, equal*

VERBOS
acabarse *to run out of*
mudarse *to move (residence)*
nevar(ie) *to snow*
prepararse *to prepare oneself*
quedarse *to stay, remain*
recoger (recojo) *to pick up*

EXPRESIONES
alguna vez *ever*
darse prisa *to hurry*
de repente *suddenly*
en seguida *at once*
hacer compras *to shop*
mientras *while*
nunca *never*
todavía *still*

*Banana and **plátano** are interchangeable terms; however, **plátano (de freír)** is applied to the kind you fry.

Examen III

Take the Listening and Speaking sections with a classmate other than one who has worked with you on *Exámenes I y II.* Do not look at what your classmate has chosen or written; rely instead on your listening and speaking skills.

Listening

Dictado. Your classmate will choose five sentences at random from previous *Observaciones*, and then read each sentence twice to you. The first time listen to the entire sentence for meaning; the second, write down what you hear during the pauses. Commas or closely associated word groups should serve to mark the pauses.

MODELO: En el Japón y Alemania, // nuestros mayores rivales en el comercio, // las compañías exportadoras pronto comenzaron // el estudio de las lenguas // para el personal de ventas internacionales. (from **Observaciones, Lesson 8**)

After completing the dictation, check your work with your classmate. Then, following the instructions above, prepare a new version of the dictation to read to him or her.

Speaking

I Tell your classmate what you did yesterday, including:

1. at what time you got up
2. where you went
3. what you studied
4. whom you saw
5. what you bought

6. what you ate and drank
7. what you read
8. what two other things you had to do
9. finally, at what time you went to bed

II Listen to each question and answer it orally. Your classmate can change the order of the sample questions below and add a few questions, too.

1. a. ¿En qué año naciste?
   b. ¿Dónde vivías de niño(a)?
   c. ¿Cuándo te graduaste de la escuela secundaria?
   d. ¿Dónde pasaban Uds. (tú y tu familia) los veranos?
2. a. ¿Quién era tu mejor amigo(a) en la escuela primaria?
   b. ¿Cómo era él (ella)?
   c. ¿A qué jugaban Uds.?
3. a. ¿A qué hora llegaste a clase hoy?
   b. ¿Qué hacía la profesora cuando entraste?
   c. ¿Qué hacían tus amigos?
   d. ¿De qué hablaron Uds. hoy?
4. a. ¿Qué libro interesante leyó Ud. el verano pasado?
   b. ¿Quiénes eran las personas principales?
   c. ¿Dónde tuvo lugar la acción?
   d. ¿Le gustó el libro? ¿Por qué?

III Situations

1. Your classmate has agreed to help out with the house chores so you must tell him or her what you want done. Make up at least five sentences that include the equivalent of these expressions in Spanish:

I want you to . . .   It's necessary that you . . .
I prefer that you . . .   I hope (that) you . . .
I wish you . . .

2. You're checking in at the Hotel Miramar. Tell your classmate, who's playing the role of the employee, what accommodations you want. Include: how many days you plan to be there; what type of room you want (bed, bathroom, etc.); at what time you need to wake up; whether or not you want the continental breakfast.

3. You're walking out of Spanish class when two Latin American students ask you how to go to the places below. Give them directions using the appropriate command forms.

the university library
the main post office downtown

4. You were in a car accident, and are explaining to the police officer what happened. Say:
   a. It was 9:30 P.M. The weather was bad. It was raining.
   b. The driver of the other car suddenly turned to the left and collided with you.[1]
   c. Your girlfriend in the car hurt[2] her head and neck. You hurt your right leg and back.
   d. You want the police officer to call a doctor.

1. **chocar conmigo:** *to collide with me, to crash*   2. **lastimarse:** *to hurt*

Writing

I Substituya la parte en cursiva en cada oración con la información entre paréntesis. Haga los cambios necesarios.

MODELO: Él es mi *amigo.* (primos) **Ellos son mis primos.**

1. a. Ella es nuestra *hija.* (hijos)
   b. *Uds.* están en su casa. (Tú)
   c. Su *carro* es azul. (maletas)
   d. *Su* apartamento está en el segundo piso. (de ellos)
2. a. Necesito ese *diccionario.* (enciclopedia)
   b. Hablábamos con ese *señor,* no aquél. (señores)
   c. ¿Prefieres esta *silla* o ésa? (asientos)
3. a. Agustín es *menos* alto que tú. (tan)
   b. *Félix* es el más trabajador de la familia. (Catalina)

II   Escoja el verbo que mejor complete cada oración y escriba la forma apropiada en el presente del indicativo.

MODELO: Ángela <u>mira</u> las fotos. (ayudar, caminar, mirar)

1. ¿Quién _____ el café? (venir, servir, cruzar)
2. Yo _____ la ropa. (ponerse, sentarse, preocuparse)
3. ¿A qué hora _____ ellos del trabajo? (llevar, salir, limpiar)
4. ¿Cuánto dinero me _____ tú? (repetir, preguntar, pedir)
5. Yo _____ ejercicios en el gimnasio. (hacer, guardar, subir)
6. Hace calor. ¿Por qué no _____ Uds. el abrigo? (mejorarse, quitarse, sentarse)
7. Nosotros _____ de casa la semana que viene. (mudarse, acabarse, prepararse)
8. Yo les _____ la verdad. (limpiar, cerrar, decir)

III   Complete las oraciones con la expresión más apropiada. Escriba el verbo en el presente del indicativo.

tener hambre   tener prisa
tener sed   tener frío
tener sueño   tener miedo

1. Los muchachos _____ porque *(because)* no duermen ocho horas.
2. Claro que tú _____ . Comes muy poco.
3. La niña no quiere estar sola. Ella _____ .
4. Deseo un refresco porque _____ .
5. La temperatura está a cero. Nosotros _____ .

IV   Cambie al mandato.

MODELO: Ud./explicarme el problema   **Explíqueme el problema.**

1. Ud./preguntarle al chófer   4. Ud./traer a sus amigos
2. Uds./venir a la reunión   5. Ud./no pagarles* a ellos
3. Uds./sentarse aquí   6. Uds./no preocuparse* por nosotros

V   Escoja la traducción correcta de la oración en inglés.

1. *I want him to go with you.*
   a. Quiero ir con Uds.
   b. Quiero que vaya con Uds.
2. *We hope to leave at eight o'clock.*
   a. Esperamos salir a las ocho.
   b. Espera que salgamos a las ocho.
3. *They're sorry (that) you are not staying longer.*
   a. Sienten no quedarse más tiempo.
   b. Sienten que no se quede más tiempo.

*¿Recuerda Ud. dónde ponemos los pronombres como **les** y **se** en los mandatos negativos?

VI Primero, decida Ud. si el contexto de la oración requiere el indicativo, el subjuntivo o el infinitivo. Después, dé la forma apropiada del verbo entre paréntesis.

1. (revisar) El Sr. Gutiérrez desea que nosotros _____ la cuenta.
2. (poder) Creo que ellos _____ ayudarte.
3. (cruzar) ¿Es necesario que la niña _____ la calle?
4. (levantarse) Tengo que _____ temprano.
5. (buscar) Preferimos que tú _____ otro lugar.
6. (divertirse) ¡Ojalá que Uds. _____ mucho!
7. (descansar) Van a _____ unos minutos.
8. (jugar) Temo que ellos no _____ muy bien al dominó.

VII ¿Pretérito o imperfecto? Traduzca al español las palabras entre paréntesis.

1. (I went) _____ al museo ayer.
2. (brought) Mercedes me _____ este regalo de Chile.
3. (We used to see) _____ a Jorge Luis todos los días.
4. (arrived) Los Acosta _____ esta mañana.
5. (was) Mirta _____ alta y tenía el pelo castaño.
6. (I was studying) Conocí a varios amigos cuando _____ en México.
7. (did you put) ¡Caramba! ¿Dónde _____ el periódico de hoy?

VIII ¿Pretérito o imperfecto? Dé la forma apropiada de los verbos entre paréntesis.

Miguel de Cervantes, autor de la incomparable novela *Don Quijote de la Mancha,* (nacer) ___1___ en España en el año 1547. De niño su familia (ser) ___2___ pobre y frecuentemente (mudarse) ___3___ de ciudad a ciudad para° mejorar su condición. Cuando Cervantes (tener) ___4___ veintidós años, (ir) ___5___ a Roma al servicio de un cardenal. Pronto (aprender) ___6___ italiano y (comenzar) ___7___ a leer las grandes obras italianas.°

    En el año 1571 Cervantes (tomar) ___8___ parte en la importante batalla naval de Lepanto, donde (distinguirse°) ___9___ por su valor. Cuando (regresar) ___10___ a España unos piratas lo° (capturar) ___11___ en el mar Mediterráneo, y lo (llevar) ___12___ a África. Finalmente, después de un largo cautiverio,° Cervantes (llegar) ___13___ a a España. Allí pasó varios años de apuro° hasta que por fin en el año 1605 (publicar) ___14___ su brillante novela, *Don Quijote de la Mancha.* Esa obra (ser) ___15___ un éxito° inmediato.

in order to

great Italian works

to distinguish oneself

him

long (period of) captivity

pasar apuro: *to go through bad times*

success

IX Vocabulario. Traduzca al español.

1. room
2. bath
3. kitchen
4. living room
5. dining room
6. orange
7. pineapple
8. apple
9. peach
10. grapefruit
11. Come in!
12. What's wrong with you?
13. Congratulations!
14. likewise
15. very grateful

Después de ver una representación de la ópera _El barbero de Sevilla_ en el Teatro Colón,[1] los señores° Ponte van a cenar a un restaurante de Buenos Aires. Están sentados y leen el menú mientras toman un aperitivo. El camarero viene a tomar la orden.

              Mr. and Mrs.

CAMARERO ¿Qué desean los señores?

SR. PONTE Por favor, para mi mujer un plato de sopa y un biftec medio asado.° Para mí un churrasco[2] bien asado y una ensalada. El postre°... lo pediremos más tarde.   *medium done / dessert*

CAMARERO ¿Me permite recomendarle una botella° de vino tinto?°   *bottle / red wine*

SRA. PONTE (A su esposo) A mí me gustaría° más tomar un espumante.°   *would like / sparkling wine*

SR. PONTE Muy bien. Espumante para la señora y vino tinto para mí.

SRA. PONTE ¡Qué divertida° estuvo la ópera! Creo que _El barbero de Sevilla_ siempre será popular.   *amusing*

SR. PONTE Tienes razón. Nunca me cansaré° de verla.   *I'll never get tired*

SRA. PONTE ¿Cuándo la pondrán° otra vez?   *will (they) put it on*

SR. PONTE Me imagino que tendremos que esperar hasta otra temporada.°   *theater season*

1. El compositor italiano Rossini (1792–1868) compuso la ópera _El barbero de Sevilla_. El Teatro Colón, en Buenos Aires, es uno de los centros culturales más famosos del mundo.
2. Churrasco is grilled steak (Argentina); barbecue.

183

¿RECUERDA UD.?

1. ¿Qué ópera vieron los Ponte?
2. ¿Dónde vieron esa ópera?
3. ¿Adónde fueron después de la ópera?
4. ¿Qué leían?
5. ¿Qué pidió el Sr. Ponte para su mujer? ¿y para él?
6. ¿Qué quería tomar ella?
7. ¿Cómo estuvo la ópera?
8. ¿Cuándo pondrán esa obra otra vez?
9. ¿Es español o italiano el apellido « Ponte »?
10. ¿Cenan tarde o temprano en la Argentina?

Restaurante La Pampa

Entremeses (Hors d'oeuvres)
jugos de frutas frescas (juices)
coctel de frutas
coctel de camarones (shrimp)
ceviche (minced raw fish, lime
   juice, onions)
sopa (soup)
gazpacho (cold soup: tomato,
   cucumber)

Ensaladas
mixta
del chef
de frutas
de atún (tuna)

Platos del día (Today's specials)
parrillada (grilled meat)
paella (rice with seafood and
   vegetables)
arroz con pollo (chicken with
   rice)
biftec
jamón asado (roasted ham)
pescado (fish)
frijoles

Postres (Desserts)
flan (custard with caramel)
torta (cake)
helados (ice creams)
frutas frescas
quesos (cheeses)

Bebidas (Beverages)
vino tinto y blanco (red
   and white wine)
cerveza (beer)
café
té caliente o helado
leche (milk)
refrescos
agua mineral (mineral
   water)

¡Buen Provecho!

ADAPTACIÓN

Tres de ustedes están en el restaurante La Pampa. Uno de Uds. debe ser
camarero(a) y los otros, clientes. Preparen un diálogo original. Pidan
algo de cada parte del menú. No se limiten Uds. a las hamburguesas y
las papas fritas (French fries). El camarero debe ofrecer sugerencias y
los clientes deben hacer preguntas; por ejemplo, ¿Qué sopa hay? ¿Para
cuántas personas es la paella? ¿Es fresco el pescado? ¿Es picante (spicy)
la comida? ¿Está incluida la propina (tip)? ¿Puede darnos cuentas separadas?, etc.

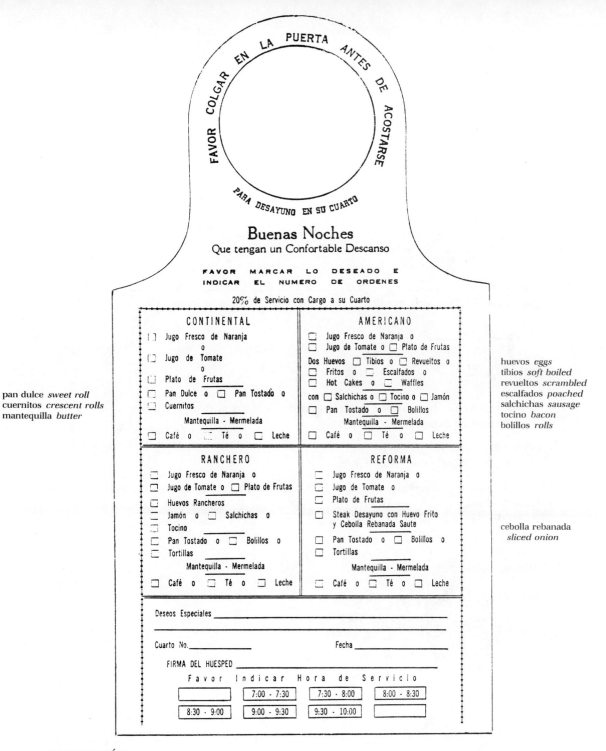

pan dulce *sweet roll*
cuernitos *crescent rolls*
mantequilla *butter*

huevos *eggs*
tibios *soft boiled*
revueltos *scrambled*
escalfados *poached*
salchichas *sausage*
tocino *bacon*
bolillos *rolls*

cebolla rebanada
sliced onion

ADAPTACIÓN

Usted se queda *(stay)* en un hotel y quiere desayunar en su cuarto. Haga
una lista de lo que desea comer.

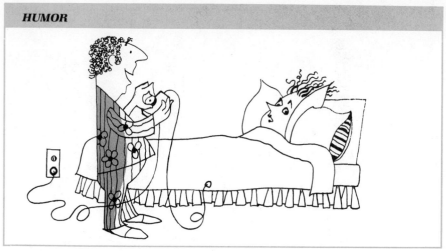

—¿Bien asado (*roasted*), mediano o crudo?

Estructura

I *El futuro*

A Up to now we have relied on the simple present and the expression **ir a** + *infinitive* to express future actions.

Pago luego.   Voy a pagar luego.
I'll pay later.   *I'm going to pay later.*

The true future *(will, won't)* in Spanish is formed by taking the entire infinitive and adding one set of endings to all verbs: **-é, -ás, -á, -emos, -éis, -án**. All the endings have an accent mark except the **nosotros**(as) form.

pagar	
pagaré (*I will, shall pay*)	pagaremos
pagarás	pagaréis
pagará	pagarán
¿Cuándo pagará Ud.?	No iremos allí.
When will you pay?	*We won't go there.*

PRÁCTICA

a   Diga los planes que tienen estas personas para el viernes o el sábado.

MODELO: nosotros: estudiar español / comer con los amigos
    El viernes   **Estudiaremos español. Comeremos con los amigos.**

1. nosotros: limpiar la casa / guardar la ropa / lavar el carro / bañar al perro / cortar la hierba (*mow the grass*) / reparar las bicicletas / y finalmente descansar un poco

2. mis padres: trabajar unas horas / ir a las tiendas / comprar la comida / preparar la cena / leer el periódico / visitar a la familia / divertirse un poco

3. yo: levantarse temprano / bañarse / desayunar cereal y café con leche / ir a la universidad / asistir a las clases / regresar a casa / comer un sándwich / ¿?

b **Situación.** Una representante de su firma en Sudamérica visita la fábrica donde usted trabaja. Ud. debe explicarle a ella como pasará el día.

MODELO: 8:30 llegar a la fábrica **A las 8:30 (usted) llegará a la fábrica.**

1. 9:00 visitar la fábrica	4. 13:00 presentar un informe
2. 10:00 hablar con el director	5. 14:00 ver las nuevas computadoras
3. 12:00 almorzar con el personal	6. 15:00 dar un paseo

B A few verbs have irregular stems in the future.

1. The following verbs replace the **e** or **i** of the infinitive with **d**.

tener: **tendré, tendrás, tendrá, tendremos,** tendréis, **tendrán**
poner: **pondré, pondrás, pondrá, pondremos,** pondréis, **pondrán**
salir: **saldré, saldrás, saldrá, saldremos,** saldréis, **saldrán**
venir: **vendré, vendrás, vendrá, vendremos,** vendréis, **vendrán**

2. These verbs drop the **e** of the infinitive.

poder: **podré, podrás, podrá, podremos,** podréis, **podrán**
saber: **sabré, sabrás, sabrá, sabremos,** sabréis, **sabrán**
querer: **querré, querrás, querrá, querremos,** querréis, **querrán**
haber*: **habré, habrás, habrá, habremos,** habréis, **habrán**

3. **Decir** and **hacer** have the stems **dir-** and **har-**.

diré, dirás, dirá, diremos, diréis, **dirán**
haré, harás, hará, haremos, haréis, **harán**

C Spanish also uses the future tense to express probability (to make a guess) in the present. Its English equivalents are *probably, I wonder,* and *must.*

¿Dónde estará Elvira?   Estará en clase ahora.
I wonder where Elvira is? Where can   She's probably in class now. She
  Elvira be?   *must be in class now.*

*Haber, discussed in the next lesson, is an auxiliary verb; **hay** (*there is, there are*) is derived from it. Compare: **hay, había, habré.**

PRÁCTICA

a   Haga oraciones nuevas según los modelos.

MODELOS: **Agustina hará café.**
      nosotros/té → **Haremos té.**
      ellos/chocolate → **Harán chocolate.**

1. **Ellos saldrán luego.**
   él/mañana
   yo/a las ocho y media
   ellas/el sábado
   nosotros/¿?
   tú/¿?
   ¿?

2. **Vendremos en carro.**
   ella/taxi
   Uds./autobús
   tú/avión
   yo/tren
   nosotros/¿?
   ¿?

3. **Mimi no podrá ir al campo.**
   yo/a las tiendas
   nosotros/al restaurante
   ellos/a la fiesta
   la gente/al cine
   ¿?

4. **Tendré que pagar.**
   ellos/cocinar
   nosotros/comer
   tú/salir
   ella/trabajar
   yo/¿?
   ¿?

5. **Cristóbal dirá muy poco.**
   yo/lo mismo de siempre
   el gobierno/la verdad
   nosotros/no... nada
   Uds./algo
   ¿?

b   Conteste las siguientes preguntas con el futuro de probabilidad para especular sobre *(about)* lo que pasa en el dibujo.

La finca *(The farm)*

Jacinto Carrillo vivirá en el campo, ¿no?

1. ¿Qué tiempo hará? ¿Hará frío?
2. ¿Qué estación será, el invierno o el verano?
3. ¿Qué hora será?
4. ¿Dónde vivirá Jacinto?
5. ¿Cuántos años tendrá él? ¿y su hija?
6. ¿Será casado o soltero?
7. ¿Qué cultivará Jacinto?
8. ¿La tierra (land) será fértil o árida?
9. ¿Qué animales habrá en la finca?
10. ¿Quién montará (probably rides) a caballo?
11. ¿Qué comerán los Carrillo?
12. ¿Con qué harán una ensalada?
13. ¿Qué condimento pondrán en la comida?
14. ¿Será el maíz para la familia o para los animales?
15. ¿Con qué harán tortillas?
16. ¿Qué dirá Jacinto?
17. Y finalmente, ¿querrá Ud. ser agricultor como Jacinto? ¿Por qué?

c   Traduzca las oraciones, usando el futuro de probabilidad.

MODELO: I wonder who knows the answer?
                 ¿Quién sabrá la respuesta?

1. I wonder what time it is?
2. You are (probably) hungry.
3. They (must) know the director.
4. Mauricio (probably) doesn't remember Mrs. Chávez.
5. Where can the children be?

d   Escriba el párrafo otra vez, cambiando las formas **ir a** + *infinitivo* al futuro.

MODELO: Voy a ver a tía Conchita.   **Veré a tía Conchita.**

El sábado vamos a visitar a nuestros tíos en el campo. Vamos a salir temprano por la mañana, y así vamos a pasar todo el día con ellos. Tío Pedro nos va a enseñar la finca y los animales. Mi hermana Julia va a querer montar a caballo. Probablemente tía Conchita va a hacer un delicioso arroz con pollo. Después de almorzar vamos a tomar una tacita (demitasse) de café, y vamos a hablar de la familia y los amigos. Seguro que nos vamos a divertir mucho en el campo.

e   Diga ocho cosas que usted hará este fin de semana. Incluya palabras como **primero, después, luego, más tarde, por la tarde, por la noche,** etc.

II *El condicional*

A The conditional expresses what *would* happen. It is formed by taking the entire infinitive (like the future) and adding one set of endings to all verbs: **-ía, -ías, -ía, -íamos, -íais, -ían.**

pagar	tener	decir
pagaría (I would pay)	tendría (I would have)	diría (I'd say)
pagarías	tendrías	dirías
pagaría	tendría	diría
pagaríamos	tendríamos	diríamos
pagaríais	tendríais	diríais
pagarían	tendrían	dirían

Iríamos más tarde.   ¡Yo no sabría qué hacer!
We would go later.   *I wouldn't know what to do!*

B The conditional is used to express:

1. A request or wish more politely.

Me **gustaría** una mesa cerca de la   **¿Podrían** Uds. regresar más tarde?
  ventana.   *Could you return later?*
I'd like a table near the window.

2. A future action or situation in relation to the past.

Los Ponte dijeron que **estarían** en casa.
The Pontes said (that) they would be home.

3. Probability in the past. Remember that English uses expressions such as *probably, I wonder,* and *must* to indicate probability.

Tendrías razón.   ¿Quién haría eso?
You were probably right. (You must   *I wonder who did that?*
  have been right.)

Do not confuse the conditional with the imperfect: when *would* means *used to* (habitual past action), the imperfect, *not* the conditional, is used.

De niños **leíamos** los cuentos de vaqueros... pero hoy no los **leeríamos**
  con tanto gusto.
As children we would (used to) read cowboy stories . . . but today we
  wouldn't read them with such pleasure.

PRÁCTICA

a Usted quiere expresar sus deseos de una manera más cortés *(polite).*
Cambie las siguientes oraciones del presente al condicional.

MODELO: ¿Puedes ayudarme? **¿Podrías ayudarme?**

1. ¿Pueden Uds. cambiarme el cheque?
2. ¿Tiene Ud. la hora?
3. Me gusta el café más tarde.
4. Prefiero hablar con los padres.
5. ¿Nos permite Ud. entrar?

b Su amiga no está segura de lo que hacían varias personas. Hagan y
contesten preguntas que indiquen probabilidad en el pasado.

MODELO: qué / tomar Sofía
Su amiga: **¿Qué tomaría Sofía?**
Usted: **Tomaría un espumante, un refresco,** etc.

1. qué / comer Marcelo
2. adónde / ir los Ponte
3. dónde / estar el profesor
4. a qué hora / llegar los estudiantes
5. dónde / poner tú el carro
6. cuánto / pagar Ud. por ese reloj
7. qué / ¿?
8. cuándo / ¿?
9. ¿?

c ¿Cómo se dice?

1. I wouldn't go out now.
2. Could you see me today?
3. I wonder who brought the bottle of red wine.
4. They were probably very thirsty.
5. Pepe Luis said (that) he would pick up the children at the movies.

III *Los pronombres de complemento directo*

A A direct object receives the action of a verb and serves to answer the
question *What?* or *Whom?* in relation to that verb.

Mariano drinks *coffee.* (direct object noun)
What does he drink?

Juanita helped *him.* (direct object pronoun)
Whom did Juanita help?

B A direct object pronoun *replaces* a direct object noun. Spanish direct object pronouns are the same as the reflexive pronouns except for the third person singular and plural.

¿**Me** entiendes?	*Do you understand me?*
Sí, **te** entiendo perfectamente.	*Yes, I understand you perfectly.*

¿Conoce Ud. a Natalia Duque?	
No, no **la** conozco.	*No, I don't know her.*

¿Trajeron Uds. los discos?	
Sí, **los** trajimos.	*Yes, we brought them.*

DIRECT OBJECT PRONOUNS

me	*me*	nos	*us*
te	*you*	os	*you*
lo*	*him, it, you* (Ud.)	los*	*them, you* (Uds.)
la	*her, it, you* (Ud.)	las	*them, you* (Uds.)

*In Spain **le, les** may replace **lo, los** for male persons.

C Object pronouns immediately precede conjugated verbs and negative commands.

¿**La** cartera? **La** compré en Buenos Aires.
The wallet? I bought it in Buenos Aires.

Por favor, ¡no **me** moleste más!
Please, don't bother me anymore!

They may also be attached to the end of infinitives.

Los voy a invitar. (Voy a invitar**los**.)
I'm going to invite them.

In affirmative commands all object pronouns (reflexive, direct, and indirect) must be attached to the verb.

¡Siénten**se** Uds.!	¡Espére**me**!	¡Pregúnte**le**!
Sit down!	*Wait for me!*	*Ask him!*

PRÁCTICA

a Usted quiere saber si su amigo(a) escribió varias cosas. Refiérase a las palabras indicadas para hacer las preguntas.

MODELO: (la carta)   Usted: **¿Escribiste la carta?**
Su amigo(a): **Sí, la escribí.**
No, no la escribí.

la fecha, el número, la dirección, las palabras, los nombres, el teléfono, ¿?

b Pregúntele a su amigo(a) si quiere ver a las siguientes personas o cosas.

> MODELO: (a Jorge Luis) Usted: **¿Quieres ver a Jorge Luis?**
> Su amigo(a): **Sí, quiero verlo.**
> **No, no quiero verlo.**

a María Teresa, al Sr. Lima, el programa de televisión, las fotos, la revista, a Clementina y Violeta, a los Pérez, ¿?

c Usted prepara una cena. Su compañero(a) quiere ayudarlo(la), pero Ud. está un poco indeciso(a) porque primero le contesta con mandatos afirmativos y luego con mandatos negativos.

> MODELOS: Compañero(a): **¿Sirvo los refrescos?**
> Usted: **Sí, sírvalos.**
> **No, no los sirva.**
> Compañero(a): **¿Me siento en esta silla?**
> Usted: **Sí, siéntese en esa silla.**
> **No, no se siente en esa silla.**

Compañero(a):

¿Sirvo el coctel?	¿Me preocupo por el postre?
¿Traigo la sopa?	¿Lavo las frutas?
¿Preparo las ensaladas?	¿Hago el café?
¿Cocino el pollo?	¿?
¿Me siento a la mesa?	

IV *Los pronombres con preposiciones*

The prepositional phrases **a mí** *(me),* **a ti** *(you),* **a él** *(him),* and so forth, can be added to a sentence for emphasis or clarification. These prepositional pronouns are the same as the subject pronouns, except for **a mí** and **a ti**.

¿Me ayudarías a mí?
Would you help me?

¿Nos vas a esperar a nosotros?
Are you going to wait for us?

Sí, te ayudaría **a ti** pero no a él.
Yes, I'd help you but not him.

No, no los voy a esperar **a Uds.**
No, I'm not going to wait for you.

Other common prepositions besides **a** include:

de *of, from, about*   **para** *(intended) for*
en *on, at*   **por** *for (the sake of), by*

(para)	**mí**	(for)	me	(para)	**nosotros (as)**	(for)	us
	ti		you		**vosotros (as)**		you
	él, ella		him, her		**ellos, ellas**		them
	Ud.		you		**Uds.**		you

The preposition **con** + **mí** or **ti** becomes **conmigo** and **contigo**, respectively.

¿Almuerzas conmigo?   **¡Claro que almuerzo contigo!**
Are you having lunch with me? *Of course I'm having lunch with you!*

PRÁCTICA

a Hágale a su amigo(a) una serie de preguntas con los siguientes verbos. Para énfasis, incluya la frase **a mí** en las preguntas.

MODELO: Usted: **¿Me entiendes a mí?**
         Su amigo(a):   **Sí, te entiendo.**
                        No, no te entiendo.

entender, ayudar, necesitar, buscar, esperar, llevar, escuchar, creer, ver, invitar

b Repitan la práctica anterior, pero esta vez permita que su amigo(a) haga las preguntas. Cambien a la forma formal e incluyan la frase **a Ud.** en las respuestas.

MODELO: Su amigo(a):   **¿Me entiende Ud.?**
         Usted: **Sí, lo (la) entiendo a Ud.**

c Ahora hágale estas preguntas a otro(a) estudiante.

1. ¿Estudias conmigo?
2. ¿Piensas en mí?
3. ¿Traes un regalo para mí?
4. ¿Me conoces bien a mí?
5. ¿Hablabas de mí?
6. ¿Vas a cenar con nosotros?
7. ¿Preguntaste por ellos?
8. ¿Alejandro se casa contigo?
9. ¿Nos esperas un minuto? ¿Dónde nos esperas?
10. ¿Nos llamarás por teléfono? ¿Cuándo nos llamarás?

d Traduzca las palabras en inglés.

1. Los Ponte van de compras con *(her, him, us, me, you [fam.])*.
2. La invitación es para *(them [m.], them [f.], me, him, you [formal])*.

OBSERVACIONES

Al leer las Observaciones trate de recordar el horario de las comidas y los diferentes platos populares.

Las comidas

La variedad de comidas en Hispanoamérica y España es increíble. Estas comidas se sirven a diferentes horas del día, pero en general son el desayuno, el almuerzo y la cena.

El desayuno es generalmente ligero:° café con leche caliente[1] o chocolate y pan con mantequilla y mermeladas. La comida principal usualmente no se sirve hasta las dos de la tarde y por eso° hay quien° come o toma algo más o menos a las once. En muchos pueblos — ya no tanto° en las capitales — las escuelas y los comercios cierran dos o tres horas por la tarde para que° la gente regrese a casa a comer con calma. Aunque° la variedad de platos es interminable en esta comida la gente toma sopa y después come arroz, carne,° frijoles, legumbres y ensalada.

light (weight)

for that reason / there are those who
not so much

so that / Although

meat

Los platos de España y de Hispanoamérica se diferencian más de la comida norteamericana en el sabor° que en las comida misma.° Los hispanos usan el ajo,° la cebolla,° la pimienta, el aceite de oliva° y otros condimentos como el comino,° el laurel y el azafrán° para darle más sabor a sus comidas. El chile y la comida picante° son, en general, más comunes en México y Guatemala. Entre los platos más populares por todo el mundo hispano se podrían nombrar la paella (España), la parrillada (Argentina y Uruguay), el arroz con pollo (Caribe), el lomo saltado[2] (Perú) y el pescado que se prepara de mil maneras por todas partes.

flavor / itself
garlic / onion / olive oil
cumin / saffron
spicy

La última comida del día es por lo general una cena ligera que no se sirve hasta las nueve o las diez de la noche. Antes de la cena — entre las cinco y las siete de la tarde — muchas familias sirven una merienda° de frutas, galletas,° queso, etc., para entretener° el estómago hasta la hora de cenar.

snack
crackers / entertain

El café (después de comer) y el vino son parte de las buenas comidas. Los postres son riquísimos,° aunque mucha gente prefiere un postre de frutas y queso. El flan, el pudín y los helados son también muy preferidos por los hispanos.

very delicious

¿Qué pensarán los hispanos de nuestros desayunos fuertes, almuerzos ligeros a las doce del día y comidas completas a las seis o siete de la tarde? Según ellos su horario satisface el apetito gradualmente, pero con el horario norteamericano hay que° esperar mucho tiempo entre comidas.

one must

1. Caliente = *hot (to the touch)*: **La sopa está caliente.** But when referring to weather or temperature, you say **Hace calor**. **2. Lomo saltado** is seasoned sirloin steak served over rice.

¿COMPRENDE UD.?

a Vocabulario. Complete las oraciones con la palabra más adecuada a la derecha.

1. Las tres comidas son el desayuno, el almuerzo y _____ .   un postre
2. El ajo y _____ son condimentos.   picante
3. Ponemos mermelada o _____ en el pan.   mantequilla
4. El flan es _____ riquísimo.   la cena
5. Una comida con muchos condimentos puede estar   el azafrán
   _____ .

b Comprensión. Complete cada oración con la mejor respuesta.

1. El desayuno de los hispanos es generalmente
   a. fuerte
   b. ligero
   c. abundante
2. Usualmente la comida principal en España e Hispanoamérica se
   sirve a
   a. las seis de la tarde
   b. las once y media de la mañana
   c. las dos de la tarde
3. Para cocinar los hispanos prefieren
   a. el aceite de oliva
   b. los productos como Crisco
   c. el queso blanco
4. La paella es un plato delicioso de
   a. Cuba
   b. el Perú
   c. España
5. La comida picante es más común en
   a. la República Dominicana
   b. México y Guatemala
   c. la Argentina y el Uruguay

Actividades

Ponemos la mesa (We set the table)

Apréndase el vocabulario a continuación. Refiérase al dibujo (*drawing*)
en la página 197.

Vocabulario

1. la pimienta	4. la copa	7. el plato	10. la cucharita
2. la sal	5. el pan	8. la servilleta	11. la cuchara
3. el vaso	6. el tenedor	9. el cuchillo	12. la taza y el platillo*

*The cup and saucer are not on the table (p. 197) because coffee is an after-dinner drink.

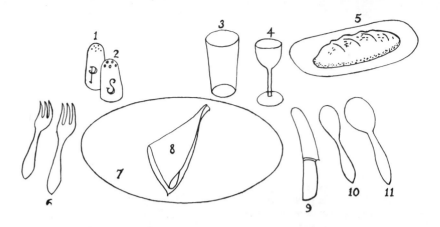

SITUACIONES

a   Usted le explica a otra persona cómo poner la mesa.

Ponga...

1. _____ inmediatamente a la derecha del plato.
2. _____ a la derecha de la cucharita.
3. _____ delante del *(in front of)* plato, cerca a la derecha.
4. _____ a la izquierda de la copa.
5. _____ a la derecha del vaso y la copa.
6. _____ y la pimienta delante del plato, a la izquierda.
7. Los dos _____ a la izquierda del plato.
8. _____ en el plato.

b   Usted va a preparar una cena especial para seis o siete buenos amigos. Prepare una lista de los comestibles *(groceries)* que tendrá que comprar. Indique cuánto comprará en kilos, libras, docenas, etc.

c   Unos amigos de Ud. piensan ir a México en el verano. ¿Qué comidas les recomendará Ud. a ellos? ¿Qué les dirá de las horas de comer?

Vocabulario

SUSTANTIVOS

LAS CARNES
el **biftec** *beefsteak*
el **cerdo** *pork*
el **pollo** *chicken*

LOS POSTRES
el **flan** *custard*
el **helado** *ice cream*
la **torta** *cake*

LAS BEBIDAS
el **agua** *water*
la **cerveza** *beer*
el **jugo (de naranja)** *(orange) juice*
la **leche** *milk*
el **té** *tea*
el **vino tinto (blanco)** *red (white) wine*

LOS UTENSILIOS
la **copa** *wine glass*
la **cuchara** *tablespoon*
la **cucharita** *teaspoon*
el **cuchillo** *knife*
el **plato** *dish*
la **taza** *cup*
el **tenedor** *fork*
la **servilleta** *napkin*
el **vaso** *(drinking) glass*

OTROS SUSTANTIVOS
el **aceite** *oil*
el **ajo** *garlic*
la **botella** *bottle*
el **camarero, la camarera** *waiter, waitress*
la **cebolla** *onion*
la **ensalada** *salad*
la **finca** *farm*
el **huevo** *egg*
la **mantequilla** *butter*
el **pescado** *fish*
la **pimienta** *pepper*
la **sal** *salt*

ADJETIVOS
asado(a) *roasted*
   bien asado *well done*
   medio asado *medium done*
crudo(a) *rare*
frito(a) *fried*
picante *spicy*

VERBOS
cenar *to dine*
cansarse *to get tired*
imaginarse (que) *to imagine (that)*

Lección 11 — *Por teléfono*

Ted Morales, agente de compras° de una compañía en Dallas, llama a la
compañía de tejidos° *El Inca* en Lima para saber por qué no ha llegado un
pedido° de artículos de lana que necesita con urgencia. El gerente de ven-
tas° de *El Inca*, Celso Vega, trata de° explicarle la razón° de la demora.

purchasing agent

textile

order

sales manager / tries to / reason

TED MORALES ¿Con el señor Vega?

CELSO VEGA A sus órdenes.

TED MORALES Sr. Vega, lo he llamado para saber si Ud. ya me ha enviado
los tejidos que le pedí a principios de° mes.

at the beginning

CELSO VEGA Sí, señor Morales. Su pedido ya salió de Cuzco por tren. Tan
pronto° llegue a Lima se lo enviaremos° en el primer barco° que salga para
allá.

As soon as / we'll send it to you / ship

TED MORALES Bien, pero prefiero que me lo envíen[1] por avión.°

by plane

CELSO VEGA Recuerde que costará más mandárselo° de esa manera.

to send it to you

TED MORALES Sí, pero así° la mercancía° vendrá directamente a Dallas.

that way / merchandise

CELSO VEGA De acuerdo.° Estoy seguro que por vía aérea° recibirá su pedido en menos de ocho días.[2]

Agreed / via airmail

TED MORALES Muy bien. Muy agradecido.

CELSO VEGA Igualmente, señor Morales. Es un placer° servirle.

pleasure

1. The forms of **enviar** *(to send)* have a written accent mark on the **i** in the present indicative and subjunctive; the **nosotros** forms do not: **envío, envías, envía, enviamos, envían,
¡Envíe Ud.!** **2.** En español decimos **ocho días** para referirnos a un período de una semana y **quince días** para dos semanas.

¿RECUERDA UD.?

1. ¿Cuál es el oficio de Ted Morales?
2. ¿En qué ciudad está él?
3. ¿Dónde está la compañía *El Inca*?
4. ¿Qué necesita Ted?
5. ¿A quién llama Ted por teléfono?
6. ¿Cuándo pidió Ted los tejidos?
7. ¿Prefiere Ted que Celso envíe la mercancía por barco o por avión?
8. ¿Cuándo recibirá Ted el pedido?
9. ¿Estará contento Ted con la explicación de Celso?
10. ¿El tono *(tone)* de la conversación es cordial u hostil? ¿agradable *(agreeable)* o desagradable? Refiérase Ud. a palabras específicas en el diálogo para apoyar *(support)* su respuesta.

SITUACIONES

1   Imagínese que Ud. es Camila Acosta y desea hablar por teléfono con Irma Solís. Usted llama y la mamá de Irma contesta. Ponga las siguientes expresiones en orden para crear *(create)* una conversación apropiada.

CAMILA

a. Entonces, por favor dígale que llame a Camila Acosta al 35-07-86, después de las tres de la tarde.
b. Con Irma Solís, por favor.
c. Gracias. Hasta luego.

LA MAMÁ DE IRMA

d. ¿Aló?*
e. Con mucho gusto.
f. Lo siento. Irma no está aquí en este momento.

2   Usted está en México y quiere llamar a los Estados Unidos. Ud. habla con la operadora. Ponga estas expresiones en orden.

USTED

a. Llamaré más tarde. Gracias.
b. Sí. Con Steve McDaniel, a pagar allá.†
c. Deseo llamar a St. Louis, Missouri.
d. 846-3215

LA OPERADORA

e. ¿Cuál es el número?
f. Bueno
g. ¿De persona a persona?
h. Lo siento. La línea está ocupada.
i. Para servirle.

3   Usted y otro(a) estudiante preparan una conversación original, basada en este problema: Ud. es gerente de ventas para Computadoras ABC en los Estados Unidos. Un cliente de Hispanoamérica llama por teléfono y se queja de *(complains)* que no ha recibido su pedido de *software* (artículos intangibles). Hable con él y explíquele la demora. Dígale cómo y cuándo Ud. enviará el pedido.

---

*Los saludos típicos por teléfono son: **Aló, Hola, Diga, Oigo, Bueno.**
†Es más barato llamar **a pagar allá** *(collect)* de México a los Estados Unidos.

Estructura

I Pronombres de complemento indirecto

A The indirect object answers the questions To whom? or For whom?.

Celso sends the order *to them*.   Celso sends *them* the order.
We're buying lunch *for the children*.   We're buying *the children* lunch.

In English the preposition is often omitted.

B Spanish indirect object pronouns are the same as the reflexive and direct object pronouns with the exception of the third person singular and plural. These become **le** and **les**, respectively, and do not indicate gender.

me *(to, for)*	*me*	**nos** *(to, for)*	*us*
te	*you*	**os**	*you*
le	*him, her, you, it*	**les**	*them, you*

C Indirect object pronouns follow the same word order in a sentence as the other object pronouns. The prepositional phrases **a mí, a ti, a él, a Diego**, etc., may be added for emphasis or clarification. Although redundant, this construction is perfectly natural in Spanish.

Yo no **les** di nada **a ellos**.
I didn't give them anything.

Le enviamos el cheque **a Gloria**.
We sent the check to Gloria.

Queremos comprar**te** algo. / **Te** queremos comprar algo.
We want to buy you something. (We want to buy something for you.)

¡Pregúnt**ele** **a ella**! ¡No **le** pregunte **a él**!
Ask her! Don't ask him!

PRÁCTICA
a Cambie los pronombres según la información entre paréntesis.

MODELO: Le di el dinero a él. (a ti)   **Te di el dinero a ti.**

1. Les di el dinero a ellos. (a ella, a Ud., a sus padres, a Sofía, a ti, a los niños, ¿?)
2. Ellos te van a servir la comida a ti. (a mí, a él, a nosotros, a los jóvenes, a Uds., a ti, ¿?)

b Refiérase a los dibujos para contestar las preguntas. (Regalar *means to give, as a gift.*)

Es el día de las madres.

Julia   Mamá   Hugo

1. unos dulces   2. una planta
(candies)

Es el aniversario de los Ramírez.

Flora   los Ramírez   Marco y Lila

1. una maleta   2. un radio

1. ¿Qué le regala Julia a su mamá?
2. ¿Le regala Julia una planta a ella?
3. ¿Qué le regala Hugo a su mamá?

1. ¿Qué les regala Flora a los Ramírez?
2. ¿Les regala Flora un televisor a ellos?
3. ¿Qué les regalan Marco y Lila?

c Situación. Usted y un amigo están en un restaurante. Ud. está perezoso(a) *(lazy)* hoy, y le pide varias cosas a él.

MODELO: ¿Me das el vaso?   **Sí, te doy el vaso.**
                                   No, no te doy el vaso.

1. ¿Me das el cuchillo?
2. ¿Me traes las cucharas?
3. ¿Me pasas la sal?
4. ¿Me sirves el vino?
5. ¿Me das la servilleta?

6. ¿Me pasas los platos?
7. ¿Me explicas el menú?
8. ¿Me pagas la cuenta?
9. ¿?

d Repitan la práctica c, usando el sujeto Ud.

MODELO: **¿Me da Ud. el vaso?**
            Sí, le doy el vaso.

e Haga un mínimo de doce oraciones, usando una palabra de cada columna. Las columnas 1 y 4 tienen que concordar *(agree).*

MODELO: (1)   (2)   (3)   (4)
          Abuela *le* preparaba unos sándwiches *a Hugo.*

1	2	3	4
Abuela	me	sirve	la sopa	a mí
	te	trae	la ensalada	a ti
	nos	preparaba	el biftec	a nosotros(as)
	le	hizo	el arroz con pollo	a él, a ella, a Ud., a Hugo
	les	cocinará	las enchiladas	a ellos, a ellas, a Uds.
		va a dar	el pescado	a los Vega, a los Lara
		lleva	los frijoles	
			unos sándwiches	

f   **Preguntas.** Escoja la mejor respuesta.

1. ¿A quién le escribes?
   a. Luis me escribe.
   b. Le escribo a Marco.
   c. Carmela le escribe a su amigo.
2. ¿Quién te pidió más dinero?
   a. Lola te pidió más.
   b. Julián le pidió más.
   c. Nora me pidió más.
3. ¿Qué les trajo Bárbara a Uds. de Sudamérica?
   a. Nos trajo unos cuchillos finos.
   b. Te trajo unas servilletas bonitas.
   c. Les trajo unos platos de madera.
4. ¿Cuándo puede Ud. enviarnos el cheque?
   a. Puede enviarle el cheque en ocho días.
   b. Pueden enviarnos el cheque la semana que viene.
   c. Puedo enviarles el cheque en quince días.
5. ¿A quién le dio Ud. los papeles?
   a. La señora me dio los papeles.
   b. Le di los papeles al señor.
   c. Los estudiantes me dieron los papeles a mí.

g   Estudie las siguientes listas de verbos y después escriba diez oraciones originales con pronombres indirectos. Debe incluir estas variaciones:

1. mandatos positivos y negativos
2. un verbo solo: ¿Me preguntas a mí? / No nos dijeron nada.
3. dos verbos: Trataremos de enviarle el pedido pronto. / Tengo que darte la dirección.

The following types of verbs often take an indirect object pronoun:

VERBS OF COMMUNICATION

preguntar	explicar
contestar	mencionar
decir	escribir

VERBS OF EXCHANGE

enviar
mandar
dar
traer
pedir
regalar
prestar *(to lend)*
devolver (ou) *(to return something, to give back)*

II *La combinación de dos complementos*

A   In Spanish, when indirect and direct object pronouns occur together, the indirect object pronoun precedes the direct.

Te las traeré mañana. (**te**:   *I'll bring them to you tomorrow.*
  indirect; **las**: *direct*)   (*them*: direct; *to you*: indirect)
No pueden reparár**melo**. (**me**:   *They can't repair it for me.* (*it*:
  indirect; **lo**: *direct*)   direct; *for me*: indirect)

A written accent mark is added if the attachment of the pronouns changes the original stress of the verb.

¡Escríbale a ella!   ¿Puedes prestármelas?
Write to her!   *Can you lend them to me?*

B   When both the indirect and direct object pronouns are in the third person, the indirect object pronouns **le** and **les** change to **se**. The prepositional phrases **a ella, al señor, a ellos,** and so on, may be added for clarity or emphasis.

INDIRECT		DIRECT
se	+	**lo, la**
		los, las

¿**Le** diste **las llaves** a ella?   — No, no **se las** di a ella.
¿Puedes explicar**les** **el problema**?   — Sí, puedo explicár**selo**.

OJO: ¿Cuál es el **se** reflexivo, el **se** impersonal y el **se** del pronombre indirecto?

a. ¿El periódico? Yo **se** lo di a ella.
b. Ellos **se** levantan temprano.
c. **Se** trabaja mucho aquí.

PRÁCTICA
a   Sustituya según los modelos.

MODELO: Me pidieron el pasaporte.   **Me lo pidieron.**

1. a. Me contestaron la carta.   *c.* Nos regalaron los discos.
   b. Te enviaré la invitación.   *d.* No me diste la dirección.

MODELO: Quiero enseñarte los regalos.   **Quiero enseñártelos.**

2. a. Quiero enseñarte la casa.   *c.* ¿Vas a traerme las cassettes? (*or* los casetes)
   b. Deben darnos el descuento, ¿no?   *d.* Prefiero regalarte la camisa.

MODELO: Déle el dinero a ella. **Déselo.**

3. *a.* Déle el cheque a él.
   b. Pídale las reservas a ellas.
   c. Enséñeles la habitación a ellos.
   d. Devuélvales las maletas a los señores.

MODELO: No le preste el carro a él. **No se lo preste.**

4. *a.* No le preste la cámara a él.
   b. No le devuelva los papeles a Flora.
   c. No les pague la cuenta a ellos.
   d. No les dé los dulces a los niños.

b En pares. Ud. le hace preguntas a su compañero(a) en el pretérito. Él (Ella) le contesta, usando los pronombres se + lo (los), la (las).

MODELO: dar / las gracias Ud.: **¿A quién le* diste las gracias?**
             Su compañero(a): **Se las di a la profesora.**

1. dar / la cuenta
2. servir / el postre
3. pedir / el coctel
4. explicar / el menú
5. traer / la ensalada
6. cambiar / la orden
7. devolver / las botellas
8. enseñar / los platos
9. pagar / el almuerzo
10. regalar / los dulces

c Repitan la práctica *b*, usando los verbos en el futuro. (Repasen el futuro, Lección 10.)

MODELO: **¿A quién le darás las gracias?**
          Se las daré a...

d Use el dibujo para contestar las preguntas.

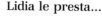

Lidia le presta...

1. ¿Qué le presta Lidia a Hernán
   — la cinta o las tijeras?
2. ¿Le presta Lidia la cinta a Tomás?
3. ¿Se la presta a Hernán?
4. ¿Te la presta a ti?
5. ¿Se la presta a Uds.?
6. ¿A quién le presta Lidia las tijeras?
7. ¿Se las presta a Hernán?
8. ¿Le presta Hernán las tijeras a Tomás? Y finalmente...
9. ¿Qué le presta Ud. a su amigo(a)?
10. ¿Qué me presta Ud. a mí? (*me = su profesor, -a*)

1. *la cinta de celofán*
2. *las tijeras*

e Refiérase al dibujo de la práctica *d* y haga ocho preguntas similares. Use los verbos **traer, devolver, dar** y los sustantivos **la revista, el diccionario, el dinero,** etc.

*When **A quién(es)** refers to an indirect object, **le (les)** follows it.

III *Los tiempos compuestos*   (*Compound or Perfect Tenses*)

The compound or perfect tenses (I *have called*, he *has eaten*, and so on)
in Spanish consist of the verb forms of **haber** plus the past participle.
This participle is formed by changing the infinitive endings **-ar** to **-ado**;
-er and **-ir** to **-ido**.

llamar → **llamado**   perder → **perdido**   ir → **ido**

When used in the perfect tenses, the past participle always ends in **-o**.

A   El presente perfecto (*The present perfect*) The present perfect tense
describes what *has* or *has not* happened. It implies that a recent past action still has bearing on the present.

¿Has llamado al Sr. Vega hoy?   Julieta ya **ha comido.**
Have you called Mr. Vega today?   *Julieta has already eaten.*

No, todavía no lo **he llamado.**
No, I still haven't called him.

Note above that Spanish verbs in the perfect tenses comprise a unit that
cannot be separated by other words such as pronouns, negative words,
and adverbs. The endings of **haber** are similar to those of the simple future; with the exception of the **vosotros** form, the accent marks are omitted: **-e, -as, -a, -emos, -éis, -an**

---

haber + participio pasado

he llamado (*I have called*)	**hemos** llamado
has llamado	**habéis** llamado
ha llamado	**han** llamado

The present perfect subjunctive is formed by the present
subjunctive of **haber** (**haya, hayas, haya, hayamos, hayáis,
hayan**) plus the past participle. It is used in place of the
present perfect indicative after expressions of emotion or
others that require the subjunctive; for example, **Siento que
hayas perdido el boleto.** (*I'm sorry you've lost the ticket.*)

PRÁCTICA
a   Diga adónde han ido las siguientes personas esta semana.

MODELO: Celso / el banco   **Celso ha ido al banco.**

1. la Sra. Lima / el teatro
2. tú / las tiendas
3. yo / el gimnasio
4. Uds. / la biblioteca
5. Aurora y yo / el concierto
6. los Salgado / la casa de sus hijos
7. ¿?
8. ¿?

b   Mencione lo que ha enviado cada persona por correo.

MODELO: Linda / paquete *(package)*   **Linda ha enviado un paquete.**

1. Ud. / una invitación
2. nosotros / un cheque
3. tú / unas tarjetas
4. la compañía / un anuncio
5. yo / unas revistas
6. ¿?

c   Usted quiere iniciar una conversación con otro(a) estudiante. Pregúntele si ha hecho *(done)* las siguientes cosas recientemente.

MODELO: jugar al tenis   **¿Has jugado al tenis recientemente?**
                           Sí, he jugado al tenis.
                           No, no he jugado...

1. visitar a la familia
2. comprar ropa nueva
3. comer en un buen restaurante
4. mudarse de casa
5. divertirse mucho
6. estar en Sudamérica
7. cambiar de trabajo
8. recibir cartas de los amigos
9. *leer un libro interesante
10. *oír un chiste
11. ¿?
12. ¿?

B   **Participios irregulares** A few verbs have irregular past participles:

ver: **visto** *(seen)*
escribir: **escrito** *(written)*
abrir: **abierto** *(opened)*
romper: **roto** *(broken)*
poner: **puesto** *(put, placed)*
hacer: **hecho** *(done, made)*
decir: **dicho** *(told, said)*

PRÁCTICA

a   Situación. Su amigo(a) es gerente de una oficina y usted es su empleado(a). Él (Ella) le hace las siguientes preguntas que Ud. debe contestar con la frase negativa No, todavía no... y los verbos en el presente perfecto. Según el contexto use Ud. los pronombres directos lo (los), la (las) e indirectos le (les).

MODELO: Amigo(a):   ¿Puso Ud. los papeles en orden?
          Usted: **No, todavía no los he puesto en orden.**

1. ¿Abrió Ud. la correspondencia?
2. ¿Les escribió Ud. a los clientes?
3. ¿Hizo las fotocopias?
4. ¿Vio Ud. a la representante de Latinoamérica?
5. ¿Le mandó Ud. los pedidos al Sr. Morales?
6. ¿Le dijo Ud. el precio a él?
7. ¿Puso el dinero en el banco?
8. ¿?

*The past participles of these verbs require an accent mark: **leído, oído.**

b ¿Qué hemos hecho? Diga tres cosas que cada una de estas personas ha hecho recientemente.

1. En la clase nosotros _____ , _____ , _____ .
2. En casa mi hermano(a) _____ , _____ , _____ .
3. En el trabajo yo _____ , _____ , _____ .

C   Los otros tiempos compuestos

The *past perfect* tense expresses what *had* happened prior to another past action. This tense is formed by the imperfect of **haber** (**había, habías, ...**) plus the past participle.

había leído	*I had read*
habías dicho	*you had said*
no había salido	*he hadn't gone out*
nos habíamos levantado	*we had gotten up*
habíais roto	*you had broken*
se habían preocupado	*they had worried*

PRÁCTICA

a   Diga lo que habían hecho estas personas antes de ocurrir los otros eventos.

MODELO: (nosotros) / ir a Wáshington / antes del verano pasado
   Habíamos ido a Wáshington antes del verano pasado.

1. ellos / visitar la capital / antes del otoño pasado
2. (tú) / estar en Europa / antes del año pasado, ¿no?
3. Flora / conocer a los Ortiz / antes que yo
4. (nosotros) / no acostarse / antes de las doce
5. (yo) / graduarse de la secundaria / antes que ellos
6. mis padres / ¿? / antes...

b   Díganos en cinco o seis oraciones a quién había visto Ud. ayer antes de llegar a casa, qué había oído Ud. y qué había estudiado (leído, escrito, etc.).

The *future* and *conditional perfect* tenses are formed with the future and conditional forms of **haber**, respectively, plus the past participle.

Habré comido.   *I will have eaten.*
Ellos se habrían cansado.   *They would have gotten tired.*

Los transportes

1. el avión
2. el tren
   el ferrocarril (railroad)
3. el barco
4. el autobús
5. el boleto*

6. el metro (subway)
7. el camión
8. el carro, el coche
9. el puente
10. la carretera (highway); el camino (road)

PRÁCTICA

a   Refiérase a los dibujos y diga la palabra que corresponde a estos números: 1, 3, 4, 7, 9, 10.

b   Escoja la palabra que *no* pertenece (belongs) en cada grupo.

1. aire: avión, helicóptero, coche
2. carretera: camión, tren, autobús
3. agua: barco, canoa, metro
4. conductor: ferrocarril, chófer, piloto
5. cine: película, multa, entrada

ADIVINANZA

¿En qué se parece (resemble) el tren a la manzana?

En que no es pera.

---

*La palabra para *ticket* es muy precisa en español. Fíjese en las traducciones: el **boleto** o el **billete**: *plane, train, boat ticket*; la **entrada**: *theater, movie ticket*; la **multa**: *traffic ticket, fine*.

OBSERVACIONES

Antes de leer las Observaciones estudie el mapa de Sudamérica. Piense en el efecto que la geografía ha tenido en el desarrollo (development) *de los modos de transporte. Note también lo siguiente:*

1. la ubicación *(location)* de las ciudades principales
2. las distancias que separan a esas ciudades
3. el flujo *(flow)* de los ríos; oeste a este; norte a sur y vice versa
4. la extensión de las montañas
5. los países con más / menos obstáculos geográficos
6. los países con costa al mar Caribe y a los océanos Pacífico y Atlántico

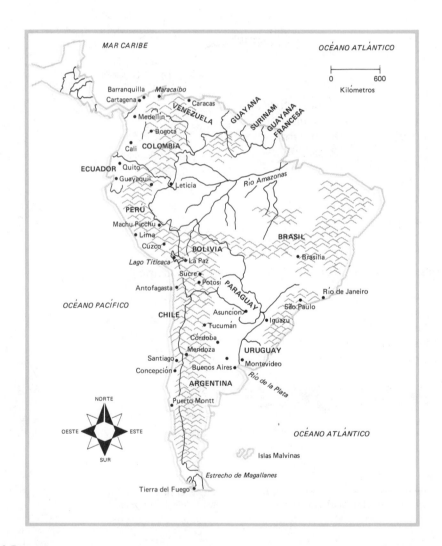

Los transportes

Hoy día Hispanoamérica cuenta con° un buen sistema de transporte. Sin embargo, la falta° de capital, los obstáculos geográficos y los fenómenos naturales como los terremotos° y las lluvias° han limitado su pleno° desarrollo.

counts on
lack
earthquakes / rains / full

España y México han desarrollado un extenso sistema de ferrocarriles, y su servicio varía de mediocre a excelente. Sudamérica, al contrario, tiene pocos ferrocarriles, particularmente en las regiones de los Andes, donde se hallan° las montañas más altas de las Américas.* Como proeza° de la ingeniería se debe notar el tren Guayaquil-Quito, que asciende a casi 5.000 metros (16.000 pies) de altitud y pasa por° sesenta y siete túneles.

are found / prowess
through

Por otra parte, el transporte aéreo ha tenido un enorme impacto en el desarrollo de Hispanoamérica. El avión ha hecho posible la exploración de regiones remotas y ha acelerado el contacto comercial y cultural entre° los países del hemisferio. Viajes° que antes habían llevado° días a causa de las montañas o la selva,° ahora llevan sólo pocas horas.

among
Trips / had taken
jungle

Algunos° ríos sudamericanos facilitan el transporte, pero otros no, por falta de centros urbanos cercanos. Este es el caso del inmenso río Amazonas. En cambio, en el sur del continente los ríos Uruguay, Paraguay y Paraná sirven de vías marítimas y además producen energía eléctrica para las ciudades y las fábricas.

Some

La Carretera Panamericana, que algún día° unirá a todos los países del hemisferio, es una realidad en algunas regiones y apenas° un sueño° en otras. La construcción y reconstrucción de esta importante vía continúa a pesar de° las dificultades económicas y las barreras° geográficas.

some day
barely / dream
in spite of / barriers

Aunque el número de vehículos particulares° aumenta más y más, el autobús es el modo de transporte más accesible para muchos. Hay buses de lujo° con todas las comodidades modernas y buses corrientes° que son menos cómodos° pero más baratos. Además, en los grandes centros urbanos el público viaja en el metro, que es eficiente y muy económico. Algunos metros son viejos y ruidosos° mientras otros como los de Buenos Aires, Santiago de Chile y la ciudad de México son más nuevos o atractivos y tienen estaciones decoradas con cuadros° y exhibiciones. En total, el transporte — terrestre, marítimo y especialmente el aéreo — seguirá siendo° esencial para el desarrollo de Hispanoamérica.

private
deluxe / ordinary
comfortable
noisy
pictures
being

¿COMPRENDE UD.?

a Vocabulario. Combine las palabras de la columna A con los correspondientes sinónimos de la columna B.

A		B	
1. seguir _____	6. tren _____	a. nación	f. lejano
2. barrera _____	7. pasar por _____	b. ferrocarril	g. construir
3. cómodo _____	8. remoto _____	c. continuar	h. confortable
4. carro _____	9. país _____	d. unir	i. coche
5. conectar _____	10. hacer _____	e. obstáculo	j. cruzar

*La Argentina, sin embargo, cuenta con un extenso sistema de ferrocarriles.

b Refiérase a la lectura para traducir estas oraciones.

1. The trip takes only a few hours.
2. Mexico counts on an extensive railroad system.
3. The Andes are the highest mountains in the Americas.
4. Latin America has especially developed air transportation.

c Comprensión. ¿Cierto o falso?

1. Los países andinos *(Andean)* cuentan con un extenso sistema de ferrocarriles.
2. La Carretera Panamericana ya une a todo el hemisferio.
3. El río Amazonas está lejos de las ciudades grandes.
4. Para ir de Buenos Aires a Bogotá una persona viajará en tren.
5. Los autobuses en Hispanoamérica pueden ser de lujo (primera clase) o corrientes (segunda clase).

Tres de las previas oraciones son falsas. Cámbielas a oraciones ciertas.

Cuando hay muchos pasajeros *(passengers)* en el autobús o el metro, se dice que **viajan como sardinas en lata.** *(They're traveling like sardines in a can.)*

Actividades

a Imagínese que usted piensa manejar *(to drive)* a México. ¿Puede identificar el significado de estas señales *(signs)*?

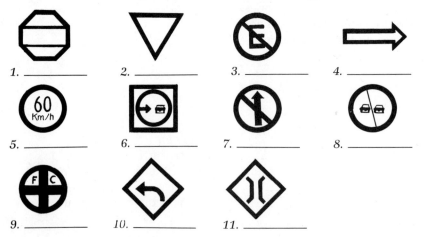

1. _____ 2. _____ 3. _____ 4. _____

5. _____ 6. _____ 7. _____ 8. _____

9. _____ 10. _____ 11. _____

Significados

a. no se estacione
b. ferrocarril, tren
c. una vía
d. máxima velocidad
e. curva
f. alto *(stop)*
g. conserve su derecha
h. no entre *(do not enter)*
i. puente angosto *(narrow bridge)*
j. no rebase *(no passing)*
k. ceda el paso *(yield)*

b **Situación.** Su carro no funciona bien y usted decide llevarlo a una gasolinera *(gas station)*. Explíquele al mecánico qué problemas tiene el carro. Después dígale lo que usted quiere que él revise o repare. Refiérase a las siguientes palabras para preparar una charla *(talk)* de diez oraciones originales.

(no)	funcionar	el motor	*(el) aire
(no)	arrancar *to start* (engine)	la transmisión	*(el) aceite
(no)	servir	la batería	*(el) agua
	revisar	los frenos *brakes*	*(la) gasolina
	reparar	el radiador	
	cambiar	el tanque	
	poner	las luces	
	limpiar	las llantas *tires*	

*Omit the definite article when referring to a portion of (some) liquid or mass. Compare:
¡Ponga el aceite! *Put the oil in!* and **¡Ponga aceite!** *Put (some) oil in!*

Vocabulario

SUSTANTIVOS
el, la **agente de compras** *purchasing agent*
el, la **agente de ventas** *sales agent*
el **avión** *airplane*
el **barco** *ship*
el **camino** *road, way*
la **carretera** *highway*
la **comodidad** *comfort*
los **dulces** *candies*
los **frenos** *brakes*
la **lana** *wool*
las **llantas** *tires*
la **mercancía** *merchandise*
el **paquete** *package*
el **pedido** *order*
el **placer** *pleasure*
el **puente** *bridge*
la **razón** *reason*
las **tijeras** *scissors*
el **viaje** *trip*

ADJETIVOS
cómodo(a) *comfortable*
estrecho(a) *narrow, tight*
ruidoso(a) *noisy*

VERBOS
contar (ue) con *to count on*
desarrollar *to develop*
devolver (ue) *to return something, give back*
enviar *to ship, send*
estacionar *to park*
mandar *to send*
manejar *to drive*
prestar *to lend*
regalar *to give a gift*
tratar de + infinitive *to try to*

EXPRESIONES
así *this way*
de acuerdo *agreed*
entre *between, among*
casi *almost*
a pagar allá *collect (call)*
por teléfono *by telephone*
por vía aérea *via airmail*
a principio de *at the beginning*
tan pronto como *as soon as*
ya *already*

PUNTOS CARDINALES (CARDINAL POINTS)
el **este** *east*
el **norte** *north*
el **oeste** *west*
el **sur** *south*

Lección 12 Las fiestas

Son casi las doce de la noche y los señores Rivera no han podido dormirse.° Sus hijos Alvarito[1] y María Elena han ido juntos° a una fiesta de despedida° y todavía no han regresado a casa.

to fall asleep / together
farewell

GRACIELA ¿No te has dormido todavía?

ÁLVARO ¡Qué va!° y no me dormiré hasta que° lleguen los muchachos.

Of course not! / until

GRACIELA Mira, mi amor,° ya no son niños. Alvarito tiene veinte y dos años y María Elena va a cumplir° veinte pasado mañana°... Vamos a celebrarlo aquí, ¿no?

love
to become ... years old / day after tomorrow

ÁLVARO ¡Ay, Dios mío!° Otra fiesta y esta vez° en mi casa. Creo que también tendrán fiesta cuando yo me muera.°

Oh, my God! / this time
I die

GRACIELA Ay, Álvaro, no me gusta que hables así.

ÁLVARO Es que° para esta familia todo es fiesta. Celebran el bautismo,° la primera comunión, el santo,[2] el cumpleaños, los quince años, el compromiso° y la boda.°

The fact is that / baptism

engagement / wedding

GRACIELA No digas[3] « celebran », di° « celebramos ». Recuerda cuánto te divertiste bailando° en el aniversario de los Martínez.

say (tú command)
dancing

ÁLVARO Sí, pero eran sus bodas de plata° y nadie° se quedó tarde.

silver anniversary / no one

GRACIELA Cálmate,° Álvaro. Voy a prepararte un vaso de leche caliente para que te duermas.

Calm down

1. The endings, **-ito(a)** and **-cito(a)** indicate smallness in size and also show affection: **Álvaro, Alvarito; mujer, mujercita** (*young, nice woman*). Compare: *John, Johnny.* Use of the diminutives depends on intimacy and dialect.   **2.** Babies are often given a saint's name, and thus may celebrate both their birthday and saint's day. For example, Francisco (Pancho) Reyes, born in August, would celebrate his birthday that month but could also celebrate his **santo** on April 2, Saint Francis' Day.   **3.** The negative **tú** commands are identical to the **tú** forms of the present subjunctive: **decir,** ¡**No digas!**; **preocuparse,** ¡**No te preocupes!**

214

¿RECUERDA UD.?

1. ¿Adónde fueron María Elena y Alvarito?
2. ¿Por qué no se duerme el Sr. Rivera?
3. ¿Cuántos años tienen los hijos?
4. ¿Qué fiestas celebran los Rivera?
5. ¿Quién es más paciente, el padre o la madre? ¿Quién es más cascarrabias (grouchy)?
6. ¿Se divirtió Álvaro en el aniversario de los Martínez? ¿Cómo pasaría Álvaro el tiempo?
7. ¿Cuántos años de casados cumplieron los Martínez?
8. ¿Qué le preparó Graciela a su esposo para calmarlo? Y usted, ¿qué toma para calmarse o dormirse?
9. ¿Cree Ud. que Graciela mima (pampers) a su esposo? Dé un ejemplo. Y usted, ¿está muy mimado(a) en casa? ¿en la clase?
10. ¿Le gusta exagerar (exagerate) a Álvaro? Dé un ejemplo. Y según usted, ¿quién es la persona más exagerada de la clase? ¿Será el profesor (la profesora)? Dé ejemplos.

ADAPTACIÓN

a   Una amiga de muchos años se muda y Ud. quiere darle una fiesta de despedida. ¿Qué planes tiene Ud.? Escoja todas las respuestas que le gusten a Ud. y añada (add) otras.

1. Voy a invitar a
   a. los amigos íntimos
   b. los abuelos
   c. los profesores
   d. ¿?
2. Serviré
   a. refrescos
   b. torta
   c. ponche
   d. ¿?
3. Durante la fiesta pienso hablar
   a. del trabajo
   b. de los deportes
   c. de los estudios
   d. ¿?
4. Voy a divertirme cuando
   a. baile
   b. cante (sing)
   c. juegue a...
   d. ¿?
5. Quiero que alguien
   a. diga unos chistes
   b. recite unos poemas
   c. enseñe unas fotos
   d. ¿?
6. Como regalo(s) de despedida le compraré
   a. un libro de español
   b. un disco
   c. perfume
   d. ¿?
7. Espero que la fiesta se termine antes de
   a. la medianoche (midnight)
   b. la una
   c. las dos
   d. ¿?

b   Compare sus respuestas con otro(a) compañero(a). ¿Hay diferencias de opinión?

Ahora imagínese que su mejor amigo(a) va a casarse. ¿Qué planes tiene Ud. para darle una despedida de soltero(a) *(bachelor's party/wedding shower)*?

c   Díganos Ud. en ocho oraciones cuándo es su cumpleaños y cómo lo celebra.

Estructura

I   *Los pronombres indirectos con los verbos* **gustar, parecer** *y* **faltar**

You have already used **me gusta(n)** and **le gusta(n)** to express *I like* and *you like.* Literally, **gustar** means *to please (to be pleasing)* and functions like that verb in English. Recall that *gustan* is used when the subject (what pleases) is plural.

Me gusta **el*** béisbol.	*I like baseball. (Baseball is pleasing to me.)*
¿Le gustan **los** deportes?	*Do you like sports? (Do sports please you?)*

> **Gustar** follows the pattern *indirect object pronoun + third person verb form + subject.*

1. With an infinitive the singular form **gusta** is always used.

Nos gusta estar aquí.   *We like to be here.*

2. The prepositional phrases **a mí, a Mariana, a Uds.,** and so on, may be added for clarity or emphasis.

A Néstor no le gustó el programa.	*Nestor didn't like the program.*
A mí me gustan las carreras de caballo.	*I like horse races.*

3. Other verbs that function similarly to **gustar** are **parecer** *(to seem)* and **faltar** *(to be lacking, missing).*

Nos parecen caras estas cosas.	*These things seem expensive to us.*
Me faltan mil pesos.	*I'm lacking a thousand pesos.*

PRÁCTICA
a   Ud. menciona las diversiones que le gustan. Use los sujetos para hacer oraciones nuevas.

MODELO: Me gusta el teatro. (las comedias)   **Me gustan las comedias.**

la música popular, la ópera, los conciertos, tocar la guitarra, dar un paseo, los deportes, ¿?

*Notice that English may omit the definite article in this construction, but Spanish may not.

b   Queremos preparar una tortilla a la española *(Spanish omelet)*, pero no tenemos los ingredientes. Diga lo que nos falta, usando las palabras entre paréntesis.

MODELO: **Nos falta el aceite.**

(las papas, la sal, los huevos, el aceite)

La tortilla española es uno de los platos más favoritos de España. Aquí tenemos una versión de esa deliciosa tortilla:

4 papas	1/2 taza de aceite
8 huevos	1/2 cucharita de sal

1. Pele° las papas y córtelas en rebanadas finas.° Fríalas° en aceite caliente hasta que estén casi doradas.° Escurra° el aceite de las papas y añada° ¼ (un cuarto de) cucharita de sal a las papas.
2. Bata° los huevos en una escudilla,° añada el resto de la sal, y échelos° en las papas para hacer una tortilla redonda.° Cocine la tortilla hasta que esté dorada por° los dos lados.° Da cuatro raciones.

Peel / slice them / Fry them
brown / Drain
add
Beat / bowl
pour them / round
along / sides

SITUACIONES

a   Ud. y su amiga van a las tiendas para comprar unos regalos. Ud. le pregunta a ella qué le parecen las cosas que va a comprar. Deben usar los sustantivos y adjetivos en la lista.

MODELO: ¿Qué te parece la camisa? *(What do you think of the shirt?; lit., How does the shirt seem to you?)*

Me parece bonita. *(I think it's pretty.; lit., It seems pretty to me.)*

Sustantivos		Adjetivos
la chaqueta	la corbata	bonito / feo
la blusa	los zapatos	caro / barato
la falda	las sandalias	grande / pequeño
el vestido	los tenis	largo / corto *(long/short)*
los pantalones	las camisetas	bueno / malo
el suéter	¿?	ancho / estrecho *(loose/tight)*
el traje		¿?

b   Ud. está en un restaurante con un(a) amigo(a). Debe preguntarle si le gustan estos platos.

MODELO: Ud: **¿Te gusta el arroz con pollo?**
        Amigo(a): **Sí, me gusta. / No, no me gusta.**

el pescado, el ceviche, los tacos, las enchiladas, la paella, los camarones, el gazpacho, las papas fritas, ¿?

c Repitan la situación b. Ahora Ud. les pregunta a dos o tres amigos si les gustan los platos.

MODELO: Ud: **¿Les gusta el arroz con pollo?**
Amigos: **Sí, nos gusta.**

IMPROVISACIÓN
Improvise usted, usando un sustantivo (singular o plural) o un infinitivo.

MODELO: A él le gusta(n)... **A él le gustan los carros de sport.**
A él le gusta hacer las compras.

(Use las frases **a mí, a ti, a Eva**, etc., al principio de las oraciones para darle énfasis al complemento indirecto.)

1. A mí me gusta(n)...
2. A ellos les falta(n)...
3. A nosotros nos parece(n)...
4. A ti no te gusta(n)...
5. ¿?

HUMOR

Siento que no te guste la música barroca *(baroque)*
pero a mis plantas les gusta mucho.

II *El subjuntivo con algunas expresiones adverbiales*

A Besides its use with the notions of request and emotion, the subjunctive is also used with expressions that signal events yet to be realized. The following adverbial expressions designate pending or provisional actions and always take the subjunctive in Spanish.

para que *so that, in order that*	**sin que** *without*
antes (de) que *before*	**con tal que** *provided (that)*

Te daré la dirección **para que** visites a mis padres.
I'll give you the address so that you'll visit my parents.

Terminaremos pronto **con tal que** Uds. nos ayuden.
We'll finish quickly provided you help us.

B   When **que** is omitted from **para, antes de** and **sin**, they become prepositions and require the *infinitive* rather than the subjunctive. This often happens when there is no change of subject in the sentence.

Lo haré **sin decir** nada.
I'll do it without saying anything.

BUT   Lo haré **sin que ellos me digan** nada.
I'll do it without their saying anything to me.

Queremos ver a Graciela **antes de irnos**.
We want to see Graciela before leaving.

BUT   Queremos ver a Graciela **antes de que ella se vaya**.
We want to see Graciela before she leaves.

PRÁCTICA

a   ¿Cómo se relacionan las expresiones de las columnas A y B?

A	B
1. Invitaremos a los Rivera	*a.* sin que tú interrumpas.
2. Te acompañaré al teatro esta noche	*b.* para que vengan a la fiesta.
3. Miguelito, quiero que me des ese vaso	*c.* antes de que lo rompas.
4. ¡Qué horror! No puedo decir nada	*d.* con tal que den una comedia buena.

b   Unos amigos invitan a María Elena a un café. Ella desea ir, pero tiene unos compromisos *(commitments)*. ¿Qué les debe decir ella a sus amigos? Use las expresiones indicadas para completar la frase.

¡Estupendo, con tal que (yo)... !

terminar el trabajo / regresar temprano / no tener otro compromiso / no estar muy ocupada / traer a mi hermano / no necesitar estudiar

c   Consuelo no sabe qué hacer con su hijo Angelito. Ella le pide consejos *(advice)* a su tía. Empiece cada pregunta con Ay, tía...

Ay, tía, ¿qué hago con Ángelito para que (él)... ?

buscar trabajo / limpiar su cuarto / guardar la ropa / no ser tan desobediente / no tocar música todo el día / casarse pronto / ¿?

d   ¿Cómo se dice en español?

1. *a.* I'll call before eating.
   b. I'll call before they eat.
2. *a.* They're coming (in order) to celebrate the anniversary.
   b. They're coming so (that) we'll celebrate the anniversary.
3. *a.* We won't leave without finishing the work.
   b. We won't leave without your friend finishing the work.

ADIVINANZA

Usted tiene una canasta *(basket)* con tres manzanas para tres niños. ¿Qué hará para darle una manzana a cada niño, y para que quede *(remain)* una manzana en la canasta?

Usted le da la última manzana con la canasta al tercer niño.

III El indicativo o el subjuntivo con otras expresiones

Both the indicative and the subjunctive may be used after the adverbial expressions below. The indicative is used when referring to events that have already occurred or generally do occur. That is, the information is considered certain and factual. The subjunctive is used when referring to events that have not yet occurred or are deemed uncertain.

---

cuando   *when, whenever*
hasta que   *until*
aunque   *although, even though*

INDICATIVE
(certainty: non-future)

Cerraron la puerta cuando
   entraron.
*They closed the door when they
   came in.*

Por lo general cierran la puerta
   cuando entran.
*Generally they close the door when
   they come in.*

Estudiamos aunque es tarde.
We're studying although it's late.

SUBJUNCTIVE
(uncertainty: future)

Cerrarán la puerta cuando **entren**.
*They'll close the door when they
   come in.*

Van a cerrar la puerta cuando
   entren.
*They're going to close the door
   when they come in.*

Estudiaremos aunque **sea** tarde.
We'll study although it may be late.

PRÁCTICA

a Use el verbo indicado para completar cada grupo de oraciones. Escoja entre el indicativo o el subjuntivo según el contexto.

1. **ver**
   a. Hablaré con Jaime cuando yo lo _____ .
   b. Voy a hablar con Jaime cuando (yo) lo _____ .
   c. Siempre hablo con Jaime cuando lo _____ .
   d. Hablé con Jaime ayer cuando lo _____ .

2. **insistir**
   a. No iremos aunque ellos _____ .
   b. No fuimos aunque ellos _____ .
   c. No vamos a ir aunque ellos _____ .

3. **regresar**
   a. Van a quedarse aquí hasta que ella _____ .
   b. Se quedarán aquí hasta que ella _____ .
   c. Se quedaron aquí hasta que ella _____ .

b ¿Cómo se dice en español?

1. I'll write when I arrive.
2. I was sixteen when I started to work.
3. We'll wait here until he calls us.
4. They won't sell the house even though you may give them a million pesos.
5. Even though I paid them last summer, they still send me the bill every month.

c Pregúntele a otro(a) estudiante.

1. a. ¿Adónde irá Ud. hoy cuando salga de clase?
   b. ¿Adónde fue ayer cuando salió de clase?
2. a. ¿Qué hará cuando llegue a casa?
   b. ¿Qué hizo ayer cuando llegó a casa?
3. a. ¿Estudiará esta noche aunque esté cansado(a)?
   b. ¿Estudió anoche aunque estaba cansado(a)?

d ¿Qué les dirá Ud. a sus amigos cuando sea:

1. el 25 de diciembre?	F	Año Nuevo
2. el día de Janucá?	E	Janucá
3. el primero de enero?	L	Navidad
4. el día de su cumpleaños?	I	Cumpleaños
	Z	Aniversario

POEMA POPULAR

Cuando tenía dinero me llamaban don* Tomás.
Ahora que no lo tengo me llaman Tomás no más *(only)*.

don, doña are titles of respect or affection used before a first name.

IV *Palabras Afirmativas y Negativas*

AFIRMATIVAS	NEGATIVAS
alguien *someone, somebody*	**nadie** *no one, nobody*
algo *something*	**nada** *nothing*
algún, alguno(a)(os)(as) *any, some (one or more from a group)*	**ningún, ninguno(a)** *none, no, not any (from a group; always singular)*
también *also, too*	**tampoco** *neither, not either*
siempre *always*	**nunca** *never*
	jamás *never, not ever*

A Unlike English, Spanish may use more than one negative in a sentence.

No compré nada.   No vimos a nadie.
I didn't buy anything.   *We didn't see anyone.*

B **Alguno** and **ninguno**, like **uno**, drop the **o** before a masculine singular noun.

> No leyó ningún informe.
> *He didn't read any report.*

BUT   ninguna persona *no person*
      algunas mujeres *some women*

C Negative expressions may be placed *before* the verb with **no** omitted. (Frequently **nadie** and **ningún, ninguno(a)** serve as subject in this case.)

Nadie se quedó allí.
No se quedó nadie allí. } *No one stayed there.*

Tampoco fueron a la reunión.
No fueron a la reunión tampoco. } *They didn't go to the reunion either*

Ninguno (de ellos) entró.
No entró ninguno (de ellos). } *None (of them) entered.*

PRÁCTICA
a   Cambie la palabra afirmativa a negativa.

MODELO: Alguien te ha llamado por teléfono.
        Nadie te ha llamado por teléfono.

1. Alguien lo ha visto a él.
2. Ellos siempre salían juntos.
3. Algo ha pasado aquí.
4. Alguno sabrá la respuesta.

5. Algunas de las muchachas vinieron en autobús.

6. Alguien preguntó por ti.

7. También le envié una invitación a Marcela.

b Repita la práctica anterior, pero esta vez use la estructura
no + verbo + otro negativo.

MODELO: **No** te ha llamado **nadie** por teléfono.

c María Elena y Alvarito trabajan en la compañía de su papá SÍ-VA.
Describa con palabras positivas la situación ahí. Después, describa ne-
gativamenta lo que pasa en NO-VA.

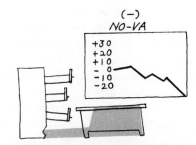

1. ¿Hay alguien en la oficina?
2. ¿Hay algo en el escritorio (*desk*)?
3. ¿Hay algo también en la pared?
4. ¿La compañía siempre gana dinero?
5. ¿Conoces a algunas de las
   personas en la oficina?

1. ¿Hay algún empleado aquí?
2. ¿Qué hay en el escritorio?
3. ¿Y en el archivo (*files*)?
4. ¿La compañía gana siempre dinero?
5. ¿Trabajas en alguna oficina de
   la universidad?

d ¿Cómo se dice en inglés?

1. No le dimos nada a él.
2. No le gustó esa foto a nadie.
3. Ellos tampoco dijeron nada.

4. No fuimos a ningún lugar.
5. Eugenio jamás toma café.
6. Algún día seremos ricos y famosos, ¿no?

e ¿Cómo se dice en español?

1. No one has paid us anything.
2. None of them has written to me.
3. Julieta always buys them something.
4. They don't ever go to the movies.

f **Opiniones.** Conteste Ud.

1. ¿Hay alguien más sociable que Ud.? ¿más estudioso(a)? ¿menos
   paciente?
2. ¿Quiénes son algunos de sus mejores amigos? ¿mejores profesores?
3. ¿Hay algo más importante que el dinero? ¿la salud? ¿la familia?
4. ¿Piensa mudarse algún día? ¿por qué?
   (Si Ud. contesta negativamente, cambie **algún día** a **nunca** o **jamás**.)
5. ¿Quiere Ud. que sus hijos asistan a esta universidad también? ¿Por qué?

La vida social

La vida social en los países hispanos tiene una fuerte orientación familiar. Por lo general casi todos los miembros de la familia participan en las fiestas sin que falten los niños y los abuelos.

Entre las fiestas familiares el cumpleaños es una de las más alegres celebraciones. Tradicionalmente los cumpleaños infantiles incluyen una piñata para que los niños se diviertan rompiéndola.° Más tarde cuando una joven cumple° quince años, los padres le dan una magnífica fiesta formal para reconocer° socialmente que su hija ya es señorita. | *breaking it* / *turns, becomes* / *to acknowledge*

Las fiestas religiosas, especialmente la Navidad, ofrecen oportunidades para reunirse° con familiares y amigos. Los hispanos celebran el 24 de diciembre, la Nochebuena,° con una estupenda cena llena de alegría y compadrería.° El seis de enero los Reyes Magos° les traen regalos a los niños. | *to get together* / *Christmas Eve* / *close companionship / Three Wise Men (the coming of the Magi)*

Para divertirse la gente frecuentemente da un paseo por las calles, plazas y parques. Con tal que tengan tiempo los amigos terminan el paseo con un aperitivo en un café o restaurante, donde continúan sus animadas conversaciones. Cuando hay carnaval las calles se convierten en un mundo° de magia y fantasía. Ahí° jóvenes y viejos cantan y bailan. | *world* / *There*

Aunque la televisión y los deportes atraen° bastante° público, a los hispanos todavía les gusta mucho ir al cine. Les gustan las películas° hispanas y también las extranjeras° de los Estados Unidos, Francia, Alemania° y otros países. | *attract / quite a bit (of)* / *films* / *foreign / Germany*

Parece que para los hispanos la vida social, particularmente los domingos con la familia, es una necesidad y no una parte incidental de la existencia.

¿COMPRENDE UD.?

a Traducción. Refiérase a las **Observaciones** para traducir estas oraciones.

1. Invite all (**toda**) the family, without missing grandmother and all the children.
2. Take the children to the park so that they'll have a good time.
3. When a young woman turns fifteen, her parents give her a formal party.
4. I'll go for a walk provided (that) I have time.
5. Although television attracts many Hispanics, they still like to go to the movies.

b Comprensión. Escoja la respuesta que mejor termine cada oración.

1. Cuando los hispanos tienen una fiesta
   a. necesitan una niñera *(babysitter)*
   b. ven la televisión
   c. incluyen a los abuelos
2. Los padres dan una magnífica fiesta cuando su hija cumple
   a. catorce años
   b. quince años
   c. dieciséis años
3. Los hispanos celebran la Nochebuena
   a. el 24 de diciembre
   b. el 25 de diciembre
   c. el primero de enero
4. Después del paseo los amigos
   a. van a la iglesia
   b. caminan por la plaza
   c. toman algo
5. Para los hispanos la vida social es
   a. incidental
   b. esencial
   c. secundaria

c **Situación.** Imagínese que Ud. está en un café al aire libre *(outdoors).* A Ud. le gusta mirar a la gente. Haga comentarios acerca de *(concerning)* cada una de estas personas.

1. Allí* va una señora muy elegante. Lleva...
2. Dos niños con uniformes de escuela cruzan la calle. Ellos...
3. Cerca de mi mesa están unos novios *(sweethearts).* Hablarán de...
4. Ahí* pasa un viejecito que vende billetes de lotería *(lottery tickets).* Tendrá... años, y...
5. Ahora veo a...

Actividades

Las crónicas sociales *(social news).* Unos amigos quieren que Ud. les traduzca estas crónicas.

QUINCEAÑERA

1. Quince años. Una animada fiesta conmemoró[1] los suspirados[2] quince años de la gentil señorita Ada Madero, hija del señor Hernando Madero y señora Rosa de Madero, siendo su dichoso[3] compañero de baile el joven Carlos Julio Gómez. Le enviamos nuestras sinceras felicitaciones a la señorita Madero.

1. *commemorated* **2.** *longed for* **3.** *being her fortunate*

2. Nacimiento. Un niño llegó al hogar[1] de Guillermo Uribe y señora Beatriz Roa de Uribe. Con este motivo han recibido numerosas felicitaciones de sus familiares y amigos.

1. synonym: **casa**

3. Reunión. Un delicioso almuerzo ofrecido por la gentil Mariana Castillo de Suárez, en su residencia de Miami, reunió a las voluntarias[1] del Centro Hispano, entidad[2] que ella preside, para coordinar detalles[3] de futuros eventos que se efectuarán[4] a beneficio del[5] *Senior Center.*

1. *volunteers* **2.** *organization* **3.** *details* **4.** *will take place* **5.** *for the benefit of*

*Ahí means *there*, not far from the speaker: ***ese** lugar **ahí**.* **Allí** means *over there*, far from the speaker: ***aquel** lugar **allí**.*

Vocabulario

SUSTANTIVOS
el **amor** *love*
el **aniversario** *anniversary*
la **boda** *wedding*
el **compromiso** *engagement, commitment*
la **despedida** *farewell*
el **escritorio** *desk*
el **mundo** *world*
la **Nochebuena** *Christmas Eve*
la **película** *motion picture, film*
el **santo** *saint's day*

ADJETIVOS
ancho(a) *wide, loose*
bastante *enough, quite a bit*
corto(a) *short*
extranjero(a) *foreign*
junto(a) *together*
largo(a) *long*

AFIRMATIVOS Y NEGATIVOS
algo *something*
alguien *someone, somebody*
algún, alguno(a)(os)(as) *some, any*
jamás *never, not ever*
nadie *no one, nobody*
ningún, ninguno(a) *none, no, not any (always singular)*
nunca *never*
tampoco *neither, not either*

VERBOS
*****atraer (atraigo)** *to attract*
calmarse *to calm (oneself) down*
cantar *to sing*
celebrar *to celebrate*
cumplir... años *to turn . . . years, to have a birthday*
dormirse (ue) *to fall asleep*
faltarle (a alguien) *to be lacking (to someone)*
gustarle (a alguien) *to be pleasing (to someone), to like*
parecerle (a alguien) *to seem (to someone)*
morirse (ue) *to die*
†**reunirse** *to get together*

EXPRESIONES
ahí *there*
allí *over there*
antes (de) (que) *before*
aunque *although, even though*
con tal que *provided (that)*
cuando *when*
después (de) *after*
¡Dios mío! *My God!, My goodness!*
Es que... *The fact is . . .*
hasta (que) *until*
para *for, in order to*
para que *so that, in order that*
pasado mañana *day after tomorrow*
¡Qué va! *Of course!*
sin (que) *without*
todavía *still*

---

*In vocab. lists denotes a verb with an irregular 1st person singular form.
†The verb forms of **reunir** have a written accent mark on the **ú** in the present indicative and subjunctive. The **nosotros** forms do not: **reúno, reúnes**, etc. **Graduarse** and **continuar** also have the accent: **me gradúo; continúo.**

Lección 13 — *Los problemas socio-políticos*

Ha Cambiado Poco la Situación de la Mujer en Diez Años: Freda B...

Argentina Restableció el Derecho de Huelga

Modifica el Banco de México las Tasas de Interés a Plazo Fijo

Arrestado en Posesión de Marihuana

Se Desplazan Fuerzas Hondureñas Hacia la Frontera con Nicaragua

Durante una reunión del Centro Internacional Universitario tres estudiantes hispanos presentan una breve charla con respecto a los problemas socio-políticos de sus respectivas regiones. Los tres tratan de ofrecer soluciones posibles para esos problemas.

Guatemala (Catalina Toledo, estudiante de medicina)

Yo quiero hablar de Centroamérica. Los conflictos allí son internacionales y no locales. Dudo que la solución de nuestros problemas sea puramente° marxista o capitalista.

    Para remediar nuestra condición, primero será preciso que mejoremos el nivel de vida° de los pobres. Segundo, no lograremos° tener estabilidad política hasta que los radicales y los reaccionarios piensen más en el bienestar° del país que en sus propios° intereses. Tercero, tenemos que recordar que no hay democracia que pueda sobrevivir° sin la lucha° vigorosa del pueblo contra la corrupción y el engaño.° Es posible cambiar las cosas con el apoyo,° con el voto, del pueblo.

La Argentina (Martín Schmidt, estudiante de ciencias políticas)

En la Argentina queremos el orden y no la represión militar. Esperamos que el gobierno civil restaure° la justicia y la estabilidad económica.

    Aunque ya estamos hartos de° las dictaduras, no olvidemos° que un gobierno fuerte y decisivo es la única° solución al desorden y al caos. Para que la democracia en la Argentina siga adelante° el gobierno no podrá dar su brazo a torcer° a los terroristas. Nosotros los argentinos debemos apoyar firmemente a nuestro presidente.

México (Lourdes Quintana, estudiante de comercio)

No creo que los problemas de mi país se solucionen° en un santiamén.° Para empezar será necesario que México desarrolle más la industria y que aumente° las exportaciones.°

purely

standard of living / won't succeed in

well-being / their own
survive / struggle
deceit
support

restores

fed up with / let's not forget
only, sole
ahead
won't be able to give an inch

solve themselves / jiffy

increase / exports

228

Nuestro nivel de vida mejorará cuando el gobierno entrene° más a los desempleados° en trabajos nuevos. Los campesinos especialmente necesitan la asistencia federal para que cultiven diferentes productos y no abandonen el campo por° la capital.

trains
unemployed

for

¿RECUERDA UD.?

a La charla de Catalina Toledo

1. ¿Cree Catalina que los problemas de Centroamérica sean puramente regionales?
2. ¿Qué será preciso mejorar primero?
3. Para ayudar a los pobres, ¿les daría Ud. asistencia económica o los entrenaría en un trabajo nuevo?
4. Según Catalina, ¿cuándo lograrán una estabilidad política en Centroamérica?
5. ¿Cree Ud. que hombres como Jorge Wáshington y Benito Juárez pensaban más en su propio bienestar que en su país?
6. ¿Recuerda Ud. algun caso de corrupción o engaño recientemente en las noticias *(news)*? ¿Había pagado alguien una mordida *(colloquial: bribe)*? ¿Cree Ud. que las mordidas son necesarias en algunos casos? Dé ejemplos si contesta que *sí*.
7. ¿Ha votado Ud. en las últimas elecciones? ¿Votó Ud. por el partido *(party)* o por el candidato?
8. ¿Si se celebraran *(were held)* las elecciones los domingos en los Estados Unidos, votarían más personas? ¿Por qué?

b La charla de Martín Schmidt

1. ¿De qué están hartos los argentinos?
2. ¿Qué tipo de gobierno tiene la Argentina ahora — una democracia o una dictadura?
3. Según Martín, ¿cuál es la única solución al desorden y al caos?
4. Si Ud. fuera juez *(If you were a judge)*, ¿cuál de estas sentencias le daría a un terrorista?
   a. Lo encarcelaría *(incarcerate)* por el resto de su vida.
   b. Lo perdonaría después de unos años de cárcel *(jail)*.
   c. Le haría pagar una multa *(fine)* severa.
   d. ¿?
5. Para que la democracia siga adelante, ¿qué no podrá hacer el gobierno argentino?
6. ¿Cree Ud. que Martín sea anarquista? ¿Por qué?

c La charla de Lourdes

1. ¿Duda Lourdes que los problemas de México se solucionen en un santiamén?
2. ¿Qué será necesario que el país desarrolle?
3. Según Lourdes, ¿cómo mejorará el nivel de vida?
4. Si Ud. fuera el gobierno, ¿les daría asistencia económica a los campesinos? ¿Por qué?

Los gobiernos

República	Monarquía	Dictadura

Presidente	Rey *(King)* Reina *(Queen)*	Dictador
Vicepresidente	Primer Ministro	Junta
Congreso	Parlamento	izquierda, derecha

NOTA CULTURAL

Las dictaduras de la izquierda o la derecha son una realidad en el mundo hispano, pero la democracia poco a poco va estableciéndose.° Costa Rica tiene una larga historia de democracia. México es básicamente democrático, aunque cuenta° principalmente con un solo partido político el PRI (Partido Revolucionario Institucional). Después de muchos años de dictadura, España en 1975 instituyó una monarquía parlamentaria. Recientemente las elecciones en la Argentina y el Uruguay le han dado nuevo ímpetu° a la democracia.

establishing itself

counts on

impetus

ADAPTACIÓN

Imagínese que Ud. es político *(politician)* y desea que el público vote por Ud. en las próximas *(next)* elecciones. Prepare un breve anuncio para la televisión donde Ud. presenta un problema y unas soluciones. Escoja su problema o refiérase a uno de éstos:

PROBLEMAS	SOLUCIONES POSIBLES
1. la economía	importar menos y exportar más
	modificar el sistema de impuestos *(taxes)*
	crear nuevas industrias
	competir(i) más agresivamente en el mercado internacional
	¿?

2. la contaminación
(pollution)

mejorar el sistema de emisión en los autos
limpiar los ríos y lagos (lakes)
multar (fine) a los contaminadores
construir o no construir plantas nucleares
¿?

3. los conflictos
internacionales

apoyar la ONU (Organización de Naciones Unidas)
dar ayuda militar, técnica o económica
boicotear (boycott) los países agresores
reducir la proliferación de las armas nucleares
¿?

MODELO*: Queridos amigos,
    problema: **El candidato del otro partido no se preocupa
        jamás por...
    Dudo que él...
    No creo que...**
    soluciones: **Yo les prometo... , ... y...
    No hay nadie que... más que yo.**
    conclusión: **Quiero que Uds....
    Espero que Uds....
    ¡Necesito su voto!**

Estructura

I   ***El subjuntivo después de los antecedentes indefinidos y negativos***
(The subjunctive after indefinite and negative antecedents)

Spanish speakers use the subjunctive in the subordinate action or clause
when referring back to a noun or pronoun (the antecedent) that is indefinite or negative.

A   **Indefinite antecedent** (unknown, hypothetical):

    ¿Conoces† una persona que **trabaje** allí?   *Do you know a person who works there?*
                                                      (unknown)

BUT   **Sí, conozco a una persona** que **trabaja** allí.   *Yes, I know a person who works there.*
                                                      (known)

B   **Negative antecedent** (nonexistent):

    No conozco a nadie‡ que trabaje allí.   *I don't know anyone who works there.*
                                                      (negative)

*Recuerde que el anuncio es propaganda. Exagere un poco. Use humor e incluya fotos, dia-
gramas o artículos de periódico.
†Note: The personal **a** is omitted when the direct object is indefinite.
‡Note: As direct objects, **nadie, alguien, ninguna persona,** etc., require the personal **a**.

PRÁCTICA

a ¿Indicativo o subjuntivo? Complete las oraciones con la forma apropiada del verbo entre paréntesis.

1. (hablar) Necesitamos una señorita que _____ bien inglés y español.
2. (estacionar) Busco al joven que _____ los carros.
3. (vivir) No hay nadie aquí que _____ cerca de esa dirección.
4. (estar) Por favor, ¡tráigame la carta que _____ en la mesa!
5. (costar) ¿Tienen Uds. algo que _____ menos de mil pesos?
6. (gustar) ¡Caramba, no hay nada que les _____ a ellos!
7. (preocuparse) Irma es la empleada que más _____ por los clientes.
8. (ir y venir) No conozco a ningún estudiante que _____ y _____ a la universidad todos los días.

b Primero conteste afirmativamente y después negativamente.

1. ¿Conoces a alguien que piense ir a México este verano?
2. ¿Tienes un libro que explique bien la gramática?
3. ¿Hay alguna persona en esta clase que sepa más que tú?
4. ¿Pasa un autobús por aquí *(by here)* que vaya al museo?

c Imagínese que usted es jefe de personal y busca trabajadores para su firma. Prepare una lista de los siete requisitos *(requirements)* más importantes que los trabajadores deben cumplir *(fulfill)*. Empiece de esta manera: **Busco trabajadores que sean responsables, que aprendan rápido, que lleguen a tiempo, que...**

d ¿Cómo se dice en español? Use **que** para traducir *who, that.*

1. There is no one who wants to go.
2. Excuse me, I need a taxi that will take me to this address.
3. Where's the money that my parents sent me?
4. Do you know anyone who cleans houses?
5. We need someone who can help us.

II El subjuntivo con expresiones de duda y negación

A To express doubt or uncertainty about some action or situation, Spanish speakers use the subjunctive.

> Dudan que Figueroa **gane** las elecciones.
> *They doubt (that) Figueroa will win the elections.*

As expressions of certainty, **no dudar, creer, estar seguro(a), es verdad,** and **es cierto** would be followed by the indicative, not the subjunctive.

> No dudo (Creo...) que ella **regresará.**
> *I don't doubt (I believe. . .) she'll return.*

As expressions of uncertainty, **es (im)posible** and **es (im)probable** take the subjunctive in both the affirmative and the negative.

¿Es posible que **pases** las vacaciones en el Caribe?
Is it possible (that) you'll spend your vacations in the Caribbean?

No es posible que las **pase** allí.
It's not possible (that) I'll spend them there.

B Similarly, speakers use the subjunctive to indicate denial or disbelief about an action.

No es verdad que Aurora **se case** con Rogelio.
It's not true that Aurora is getting married to Rogelio.

No creo que ellos **comprendan** los problemas.
I don't believe (that) they understand the problems.

¿Creer que...? may take either the indicative or subjunctive, depending on the speaker's desire to express certainty or doubt.

¿Crees que ellos protestarán? *(certainty)*
¿Crees que protesten? *(doubt)*

PRÁCTICA

a Usted desea saber qué opinión tiene su compañero de varias personas. Su compañero parece ser muy indeciso porque primero le contesta positivamente y después negativamente. Refiérase a la lista para hacer y contestar las preguntas.

MODELO: Usted: **¿Crees que Camila sea puntual?**
    Su compañero(a): **Sí, creo que es puntual. No, no creo que sea puntual.**

Lista:

1. Timoteo / expresivo
2. Elisa / amable
3. Susita / jovial
4. los Navarro / responsables
5. tus amigos / muy serios
6. la profesora / muy estricta
7. yo / razonable
8. ellas / simpáticas
9. mi amigo y yo / justos
10. ¿?
11. ¿?

b ¿Indicativo o subjuntivo? Complete con la forma apropiada del verbo entre paréntesis.

1. (estar) Dudo que Elisa _____ en casa ahora.
2. (ir) ¿Será posible que Uds. _____ a Sudamérica este año?
3. (tener) Creen que tú _____ razón.
4. (hacer) Es imposible que yo lo _____ todo solo.
5. (doblar) Ramona está segura de que nosotros _____ aquí.
6. (acostarse) No creo que los Gutiérrez _____ antes de las doce.
7. (conocer) ¿Crees que ellos _____ a Omar? Yo lo dudo.

c Las universidades: una encuesta *(a survey)*. Formen grupos de tres estudiantes. El primero les hace a Uds. las siguientes preguntas; el segundo anota *(jots down)* sus respuestas; y luego el tercero le presenta a la clase el consenso del grupo, comenzando con la frase: (**No**) **Creemos que...**

1. ¿Crees que es bueno tener materias electivas? ¿y requisitos? ¿Cuáles deben ser los requisitos?
2. ¿Prefieres que la asistencia *(attendance)* a clase sea obligatoria o no? ¿Por qué?
3. ¿Qué exámenes temes que sean más difíciles — los de español o los de matemáticas? ¿los de biología o los de historia?
4. ¿Es mejor que las universidades preparen a individuos cultos *(learned individuals)* o a especialistas? Incluyan Uds. dos o tres razones *(reasons)*.
5. ¿Es posible que las universidades den mucho énfasis a la vida social? ¿a los deportes? ¿a los exámenes? Mencionen Uds. ejemplos específicos.

d ¿Cómo se dice?

1. I don't believe (that) Lidia speaks English well.
2. The prices? I'm sure the company will raise them.
3. It's possible (that) the conservatives (**los conservadores**) will win the elections.
4. I doubt that Pepita is older than Alonso.
5. Do you think (that) the children are hungry? (I doubt it.)

III *El imperfecto (pasado) del subjuntivo*

The past subjunctive is used for past actions, generally under the same rules that apply to the present subjunctive, that is, after:

1. expressions of request and emotion
2. adverbial conjunctions designating pending or provisional actions
3. expressions of doubt, denial and disbelief
4. indefinite and negative antecedents

To form the imperfect subjunctive, take the third person plural (**Uds.**) form of the preterite and change the **-o** in the ending to **-a.**

llamar (llamarón)	**poder** (pudierón)	**ir / ser** (fuerón)
llamara	pudiera	fuera
llamaras	pudieras	fueras
llamara	pudiera	fuera
llamáramos	pudiéramos	fuéramos
llamarais	pudierais	fuerais
llamaran	pudieran	fueran

Quiero que Uds. llamen.	I want you to call.
Quería que Uds. **llamaran.**	I wanted you to call.
Te doy el dinero para que pagues las cuentas.	I'm giving you the money so that you'll pay the bills.
Te di el dinero para que **pagaras** las cuentas.	I gave you the money so that you would (might) pay the bills.
Buscan una persona que sirva de intérprete.	They're looking for a person who'll serve as interpreter.
Buscarían una persona que **sirviera** de intérprete.	They were probably looking for a person who would (might) serve as interpreter.

The imperfect subjunctive can be translated with the helping verbs *would* or *might* depending on the context. Notice that in Spanish when the main clause is in the past, the subordinate clause (with the subjunctive) is also in the past.

PRÁCTICA

a Hágale preguntas a un(a) compañero(a), usando los verbos entre paréntesis.

MODELO: Usted: ¿Qué querías que (yo) leyera?
Compañero(a): **Quería que leyeras esta página.**

1. ¿Qué querías que (yo) leyera? (estudiara, escribiera, trajera, viera, preparara, ¿?)
2. ¿Dudabas que (yo) regresara? (manejara, cocinara, bailara, me mudara, me preocupara por ti, ¿?)
3. ¿Hablarías con la profesora antes de que (yo) terminara? (empezara, llegara, saliera, viniera, pudiera, ¿?)

b Situación. Usted está en un restaurante y no está contento(a) con el servicio. Combine las listas A y B para expresarle su disgusto *(displeasure)* al camarero. Haga un mínimo de ocho oraciones diferentes.

MODELO: **Le pedí que me asara la carne un poco y no mucho.**
(I asked you to roast the meat for me a little, not a lot.)

A	B
Quería que me...	traer vino tinto y no blanco
Le pedí que me...	servir pollo y no jamón
Esperaba que nos...	preparar una ensalada y no un sándwich
No creía que nos...	dar un cuchillo y no...
Dudaba que me...	cocinar... y no...
Sería posible que me...	calentar *(to warm)*... y no...
	enfriar... y no...
	cobrar *(charge)*... y no...
	¿?

IV *Claúsulas con si*   (If-clauses)

Speakers also use the past subjunctive in **si** *(if)* clauses to express situations that are contrary to fact or unlikely to happen. The verb in the clause expressing the result is in the *conditional*.

Si yo fuera tú, no le diría nada a él.
If I were you, I wouldn't tell him anything.

Si tuviéramos tiempo, iríamos contigo.
If we had the time, we'd go with you.

> **Si** + imperfect subjunctive + conditional
> (contrary-to-fact clause)   (result clause)

However, when a situation is considered factual or likely to happen, the indicative is used.

Si voy al cine, invitaré a mis primos.
If I go to the movies, I'll invite my cousins.

PRÁCTICA

a   Formen grupos de tres estudiantes. El primero hace las preguntas, el segundo las contesta y el tercero repite las respuestas.

MODELO: Primero: **Si tuvieras un millón de dólares, ¿qué harías?**
Segundo: **Pues, si tuviera un millón de dólares, le daría una parte a mi familia, compraría un carro de sport, pasaría unas vacaciones en...**
Tercero: **Él (Ella) dijo que si tuviera un millón de dólares, le daría...**

1. Si fueras profesor(a), ¿qué materias enseñarías?
2. Si pudieras ser una famosa figura política, ¿quién serías?
3. Si pudieras hacer un viaje, ¿adónde te gustaría ir?
4. Si sólo pudieras leer dos o tres libros este año, ¿qué libros leerías?
5. Si sólo fueras al cine dos o tres veces este año, ¿qué películas verías?
6. Si estuvieras en una isla tropical desierta, ¿qué harías para pasar el tiempo?
7. Si alguien llega tarde a clase, ¿qué dice la profesora normalmente?
8. Si tú no sabes bien la lección, ¿qué le dices al profesor?

b   ¿Qué haría Ud. en estas situaciones?

1. en el aeropuerto: ¿Qué haría si perdiera la conexión de un vuelo con otro? ¿si la compañía perdiera sus maletas? ¿si un terrorista tomara control del avión?

2. en la tienda: ¿Qué le diría a la dependiente si Ud. devolviera una camisa con un defecto? ¿si no tuviera el recibo? ¿Qué le compraría a su novio(a) *(sweetheart)* si fuera el cumpleaños de él (ella)? ¿Qué haría Ud. si no tuviera dinero para pagar las compras?

OBSERVACIONES

*Lea el siguiente ensayo (essay) que escribió una estudiante para un examen de ciencias políticas. La pregunta era: **Los problemas socio-políticos en Hispanoamérica.** Describa cómo comenzaron esos problemas y ofrezca (offer) algunas soluciones.*

Dudo que los problemas socio-políticos de Hispanoamérica se solucionen de hoy a mañana.° Creo que esos problemas son el resultado° de la geografía, historia y economía de esos países. Antes de las guerras° de independencia las distancias y las barreras geográficas habían formado regiones naturalmente separadas. Me parece que esa separación geográfica, combinada con diferencias étnicas, le dio a cada nación un carácter individual. Por esas razones es posible que México sea tan diferente de la Argentina y Costa Rica de Guatemala.

    Durante los tiempos coloniales los hispanoamericanos tuvieron poca oportunidad de aprender a gobernarse porque casi todos los administradores eran de España. Esto fomentó° el paternalismo y el personalismo.* Después de la independencia varios países, en busca de° la estabilidad política, pasaron a manos de dictadores. No es raro° que un pueblo descontento con la discordia civil y la injusticia social siga un líder° que le prometa mejorar su condición. Lo malo es que luego ese pueblo termine dominado por un tirano.

    Es verdad que hoy día la industrialización ha aumentado la clase media urbana, pero no lo suficiente.° Todavía existe una discrepancia enorme entre los ricos y los pobres. No creo que la industria haya creado° los empleos necesarios para la multitud de gente sin especialización. Me parece que la solución, aunque no sea fácil, está en reducir el gran desnivel° económico entre las clases. También es preciso que políticamente se integren° las posiciones extremas de los ultraconservadores y ultrarradicales. Es posible que la estabilidad política y la democracia coexistan de un grado a otro como° se nota en México, Costa Rica, Venezuela y España.

overnight / result
wars

fostered
in search of
unusual
leader

sufficiently
has created

imbalance
integrate

as

*el personalismo: having "connections" with the appropriate official

¿COMPRENDE UD.?

a Vocabulario. Combine las palabras de la columna A con los correspondientes sinónimos de la columna B.

A	B
1. formar _____	*a.* trabajo
2. dominar _____	*b.* personas
3. guerra _____	*c.* racial
4. fomentar _____	*d.* crear
5. la gente _____	*e.* unir
6. preciso _____	*f.* luego
7. integrar _____	*g.* conflicto militar
8. después _____	*h.* necesario
9. étnico _____	*i.* estimular
10. empleo _____	*j.* controlar

b Comprensión. Escoja la mejor respuesta según el ensayo.

1. Esto contribuye a la separación en Hispanoamérica.
    a. la religión
    b. la geografía
    c. la lengua

2. Generalmente *no* fue parte del colonialismo.
    a. el paternalismo
    b. el monopolio
    c. la autonomía

3. Después de las guerras de independencia las nuevas naciones se convirtieron en
    a. dictaduras
    b. democracias
    c. monarquías

4. La industria en Hispanoamérica *no*
    a. ha aumentado la clase media
    b. ha atraído *(attracted)* los campesinos a la ciudad
    c. ha creado suficientes trabajos

5. La ayuda de amigos o conexiones en el gobierno o el comercio se llama
    a. nepotismo
    b. personalismo
    c. magnetismo

Actividades

Imagínese que Ud. está en una tertulia *(social gathering)* donde hay personas de diferentes países hispanos. Haga el papel de un(a) hispano(a) y díganos algo de Ud. y su país. Consulte la biblioteca, específicamente *The Area Handbook, The Almanac* y otros libros apropiados. Si es posible consulte con una persona de ese país.

MODELO: **Me llamo Norma Miranda y Llorens.**
Trabajo en la Compañía...
Soy de...
Mi país tiene un área de...
La población es... La mayoría vive en...
Producimos... Comerciamos con...
El sistema de gobierno es...
Algunas personas prominentes son...

Vocabulario

SUSTANTIVOS
el **apoyo** *support*
los **capitalistas** *capitalists*
los **comunistas** *communists*
la **contaminación** *pollution*
el **desempleado,** la **desempleada** *unemployed*
la **dictadura** *dictatorship*
las **elecciones** *elections*
el **engaño** *deceit*
la **guerra** *war*
el, la **juez** *judge*
los **impuestos** *taxes*
el **líder** *leader*
la **lucha** *struggle*
las **noticias** *news*
el **partido político** *political party*
la **reina,** el **rey** *queen, king*
el **resultado** *result*
el **voto** *vote*

ADJETIVO
culto(a) *learned, educated*

VERBOS
apoyar *to support*
aumentar *to increase*
crear *to create*
discutir *to discuss, argue*
dudar *to doubt*
ganar *to win, earn*
mejorar *to improve*
ofrecer (zc) *to offer*
olvidar *to forget*
proteger (j) *to protect*
reducir (zc) *to reduce*
solucionar *to solve*
votar *to vote*

EXPRESIONES
adelante *ahead*
el **nivel de vida** *standard of living*
es raro *it's strange, unusual*
estar harto(a) de *to be fed up with*
estar seguro(a) *to be sure*
lo suficiente *sufficient (amount)*
por esa razón *for that reason*
que *who, that*

14 *Las obras maestras* (Masterpieces)

España y Latinoamérica han creado° formidables obras maestras en el arte, la música y la literatura. Estas obras generalmente han sido° realistas y espontáneas, y han reflejado° el espíritu del pueblo.

have created
have been
have reflected

El arte

En los siglos° XVI–XVII* España tuvo excelentes pintores.° El Greco pintó° cuadros° intensamentes religiosos. Empleó° colores claros y oscuros,° modificando la realidad para representar la verdadera alma° del sujeto.° Diego Velázquez se destacó° por su realismo y por su énfasis en la perspectiva. Sus sujetos son dignos° y admirables. Un siglo más tarde Francisco de Goya se hizo° famoso por su técnica impresionista y por sus cuadros dramáticos donde atacaba° la decadencia política y social de su país. Su cuadro *Los fusilamientos*° *del 3 de mayo* (1808) describe gráficamente el horror de la invasión napoleónica de España.

centuries / painters / painted
pictures / Used / light and dark
soul / subject
stood out
dignified
became
attacked
shootings

*Ordinal numbers beyond *tenth* (**décimo**) are rarely used in *spoken* Spanish. Read XI as **once**, XII as **doce**, and so forth.

El entierro (burial) *del conde* (count) *de Orgaz* es la obra maestra de El Greco.

Los fusilamientos del 3 de mayo, de Francisco de Goya, dramatiza los horrores de la guerra.

Las doncellas de Avignon, de Pablo Picasso, emplea figuras geométricas para representar las figuras humanas.

En el siglo XX los españoles Pablo Picasso y Salvador Dalí han represen- _from_
tado la realidad desde° un punto de vista que desfigura lo normal para obli-
garnos° a ver la anormalidad de la época. Picasso, sin duda, es el pintor _force us_
que más ha influído en el arte contemporáneo. Con su obra *Las doncellas*° _young ladies_
de Avignon (1907) se inició el cubismo. En ese cuadro Picasso deformó radi-
calmente el sujeto — por medio de° círculos, rectángulos y triángulos — _by means of_
para hacernos ver las figuras desde diferentes perspectivas. Luego Dalí, en
sus obras cubistas y surrealistas, nos ha representado el mundo de los
sueños° y los pensamientos.° _dreams / thoughts_

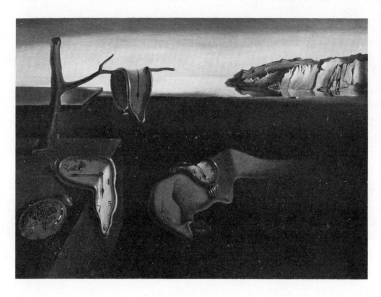

La persistencia de la memoria, de Salvador Dalí, es una de las obras más prominentes del surrealismo.

La América precolombina° produjo° excelentes obras de arte, especialmente en la arquitectura y la escultura. *La piedra° del Sol,* calendario azteca, es una de las esculturas más conocidas. Desde° el principio los pintores hispanoamericanos combinaron temas° indígenas con las técnicas europeas. En la primera mitad° del siglo XX los célebres pintores mexicanos Diego Rivera, José Clemente Orozco y David Alfaro Siqueiros adaptaron esa combinación para crear una extensa serie de pinturas murales que simbolizan las preocupaciones sociales y políticas del pueblo.

pre-Columbian / produced
stone
Since
themes
half

La piedra del Sol representa
conceptos extraordinarios del tiempo.

Cerámica precolombina,
Perú.

Pintura mural de David Alfaro Siqueiros
en la Ciudad Universitaria.

Plácido Domingo, distinguido
tenor español de la Ópera
Metropolitana.

Andrés Segovia restableció
la guitarra como (as) instrumento
de concierto.

La música

Los hispanos se distinguen° por su amor a la música. Entre° los más famosos compositores de la música moderna española se encuentran° Isaac
Albéniz, creador de la suite *Iberia*, y Manuel de Falla, bien conocido por su
encantadora° *Danza ritual del fuego.*° El guitarrista Andrés Segovia y el vio-
loncelista Pablo Casals son otros prodigiosos músicos españoles. Carlos
Chávez, de México, se ha distinguido universalmente por sus vigorosas
composiciones que incorporan la música ritual indígena. Otros hispanoamericanos de fama internacional son: los mexicanos Agustín Lara, compositor de *Granada*; Armando Manzanero, creador de numerosas canciones
populares; el cubano Ernesto Lecuona, compositor de *Siboney* y *Mala-
gueña;* y Claudio Arrau, gran pianista chileno.

*distinguish themselves /
  Among
are found*

enchanting / Fire Dance

La literatura

La literatura se distingue desde sus
comienzos° por un genuino realismo
en el que° toda clase de personajes°
viven su vida y cuentan° su historia. El
Cid y el novelesco Don Quijote son
incomparables personajes clásicos de
la literatura española. Esos personajes
se enfrentaron° a la realidad con
cierto realismo e idealismo, ven-
ciendo° unas veces y perdiendo otras.

beginnings

in which / characters
tell

faced

conquering

Miguel de Cervantes, autor de
Don Quijote de la Mancha, contempla
desde arriba (top) a Don Quijote
y a su inseparable compañero
Sancho Panza.

Durante la época colonial la monja° Sor° Juana Inés de la Cruz fue la figura literaria más notable de Hispanoamérica. Defendió el derecho° de la mujer a participar en las actividades intelectuales y religiosas cuando esa causa no era popular.

    En la segunda mitad del siglo XIX un grupo de poetas hispanoamericanos, entre los cuales sobresalía° Rubén Darío (Nicaragua), inició el movimiento literario llamado Modernismo. Ese movimiento le dio a la poesía una nueva musicalidad y sensibilidad desconocidas° hasta entonces. Durante esa época la novela realista estaba en su apogeo.° Entre los novelistas españoles, Benito Pérez Galdós se destacó por su enorme producción literaria y su viva° descripción de las circunstancias sociales de España.

    La tradición realista continuó en el siglo XX. Las novelas hispanoamericanas anteriores a 1950 generalmente son documentales que denuncian° las deplorables condiciones político-económicas del pueblo. En años más recientes, los cuentistas° y novelistas, aunque inspirados en la realidad, se han interesado más en explorar la naturaleza° humana. Jorge Luis Borges (la Argentina), Mario Vargas Llosa (el Perú) y Gabriel García Márquez (Colombia) — por medio de su técnica narrativa — han escrito verdaderas obras maestras.

nun / Sister
right

stood out

unknown
apogee

lively

denounce

short-story writers
nature

Gabriel García Márquez, famoso novelista y ganador del Premio Nóbel.

Gabriela Mistral, eminente poetisa chilena y ganadora del Premio Nóbel.

¿COMPRENDE UD.?

a Busque en la columna de la derecha el antónimo de cada palabra en la columna de la izquierda.

MODELO: feo **bonito**

1. claro   *a.* imaginario
2. normal   *b.* indigno
3. digno   *c.* muerto
4. encontrar   *d.* desconocido
5. realista   *e.* anormal
6. conocido   *f.* oscuro
7. vivo   *g.* perder

b Complete las oraciones con la expresión más apropiada.

amor   se ha hecho   los sueños
ha creado   desde   la época
un cuadro   vencía

1. Dalí _____ numerosas obras surrealistas.
2. Los surrealistas tratan de interpretar _____ .
3. Plácido Domingo _____ un distinguido cantante de ópera.
4. Los hispanos sienten gran _____ por la música.
5. Sor Juana vivió durante _____ colonial.
6. Las obras de Picasso deben contemplarse _____ diferentes puntos de vista.
7. *El entierro del conde de Orgaz* es _____ famoso de El Greco.
8. A veces creemos que Don Quijote _____ la realidad sórdida.

c Identifique a las siguientes personas como **pintor, músico o escritor.**

1. Picasso   6. El Greco
2. Cervantes   7. García Márquez
3. Darío   8. Andrés Segovia
4. Goya   9. Borges
5. Albéniz   10. Velázquez

d Complete las oraciones.

1. La obra maestra de Velázquez es...
2. *Los fusilamientos del 3 de mayo* es del pintor...
3. El pintor que ha influido más en el arte contemporáneo es...
4. Rivera, Orozco y Siqueiros pintaron una extensa serie de...
5. El compositor de *La danza ritual del fuego* es...
6. La literatura hispana se distingue desde sus comienzos por...
7. Dos personajes clásicos de la literatura española son...
8. Sor Juana de la Cruz defendió...
9. Las novelas hispanoamericanas anteriores a 1950 denuncian...
10. Tres famosos escritores contemporáneos de Hispanoamérica son...

Las meninas (*Ladies in Waiting*) es la obra maestra de Velázquez.

e **Interpretación.** *Las meninas* es una maravillosa combinación de realismo y perspectiva artística. Refiérase Ud. a ese cuadro, y conteste las siguientes preguntas. Después compare sus respuestas o interpretación con otro(a) estudiante.

1. ¿Quién será el pintor que está a la izquierda?
2. ¿Crees que el señor en la puerta va a entrar o salir?
3. ¿Crees que las dos figuras en el fondo *(rear)* son imágenes en un cuadro o en un espejo *(mirror)*?
4. ¿Por *(Through)* dónde entra la luz en el cuadro?
5. ¿Cómo son las caras de las personas?
6. ¿A quiénes mira el pintor? ¿A quiénes pintará?

f **Poesía** *(Poetry).* No es raro que de vez en cuando *(now and then)* los hispanos reciten algunos de sus poemas favoritos en las tertulias o las reuniones. Apréndase Ud. los siguientes versos de memoria, y después vamos a ver *(let's see)* quién da la mejor interpretación en clase.

Rimas[1]

Por una mirada,[2] un mundo
por una sonrisa,[3] un cielo[4]
por un beso[5]... ¡yo no sé
que te diera[6] por un beso!

Gustavo Adolfo Bécquer
(España, 1836–1870)

1. *Poems (Rhymes)*   2. *For a glance*
3. *smile*   4. *sky*   5. *kiss*
6. *I'd give*

Cuadros y ángulos[1]

Casas enfiladas,[2] casas enfiladas,
casas enfiladas,
Cuadrados, cuadrados, cuadrados.
Casas enfiladas.
Las gentes ya tienen el alma[3] cuadrada,
ideas en fila[4]
y ángulo en la espalda.[5]
Yo misma he vertido[6] ayer una lágrima,[7]
Dios mío, cuadrada.

Alfonsina Storni
(Argentina, 1892–1938)

1. *Squares and angles*   2. *Houses in a row*
3. *soul*   4. *in a row*   5. *(one's) back*
6. *I myself shed*   7. *tear*

Vocabulario

SUSTANTIVOS
el **cuadro** *picture*
el **derecho** *right*
la **época** *period, era*
la **mitad** *half*
la **obra** *work*
la **obra maestra** *masterpiece*
el **pintor**, la **pintora** *painter*
el **pueblo** *people, town*
el **siglo** *century*
los **sueños** *dreams*

ADJETIVOS
claro(a) *light (color)*
desconocido(a) *unknown*

digno(a) *worthy, dignified*
oscuro(a) *dark*
vivo(a) *alive, lively*

VERBOS
contar (ue) *to count, tell*
distinguir *to distinguish*
encontrar (ue) *to find*
hacerse *to become*
pintar *to paint*
vencer (z) *to conquer*

EXPRESIONES
desde *from, since (a certain time)*
entre *between, among*

Examen IV

I   Tell your classmate about a trip you plan to take to a national park. Include:

1. when and where you will go
2. how far it is
3. who will be going with you and in whose car
4. what you will see in the park
5. what you will do there (swim, go for a walk, ride a horse, etc.)
6. what you will have for lunch
7. what you will wear
8. how long you will stay there
    Say also:
9. that you will have a good time
10. that you want him (her) to go with you

II   Make up five questions in the present perfect for each situation.

1. An employer asking an employee: "Have you done . . . ? Have you written to . . . ?" Use the Ud. form.
2. A parent asking a child: "Have you gotten up? Have you taken a bath?," etc. Use the **tú** form.

III   Say five things you would do or change if you were president of the nation, beginning your sentence with **Si yo fuera...**

IV   Imagine that a visitor from Spain asks you (a travel agent) about traveling from New York to California. Answer his or her questions.

1. ¿Sería mejor ir en avión o en tren?
2. ¿Cuánto costaría un boleto de idea y vuelta *(round trip)*?
3. ¿Cuántos días tendría yo que pasar en California para que la compañía me diera un descuento?
4. ¿Qué días podría ir y venir?
5. ¿Quién me llevaría al aeropuerto?

V   Your classmate has a bad memory and asks you basically the same question twice. Refer to the information in parentheses to ask and answer the questions in the preterite. Use the formal forms of the pronouns and verbs.

MODELO: (dar / el cuaderno)
　　　　　　Compañero(a): **¿A quién le dio Ud. el cuaderno?**
　　　　　　Usted: **Le di el cuaderno a Ud.**
　　　　　　Compañero(a): **¿Me lo dio a mí?**
　　　　　　Usted: **Sí, se lo di a Ud.**

1. devolver / los papeles   3. dar / las instrucciones
2. prestar / el bolígrafo   4. enseñar / la foto

Switch roles and repeat the previous exercise. Use the familiar forms this time.

MODELO: Compañero(a): **¿A quién le diste el cuaderno?**
          Tú: **Te lo di a ti.**
          Compañero(a): **¿ ... a mí?**
          Tú: **Sí,...**

Writing

I **Pronombres directos e indirectos.** Cambie las palabras en cursiva a pronombres y después escriba la oración otra vez.

MODELO: Le prestamos *el carro*. **Se lo prestamos.**

1. Les enseñaré *la casa*.
2. Te traje *el periódico*.
3. No entiendo *a la Sra. de Morales*.
4. Deben darle *el boleto* a Ud.
5. ¿Conoces *a mis amigas*?
6. Patricia nos ha preparado *unos sándwiches*.
7. ¡Envíeles *los paquetes* por correo!
8. ¡No me mencionen *ese nombre* más!

II **¿Indicativo, subjuntivo o infinitivo?** Complete con la forma apropiada del verbo entre paréntesis. Note el tiempo (tense) que el contexto requiere.

1. (llamar) Emilia siempre nos _____ cuando llega a casa.
2. (tener) Ojalá que Uds. _____ buena suerte.
3. (pedir) ¿Prefieres que yo _____ algo?
4. (manejar) Es verdad que Lorenzo _____ como loco.
5. (olvidar) No creo que ellos te _____ jamás.
6. (decir) Los muchachos se fueron sin _____ adiós.
7. (pintar) Mamá quería que nosotros _____ la casa.
8. (escribir) ¿Conoces a alguien que _____ programas para las computadoras?
9. (bajar) Aunque el vendedor _____ el precio, no compraré ese televisor.
10. (cometer) Dudábamos que tú _____ ese error.
11. (reunirse) Tenemos que _____ este viernes.
12. (ser) No hay nada que _____ difícil para ella.
13. (comprender) Les expliqué todo despacio para que ellos me _____ bien.
14. (aumentar) Es posible que el gobierno _____ los impuestos.
15. (regalar) ¿Dónde están los dulces que Uds. me _____ para mi cumpleaños?
16. (perder) ¡Váyanse en taxi para no _____ tiempo!
17. (crear) Será mejor que hables con don Julio antes de que él _____ más problemas.
18. (hacer) Te daré un beso con tal que me _____ mi plato favorito.

III   Traduzca al español las palabras entre paréntesis.

1. *(I would like)* *A mí _____ invitarlos a almorzar.
2. *(We gave it to you)* ¿La tarjeta? Nosotros _____ a Ud.
3. *(I still haven't seen him)* Todavía no _____ .
4. *(Are we lacking)* ¿Qué documentos _____ ?
5. *(when Rita turns fifteen)* Tendremos tremenda fiesta _____ .
6. *(anything)* No me dijiste _____ .
7. *(none of them)* ¿Esas canciones? No sé cantar _____ .
8. *(might offer us)* Buscábamos una compañía que _____ mejor precio.
9. *(if I had time)* Iría a la reunión _____ .
10. *(made)* Habían _____ un postre delicioso.
11. *(count on you)* ¿Podríamos _____ ?
12. *(lend them to me)* Sí, las tijeras. ¡Por favor, _____ Ud.!

IV   Vocabulario

a   **La mesa.** Usted tiene invitados a cenar esta noche. Mencione ocho utensilios que pondrá en la mesa.

b   **La cena.** Haga una lista de ocho cosas que les servirá a sus invitados. Empiece con el coctel, después el plato principal y finalmente el postre y las bebidas.

c   **Expresiones.** Traduzca al español.

1. a well-done steak
2. orange juice
3. collect call
4. the highway
5. the bridge
6. ahead
7. to try to
8. the picture
9. light and dark
10. wide not narrow
11. at the beginning
12. love

V   **Las obras maestras.** Refiérase a las siguientes listas y escriba oraciones donde Ud. relacione las personas con su obra o profesión.

MODELO: Goya pintó...
      Vargas Llosa y García Márquez eran...

1. Goya
2. El Greco
3. Manuel de Falla
4. Cervantes
5. Picasso
6. Velázquez

a. *Las meninas*
b. *El entierro del conde de Orgaz*
c. *Las doncellas de Avignon*
d. *La danza ritual del fuego*
e. *Los fusilamientos del 3 de mayo*
f. *Don Quijote de la Mancha*

1. Vargas Llosa, García Márquez
2. El Cid, Don Quijote
3. Darío, Mistral
4. Albéniz, Segovia
5. Rivera, Orozco, Siqueiros

a. *artistas de pinturas murales*
b. *escritores contemporáneos*
c. *músicos famosos*
d. *personajes de la literatura*
e. *poeta y poetisa eminentes*

*Don't use **quisiera** with this construction.

Otras consideraciones

Forms not studied specifically in the text

I   *Los mandatos familiares.*

Negative **tú** commands use the present subjunctive. Regular affirmative **tú** commands are identical to the third–person singular (**él**) of the present indicative. Placement of object pronouns is the same as with the **Ud(s).** commands. (Review pages 125–128.)

	MANDATOS	
	Afirmativos	**Negativos**
Formal	¡**Hable (Ud.)!** ¡**Coma!** ¡**Traiga!** ¡**Levántese!** ¡**Dígame!**	¡**No hable (Ud.)!** ¡**No se levante!** ¡**No me diga!**
Familiar	¡**Habla** (tú)! ¡**Come!** ¡**Trae!** ¡**Levántate!** *Irregulares:* decir **di** ¡**Dime!** venir **ven** tener **ten** ver **ve** poner **pon** ¡**Ponte la chaqueta!** salir **sal** hacer **haz** ser **sé**	¡**No hables** (tú)! ¡**No te levantes!** ¡**No te pongas la chaqueta!** ¡**No seas malo!**

Formal commands, as well as familiar negative commands, use present subjunctive forms.

SITUACIÓN

Imagínese que hoy Ud. cuida *(take care)* a Pedrito, un niñito de ocho años. Dígale diez mandatos, algunos afirmativos y otros negativos.

MODELO: Pedrito, ¡**abre la puerta!**   ¡**no la abras!**
　　　　　Pedrito, ¡**ponte el pijama!**   ¡**no te lo pongas!**

251

II *Los tiempos progresivos*

The progressive tenses emphasize an action in progress at a given moment.

¿Qué **está haciendo Ud.** ahora?	*What are you doing now?*
Estoy estudiando un poco.	*I'm studying a little.*
¿A quién **le**[1] **estabas escribiendo**?	*To whom were you writing?*
Estaba escribiéndole[1] a Mayra.	*I was writing to Mayra.*

> The progressives consist of a conjugated form of **estar** plus the present participle, which is formed by adding **-ando** to the stem of **-ar** verbs and **-iendo** to the stem of **-er** and **-ir** verbs.

hablar	**hablando**	leer	**leyendo**[2]
comer	**comiendo**	oír	**oyendo**
escribir	**escribiendo**	decir	**diciendo**[3]
		dormir	**durmiendo**[3]

Remember that Spanish uses the simple present to indicate immediate future actions and to describe actions someone is doing over a period of time, but not necessarily at this moment.

Me mudo este verano.	*I'm moving this summer.*
¿Trabajan Uds. en una clínica?	*Are you working in a clinic?*

PRÁCTICA

a Cambie según el modelo.

MODELO: Estudio frecuentemente. **Pero no estoy estudiando ahora.**

1. Descanso frecuentemente.
2. Leo frecuentemente.
3. Corro mucho.
4. Me preocupo mucho.
5. Los ayudo generalmente.

b ¿Qué están haciendo estas personas ahora? Use el presente progresivo de los verbos a la derecha para contestar.

1. el, la chofer — cuidar a los niños
2. la enfermera — pintar un cuadro
3. el, la artista — escuchar y hablar
4. la niñera — manejar
5. el niño — dormir
6. su profesor(a) — ponerle una inyección al paciente
7. sus compañeros — pensar en...
8. usted — ¿?

[1] Object pronouns can either be attached to the end of the participle or placed before *estar*.
[2] An unstressed **-i** between vowels becomes **-y**.
[3] Stem-changing **-ir** verbs change the **e** to **i**, and the **o** to **u**. See also Los Verbos, page 261.

III *Las preposiciones para y por.*

Depending on the context, the meaning of both **por** y **para** in English is *for*. However, these prepositions cannot be interchanged without affecting the meaning.

A **Para** is equivalent to *for* with these meanings:

1. *destination (place, time), intended for*

Salieron **para** el centro.	*They left for downtown.*
Lo necesito **para** la una.	*I need it for (by) one o'clock.*
¿**Para** quién es esto?	*Whom is this for?*

2. *in order to*

Me senté adelante **para** ver mejor.	*I sat up front in order to see better.*
Estudia **para** (ser) maestro.	*He's studying (in order) to be a teacher.*

3. *in the employment of*

Trabajan **para** una casa editorial.	*They work for a publishing house.*

B **Por** is equivalent to *for* with these meanings:

1. *for (the sake of), because of*

Se sacrifican mucho **por** sus hijos.	*They sacrifice a lot for their children.*
Nos quedamos en casa **por** la tormenta.	*We stayed home because of the storm.*

2. *in exchange for*

Le di 50.000 pesos **por** el anillo.	*I gave her 50,000 pesos for the ring.*

Other meanings of **por**:

1. *through, along*

¡Entren **por** aquí!	*Enter through here!*
Caminamos por la calle Obispo.	*We walked along Bishop St.*

2. *per* (units of measure)

Vamos a ochenta kilómetros **por** hora.	*We're going eighty kilometers per hour.*
Las frutas se venden **por** kilo.	*The fruits are sold by the kilo.*

3. *during (in)* the morning, afternoon and so on

Hago ejercicios **por** la tarde.	*I exercise in the afternoon.*

4. in several set expressions

por Dios	*for heaven's sake*	**por fin**	*finally*
por ejemplo	*for example*	**¿por qué?**	*why?*
por eso	*that's why*	**por teléfono**	*by telephone*
por favor	*please*		

PRÁCTICA

a   Conteste Ud.

1. ¿Estudia Ud. para computista? ¿para contador *(accountant)*?
2. ¿Prefiere estudiar por la mañana o por la tarde?
3. ¿A cuántas millas (o kilómetros) por hora maneja en el campo? ¿en la ciudad?
4. ¿Cuántos dólares pagó por su carro? ¿por su reloj?
5. ¿Por dónde le gusta caminar?
6. ¿Para quién va a comprar un regalo?
7. ¿Cuántas veces *(times)* por semana va al supermercado?
8. ¿Para cuándo se graduará?

b   Complete con **por**, **para**, o nada, según sea necesario.

1. Trabajan _____ una compañía extranjera.
2. Estoy nervioso _____ el examen.
3. Saldremos _____ España en diciembre.
4. Buscaba _____ lugar tranquilo.
5. Las reservaciones son _____ el primero de julio.
6. Viviré con una familia hispana _____ conversar más en español.
7. Esperamos _____ el autobús.
8. _____ favor, llámeme _____ teléfono.

IV *Las formas posesivas enfáticas*

To emphasize possession, Spanish speakers use stressed possessives, also called the long forms of possessive adjectives.

mío *(a, os, as)*	*my, mine, of mine*
tuyo *(a, os, as)*	*yours, of yours*
suyo *(a, os, as)*	*his, of his; hers, of hers; yours* (de Ud., de Uds.), *of yours; theirs, of theirs*
nuestro *(a, os, as)*	*ours, of ours*
vuestro *(a, os, as)*	*yours, of yours*

¿Las llaves? No son **mías**. Son **tuyas**.	*The keys? They aren't mine. They're yours.*
¿Los amigos de Julia? Sí, conocí a unos amigos **suyos**.	*Julia's friends? Yes, I met some friends of hers.*

Note that the possessives agree in number and gender with the thing possessed and not the owner. To clarify the possessor, **suyo (a, os, as)** may be replaced by **de él, de ella, de Ud., de ellos, de Uds.**

Este asiento es de ella, no de él.   *This seat is hers, not his.*

PRÁCTICA

a   Haga los cambios según el modelo.

MODELO: Son mis papeles.   **Son unos papeles míos.**
                             Son míos.

1. Son mis cartas.   5. Era mi profesora.
2. Son nuestros amigos.   6. Eran sus cuentas.
3. Es tu revista.   7. Son tus periódicos.
4. Es su cuaderno.   8. Son sus exámenes.

b   ¿Cómo se dice en español?

1. This pen is mine, not yours.
2. These suitcases are his, not hers.
3. He's a friend of ours and of theirs, too.

c   Hágale estas preguntas a su compañero(a). Él (ella) debe contestarle con un posesivo enfático.

MODELO: Usted: ¿Quieres comer en mi casa o en la tuya?
             Él (ella): **Quiero comer en la mía (*or* en la tuya).**

1. ¿Quieres dar un paseo en mi carro o en el tuyo?
2. ¿Deseas usar mi máquina de escribir o la tuya?
3. ¿Cuáles son más difíciles, mis clases o las tuyas?
4. ¿Quiénes son más amables, mis profesores o los tuyos?

Apéndices

Respuestas de los Exámenes I–IV

EXAMEN I   *LISTENING–DICTADO*   **I.** Answers vary; **II.** 1. cuarenta y seis-setenta y cuatro-cero siete; 2–3. Answers vary; **III.** 1. seiscientos cincuenta pesos; 2–5. Answers vary; **IV.** 1. hache-e-erre-e-ere-a; 2–5. Answers vary. *SPEAKING* **I.** Answers vary. 1. Estoy bien; 2. Hace buen tiempo; 3. Son las tres; 4. Mi cumpleaños es el dos de mayo; 5. Sí, soy estudiante; 6. Tengo dos hermanos; 7. Mi carro es negro; 8. El almuerzo es a las ocho; 9. Me gusta el béisbol. **II.** Possible questions given. **III.** Answers vary. 1. Me llamo...; 2. Soy de...; 3.Soy..; 4. El lunes tengo... a las diez de la mañana. 5. Me gusta...; No me gusta... *WRITING* **I.** 1. Son las dos y media de la tarde; 2. Son las diez menos quince (cuarto) de la noche; 3. Son las siete en punto de la mañana. **II.** 1. el ocho de noviembre de mil quinientos diecinueve; 2. el catorce de julio de mil setecientos noventa y nueve; 3. el veinte de enero de mil novecientos ochenta y uno. **III.** 1. Buenos días, Señora Gómez; 2. Muchas gracias; 3. Hace calor aquí en el verano; 4. Hay veinticuatro estudiantes aquí; 5. Mi prima Marta es muy simpática; 6. Hasta mañana; 7. Tengo el pelo castaño y los ojos verdes; 8. Con permiso; 9. ¿Cuánto cuesta? *CULTURA* 1. Sí; 2. No; 3. Sí; 4. No. *READING* **I.** 1. e; 2. d; 3. a; 4. b. **II.** 1. llamo; 2. Soy; 3. el; 4. día; 5. tengo; 6. fecha; 7. patriótica; 8. gustan.

EXAMEN II   *LISTENING–DICTADO: Answers vary* *SPEAKING* **I.** 1. Carlos entra; 2. Alicia y Diego bailan; 3. Tú cocinas; 4. Nosotros leemos; 5. Yo me baño; **II.** Answers vary. 1. Me levanto...; 2. Voy a...; 3. Almuerzo...; 4. Hablo con...; 5. Leo...; 6. Juego a...; 7. Answers vary; 8. Me acuesto... **III.** Answers vary. **IV.** 1. Tengo dolor de garganta; 2. Tengo dolor de oído; 3. Tengo dolor de cabeza; 4. Tengo dolor de espalda; 5. Tengo dolor de estómago. *WRITING* **I.** Answers vary. May include: la oreja, la mano, el brazo, el pie, la pierna, el pecho, el corazón, la nariz, etc. **II.** 1. busca; 2. comprendes; 3. debemos; 4. cree; 5. hablan; 6. me siento; 7. pueden; 8. vemos; 9. sé; 10. da. **III.** 1. ¿A qué hora llega Ud.? Llego a...; 2. ¿Qué refresco tomas tú? Tomo...; 3. ¿Dónde está la profesora? Está...; 4. ¿A qué clases asistes tú? Asisto a...; 5. ¿A quién esperan Uds.? Esperamos a...; 6. ¿A qué juegas tú? Juego.... **IV.** 1. Lupita tiene los ojos castaños; 2. Vamos al parque; 3. Josefina es española; 4. La carta es del esposo; 5. Tienes mucho dinero mexicano; 6. Yo me pongo el abrigo; 7. Berta y Mariana quieren ir de compras; 8. Arturo es un buen estudiante; 9. Buscamos al Sr. Ruiz; 10. La hermana es joven y guapa; 11. Viven en una casa de madera; 12. Me gusta la fiesta. **V.** 1. es; 2. es; 3. está; 4. es; 5. están; 6. es; 7. está. **VI.** Answers vary. 1. El departamento de muebles está a la derecha; 2. La librería está derecho; 3. El departamento de ropa está arriba; 4. La zapatería está a la izquierda; 5. Los baños están abajo. **VII.** Answers vary; **VIII.** 1. ¿Cómo están Uds.?; 2. Somos de los Estados Unidos; 3. ¿Habla Ud. inglés?; 4. ¿Dónde trabajas?; 5. ¿Te diviertes en la clase de español?; 6. ¿En qué puedo servirle?; 7. Quiero probarme los pantalones azules; 8. Aquí se come temprano; 9. ¿A quién esperas?; 10. Sabes jugar al tenis, ¿no?; 11. Perdóneme, estoy perdido(a); 12. Deben ver a la Sra. Flores hoy. *READING* 1. cree; 2. vivir; 3. hispana; 4. tienen; 5. novela; 6. del; 7. toda; 8. entre.

EXAMEN III   *LISTENING–DICTADO: Answers vary* *SPEAKING* **I.** Answers vary but the first person preterite of the verb should be used. 1. me levanté; 2. fui; 3. estudié; 4. vi; 5. compré; 6. comí y tomé; 7. leí; 8–9. Answers vary; 10. me acosté. **II.** Answers vary. **III.** 1. Answers vary. Possible verbs: quiero que; prefiero que; deseo que; es necesario que; espero que; etc. 2. Answers vary; 3. Answers vary; 4. a. Eran las nueve de la noche. Hacía mal tiempo. Llovía. b. El chófer del otro auto dobló de repente a la izquierda y chocó conmigo; c. Mi amiga se lastimó la cabeza y el cuello. Yo me lastimé la pierna derecha y la espalda; d. Quiero que llame a un médico. *WRITING* **I.** 1a. Ellos son nuestros hijos; b. Tú estás en tu casa; c. Sus maletas son azules; d. El apartamento de ellos está en el segundo piso; 2a. Necesito esa enciclopedia; b. Hablábamos con esos señores, no aquéllos; c. ¿Prefieres estos asientos o ésos?; 3a. Augustín es tan alto como tú; b. Catalina es la más ambiciosa de la familia. **II.** 1. sirve; 2. me pongo; 3. salen; 4. pides; 5. hago; 6. se quitan; 7. nos mudamos; 8. digo. **III.** 1. tienen sueño; 2. tienes hambre; 3. tiene miedo; 4. tengo sed; 5. tenemos frío. **IV.** 1. Pregúntele al chofer; 2. Vengan a la reunión; 3. Siéntense aquí; 4. Traiga a sus amigos; 5. No les pague a ellos; 6. No se preocupen por nosotros. **V.** 1. b; 2. a; 3. b. **VI.** 1. revisemos; 2. pueden; 3. cruce; 4. levantarme; 5. busques; 6. se diviertan; 7. descansar; 8. jueguen. **VII.** 1. Fui; 2. trajo; 3. Veíamos; 4. llegaron; 5. era; 6. estudiaba; 7. pusiste. **VIII.** 1. nació; 2. era; 3. se mudaba; 4. tenía; 5. fue; 6. aprendió; 7. comenzó; 8. tomó; 9. se distinguió; 10. regresaba; 11. capturaron; 12. llevaron; 13. llegó; 14. publicó; 15. fue. **IX.** 1. el cuarto / la habitación; 2. el baño; 3. la cocina; 4. la sala; 5. el comedor; 6. la naranja / la china; 7. la piña; 8. la manzana; 9. el melocotón / durazno; 10. la toronja; 11. ¡Pase!; 12. ¿Qué le pasa?; 13. ¡Felicitaciones!; 14. igualmente; 15. muy agradecido.

EXAMEN IV   *SPEAKING* **I.** Answers vary; **II.** 1. Answers vary. ¿Ha hecho...?, ¿Ha escrito a...? 2. Answers vary. ¿Te has levantado?, ¿Te has bañado...? **III.** Answers vary. **IV.** Answers vary. **V.** 1. **Compañero:** ¿A quién le devolvió Ud. los papeles?; **Ud.:** Le devolví los papeles a Ud.; **Compañero:** ¿Me los devolvió Ud. a mí?; **Ud.:** Sí, se los devolví a Ud.; 2. **Compañero:** ¿A quién le prestó Ud. el bolígrafo?; **Ud.:** Le presté el bolígrafo a Ud.; **Compañero:** ¿Me lo prestó a mí?; **Ud.:** Sí, se lo presté a Ud.; 3. **Compañero:** ¿A quién le dijo Ud. las instrucciones? **Ud.:** Le dije las instrucciones a Ud.; **Compañero:** ¿Me las dijo a mí?; **Ud.:** Sí, se las dije a Ud. 4. **Compañero:** ¿A quién le enseñó la foto?; **Ud.:** Le enseñé la foto a Ud.; **Compañero:** ¿Me la enseñó a mí?; **Ud.:** Sí, se la enseñé a Ud.. Second time: 1. **Compañero:** ¿A quién le devolviste los papeles?; **Ud.:** Te devolví los papeles a ti; **Compañero:** ¿Me los devolviste a mí?; **Ud.:** Sí, te los devolví a ti; 2. **Compañero:** ¿A quién le prestaste el bolígrafo?; **Ud.:** Te presté el boligrafo a ti; **Compañero:** ¿Me lo prestaste a mí?; **Ud.:** Sí, te lo presté a ti; 3. **Compañero:** ¿A quién le dijiste las instrucciones?; **Ud.:** Te dije las instrucciones a ti; **Compañero:** ¿Me las dijiste a mí?; **Ud.:** Sí, te las dije a ti; 4. **Compañero:** ¿A quién le enseñaste la foto?; **Ud.:** Te enseñé la foto a ti; **Compañero:** ¿Me la enseñaste a mí?; **Ud.:** Sí, te la enseñé a ti. *WRITING* **I.** 1. Se la enseñaré; 2. Te lo traje; 3. No la entiendo; 4. Deben dárselo a Ud.; 5. ¿Las conoces?; 6. Patricia nos los ha preparado; 7. ¡Envíeselos por correo!; 8. ¡No me lo mencionen más! **II.** 1. llama; 2. tengan; 3. pida; 4. maneja; 5. olviden; 6. decir; 7. pintáramos; 8. escriba; 9. baje; 10. cometieras; 11. reunirnos; 12. sea; 13. comprendieran; 14. aumente; 15. regalaron; 16. perder; 17. cree; 18. hagas. **III.** 1. me gustaría; 2. se la dimos; 3. lo he visto; 4. nos faltan; 5. cuando Rita cumpla quince años; 6. nada; 7. ninguna de ellas; 8. nos ofreciera; 9. si tuviera tiempo; 10. hecho; 11. contar contigo; 12. préstemelas. **IV.** a. Answers vary. May include: los platos, los tenedores, los cuchillos, las cucharas, las cucharitas, las servilletas, los copas, las tazas, etc.; b. Answers vary. May include: el coctel, la sopa, la ensalada, el pescado, la carne, las legumbres, la salsa, el helado, etc. c. 1. Un bistec bien asado; 2. jugo de naranja; 3. una llamada a pagar allá; 4. la carretera; 5. el puente; 6. todo derecho; 7. tratar de; 8. el cuadro; 9. claro y oscuro; 10. ancho no estrecho; 11. al principio; 12. el amor. *LAS OBRAS MAESTRAS* **A.** 1. e; 2. b; 3. d; 4. f; 5. c; 6. a. **B.** 1. b; 2. d; 3. e; 4. c; 5. a.

Los verbos

Stem-changing and spelling-changing verbs

In the following list, the numbers in parenthesis indicate that the conjugated verb forms appear in the charts on pages 264–273.

Stem-changing verbs

1. Verbs ending in -ar and -er

e to ie	o to ue
ascender	acostarse
cerrar	almorzar
comenzar[1]	contar (3)
defender	costar
despertarse	devolver
empezar (8)	doler
encender	encontrar
entender	jugar[2] (13)
negar	llover
pensar (17)	mover
perder (18)	poder (19)
querer (21)	probarse
sembrar	recordar
sentarse	volver (30)

2. Verbs ending in -ir

e to ie	o to ue	e to i
divertirse (6)	dormir (7)	decir (5)
invertir	morir	pedir (16)
preferir		repetir
referir		seguir[3]
requerir		servir
sentirse (24)		vestirse

[1]See Spelling-changing verbs z to c, pp. 127–150.
[2]See Spelling-changing verbs, pp. 127–150.
[3]See Spelling-changing verbs gu to g, p. 114.

Spelling-changing verbs

1. c to qu
Verbs that end in -car change c to qu before e:
¿Busque Ud.!   (Yo) Busqué ayer.
Other verbs: practicar, tocar, sacar

2. z to c
Verbs that end in -zar change z to c before e:
¡Comience Ud.!   (Yo) Comencé ayer.
Other verbs: almorzar, comenzar, cruzar

3. g to gu
Verbs that end in -gar change g to gu before e:
¡Juegen!   No jugué ayer.
Other verbs: llegar, pagar

4. gu to g
Verbs that end in -guir change gu to g before a and o:
¡Siga Ud.!   (Yo) Sigo hablando ahora.
Other verbs: conseguir, distinguir

5. g to j
Verbs that end in -ger or -gir change g to j before a and o:
¡Recojan Uds.!   (Yo) Recojo ahora.
Other verbs: proteger, dirigir

6. i to y
Verbs that end in -eer, the unstressed i between vowels becomes y:
Leyó mucho.   ¡Te dije que no leyeras!
Other examples: creer (see leer (14).
The verb oír (15), also changes i to y:
¿Oyes tú bien?   ¿Oyeron el anuncio?

Regular verbs

Simple tenses

	INDICATIVE				
INFINITIVE	*Present*	*Imperfect*	*Preterite*	*Future*	*Conditional*
hablar	hablo	hablaba	hablé	hablaré	hablaría
	hablas	hablabas	hablaste	hablarás	hablarías
	habla	hablaba	habló	hablará	hablaría
	hablamos	hablábamos	hablamos	hablaremos	hablaríamos
	habláis	hablabais	hablasteis	hablaréis	hablaríais
	hablan	hablaban	hablaron	hablarán	hablarían
comer	como	comía	comí	comeré	comería
	comes	comías	comiste	comerás	comerías
	come	comía	comió	comerá	comería
	comemos	comíamos	comimos	comeremos	comeríamos
	coméis	comíais	comisteis	comeréis	comeríais
	comen	comían	comieron	comerán	comerían
vivir	vivo	vivía	viví	viviré	viviría
	vives	vivías	viviste	vivirás	vivirías
	vive	vivía	vivió	vivirá	viviría
	vivimos	vivíamos	vivimos	viviremos	viviríamos
	vivís	vivíais	vivisteis	viviréis	viviríais
	viven	vivían	vivieron	vivirán	vivirían

Perfect tenses

	INDICATIVE			
PAST PARTICIPLE	*Present perfect*	*Past perfect*	*Future perfect*	*Conditional perfect*
hablado	he hablado	había hablado	habré hablado	habría hablado
	has hablado	habías hablado	habrás hablado	habrías hablado
	ha hablado	había hablado	habrá hablado	habría hablado
	hemos hablado	habíamos hablado	habremos hablado	habríamos hablado
	habéis hablado	habíais hablado	habréis hablado	habríais hablado
	han hablado	habían hablado	habrán hablado	habrían hablado
comido	he comido	había comido	habré comido	habría comido
	has comido	habías comido	habrás comido	habrías comido
	ha comido	había comido	habrá comido	habría comido
	hemos comido	habíamos comido	habremos comido	habríamos comido
	habéis comido	habíais comido	habréis comido	habríais comido
	han comido	habían comido	habrán comido	habrían comido
vivido	he vivido	había vivido	habré vivido	habría vivido
	has vivido	habías vivido	habrás vivido	habrías vivido
	ha vivido	había vivido	habrá vivido	habría vivido
	hemos vivido	habíamos vivido	habremos vivido	habríamos vivido
	habéis vivido	habíais vivido	habréis vivido	habríais vivido
	han vivido	habían vivido	habrán vivido	habrían vivido

	SUBJUNCTIVE	COMMANDS
Present	Imperfect	
hable	hablara (-se)[1]	—
hables	hablaras (-ses)	habla (no hables)
hable	hablara (-se)	hable
hablemos	habláramos (-semos)	hablemos
habléis	hablarais (-seis)	hablad (no habléis)
hablen	hablaran (-sen)	hablen
coma	comiera (-se)	—
comas	comieras (-ses)	come (no comas)
coma	comiera (-se)	coma
comamos	comiéramos (-semos)	comamos
comáis	comierais (-seis)	comed (no comáis)
coman	comieran (-sen)	coman
viva	viviera (-se)	—
vivas	vivieras (-ses)	vive (no vivas)
viva	viviera (-se)	viva
vivamos	viviéramos (-semos)	vivamos
viváis	vivierais (-seis)	vivid (no viváis)
vivan	vivieran (-sen)	vivan

[1]The -se alternate forms (hablase, hablases...) are less commonly used.

Progressive tenses

	SUBJUNCTIVE			INDICATIVE	
			PRESENT PARTICIPLE		
Present perfect	Past perfect			Present	Past
haya hablado	hubiera (-se) hablado		hablando	estoy hablando	estaba hablando
hayas hablado	hubieras (-ses) hablado			estás hablando	estabas hablando
haya hablado	hubiera (-se) hablado			está hablando	estaba hablando
hayamos hablado	hubiéramos (-semos) hablado			estamos hablando	estábamos hablando
hayáis hablado	hubierais (-seis) hablado			estáis hablando	estabais hablando
hayan hablado	hubieran (-sen) hablado			están hablando	estaban hablando
haya comido	hubiera (-se) comido		comiendo	estoy comiendo	estaba comiendo
hayas comido	hubieras (-ses) comido			estás comiendo	estabas comiendo
haya comido	hubiera (-se) comido			está comiendo	estaba comiendo
hayamos comido	hubiéramos (-semos) comido			estamos comiendo	estábamos comiendo
hayáis comido	hubierais (-seis) comido			estáis comiendo	estabais comiendo
hayan comido	hubieran (-sen) comido			están comiendo	estaban comiendo
haya vivido	hubiera (-se) vivido		viviendo	estoy viviendo	estaba viviendo
hayas vivido	hubieras (-ses) vivido			estás viviendo	estabas viviendo
haya vivido	hubiera (-se) vivido			está viviendo	estaba viviendo
hayamos vivido	hubiéramos (-semos) vivido			estamos viviendo	estábamos viviendo
hayáis vivido	hubierais (-seis) vivido			estáis viviendo	estabais viviendo
hayan vivido	hubieran (-sen) vivido			están viviendo	estaban viviendo

Irregular, stem-changing and spelling-changing verbs

	INDICATIVE				
INFINITIVE	*Present*	*Imperfect*	*Preterite*	*Future*	*Conditional*
1. andar	ando	andaba	anduve	andaré	andaría
	andas	andabas	anduviste	andarás	andarías
	anda	andaba	anduvo	andará	andaría
	andamos	andábamos	anduvimos	andaremos	andaríamos
	andáis	andabais	anduvisteis	andaréis	andaríais
	andan	andaban	anduvieron	andarán	andarían
2. conocer	conozco	conocía	conocí	conoceré	conocería
	conoces	conocías	conociste	conocerás	conocerías
	conoce	conocía	conoció	conocerá	conocería
	conocemos	conocíamos	conocimos	conoceremos	conoceríamos
	conocéis	conocíais	conocisteis	conoceréis	conoceríais
	conocen	conocían	conocieron	conocerán	conocerían
3. contar	cuento	contaba	conté	contaré	contaría
	cuentas	contabas	contaste	contarás	contarías
	cuenta	contaba	contó	contará	contaría
	contamos	contábamos	contamos	contaremos	contaríamos
	contáis	contabais	contasteis	contaréis	contaríais
	cuentan	contaban	contaron	contarán	contarían
4. dar	doy	daba	di	daré	daría
	das	dabas	diste	darás	darías
	da	daba	dio	dará	daría
	damos	dábamos	dimos	daremos	daríamos
	dais	dabais	disteis	daréis	daríais
	dan	daban	dieron	darán	darían
5. decir	digo	decía	dije	diré	diría
	dices	decías	dijiste	dirás	dirías
	dice	decía	dijo	dirá	diría
	decimos	decíamos	dijimos	diremos	diríamos
	decís	decíais	dijisteis	diréis	diríais
	dicen	decían	dijeron	dirán	dirían
6. divertirse	me divierto	divertía	divertí	divertiré	divertiría
	te diviertes	divertías	divertiste	divertirás	divertirías
	se divierte	divertía	divirtió	divertirá	divertiría
	nos divertimos	divertíamos	divertimos	divertiremos	divertiríamos
	os divertís	divertíais	divertisteis	divertiréis	divertiríais
	se divierten	divertían	divirtieron	divertirán	divertirían

Present	Imperfect			Present	Past
ande	anduviera (-se)	—		andando	andado
andes	anduvieras (-ses)	anda (no andes)			
ande	anduviera (-se)	ande			
andemos	anduviéramos (-semos)	andemos			
andéis	anduvierais (-seis)	andad (no andéis)			
anden	anduvieran (-sen)	anden			
conozca	conociera (-se)	—		conociendo	conocido
conozcas	conocieras (-ses)	conoce (no conozcas)			
conozca	conociera (-se)	conozca			
conozcamos	conociéramos (-semos)	conozcamos			
conozcáis	conocierais (-seis)	conoced (no conozcáis)			
conozcan	conocieran (-sen)	conozcan			
cuente	contara (-se)	—		contando	contado
cuentes	contaras (-ses)	cuenta (no cuentes)			
cuente	contara (-se)	cuente			
contemos	contáramos (-semos)	contemos			
contéis	contarais (-seis)	contad (no contéis)			
cuenten	contaran (-sen)	cuenten			
dé	diera (-se)	—		dando	dado
des	dieras (-ses)	da (no des)			
dé	diera (-se)	dé			
demos	diéramos (-semos)	demos			
deis	dierais (-seis)	dad (no deis)			
den	dieran (-sen)	den			
diga	dijera (-se)	—		diciendo	dicho
digas	dijeras (-ses)	di (no digas)			
diga	dijera (-se)	diga			
digamos	dijéramos (-semos)	digamos			
digáis	dijerais (-seis)	decid (no digáis)			
digan	dijeran (-sen)	digan			
divierta	divirtiera (-se)	—		divirtiendo	divertido
diviertas	divirtieras (-ses)	diviértete (no te diviertas)			
divierta	divirtiera (-se)	diviértase			
divirtamos	divirtiéramos (-semos)	divirtámonos			
divirtáis	divirtierais (-seis)	divertíos (no os divirtáis)			
diviertan	divirtieran (-sen)	diviértanse			

Irregular, stem-changing and spelling-changing verbs

		INDICATIVE			
INFINITIVE	*Present*	*Imperfect*	*Preterite*	*Future*	*Conditional*
7. dormir	duermo	dormía	dormí	dormiré	dormiría
	duermes	dormías	dormiste	dormirás	dormirías
	duerme	dormía	durmió	dormirá	dormiría
	dormimos	dormíamos	dormimos	dormiremos	dormiríamos
	dormís	dormíais	dormisteis	dormiréis	dormiríais
	duermen	dormían	durmieron	dormirán	dormirían
8. empezar	empiezo	empezaba	empecé	empezaré	empezaría
	empiezas	empezabas	empezaste	empezarás	empezarías
	empieza	empezaba	empezó	empezará	empezaría
	empezamos	empezábamos	empezamos	empezaremos	empezaríamos
	empezáis	empezabais	empezasteis	empezaréis	empezaríais
	empiezan	empezaban	empezaron	empezarán	empezarían
9. estar	estoy	estaba	estuve	estaré	estaría
	estás	estabas	estuviste	estarás	estarías
	está	estaba	estuvo	estará	estaría
	estamos	estábamos	estuvimos	estaremos	estaríamos
	estáis	estabais	estuvisteis	estaréis	estaríais
	están	estaban	estuvieron	estarán	estarían
10. haber	he	había	hube	habré	habría
	has	habías	hubiste	habrás	habrías
	ha	había	hubo	habrá	habría
	hemos	habíamos	hubimos	habremos	habríamos
	habéis	habíais	hubisteis	habréis	habríais
	han	habían	hubieron	habrán	habrían
11. hacer	hago	hacía	hice	haré	haría
	haces	hacías	hiciste	harás	harías
	hace	hacía	hizo	hará	haría
	hacemos	hacíamos	hicimos	haremos	haríamos
	hacéis	hacíais	hicisteis	haréis	haríais
	hacen	hacían	hicieron	harán	harían
12. ir	voy	iba	fui	iré	iría
	vas	ibas	fuiste	irás	irías
	va	iba	fue	irá	iría
	vamos	íbamos	fuimos	iremos	iríamos
	vais	ibais	fuisteis	iréis	iríais
	van	iban	fueron	irán	irían

Present	Imperfect		Present	Past
duerma	durmiera (-se)	—	durmiendo	dormido
duermas	durmieras (-ses)	duerme (no duermas)		
duerma	durmiera (-se)	duerma		
durmamos	durmiéramos (-semos)	durmamos		
durmáis	durmierais (-seis)	dormid (no durmáis)		
duerman	durmieran (-sen)	duerman		
empiece	empezara (-se)	—	empezando	empezado
empieces	empezaras (-ses)	empieza (no empieces)		
empiece	empezara (-se)	empiece		
empecemos	empezáramos (-semos)	empecemos		
empecéis	empezarais (-seis)	empezad (no empecéis)		
empiecen	empezaran (sen)	empiecen		
esté	estuviera (-se)	—	estando	estado
estés	estuvieras (-ses)	está (no estés)		
esté	estuviera (-se)	esté		
estemos	estuviéramos (-semos)	estemos		
estéis	estuvierais (-seis)	estad (no estéis)		
estén	estuvieran (-sen)	estén		
haya	hubiera (-se)	—	habiendo	habido
hayas	hubieras (-ses)	he (no hayas)		
haya	hubiera (-se)	haya		
hayamos	hubiéramos (-semos)	hayamos		
hayáis	hubierais (-seis)	habed (no hayáis)		
hayan	hubieran (-sen)	hayan		
haga	hiciera (-se)	—	haciendo	hecho
hagas	hicieras (-ses)	haz (no hagas)		
haga	hiciera (-se)	haga		
hagamos	hiciéramos (-semos)	hagamos		
hagáis	hicierais (-seis)	haced (no hagáis)		
hagan	hicieran (-sen)	hagan		
vaya	fuera (-se)	—	yendo	ido
vayas	fueras (-ses)	ve (no vayas)		
vaya	fuera (-se)	vaya		
vayamos	fuéramos (-semos)	vayamos		
vayáis	fuerais (-seis)	id (no vayáis)		
vayan	fueran (-sen)	vayan		

Irregular, stem-changing and spelling-changing verbs

		INDICATIVE			
INFINITIVE	Present	Imperfect	Preterite	Future	Conditional
13. jugar	juego	jugaba	jugué	jugaré	jugaría
	juegas	jugabas	jugaste	jugarás	jugarías
	juega	jugaba	jugó	jugará	jugaría
	jugamos	jugábamos	jugamos	jugaremos	jugaríamos
	jugáis	jugabais	jugasteis	jugaréis	jugaríais
	juegan	jugaban	jugaron	jugarán	jugarían
14. leer	leo	leía	leí	leeré	leería
	lees	leías	leíste	leerás	leerías
	lee	leía	leyó	leerá	leería
	leemos	leíamos	leímos	leeremos	leeríamos
	leéis	leíais	leísteis	leeréis	leeríais
	leen	leían	leyeron	leerán	leerían
15. oir	oigo	oía	oí	oiré	oiría
	oyes	oías	oíste	oirás	oirías
	oye	oía	oyó	oirá	oiría
	oímos	oíamos	oímos	oiremos	oiríamos
	oís	oíais	oísteis	oiréis	oiríais
	oyen	oían	oyeron	oirán	oirían
16. pedir	pido	pedía	pedí	pediré	pediría
	pides	pedías	pediste	pedirás	pedirías
	pide	pedía	pidió	pedirá	pediría
	pedimos	pedíamos	pedimos	pediremos	pediríamos
	pedís	pedíais	pedisteis	pediréis	pediríais
	piden	pedían	pidieron	pedirán	pedirían
17. pensar	pienso	pensaba	pensé	pensaré	pensaría
	piensas	pensabas	pensaste	pensarás	pensarías
	piensa	pensaba	pensó	pensará	pensaría
	pensamos	pensábamos	pensamos	pensaremos	pensaríamos
	pensáis	pensabais	pensasteis	pensaréis	pensaríais
	piensan	pensaban	pensaron	pensarán	pensarían
18. perder	pierdo	perdía	perdí	perderé	perdería
	pierdes	perdías	perdiste	perderás	perderías
	pierde	perdía	perdío	perderá	perdería
	perdemos	perdíamos	perdimos	perderemos	perderíamos
	perdéis	perdíais	perdisteis	perderéis	perderíais
	pierden	perdían	perdieron	perderán	perderían

	SUBJUNCTIVE		COMMANDS	PARTICIPLES	
Present	*Imperfect*			*Present*	*Past*
juegue	jugara (-se)	—		jugando	jugado
juegues	jugaras (-ses)	juega (no juegues)			
juegue	jugara (-se)	juegue			
juguemos	jugáramos (-semos)	juguemos			
juguéis	jugarais (-seis)	jugad (no juguéis)			
jueguen	jugaran (-sen)	jueguen			
lea	leyera (-se)	—		leyendo	leído
leas	leyeras (-ses)	lee (no leas)			
lea	leyera (-se)	lea			
leamos	leyéramos (-semos)	leamos			
leáis	leyerais (-seis)	leed (no leáis)			
lean	leyeran (-sen)	lean			
oiga	oyera (-se)	—		oyendo	oído
oigas	oyeras (-ses)	oye (no oigas)			
oiga	oyera (-se)	oiga			
oigamos	oyéramos (-semos)	oigamos			
oigáis	oyerais (-seis)	oíd (no oigáis)			
oigan	oyeran (-sen)	oigan			
pida	pidiera (-se)	—		pidiendo	pedido
pidas	pidieras (-ses)	pide (no pidas)			
pida	pidiera (-se)	pida			
pidamos	pidiéramos (-semos)	pidamos			
pidáis	pidierais (-seis)	pedid (no pidáis)			
pidan	pidieran (-sen)	pidan			
piense	pensara (-se)	—		pensando	pensado
pienses	pensaras (-ses)	piensa (no pienses)			
piense	pensara (-se)	piense			
pensemos	pensáramos (-semos)	pensemos			
penséis	pensarais (-seis)	pensad (no penséis)			
piensen	pensaran (-sen)	piensen			
pierda	perdiera (-se)	—		perdiendo	perdido
pierdas	perdieras (-ses)	pierde (no pierdas)			
pierda	perdiera (-se)	pierda			
perdamos	perdiéramos (-semos)	perdamos			
perdáis	perdierais (-seis)	perded (no perdáis)			
pierdan	perdieran (-sen)	pierdan			

Irregular, stem-changing and spelling-changing verbs

INFINITIVE	Present	Imperfect	Preterite	Future	Conditional
19. poder	puedo	podía	pude	podré	podría
	puedes	podías	pudiste	podrás	podrías
	puede	podía	pudo	podrá	podría
	podemos	podíamos	pudimos	podremos	podríamos
	podéis	podíais	pudisteis	podréis	podríais
	pueden	podían	pudieron	podrán	podrían
20. poner	pongo	ponía	puse	pondré	pondría
	pones	ponías	pusiste	pondrás	pondrías
	pone	ponía	puso	pondrá	pondría
	ponemos	poníamos	pusimos	pondremos	pondríamos
	ponéis	poníais	pusisteis	pondréis	pondríais
	ponen	ponían	pusieron	pondrán	pondrían
21. querer	quiero	quería	quise	querré	querría
	quieres	querías	quisiste	querrás	querrías
	quiere	quería	quiso	querrá	querría
	queremos	queríamos	quisimos	querremos	querríamos
	queréis	queríais	quisisteis	querréis	querríais
	quieren	querían	quisieron	querrán	querrían
22. saber	sé	sabía	supe	sabré	sabría
	sabes	sabías	supiste	sabrás	sabrías
	sabe	sabía	supo	sabrá	sabría
	sabemos	sabíamos	supimos	sabremos	sabríamos
	sabéis	sabíais	supisteis	sabréis	sabríais
	saben	sabían	supieron	sabrán	sabrían
23. salir	salgo	salía	salí	saldré	saldría
	sales	salías	saliste	saldrás	saldrías
	sale	salía	salió	saldrá	saldría
	salimos	salíamos	salimos	saldremos	saldríamos
	salís	salíais	salisteis	saldréis	saldríais
	salen	salían	salieron	saldrán	saldrían
24. sentir	siento	sentía	sentí	sentiré	sentiría
	sientes	sentías	sentiste	sentirás	sentirías
	siente	sentía	sintió	sentirá	sentiría
	sentimos	sentíamos	sentimos	sentiremos	sentiríamos
	sentís	sentíais	sentisteis	sentiréis	sentiríais
	sienten	sentían	sintieron	sentirán	sentirían

	SUBJUNCTIVE	COMMANDS	PARTICIPLES	
Present	Imperfect		Present	Past
pueda	pudiera (-se)		pudiendo	podido
puedas	pudieras (-ses)			
pueda	pudiera (-se)			
podamos	pudiéramos (-semos)			
podáis	pudierais (-seis)			
puedan	pudieran (-sen)			
ponga	pusiera (-se)	—	poniendo	puesto
pongas	pusieras (-ses)	pon (no pongas)		
ponga	pusiera (-se)	ponga		
pongamos	pusiéramos (-semos)	pongamos		
pongáis	pusierais (-seis)	poned (no pongáis)		
pongan	pusieran (-sen)	pongan		
quiera	quisiera (-se)	—	queriendo	querido
quieras	quisieras (-ses)	quiere (no quieras)		
quiera	quisiera (-se)	quiera		
queramos	quisiéramos (-semos)	queramos		
queráis	quisierais (-seis)	quered (no queráis)		
quieran	quisieran (-sen)	quieran		
sepa	supiera (-se)	—	sabiendo	sabido
sepas	supieras (-ses)	sabe (no sepas)		
sepa	supiera (-se)	sepa		
sepamos	supiéramos (-semos)	sepamos		
sepáis	supierais (-seis)	sabed (no sepáis)		
sepan	supieran (-sen)	sepan		
salga	saliera (-se)	—	saliendo	salido
salgas	salieras (-ses)	sal (no salgas)		
salga	saliera (-se)	salga		
salgamos	saliéramos (-semos)	salgamos		
salgáis	salierais (-seis)	salid (no salgáis)		
salgan	salieran (-sen)	salgan		
sienta	sintiera (-se)	—	sintiendo	sentido
sientas	sintieras (-ses)	siente (no sientas)		
sienta	sintiera (-se)	sienta		
sintamos	sintiéramos (-semos)	sintamos		
sintáis	sintierais (-seis)	sentid (no sintáis)		
sientan	sintieran (-sen)	sientan		

Irregular, stem-changing and spelling-changing verbs

		INDICATIVE		
INFINITIVE	*Present*	*Imperfect*	*Preterite*	*Future*	*Conditional*
25. ser	soy	era	fui	seré	sería
	eres	eras	fuiste	serás	serías
	es	era	fue	será	sería
	somos	éramos	fuimos	seremos	seríamos
	sois	erais	fuisteis	seréis	seríais
	son	eran	fueron	serán	serían
26. tener	tengo	tenía	tuve	tendré	tendría
	tienes	tenías	tuviste	tendrás	tendrías
	tiene	tenía	tuvo	tendrá	tendría
	tenemos	teníamos	tuvimos	tendremos	tendríamos
	tenéis	teníais	tuvisteis	tendréis	tendríais
	tienen	tenían	tuvieron	tendrán	tendrían
27. traer	traigo	traía	traje	traeré	traería
	traes	traías	trajiste	traerás	traerías
	trae	traía	trajo	traerá	traería
	traemos	traíamos	trajimos	traeremos	traeríamos
	traéis	traíais	trajisteis	traeréis	traeríais
	traen	traían	trajeron	traerán	traerían
28. venir	vengo	venía	vine	vendré	vendría
	vienes	venías	viniste	vendrás	vendrías
	viene	venía	vino	vendrá	vendría
	venimos	veníamos	vinimos	vendremos	vendríamos
	venís	veníais	vinisteis	vendréis	vendríais
	vienen	venían	vinieron	vendrán	vendrían
29. ver	veo	veía	vi	veré	vería
	ves	veías	viste	verás	verías
	ve	veía	vio	verá	vería
	vemos	veíamos	vimos	veremos	veríamos
	veis	veíais	visteis	veréis	veríais
	ven	veían	vieron	verán	verían
30. volver	vuelvo	volvía	volví	volveré	volvería
	vuelves	volvías	volviste	volverás	volverías
	vuelve	volvía	volvió	volverá	volvería
	volvemos	volvíamos	volvimos	volveremos	volveríamos
	volvéis	volvíais	volvisteis	volveréis	volveríais
	vuelven	volvían	volvieron	volverán	volverían

	SUBJUNCTIVE	COMMANDS		PARTICIPLES	
Present	Imperfect			Present	Past
sea	fuera (-se)	—		siendo	sido
seas	fueras (-ses)	sé (no seas)			
sea	fuera (-se)	sea			
seamos	fuéramos (-semos)	seamos			
seáis	fuerais (-seis)	sed (no seáis)			
sean	fueran (-sen)	sean			
tenga	tuviera (-se)	—		teniendo	tenido
tengas	tuvieras (-ses)	ten (no tengas)			
tenga	tuviera (-se)	tenga			
tengamos	tuviéramos (-semos)	tengamos			
tengáis	tuvierais (-seis)	tened (no tengáis)			
tengan	tuvieran (-sen)	tengan			
traiga	trajera (-se)	—		trayendo	traído
traigas	trajeras (-ses)	trae (no traigas)			
traiga	trajera (-se)	traiga			
traigamos	trajéramos (-semos)	traigamos			
traigáis	trajerais (-seis)	traed (no traigáis)			
traigan	trajeran (-sen)	traigan			
venga	viniera (-se)	—		viniendo	venido
vengas	vinieras (-ses)	ven (no vengas)			
venga	viniera (-se)	venga			
vengamos	viniéramos (-semos)	vengamos			
vengáis	vinierais (-seis)	venid (no vengáis)			
vengan	vinieran (-sen)	vengan			
vea	viera (-se)	—		viendo	visto
veas	vieras (-ses)	ve (no veas)			
vea	viera (-se)	vea			
veamos	viéramos (-semos)	veamos			
veáis	vierais (-seis)	ved (no veáis)			
vean	vieran (-sen)	vean			
vuelva	volviera (-se)	—		volviendo	vuelto
vuelvas	volvieras (-ses)	vuelve (no vuelvas)			
vuelva	volviera (-se)	vuelva			
volvamos	volviéramos (-semos)	volvamos			
volváis	volvierais (-seis)	volved (no volváis)			
vuelvan	volvieran (-sen)	vuelvan			

Vocabulario

The Spanish-English, English-Spanish vocabularies include all the words that appear in the text, except most proper nouns and conjugated verb forms. The ENGLISH-SPANISH vocabulary includes all the words and expressions listed in the Vocabulario sections as well as those used in the exercises.

The gender of nouns is indicated with the definite article. The alphabetization follows the Spanish word pattern with CH after C, LL after L, and Ñ after N. Stem changes in verbs are indicated by (ie), (ue), or (i). A (zc) after an infinitive indicates that the YO form of the present tense has this irregularity.

The following abbreviations are used:

adj	adjective
adv	adverb
contr	contraction
dir obj	direct object
f	feminine
fam	familiar
ind obj	indirect object
inf	infinitive
m	masculine
obj of prep	object of preposition
pl	plural
prep	preposition
rel pron	relative pronoun
sing	singular

A

a to; a
a personal a
abajo below
abandonar to abandon
abierto, -a open
el **abogado,** la **abogada** lawyer
abrazar to embrace
el **abrazo** embrace, hug
el **abrigo** coat
abril April
abrir to open
la **abuela** grandmother
el **abuelo** grandfather; los **abuelos** grandparents
la **abundancia** abundance
aburrido, -a bored
acabar to finish
acabar de + *inf* to have just
acabarse to exhaust, to finish
académico, -a academic
accesible accessible
el **accidente** accident
la **acción** action, deed
el **aceite** oil
el **aceite de oliva** olive oil
acelerar to accelerate
la **acentuación** accentuation
aceptar to accept
la **acera** sidewalk
acerca de concerning
acercarse to approach, come near
aclarar to clarify
acompañar to accompany
acordar (ue) to agree
acostarse to go to bed
acostumbrarse to get used to
la **actitud** attitude
la **actividad** activity
el **acto** act; **activo, -a** active
la **actriz** actress
actual present (day)
acuerdo agreement; **de —** agreed, OK, all right
adaptar to adapt
adecuado adequate
adelantar to advance
adelante ahead
el **adelanto** advancement
además besides; **— de** in addition to
adicional additional
adiós good bye
la **adivinanza** riddle

adivinar to guess
el **adjetivo** adjective
la **administración** administration, management
el **administrador,** la **administradora** manager
administrar to administer
admirable admirable
admisión admission
adonde (to) where
adoptar to adopt
la **aduana** customs
aéreo aerial, by air
el **aeropuerto** airport
afectuoso, -a affectionate
afeitarse to shave
el **aficionado,** la **aficionada** amateur
afirmativamente affirmatively
afirmativo, -a affirmative
afortunado, -a fortunate
afuera outside
las **afueras** outskirts, suburbs
la **agencia** agency; **agencia de turismo** travel agency
el, la **agente de compras** purchasing agent
ágil agile
agosto August
agradecer (zc) to be grateful
agradecido, -a grateful
la **agresión** aggression
agresivamente aggressively
agresor, -a aggressor
agrícola agricultural
el **agricultor** farmer
la **agricultura** agriculture
el **agrónomo** agronomist
el **agua** water
el **aguacate** avocado
ahora now
ahorrar to save money
el **aire** air; **— acondicionado** air conditioned
el **ajedrez** chess
el **ajo** garlic
el **ajo** garlic
alcanzar to reach
el **alcohol** alcohol
alegrarse de to be happy about, glad to . . .
alegre happy
la **alegría** happiness, joy
el **alemán** german
Alemania Germany
alérgico, -a allergic
el **alfabeto** alphabet
alfarería pottery
el **álgebra** algebra

algo something
el **algodón** cotton
alguien someone, somebody
algún some (singular)
alguno, -a, -os, -as some; **alguna vez** some time
el **aliado,** la **aliada** ally
alimentar to feed
alimenticio nutritious, of food value
el **alimento** food, nourishment
allá, allí there
el **alma** soul
el **almacén** department store
almorzar (ue) to eat lunch
el **almuerzo** lunch
aló hello (phone)
el **alquiler** rent; **alquilar** to rent
la **altitud** altitude, height
alto, -a tall
alrededor de around
el **ama de casa** housewife
amable friendly, pleasant
amar to love
amarillo yellow
la **ambición** ambition
ambicioso, -a ambitious
el **ambiente** environment
ambigüo, -a ambiguous
ambos, ambas both
amenidades amenities
América del Norte North America
América del Sur South America
americano, -a American
el **amigo,** la **amiga** friend
la **amistad** friendship
el **amor** love
anaranjado, -a orange (color)
anarquista anarquist
anciano, -a elderly, old
ancho, -a wide
andar to walk, to work, to run (as in a watch)
andino, -a Andean
la **anestesia** anesthesia
anglosajón Anglo-Saxon
angosto, -a narrow
el **ángulo** angle
el **anillo** ring
animado, -a animated, lively
el **animal** animal
animar to encourage, to animate
el **aniversario** anniversary
anoche last night
anormal abnormal
anormalidad abnormality
anotar to make a note of
el **antecedente** antecedent
anteojos spectacles, glasses

el **antepasado** ancestor
anterior previous, before
antes (de) before
antibiótico antibiotic
antiguo, -a old, ancient; former
antipático, -a disagreeable
antropología anthropology
anual annual
anunciar to announce
el **anuncio** announcement; advertisement
añadir to add
el **año** year; **Año Nuevo** New Year
apagar to turn off, out
aparato appliance
aparecer (zc) to appear
el **apartamento** apartment
aparte aside
el **apellido** surname, last name
apenas hardly
el **aperitivo** appetizer
el **apetito** appetite
aplaudir to applaud
el **apogeo** apogee
apoyar to support
el **apoyo** support
aprender to learn
aprobar (ue) to approve, to pass a subject
apropiado, -a appropriate
aprovechar to take advantage of
apuntar to take notes
los **apuntes** (class) notes
el **apuro** predicament
aquel, aquella that; **aquél, aquélla** that one (pron)
aquí here
arable arable
el **árbol** tree
archivar to file
el **archivo** file, archive
el **área** area
la **arena** sand; bull ring
argentino, -a Argentine
árido, -a arid
aritmética arithmetic
el **arma** (f) weapon, arm
el **armamento** armament
el, la **arquitecto** architect
el **arte** art
artesanía craft
el **artesano,** la **artesana** artisan
el **artículo** article
el, la **artista** artist
artístico, -a artistic
arrancar to uproot, to tear out
arreglar to arrange, fix, repair
arriba upstairs, higher up
el **arroz** rice

asado, -a roasted
ascender (ie) to promote
así this way, thus
el asiento seat
la asistencia attendance
asistir a to attend to
asociar to associate
el aspecto aspect
astronomía astronomy
asumir to assume, to take upon oneself
el asunto subject matter, issue
atacar to attack
el ataque attack
la atención attention
atender (ie) to take care of, to attend
atentamente attentively
el Atlántico Atlantic
el, la atleta athlete
atractivo, -a attractive
atraer to attract
atrás behind
el atraso backwardness
atreverse (a) to dare (to)
el atún tuna
la audiencia audience
aumentar to increase, add
aún still, yet
aunque though, although
el auto car, auto
el autobús bus
el automóvil automobile
la autonomía autonomy
el autor, la autora author
autorizar authorize
avanzar to advance
la avenida avenue
la aventura adventure
el avión airplane
ayer yesterday
ayudar to help
el, la ayudante assistant
el azúcar sugar
el azafrán saffron (spice)
azul blue

B

bailar to dance
el baile dance
bajar to lower, to go down, descend
bajo, -a short
la banana banana, plantain
el banco bank; bench
el banquero, la banquera banker

el banquete banquet
bañarse to bathe
el baño bath, bathroom
barato, -a cheap
la barbería barber shop
el barco ship
la barrera barrier
la barriga belly
basado, -a supported, based
basar to base, to support
básico, -a basic
el básquetbol basketball
bastante enough, quite a bit
la basura trash, garbage
la batalla battle
la batería battery
batir to beat, scramble
el bautismo baptism
bautizar to baptise
el béisbol baseball
las bellas artes fine arts
el beneficio benefit
besar to kiss
el beso kiss
la biblioteca library
la bicicleta bicycle
bien well, fine, all right
bienestar welfare
bienvenido, -a welcome
el biftec beefsteak
el billette bill, ticket; billetes de lotería lottery tickets
biográfico, -a biographic
la biología biology
el bisté(c) steak
blanco, -a white
la blusa blouse
la boca mouth
la boda wedding; boda de plata 25th wedding anniver-sary
boicotear to boycott
el boleto ticket
el bolígrafo ballpoint pen
el bolillo roll
la bolsa handbag, bag, stock market
bonito, -a pretty
las botas boots
la botella bottle
el boxeo boxing
el brazo arm
breve brief, short
buen(o), -a good
buenos días good morning; buenas tardes good after-noon; buenas noches good night
el bulevar boulevard
la burocracia bureaucracy
buscar to look for

C

el **caballero** gentleman
el **caballo** horse
la **cabeza** head
el **cacao** cocoa
cada each
caer caigo to fall
el **café** coffee; small restaurant
la **cafetera** coffee pot
la **cafetería** coffee shop
los **calcetines** socks
calcular to calculate
la **calefacción** heating
el **calendario** calendar
calentar (ie) to warm, to heat
la **calidad** quality
caliente hot
el **calor** heat
la **caloría** calorie
callar(se) to be quiet
la **calle** street
la **calma** calm, calmness
calmarse to calm down
la **cama** bed; **cama de matrimonio** double bed
la **cámara** camera
el **camarero,** la **camarera** waiter, waitress
el **camarón** shrimp
cambiar to change, to exchange
el **cambio** change
caminar to walk
el **camino** road
el **camión** truck; bus (Mexico)
la **camisa** shirt
la **camiseta** undershirt, t-shirt
el **campesino,** la **campesina** farmer, peasant
el **campo** countryside
el **canal** channel; canal
la **canasta** basket
el **cáncer** cancer
la **canción** song
el **cancionero** songbook
el **candidato,** la **candidata** candidate
la **canoa** canoe
cansado, -a tired
cansarse to get tired
el, la **cantante** singer
cantar to sing
el **caos** chaos
la **capacidad** capacity
capaz capable
la **capital** capital (city)
el, la **capitalista** capitalist
capturar to capture
la **cara** face
el **carácter** character
la **característica** characteristic

¡Caramba! Golly!
el **cardenal** cardinal
el **cariño** affection, love
el **carnaval** carnival; mardigras
la **carne** meat
la **cara** face
caro, -a expensive
el **carpintero,** la **carpintera** carpenter
la **carta** letter
la **cartera** wallet
el **cartero** mailman
la **carrera** career; race
la **carretera** highway
el **carro** car
la **casa** house, home; **en —** at home
casado, -a married
casarse to get married; **— con** to be married to
cascarrabias grouchy
casi almost
la **casucha** hut
el **catarro** cold (illness)
la **catedral** cathedral
católico, -a Catholic
catorce fourteen
la **causa** cause; **a — de** on account of
el **cautiverio** captivity or confinement
la **cebolla** onion
ceder to yield
la **celebración** celebration
celebrar to celebrate
célebre famous
la **cena** dinner, supper
cenar to dine
central central
céntrico, -a central
el **centro** downtown, center; el **— comercial** shopping center
Centroamérica Central America (**América Central**)
cerca (de) near
el **cerdo** pig; **carne de—** pork meat
el **cereal** cereal
cero zero
la **cerveza** beer
cerrado, -a closed
cerrar (ie) to close
el **césped** lawn
el **ceviche** raw fish dish
el **ciclón** hurricane
el **cielo** sky; heaven
cien, ciento one hundred; **por—** percent
la **ciencia** science
cierto, -a certain, sure
cinco five
cincuenta fifty
el **cine** movie house

la **cinta** ribbon; **—de celofán** Scotch tape; **—magnética** magnetic tape

el **cinturón** belt

el **círculo** circle

la **circunstancia** circumstance

la **cirujía** surgery

la **cita** appointment, date

la **ciudad** city

civil civil

la **civilización** civilization

claro, -a clear, light

claro of course

la **clase** class; type

clásico, -a classic

la **claúsula** clause, sentence

el **clérigo** clergy

el, la **cliente** customer, client

la **clínica** clinic

el **club** club

cobrar to collect

la **cocina** kitchen

cocinar to cook

el **coco** coconut

el **coctel** cocktail

el **coche** car

coexistir to coexist

coger (j) to pick up, hold

cognado cognate

la **cola** line, queue

el **colegio** school

colgar (ue) to hang

la **colonia** cologne, colony

colonial colonial

el **color** color

la **combinación** combination

combinar to combine

la **comedia** comedy, play; farce

el **comedor** dining room

comentar to comment

el **comentario** commentary, comment

comenzar (ie) to begin

comer to eat

comercial commercial

el **comerciante** merchant, businessman

comerciar to trade, to deal

el **comercio** business, trade, commerce

los **comestibles** groceries

cómico, -a comic

la **comida** dinner; food

el **comienzo** beginning, origin

el **comino** cumin

como since, as, like

¿cómo? how? what?; **¿— está?** how are you?; **¿—le va?** How goes it?; **¡— no!** Of course!; **¿—se llama?** what is your name?

la **comodidad** comfort

cómodo, -a comfortable

la **compadrería** fellowship

el **compañero,** la **compañera** companion, friend, mate; el **compañero de clase,** la **compañera de clase** classmate

la **compañía** company

la **comparación** comparison

comparar to compare

compartir to share

competente competent

la **competición** competition

el **competidor,** la **competidora** competitor

competir(i) to compete

complejo, -a complex

completar to complete

componer (compongo) to compose

el **comportamiento** behavior

la **composición** composition

el **compositor,** la **compositora** composer

comprar to buy, to shop

las **compras** purchases

comprender to understand, comprehend

la **comprensión** understanding, comprehension

el **compromiso** engagement, commitment

compuesto, -a compound

la **computación** computer science

la **computadora** computer

común common

la **comunicación** communication

comunicar to communicate

la **comunidad** community

la **comunión** communion

comunista communist

con with

con tal que so that, provided that

el **concepto** concept

el **concierto** concert

la **conclusión** conclusion

concordar (ue) to agree (grammar)

el **conde** earl, count

la **condición** condition

el **condimento** condiment, spice

conducir (zc) to drive, conduct

el **conductor,** la **conductora** conductor

conectar to connect

la **conexión** connection

la **conferencia** conference

la **confianza** trust, confidence; familiarity

confiar en to trust in

el **conflicto** conflict

confortable comfortable

conmemorar commemorate

conmigo with me

conocer (zc) to be acquainted with, to meet

conocido, -a known, famous

el **conocimiento** knowledge

la **conquista** conquest
el **conquistador,** la **conquistadora** conqueror
conquistar to conquer
conseguir (i) to get, to obtain
el **consejo** advice
el **consenso** consensus
conservar to keep, to preserve
considerar to consider
consultar to consult
la **constitución** constitution
construir (construyo) to construct, to build
el **consumidor** consumer
la **contabilidad** accounting
el **contacto** contact
la **contaminación** pollution
contaminado, -a polluted
contar (ue) to count; — **con** to count on
contemplar contemplate
contemporáneo, -a contemporaneous, contemporary
contento, -a content
contestar to answer
el **contexto** context
contigo with you
continuar (continúo) to continue
contrario, -a contrary
contribuir (contribuyo) to contribute
el **control** control, checkpoint
controlar to control
convencer (z) to convince
conversar to converse
convertir (ie) to convert
cooperar to cooperate
coordinar to coordinate
la **copa** wine glass
el **corazón** heart
la **corbata** tie
cordial cordial
el **corredor** runner
el **correo** mail
correr to run
la **correspondencia** correspondence
el **corresponsal** reporter, correspondent
la **corrida de toros** bull fight
corriente current
la **corrupción** corruption
cortar to cut
cortés courteous
la **cortesía** courtesy
corto short (in length)
la **cosa** thing
la **cosecha** harvest; **cosechar** to harvest
cosmético, -a cosmetic
la **costa** coast
costar (ue) to cost
la **costumbre** custom
creado, -a created

creador, -a creative; creator
crear to create
creer to believe
la **crema** cream
la **crisis** crisis
el **crítico,** la **crítica** critic
la **crónica** chronicle
crudo, -a raw
la **cruz** cross
cruzar to cross
el **cuaderno** notebook
la **cuadra** city block
cuadrado, -a square
el **cuadro** square; painting
¿**cuál (es)?** which; relative pron. **cual (es)**
¿**cuándo?** when?
¿**cuánto? ¿cuánta?** how much?
¿**cuántos? ¿cuántas?** how many?
cuarenta forty
el **cuarto** room; quarter, fourth
cuatro four
cuatrocientos four hundred
cubrir to cover
la **cuchara** spoon
la **cucharilla** tea spoon
el **cuchillo** knife
la **cuenta** bill, account
el **cuento** short story
el, la **cuentista** short story writer
el **cuernito** crescent rolls
el **cuero** leather
el **cuerpo** body
la **cuestión** issue
cuidado; cuidadoso, -a careful
cuidar to take care of
la **culpa** blame; guilt
cultivar to cultivate
el **cultivo** cultivation
culto, -a learned, educated
la **cultura** culture
el **cumpleaños** birthday
cumplir to fulfill, to complete; **cumplir años** to have a birthday
el **cura** priest
la **cura** cure
curioso, -a curious
curso course; school year
la **curva** curve
cuyo, -a, -os, -as whose

CH
el **chaleco** vest, jacket
la **chaqueta** jacket
la **charla** a little chat
charlar to converse, to chat

el **cheque**   check
la **chica**   girl
el **chico**   boy
el **chisme**   gossip
el **chiste**   joke
chocar   to collide, crash
el **chocolate**   chocolate
el, la **chofer / chófer**   chauffeur
el **chorizo**   sausage
el **churrasco**   roasted meat, barbecue
el **churro**   breakfast fritter (Spain)

D

la **dama**   lady, dame
la **danza**   dance
daño   harm, damage
dar   to give; — **un paseo**   to take a walk
darse prisa   to hurry
de   of, from; — **nada**   you are welcome; — **repente**
   suddenly
debajo de   underneath
deber   ought or should; to owe; **el —**   duty
debilitar   to debilitate
la **decadencia**   decadence
decaer   to decline
décimo, -a   tenth
decir (i)   to tell, to say
decisivo, -a   decisive
declarar   to declare
decorar   to decorate
el **dedo**   finger, — **del pie**   toe
el **defecto**   defect
defender (ie)   to defend
deformar   to deform
dejar   to leave, abandon; — **de**   to cease
delante de   in front of
delgado, -a   thin
delicioso, -a   delicious
demasiado, -a   too much
la **democracia**   democracy
la **demora**   delay; **demorar**   to delay
dentro de   inside; within
denunciar   to denounce
el **departamento**   department
depender de   to depend on
el **dependiente, la dependienta**   sales clerk
deplorable   deplorable
deportar   to deport
el **deporte**   sport
la **derecha**   right
el **derecho**   right; law
desagradable   unpleasant, disagreeable
desaparecer (zc)   to disappear
desarrollar   to develop
el **desarrollo**   development
desayunar   to have breakfast

el **desayuno**   breakfast
descafeinado, -a   decaffeinated
descansar   to rest
el **descanso**   rest; break
desconocido, -a   unknown
descontento, -a   discontent
describir   to describe
la **descripción**   description
el **descubrimiento**   discovery
descubrir   to discover
el **descuento**   discount
desde   from
desear   to wish, to desire
el **desempleado, la desempleada**   unemployed
el **desempleo**   unemployment
desfigurar   to disfigure
el **desfile**   parade
el **desierto**   wilderness, desert; deserted
el **desnivel**   imbalance, unevenness
desnudo, -a   bare, naked; **hombro —**   bare shoulder
desobediente   disobedient
desorden   disorder
desorganizado, -a   disorganized
despacio, -a   slow
el **despacho**   private office
la **despedida**   farewell; **despedida de soltero**   bachelor's
   party
el **desperdicio**   waste
despertar (ie)   to wake up
después de   after
destacarse   to be outstanding
desventaja   disadvantage
el **detalle**   detail
el **detective**   detective
detener   to detain
determinado, -a   determined
detrás de   behind
la **deuda**   debt
devolver (ue)   to give back, return
el **día**   day; **todo el —**   all day long; **todos los días**
   every day
el **diagrama**   diagram
el **diálogo**   dialog
el **diario**   newspaper; daily; diary
el **dibujo**   drawing
el **diccionario**   dictionary
diciembre   December
el **dictado**   dictation
el **dictador**   dictator
la **dictadura**   dictatorship
dicho   said
dichoso, -a   lucky
diecinueve   nineteen
dieciocho   eighteen
dieciséis   sixteen
diecisiete   seventeen

el **diente** tooth
la **dieta** diet
diez ten
la **diferencia** difference
diferente different
difícil difficult
la **dificultad** difficulty
digno, -a worthy
dinámico, -a dynamic
el **dinero** money
Dios God; ¡— **mío!** My God!
diplomarse to graduate; receive a diploma
la **dirección** address; direction
directamente directly
directo, -a direct
el **director,** la **directora** director; school principal
dirigirse (j) to go toward
la **disciplina** discipline
el **disco** record, disk
la **discordia** discord
la **discrepancia** discrepancy
discreto, -a discreet
discutir to discuss, to argue
el **disgusto** displeasure, annoyance
la **distancia** distance
distinguir to distinguish
el **distribuidor** distributor
el **distrito** district
diverso, -a diverse
divertido, -a amusing
divertirse (ie) to have a good time
doblar to double
doble double
doce twelve
la **docena** dozen
el **doctor,** la **doctora** doctor
el **documento** document
el **dólar** dollar
doler (ue) to ache
el **dolor** ache, pain
dominar to dominate
domingo Sunday, **el —** on Sunday, los **domingos** on
  Sundays
el **dominó** domino
donar to donate
¿dónde? where?
dorado, -a golden
dorar to brown
dormir (ue) to sleep, **dormirse** to fall asleep
el **dormitorio** bedroom
dramáticamente dramatically
la **droga** drug
dos two
doscientos two hundred
dudar to doubt
el **dueño** owner

dulce sweet; los **dulces** candy
durante during
durar to last
duro, -a hard

E

e and (before words with an initial i-hi sound)
la **economía** economy
el, la **economista** economist
el **ecuador** equator
echar to pour
echar de menos to miss (emotionally)
la **edad** age
el **edificio** building
la **educación** education; good manners
educar to educate
EE.UU. U.S.A.
efectivamente really, in fact
el **efecto** effect
efectuar to take place
eficaz efficient
eficiente efficient
el **ejemplo** example
el **ejercicio** exercise
el **ejército** army
él he (after prep.) him
el the
la **elección** election
electivo, -a elective
la **electricidad** electricity
elegante elegant
elegir (i) to elect
el **elemento** element
eliminar to eliminate
ella she (after *prep*) her
ellos, ellas they (after *prep*) them
el **embajador** ambassador
la **emergencia** emergency
eminente eminent
la **emisión** emission
la **emoción** emotion
emocionarse to get excited
el **emperador** emperor
empezar (ie) to begin
el **empleado** employee
emplear to employ
el **empleo** employment
la **empresa** company, firm, enterprise
en in, on, at
enamorarse de to fall in love
encantador, -a charming
el **encanto** charm
encarcelar to jail, imprison
encender (ie) to turn on
encontrar (ue) to find
la **encuesta** survey

la **enchilada** enchilada
la **energía** energy
enero January
el **énfasis** emphasis
enfermarse to get sick
la **enfermedad** illness
la **enfermería** infirmary
el **enfermero,** la **enfermera** nurse
enfermo, -a ill, sick
enfilado, -a lined in a row
enfrentarse to face; confront
enfriar to cool, to chill
engañar to deceive
engaño deceit
enojado, -a angry
enojarse to become angry
enorme huge, enormous
la **ensalada** salad
ensayar to rehearse
el **ensayo** essay; rehearsal
en seguida at once, immediately
la **enseñanza** teaching, instruction
enseñar to teach
entender (ie) to understand
la **entidad** entity, society
el **entierro** burial
entonces then; well, so
la **entrada** entrance; admission ticket
entrar to enter
entre between, among
los **entremeses** hors d'œuvres
el **entrenamiento** training
entrenar to train
entretener to entertain
la **entrevista** interview
entrevistar to interview
entusiasmado, -a enthusiastic, enthused
enviar to send, to ship
la **época** epoch, period
el **equilibrio** balance, equilibrium
el **equipaje** luggage
el **equipo** equipment, team
equivalente equivalent
equivocarse to make a mistake
errar to err
el **error** error
es (form of ser) he, she, it is; **¿— usted?** are you? **—que** is that
la **escalera** stair; ladder
escalfado, -a poached
escapar (se) to escape
escaso, -a scarce
la **escena** scene
el **esclavo,** la **esclava** slave
escoger(j) to choose
escribir to write

el **escritor,** la **escritora** writer, author
el **escritorio** desk
escuchar to listen
la **escudilla** bowl
la **escuela** school
la **escultura** sculpture
escurrir to drain
ese, esa that (pl) **esos, esas** those
ése, ésa (pron) that one (pl) **ésos, ésas** those ones
esencial essential
el **esfuerzo** effort
eso that, **a eso de** + *time* around, about
el **espacio** space
la **espada** sword
la **espalda** back (of a person)
España Spain
el **español** Spanish (language), Spaniard
español, -a Spanish
especial special
la **especialización** major; specialization
específicamente specifically
específico, -a specific
el **espectáculo** show
especular to speculate; to ponder
el **espejo** mirror
la **esperanza** hope
esperar to wait for, to hope
espléndido, -a splendid
espontáneo, -a spontaneous
el **esposo,** la **esposa** husband, wife
espumante bubbling (wine); foaming
esquiar (esquío) to ski
esta this; **— noche** tonight
ésta this one
la **estabilidad** stability
establecer (zc) to establish
la **estación** season, station
estacionar to park
el **estado** state, condition
los **Estados Unidos** United States
estar to be in a place or condition; **— de acuerdo** to agree; **— de vacaciones** to be on vacation; **— listo, -a** to be ready; **— harto, -a** to be fed up
este, esta this; **estos, estas** these
éste, ésta (pron) this one; **éstos, éstas** these
el **este** east
el **estéreo** stereo
el **estereotipo** stereotype
el **estilo** style
estimado, -a estimated, dear
estimar to estimate
estimular to stimulate
esto this (neuter)
el **estómago** stomach
estrecho, -a narrow, tight
estricto, -a strict

la **estructura** structure
el, la **estudiante** student
estudiantil (*adj*) student
estudiar to study; — **para** to study to be
el **estudio** study
estudioso, -a studious
estupendo, -a great
étnico, -a ethnic
Europa Europe
europeo, -a European
el **evento** event
evidente evident
evitar to avoid
exacto, -a exact, exactly
exagerar to exaggerate
el **examen** test
examinar to examine, test
excelente excellent
la **excursión** outing, excursion
la **excusa** excuse
la **exhibición** art show; exhibition
exigente demanding
exigir to demand
la **existencia** existence
existir to exist
el **éxito** success
la **experiencia** experience
la **explicación** explanation
explicar to explain
explorar to explore
la **exploración** exploration
el **explorador** boy scout; explorer
explotar to exploit
el **exportador** exporter
exportar to export
expresar to express
la **expresión** expression
expresivo, -a expressive
extender (ie) to extend
extenso, -a extensive
el **extranjero**, la **extranjera** foreigner
extraordinario, -a extraordinary
extremo, -a extreme

F
la **fábrica** factory
el, la **fabricante** manufacturer, maker
fabuloso, -a fabulous
fácil easy
facilitar to facilitate, make easy
el **factor** factor
la **falda** skirt
falso, -a false
la **falta** lack, need; **hacer—** to lack
faltar to lack
la **fama** fame

la **familia** family
familiarizarse to become familiar
famoso, -a famous
la **fantasía** fantasy
fantástico, -a fantastic
farmacéutico, -a pharmaceutical
la **farmacia** pharmacy
el, la **farmacista** pharmacist
el **favor** favor; **—de** + *inf* please
favorito, -a favorite
febrero February
la **fecha** date (calendar)
la **federación** federation
la **felicidad** happiness
las **felicitaciones** congratulations
felicitar to congratulate
femenino, -a feminine
el **fenómeno** phenomenon
feo, -a ugly
el **ferrocarril** railroad
fértil fertile
la **fiebre** fever
fiel faithful, loyal
la **fiesta** party; **día de—** holiday; **— de despedida**
    farewell party
la **figura** figure
fijarse to note, pay attention
fijo, -a fixed
la **fila** row
la **filosofía** philosophy; **—y letras** humanities
el **filtro** filter
el **fin** end; **—de semana** weekend
final (*adj*) end
finalmente finally
la **finca** farm
fino, -a fine; refined
la **firma** signature, firm
firmemente firmly
la **física** physics
físico, -a physical
flaco, -a thin, skinny
el **flan** Spanish custard
flexible flexible
la **flor** flower
el **flujo** flow
el **folleto** brochure
fomentar to foster
el **fondo** bottom; background
formal formal
formar to form
formidable formidable
la **fortaleza** strength, fortress
la **fortuna** fortune; good luck
la **foto** photo; **fotografía** photograph
fragante fragrant
frágil fragile

el **francés** French (language)
Francia France
la **frase** phrase
la **frecuencia** frequency
frecuentemente frequently
freír (i) to fry
los **frenos** brakes
la **frente** forehead; **en — de** across from, in front of
la **fresa** strawberry
fresco, -a fresh; **hace —** It is cool
los **frijoles** beans
frío, -a cold
frito, -a fried
la **frontera** border
la **fruta** fruit
el **fuego** fire
la **fuente** fountain; source
fuera outside; **—de** (*prep.*) outside
fuerte strong
la **fuerza** force
fumar to smoke
funcionar to function
fundir to fund, to cost
el **fusilamiento** execution by firing squad
el **fútbol** soccer
el **futuro** future

G

la **galería** gallery
la **galleta** cracker; **galletitas dulces** cookies
la **ganadería** livestock industry
el **ganado** cattle; stock
el **ganador,** la **ganadora** winner
ganar to earn, win
el **garage** garage
la **garganta** throat
la **gasolinera** gas station
gastar to spend (money)
el **gasto** expense
el **gato** cat
el **gazpacho** cold vegetable soup (Spain)
la **generación** generation
general general
generalmente generally
generoso, -a generous
la **gente** people
gentil genteel
genuino, -a genuine
la **geografía** geography
geográfico, -a geographic
la **geología** geology
el, la **gerente** manager; **— de ventas** sales manager
el **gesto** gesture, expression
el **gigante** giant
el **gimnasio** gymnasium
la **glorieta** traffic circle

el **gobernador,** la **gobernadora** governor
gobernar (ie) to govern
el **gobierno** government
el **golf** golf
el **golpe** blow; **— de estado** coup d'etat
gordo, -a fat
la **gorra** cap
gozar de to enjoy
la **grabadora** tape recorder
grabar to record; to engrave
gracias thank you
el **grado** grade; degree
la **graduación** graduation
gradualmente gradually
graduarse (me gradúo) to graduate
gráfico, -a graphic
la **gramática** grammar
grande (gran) great, big
el **grano** grain
grato, -a pleasant
grave grave
la **gripe** flu
gris grey
gritar to cry, shout, scream
el **grupo** group
el **guante** glove
guapo, -a handsome, good looking
guardar to guard; to keep; to save
la **guayaba** guava (tropical fruit)
la **guerra** war
el **guerrero** warrior
la **guerrilla** guerrilla (hit–and–run warfare)
el, la **guía** guide; la **— de teléfonos** phone book
guiar (guío) to guide
los **guisantes** peas
la **guitarra** guitar
gustar to please, to like
el **gusto** taste, pleasure

H

haber to have (auxiliary)
la **habilidad** ability
la **habitación** bedroom; room
el **habitante** inhabitant
hablar to speak
hablador, -a talkative
hace buen tiempo it is nice out; **— calor** it is hot;
  — frío it is cold; **— viento** it is windy
hacer to make, do; **— daño** to hurt; **— compras** to
  shop; **— las maletas** to pack (suitcases)
hacerse to become
hacia toward
hallar to find
el **hambre** *f* hunger; **tener —** to be hungry

hasta until, even; **— luego** see you later; **— mañana** see you tomorrow; **— pronto** see you soon

hay there is, there are; **— que** it's necessary

hecho done; **— a mano** hand made

la **helada** freeze; frost

el **helado** ice cream

el **helicóptero** helicopter

el **hemisferio** hemisphere

heredar to inherit

la **herencia** inheritance

la **hermana** sister; el **hermano** brother

hermoso, -a beautiful

el **héroe** hero

la **heroína** heroine

el **hielo** ice

la **hierba** grass

el **hierro** iron

el **hijo** son; la **hija** daughter; child

hipocondríaco, -a hypochondriac

hispánico, -a Hispanic

Hispanoamérica Spanish America

la **historia** history

histórico, -a historical

el **hogar** home; fireplace

la **hoja** leaf; **— de papel** sheet of paper

hola hello

el **hombre** man; **— de negocios** businessman

la **hora** hour; ¿**Qué — es?** What time is it?

el **horario** schedule

el **horno** oven; **— de micro–ondas** microwave oven

el **horror** horror

el **hospital** hospital

el **hostelero,** la **hostelera** innkeeper

hostil hostile

el **hotel** hotel

hoy today; **— día** nowadays

la **huelga** strike

el **huésped** guest

el **hueso** bone

el **huevo** egg

huir (huyo) to flee

humano, -a human

húmedo, -a humid

el **humor** humor

el **huracán** hurricane

I

la **idea** idea

el **ideal** ideal

la **iglesia** church

igual equal; **— a** the same as

la **igualdad** equality

igualmente likewise

ilegal illegal

la **ilusión** illusion

la **imagen** image

la **imaginación** imagination

imaginario, -a imaginary

imaginarse (que) to imagine (that)

imitar to imitate

el **impacto** impact

imperfecto, -a imperfect

el **imperio** empire

el **impermeable** raincoat

impersonal impersonal

implantar implant

la **importancia** importance

importante important

importar to be important, to matter; to import

imposible impossible

la **impresión** impression

impresionante impressive

impresionista impressionistic

los **impuestos** taxes

incidental incidental

incluir (incluyo) to include

incomparable incomparable

inconsistente inconsistant

increíble incredible

indeciso, -a undecided, indecisive

la **independencia** independence

independiente independent

indicar to indicate

el **indicativo** indicative

el **índice** index

indígena indigenous, native

indigno, -a unworthy

indio, -a indian

indirecto, -a indirect

indispensable indispensable

el **individuo** individual

la **industria** industry

la **industrialización** industrialization

industrializado, -a industrialized

inepto, -a inept

infantil infantile

inferior inferior

la **inflación** inflation

la **influencia** influence

influiren (influyo) to influence

la **información** information

informar to inform

el **informe** report

la **ingeniería** engineering

el **ingeniero,** la **ingeniera** engineer

el **inglés,** la **inglesa** English

el **ingrediente** ingredient

iniciar to initiate

la **injusticia** injustice

inmediatamente immediately

inmediato, -a immediate

inmenso, -a immense, huge
la **inmigración** immigration
inmigrante inmigrant
innovador, -a innovator
insensible insensible
insistir en to insist
inspirado, -a inspired
la **institución** institution
la **instrucción** instruction
instruir (instruyo) to instruct
el **instrumento** instrument
insuficiente insufficient
integrar to integrate
intelectual intellectual
inteligente intelligent
la **intención** intention
intenso, -a intense
el **intercambio** exchange
el **interés** interest
interesante interesting
interesar to interest
el **interior** interior
interminable interminable
internacional international
la **interpretación** interpretation
interpretar to interpret
el, la **intérprete** interpreter
interrogativo, -a interrogative
interrumpir to interrupt
la **interrupción** interruption
la **intervención** intervention
intimar to intimate
íntimo, -a intimate
inútil useless
la **invasión** invasion
invertir (ie) to invest
investigar to investigate
el **invierno** winter
la **invitación** invitation
invitar to invite
ir to go; **— de compras** to go shopping
irse to go away
la **isla** island
Italia Italy
el **itinerario** itinerary
la **izquierda** left

J

el **jabón** soap
el **jai-alai** Basque game similar to handball
jamás never, ever
el **jamón** ham
Janucá Hannukah
el **Japón** Japan
japonés, japonesa Japanese
el **jardín** garden

el **jefe,** la **jefa** boss
joven young; el **—,** la **—** young man, young woman
jovial jovial
joya jewel
el **juego** game, set
jueves Thursday; el (los) **—** on Thursday(s)
el, la **juez** judge
el **jugador,** la **jugadora** player; gambler
jugar (ue) to play games
el **jugo** juice
julio July
junio June
la **junta** board; ruling group
juntos, -as together; **junto a** next to
justo, -a just, fair
la **justicia** justice
la **juventud** youth

K

el **kilo** kilo, kilogram
el **kilómetro** kilometer
el **kindergarten** kindergarten

L

la the
el **labio** lip
la **labor** job, work
el **laboratorio** laboratory
lado side; **al — de** beside, next to
el **lago** lake
la **lámpara** lamp
la **lana** wool
el **lápiz** pencil
largo, -a long
la **lástima** pity, shame; **¡Qué —!** Too bad!
lastimarse to hurt
el **latifundio** very large landholding
latino, -a Latin
latinoamericano, -a Latin American
el **laurel** bay leaf (spice); laurel
lavar to wash
lavarse to wash oneself
laxante laxative
el **lazo** bond; lasso
le to, (for, from) you, him, her
la **lección** lesson
lector reader
la **lectura** reading
la **leche** milk
la **lechuga** lettuce
leer to read
legítimo, -a legitimate
la **legumbre** vegetable
lejos far
lejos de far from
la **lengua** language, tongue
les to (from, for) them, you

la **leucemia**   leukemia
levantar   to lift
levantarse   to get up
la **ley,** las **leyes**   law, laws
liberar   to liberate
la **libertad**   liberty, freedom
la **libra**   pound
libre   free
la **librería**   bookstore
el **libro**   book
el **líder**   leader
ligero   light weight
limitar   to limit
la **limonada**   lemonade
limpiar   to clean
limpio, -a   clean
lindo, -a   pretty, lovely
la **línea**   line
liquidación   liquidation, clearance sale
lisonjero, -a   flattering
la **lista**   list, class roll
listo, -a   ready; smart
literario, -a   literary
la **literatura**   literature
lo   him, you, it
lo que   what
local   local
loco, -a   crazy
lógico, -a   logic
el **lomo**   back (**de un animal, de un cuchillo**);   bookspine
el **loro**   parrot
los, las   the; them, you
la **lotería**   lottery
la **lucha**   struggle, fight, battle
luchar   to struggle
luego   later; **hasta —**   see you later
el **lugar**   place
la **luna**   moon
lunes   Monday; el **—**   on Monday
la **luz**   light

LL

la **llama**   flame; **llama**   (animal)
la **llamada**   call
llamar   to call
llamarse   to be called; named
el **llano**   plain (flat lands)
las **llantas**   tires
la **llave**   key
la **llegada**   arrival
llegar   to arrive; **— a ser**   to become
llenar   to fill (out)
llevar   to take, carry; to wear
llorar   to weep, cry
llover (ue)   to rain
la **lluvia**   rain

M

el **machismo**   "machismo" exaggerated masculine characteristics
macho   male of the animal species; courageous
la **madera**   wood
la **madre**   mother
el **maestro,** la **maestra**   teacher
la **magia**   magic
el **magnetismo**   magnetismo
magnífico, -a   magnificent
el **maíz**   corn
mal   bad, badly, evil, ill
la **maleta**   suitcase
malo, -a   bad
mandar   to send, to command
el **mandato**   command (grammar)
manejar   to drive
la **manera**   manner, way; **de — que**   so that
el **mango**   mango (tropical fruit)
la **manga**   sleeve
la **mano**   hand; **dar la —**   to shake hands
mantener   to maintain
la **mantequilla**   butter
la **manufactura**   manufacture
la **manzana**   apple
mañana   tomorrow; **la —**   morning; **de la —**   a.m., in the morning; **— por la —**   tomorrow morning
el **mapa**   map
la **maquinaria**   machinery
el **mar**   sea
maravilloso, -a   marvelous
marcar   to brand, to mark
el **marido**   husband
el **marisco**   shellfish
marítimo, -a   maritime
marrón   brown
martes   Tuesday; **el, (los) —**   on Tuesday(s)
marxista   Marxist
marzo   March
más   more, plus; **— de**   more than + number; **— que**   more than
masculino, -a   masculine
las **matemáticas**   mathematics
la **materia**   subject (academic); matter
matricularse   to register (for school)
el **matrimonio**   wedding, married couple
el **mausoleo**   burial place
máximo, -a   maximum
maya   Mayan
mayo   May
mayor   older, **el —**   the oldest
la **mayoría**   majority
mayormente   mostly
me   me; to (for, from) me
el **mecánico**   mechanic; la **mecánica**   mechanics
la **media**   stocking

la **medianoche** midnight
la **medicina** medicine
el, la **médico** physician
media half-past; **clase —** middle class
medio half; middle
mediocre mediocre
el **mediodía** noon
los **medios** means
mejor better; **el —** the best
mejorar to improve
el **melocotón** peach
la **memoria** memory; **aprender de —** to learn by heart
mencionar to mention
la **menina** little girl, damsel
menor younger; **el, la —** the youngest
menos less; (time) till; **— de** + number less than
el **menú (la lista)** menu
el **mercado** market
la **mercancía** merchandise
merecer (zc) to deserve
la **merienda** afternoon snack; picnic
la **mermelada** marmalade
el **mes** month
la **mesa** table
mestizo, -a mestizo (of mixed Indian-European background)
el **metal** metal
meter to put in
el **metro** subway; meter
el **método** method
el **mexicano**, la **mexicana** Mexican
mezclar to mix
mi, mis my
mí me (after prep)
el **miedo** fear; **tener —** to be afraid
el **miembro** member
mientras while
miércoles Wednesday; el (los) **miércoles** on Wednesday(s)
la **migración** migration
mil thousand
militar to be an active member, to militate; military
millón million
mimar to pamper
la **mina** mine
el **mineral** mineral
la **minería** mining
el **minifundio** small farm
mínimo, -a minimum, least
la **minoría** minority
el **minuto** minute
mío, -a mine
la **mirada** look; glance
mirar to look at
mismo, -a same
la **mitad** half

mixto, -a mixed
la **moda** fashion
el **modelo** model
moderado, -a moderate
el **modernismo** modernism
moderno, -a modern
modificar to modify
el **modo** method
molestar to bother
el **momento** moment
el **monarca** monarch, king
la **monarquía** monarchy
la **moneda** currency; coin
la **monja** nun; el **monje** monk
la **montaña** mountain
montar to mount; get on; **— a caballo** ride a horse; **— en bicicleta** to ride a bicycle
el **monte** mountain, woods
el **monumento** monument
la **mordida** bribe (Mexico); bite
moreno, -a brown, brunette, dark skinned
morir, morirse (ue) to die
los **Moros** Moors
mostrar (ue) to show
motivar to motivate
el **motivo** motive
la **motocicleta** motorcycle
el **motor** motor
mover (ue) to move
el **movimiento** movement
la **muchacha** girl
el **muchacho** boy
mucho, -a much; **— gusto** very glad to meet you
muchos, -as many; **muchas gracias** many thanks
mudarse to move (residence)
los **muebles** furniture
la **muerte** death
muerto, -a dead
la **muestra** sample
la **mujer** woman; wife (fam.)
la **multa** fine; penalty
multar to fine
multinacional multinational
la **multitud** multitude
el **mundo** world; **todo el —** everybody
la **muñeca** doll
el **mural** mural
el, la **muralista** painter of murals; muralist
el **museo** museum
la **música** music
musical musical
la **musicalidad** musicality
el, la **músico** musician
mutuo, -a mutual
muy very; **— bien** very well

N

nacer (zc) to be born
el **nacimiento** birth
la **nación** nation
nacional national
nada nothing; **de —** you are welcome
nadar to swim
nadie nobody, no one
la **naranja** orange
la **nariz** nose
la **narrativa** narrative
la **natación** swimming
la **natalidad** birth rate
natural natural
la **naturaleza** nature
naturalmente naturally
naval naval
Las **Navidades** Christmas Season
necesario, -a necessary
la **necesidad** necessity
necesitar to need
negar (ie) to deny
negativo, -a negative
negativamente negatively
el **negocio** business, company; los **negocios** business
negro, -a black
el **nepotismo** nepotism
nervioso, -a nervous
la **nevada** snowfall
nevar (ie) to snow
ni nor, or; **ni... ni** neither . . . nor
la **nieve** snow
ningún, ninguno none
la **niña** girl child
la **niñera** babysitter
el **niño** boy child
el **nivel** level
no no, not
la **noche** evening, night; **Buenas noches** Good evening, good night; **de la —** p.m.; **por la —** at night
la **Nochebuena** Christmas Eve
el **nombre** name
noroeste northwest
normal normal
el **norte** north
norteamericano, -a North American
nos us, to for us
nosotros, nosotras we (after prep) us
la **nota** note, grade
notable outstanding; B grade in Hispanic scale
notar to note
la **noticia** notice; **las noticias** news
el **noticiero** newscast
noveno ninth
novecientos nine hundred
la **novela** novel
el, la **novelista** novelist
noventa ninety
noviembre November
el **novio,** la **novia** boyfriend, girlfriend; groom, bride
la **nube** cloud
nuclear nuclear
nuestro, -a our, ours
nueve nine
nuevo, -a new
el **número** number
numeroso, -a numerous
nunca never
la **nutrición** nutrition

O

o or
obedecer (zc) to obey
obligar to obligate
obligatorio, -a obligatory, required
el **objeto** object
la **obra** work
el **obrero** worker
observar to observe
el **obstáculo** obstacle
obtener (ie) to obtain
la **ocasión** occasion
el **océano** ocean
ochenta eighty
ocho eight
ochocientos eight hundred
octavo, -a eighth
octubre October
la **ocupación** occupation
ocupado, -a occupied, busy
ocurrir to occur
odiar to hate
el **odio** hatred
el **oeste** west
la **oferta** offer
oficial official; **el —** army officer
la **oficina** office
el **oficio** trade, occupation
ofrecer (zc) to offer
el **oído** (inner) ear
oír to hear
ojalá I hope, Would that
el **ojo** eye
oler (ue) to smell
el **olor** smell, odor
olvidar to forget; **olvidarse de** to forget about
once eleven
la **opción** option
la **ópera** opera
operar to operate
la **operación** operation; surgery
el **operador,** la **operadora** operator

opinar   to have, give an opinion
la **opinión**   opinion
oponerse a (me opongo)   to oppose
la **oportunidad**   opportunity, chance
la **oposición**   opposition
optimista   optimist
la **oración**   speech, oration
oral   oral
la **oratoria**   oratory, speech class
la **orden**   order, command; **el —**   order
ordenar   to order, to command; to put in order
la **oreja**   ear (outer)
organizar   to organize
la **orientación**   orientation
orientar   to orient, to inform
el **orgullo**   pride
el **origen**   origin
original   original
el **ornamento**   ornament
el **oro**   gold
os   you, to, for you
oscuro, -a   dark
el **otoño**   autumn, fall
otro, -a   other, another; **otra vez**   again

P

la **paciencia**   patience
el, la **paciente**   patient
el **padre**   father; los **padres**   parents
la **paella**   Spanish dish of rice, chicken, seafood, etc.
pagar   to pay; **a — allá**   collect call
la **página**   page
el **país**   country, nation
la **palabra**   word
el **palacio**   palace
pálido, -a   pale
el **pan**   bread
el **panorama**   panorama
los **pantalones**   pants
las **pantimedias**   pantyhose
el **Papa**   Pope
la **papa**   potato
el **papá**   father
la **papaya**   papaya (tropical fruit)
el **papel**   paper
el **paquete**   package
par   couple; even number
para   for, **—** + *inf*   in order to
el **paraguas**   umbrella
paralizar   to paralyze
parar   to stop
pararse   to stand up
pardo, -a   brown
parecer (zc)   to seem; **— se**   to look alike, resemble
la **pared**   wall

el **paréntesis**   parenthesis
el **pariente**   relative (family)
el **parque**   park
la **parrillada**   grilled meat (**Argentina**)
el **párrafo**   paragraph
la **parte**   part
participar   to participate
particular   private, particular
particularmente   particularly
el **partido**   political party; game
partir   to leave, depart
pasado, -a   past; **— mañana**   day after tomorrow
el **pasajero**   passenger
el **pasaporte**   passport
pasar   to spend time; to happen
el **pasatiempo**   pastime, hobby
pasear   to take a walk, ride
el **paseo**   a walk; **dar un —**   to take a walk (ride)
el **paso**   step; way
el **pastel**   cake, pie
el **paternalismo**   paternalism
patinar   to skate
el **patio**   patio
la **patria**   fatherland
la **paz**   peace
la **pediatría**   pediatrics
el **pecho**   chest
el **pedido**   order (for goods)
pedir (i)   to ask for (something); **— prestado**   to borrow
peinarse   to comb one's hair
pelar   to peel
la **película**   motion picture, film, movie
el **peligro**   danger
el **pelo**   hair
la **pelota**   ball
pendiente   pending, hanging
la **península**   peninsula
el **pensamiento**   thought
pensar (ie)   to think; **— en**   to think about; **—** + *inf*   to plan, intend to
peor   worse; el **—**   the worst
pequeño, -a   small
la **pera**   pear
perder (ie)   to lose
perdido, -a   lost
perdón, perdóneme   Excuse me, I am sorry
perdonar   to forgive
perezoso, -a   lazy
perfectamente   perfectly
el **perfume**   perfume
el **periódico**   newspaper
el **periodismo**   journalism
el, la **periodista**   journalist
el **período**   period (of time)
el **permiso**   permission, permit; **con —**   excuse me
permitir   to allow, to permit

pero but
el **perro** dog
la **persistencia** persistence
la **persona** person
el **personaje** character, personage
el **personal** personnel
la **personalidad** personality
el **personalismo** personalism
la **perspectiva** perspective
la **persuación** persuasion
persuadir to persuade
pertenecer (zc) to belong
pesado, -a heavy
pesar to weigh; **a — de** in spite of
el **pescado** fish
pescar to fish
la **peseta** monetary unit in Spain
el **peso** monetary unit; weight
el **petróleo** petroleum
el, la **pianista** pianist
el **piano** piano
picante spicy hot
el **pie** foot
la **piel** skin
la **pierna** leg
el **piloto** pilot
la **pimienta** pepper
el **pino** pine tree
pintar to paint
el **pintor,** la **pintora** painter
la **pintura** painting; paint
la **piña** pineapple
la **piñata** piñata
el **pirata** pirate
piropear to flatter in a flirting manner
el **piropo** flirtaceous compliment
el **piso** floor
la **pizarra** chalkboard
el **placer** pleasure
el **plan** plan
plano, -a flat, plane
la **planta** plant
la **plata** silver
el **plátano** banana, plantain
el **plato** plate, dish; **— de sopa** bowl of soup
la **playa** beach
la **plaza** square
pleno, -a full (literary)
el **plomero** plumber
la **pluma** pen
plural plural
la **población** population
pobre poor
la **pobreza** poverty
poco, -a little; **un poquito de** a little bit of
pocos, -as few

poder (ue) to be able to
el **poder** power
el **poema** poem
la **poesía** poetry
el **poeta** poet
la **poetisa** woman poet
la **policía** police force; el **—** policeman; la **mujer —** police woman
la **política** politics
políticamente politically
el **pollo** chicken
el **ponche** punch (drink)
poner (pongo) to put, to place
ponerse to put on; to become (suddenly); **— a** to start
popular popular
por by, along, for; **— ciento** percent; **— favor** please; **— la mañana, tarde, noche** in the morning, afternoon, evening
por eso that is why, therefore
¿por qué? why
porque because
el **portal** portico, arcade
poseer to possess, to have
la **posesión** possession
posesivo, -a possessive
posible possible
la **posición** position
positivo, -a positive
el **postre** dessert
practicar to practice
práctico, -a practical
el **precio** price
precioso, -a precious
preciso, -a precise
predominar to predominate
preferir (ie) to prefer
la **pregunta** question
preguntar to ask (a question)
la **prensa** press
preocupado, -a preoccupied
preocuparse (de) to worry (about)
preparar to prepare; **— se** to prepare oneself
la **presentación** presentation
presentar to present, to introduce (a person) socially
preservar to preserve
el **presidente** president
presidir to preside over, to chair
prestar to lend; **— atención** to pay attention
prestigioso, -a prestigious, renouned
el **pretérito** preterite
previo, -a previous
la **primavera** spring
primero, -a first
el **primo,** la **prima** cousin
principal main
principalmente mainly, principally

el **principio** beginning; al — at the beginning
la **prioridad** priority
la **prisa** haste, hurry; **tener —** to be in a hurry
la **probabilidad** probability
probar (ue) to taste, to try; **— se** to try on (clothes)
el **problema** problem
la **procesión** procession
prodigioso, -a prodigious
producir (zc) to produce
la **producción** production
el **producto** product
la **proeza** prowess
la **profesión** profession
profesional professional
el **profesor,** la **profesora** professor
el **programa** program
progresar to make progress
el **progreso** progress
prohibido, -a prohibited
la **proliferación** proliferation
la **promesa** promise
prometer to promise
prominente prominent
el **pronombre** pronoun
pronto soon, at once
pronunciar to pronounce
la **pronunciación** pronunciation
la **propaganda** publicity; propaganda
la **propina** tip
proponer (propongo) to propose
proporcionar to furnish, to provide
el **propósito** purpose; **a —** by the way
la **prosperidad** prosperity
próspero, -a prosperous
proteger (j) to protect
protestar to protest
protocolo protocol
la **provincia** province
provocar to provoke, to avoid
próximo, -a next (upcoming)
proyectar to project
la **prueba** test, quiz
la **(p)sicología** psychology
la **publicidad** publicity, advertising
público, -a public
el **pudín** pudding
el **pueblo** town; people
el **puente** bridge
la **puerta** door
puesto put, placed
puertorriqueño, -a Puerto Rican
pues well, then
el **puesto** job
el **pulmón** lung
el **punto** point; **en —** on the dot **— de vista** point of view; period, dot

puntual punctual
el **pupitre** student desk
puro, -a pure

Q

que that, who, whom, than
¿qué? what?; **¿Qué tal?** How are you?
quedarse to stay
los **quehaceres** chores, duties, tasks, homework
quejarse (de) to complain (about)
querer (ie) to want, wish, love; **— decir** to mean
querido, -a dear
el **queso** cheese
quien (es) who, whom
¿quién (es)? who (is it)? **¿a —?** to whom?; **¿de —?** whose?
la **química** chemistry
quince fifteen
quinientos five hundred
quitar to take away
quizás perhaps

R

racial racial
la **ración** portion, ration
el **radiator** radiator
radical radical
el, la **radio** radio
la **radiografía** x rays
la **raíz** root
ranchero, -a rancher
el **rancho** ranch
rápido, -a fast
raro, -a rare, unusual
el **rascacielos** skyscraper
el **rasgo** feature, trait
el **rato** while, little while
la **raya** line
la **raza** race
la **razón** reason; **tener —** to be right
razonable reasonable
reaccionario, -a reactionary
real real, royal
la **realidad** reality
el **realismo** realism
realista realistic
realizar to fulfill, carry out, realize
la **rebanada** slice
rebasar to pass (another vehicle)
el **recado** message
la **recepción** reception
la **receta** recipe
recibir to receive
el **recibo** receipt, bill
reciente recent, new
recientemente recently
recitar to recite

recoger (j)   to pick up, to gather
recomendar (ie)   to recommend
reconciliar   to reconcile
reconocer (zc)   to acknowledge
la reconstrucción   reconstruction
recordar (ue)   to remember
recorrer   to run through
el recreo   recreation
el rectángulo   rectangle
el recuerdo   souvenir; memory
el recurso   resource
el redactor   editor
redondo, -a   round
reducir (zc)   to reduce
referir (ie)   to refer; referirse a   to refer to
la reforma   reform
el refrán   proverb, saying
el refresco   refreshment, soft drink
el refrigerador   refrigerator
regalar   to give as a gift
el regalo   gift
el regateo   bartering
la región   region
el registro   registration, registry
regresar   to come back, return
regular   regular
la reina   queen
reír (i)   to laugh
reírse de (i)   to laugh at
la relación   relation
relatar   to narrate, tell
la religión   religion
religioso, -a   religious
el reloj   clock, watch
el remedio   remedy
remoto, -a   remote
reparar   to repair
repasar   to review
repetir (i)   to repeat
la representación   representation
el, la representante   representative; congressman
representar   to represent
la represión   repression
la república   republic
requerir (ie)   to require
el requisito   requirement
la reserva   reservation, reserve
la reservación   reservation
reservado, -a   reserved, held back
la residencia   residence; — estudiantil   college dorm
respectivo, -a   respective
respetar   to respect
el respeto   respect; faltar al —   to be disrespectful
respirar   to breathe
la respuesta   answer
responder   to respond, to answer

la responsabilidad   responsability
responsable   responsible
restaurar   to restore
el restaurante   restaurant
el resto   the rest
el resultado   result
resultar   to result
el resumen   summary
resumir   to summarize
la reunión   reunion, gathering
reunirse   to meet, get together
revisar   to revise; to correct
la revista   magazine
la revolución   revolution
revuelto, -a   scrambled
el rey   king
Los Reyes Magos   Three Wise Men
rico, -a   rich
el riesgo   risk
el río   river
la riqueza   riches, wealthy
riquísimo, -a   very rich
el ritmo   rhythm
ritual   ritual
el, la rival   rival
el robo   robbery, theft
rodear   to surround
la rodilla   knee
rojo, -a   red
romper   to break, tear
la ropa   clothing
la rosa   rose; color —   pink
rosado, -a   pink
roto, -a   broken
rubio, -a   blonde
el ruido   noise; ruidoso   noisy
la ruina   ruin
rural   rural
la rutina   routine

S

sábado   Saturday; el (los) —   on Saturday(s)
saber   to know (facts); — + inf   to know how to
la sabiduría   wisdom
el sabor   flavor
sabroso, -a   tasty, delicious
sacar   to take out
el saco   coat
el sacrificio   sacrifice
la sal   salt
la sala   living room
la salchicha   sausage
la salida   exit
salir   to leave, go out
la salud   health; ¡Salud!   God bless you!
saludar   to greet, to salute

las **sandalias**   sandals
el **sándwich**   sandwich
la **sangre**   blood
el **santiamén**   jiffy
santo   holy, saint; **día del —**   Saint's Day
el **sarape**   shawl
sarcástico, -a   sarcastic
la **sardina**   sardine
la **sartén**   frying pan
la **satisfacción**   satisfaction
se   himself, herself, yourself (reflexive)
la **secadora**   dryer
la **sección**   section
el **secretario**, la **secretaria**   secretary
el **secuestro**   kidnapping
secundario, -a   secondary
la **sed**   thirst; **tener —**   to be thirsty
la **seda**   silk
seguir (i)   to follow, continue
según   according to
segundo, -a   second
seguro, -a   sure
seis   six
seiscientos   six hundred
la **selección**   choice, selection
seleccionar   to choose, select
la **selva**   jungle
el **sello**   seal; **— de correos**   post stamp
el **semáforo**   traffic light
la **semana**   week; la **— pasada**   last week, la **— próxima**
   next week
la **semejanza**   similarity
el **semestre**   semester
el **seminario**   seminar; seminary
sencillo, -a   simple
señor, Sr.   mister, sir; el **Señor**   the Lord
señora, Sra.   Mrs., madam
señorita, Srta.   Miss
la **sensibilidad**   sensibility
sentarse (ie)   to sit down
sentimental   sentimental
sentir (ie)   to feel, to regret; **sentirse bien (mal)**   to feel
   fine (bad); **lo siento**   I am sorry
la **señal**   signal
la **separación**   separation
separado, -a   separate, apart
separar   to separate
septiembre   September
séptimo, -a   seventh
la **sequía**   drought
ser   to be (typical)
la **serie**   series, sequence
serio, -a   serious; **en —**   seriously
el **servicio**   service
la **servilleta**   napkin
servir (i)   to serve

sesenta   sixty
setecientos   seven hundred
setenta   seventy
severo, -a   severe
el **sexo**   sex
sexto, -a   sixth
sí   yes, certainly
si   if
siempre   always; **— que**   whenever
la **siesta**   nap
siete   seven
el **siglo**   century; **Siglo de oro**   Golden Age
el **significado**   meaning
significar   to mean, signify
siguiente   following, next
la **sílaba**   syllable
el **silencio**   silence
la **silla**   chair
simbolizar   to symbolize
el **símbolo**   symbol
similar   similar
simpático, -a   nice, pleasant (person)
sin   without; **sin embargo**   nevertheless
sincero, -a   sincere
el **sindicato**   worker's union, syndicate
singular   singular
sino   but (contrast)
el **sinónimo**   synonym; *adj* synonymous
el **sistema**   system
el **sitio**   place, site
la **situación**   situation
situado, -a   situated
sobre   on, about
el **sobre**   envelope
sobrevivir   to survive
la **sobrina**   niece
el **sobrino**   nephew
social   social
sociable   sociable
socialmente   socially
la **sociedad**   society
la **sociología**   sociology
el **sofá**   sofa
el **sol**   sun; **Sol (es)**   Peruvian currency
solamente   only
el **soldado**   soldier
la **solicitud**   application
sólido, -a   solid
solo, -a   alone
sólo   only
soltero, -a   single
la **solución**   solution
solucionar   to solve
la **sombra**   shade, shadow
el **sombrero**   hat
sonar (ue)   to sound

la **sonrisa**   smile

soñar (con) (ue)   to dream (about)

la **sopa**   soup

soportar   to put up with, to bear; to support

sórdido, -a   sordid

sordo, -a   deaf

sorprender   to surprise

sospechar   to suspect

sospechoso, -a   suspicious

su(s)   your, his, her, its, their

suave   soft

subir   to go up to climb

el **subjuntivo**   subjunctive

subrayado, -a   underlined

subyugar   to subjugate

sucio, -a   dirty

la **sucursal**   branch office

el **sueldo**   salary

el **sueño**   dream; **tener —**   to be sleepy

la **suerte**   luck

el **suéter**   sweater

suficiente   enough, sufficient

la **sugerencia**   suggestion

sugerir (ie)   to suggest

el **sujeto**   subject

sumamente   very, highly

superior   superior

el **supermercado**   supermarket

el **supervisor,** la **supervisora**   supervisor

suponer (supongo)   to suppose

el **sur**   south

surgir   to spurt up, to come on

surrealista   surrealist

suspirado, -a   longed for

el **sustantivo**   noun

suyo, -a, -os, -as   your(s), his, her(s), its, their(s)

T

el **tabaco**   tobacco

el **taco**   taco

el **tacto**   touch, tact

tal   such; **¿Qué tal?**   How goes it?

el **talco**   talc

tal como   such as; **tal vez**   perhaps

la **talla**   size (clothing)

también   also, too

tampoco   neither

tan   so; **tan... como**   as . . . as

tanto   so much (many); **— como**   as much as

el **tanque**   tank

tarde   late; la **tarde**   afternoon; de la **—**   p.m.,   in the afternoon; **por la —**   in the afternoon

la **tarea**   homework, chore

la **tarjeta**   card

la **taza**   cup

te   you; (for, to) you

el **té**   tea

el **teatro**   theatre

la **técnica**   technique

el **técnico**   technician

el **tejido**   textile, weaving

el **teléfono**   telephone

la **telenovela**   soap opera

la **televisión**   television; la **"tele"** TV

el **televisor**   TV set, el **— a colores**   color set

el **tema**   theme, subject

el **temblor**   tremor

temer   to fear, to be afraid of

la **temperatura**   temperature

el **templo**   temple

la **temporada**   season

temprano   early

el **tenedor**   fork; el **— de libros**   bookkeeper

tener (ie)   to have; **— ...años**   to be . . . years old; **— calor** to be hot; **— cuidado**   to be careful; **— frío**   to be cold; **— ganas de** + *inf* to feel like; **— hambre**   to be hungry; **— miedo**   to be afraid; **— que** + *inf* to have to; **— razón**   to be right; **— sed**   to be thirsty; **— sueño**   to be sleepy; **— la suerte**   to be lucky

el **tenis**   tennis

tercer(o), -a   third

terminar   to finish

el **terremoto**   earthquake

el **territorio**   territory

el, la **terrorista**   terrorist

la **tertulia**   social gathering

el **textil**   textile

la **tía**   aunt

tibio   soft boiled

el **tiempo**   weather; time

la **tienda**   store

la **tierra**   land, earth

las **tijeras**   scissors

tímido, -a   timid

tinto   red (wine)

el **tío**   uncle; los **tíos**   uncle and aunt

típico, -a   typical, customary

el **tipo**   type

el **tirano**   tyrant

el **título**   title

la **tiza**   chalk

el **tocadiscos**   record player

tocar   to touch, to play (an instrument)

el **tocino**   bacon

todavía   still; **todavía no**   not yet

todo   all; **— el mundo**   everyone; **— el día**   all day long; **todos los días**   every day

tolerante   tolerant

tomar   to drink, to take

el **tomate**   tomato

el **tono**   tone

el **tonto**   fool

torcer (ue) (tuerzo) to twist, turn
la **tormenta** storm
el **tornado** tornado, twister
el **toro** bull
la **toronja** grapefruit
la **torta** cake
la **tortilla** omelet; cornmeal cake
la **tos** cough
toser to cough
la **tostada** toast; tortilla with meat, beans, etc.
la **tostadora** toaster
trabajar to work
trabajador, -a worker, laborer; *adj* hard-working
el **trabajo** work, job, occupation
el **trabalenguas** tongue-twister
la **tradición** tradition
tradicionalmente traditionally
traducir (zc) to translate
traer to bring
el **tráfico** traffic
el **traje** suit, outfit; — **de baño** bathing suit
el **tranquilizante** tranquilizer
tranquilo, -a tranquil, quiet, calm
la **transmisión** transmission
el **transporte** transportation
el **tratamiento** treatment
tratar (de) to try (to)
tratarse de to deal with
trece thirteen
treinta thirty
tremendo, -a tremendous, terrific
el **tren** train
tres three
trescientos three hundred
el **triángulo** triangle
la **tribu** tribe
el **tributo** tribute
el **trigo** wheat
triste sad
tropical tropical
tú you (familiar)
tu, tus your (possessive)
la **tumba** tomb
el **turismo** tourism
el, la **turista** tourist
turnarse to take turns
el **turno** turn
tuyo, -a, -os, -as yours

U

la **ubicación** location
último, -a last
un, una a, an
único, -a only
unido, -a united

el **uniforme** uniform
unir to unite, to join, connect
universal universal
la **universidad** university
universitario, -a (*adj*) university
uno one
unos, unas some, several
urbano, -a urban
la **urgencia** urgency
urgente urgent
usado, -a used
usar to use
usted, Ud. you (formal)
ustedes, Uds. you (formal, *pl*)
usual usual
útil useful
utilizar to utilize
la **uva** grape

V

las **vacaciones** vacation; de — on vacation
vacío, -a empty
valer to be worth
valiente valiant, courageous
el **valle** valley
el **valor** courage; value
¡Vamos! Let's go; Come on!
el **vaquero** cowboy
la **variación** variation, divergence
variar (varío) to vary
la **variedad** variety
varios, -a several
vasco Basque
el **vaso** (drinking) glass
el **vecino, la vecina** neighbor
vegetal vegetable
veinte twenty
la **velocidad** speed
vencer (venzo) to conquer, to defeat
el **vendedor, la vendedora** sales person
vender to sell
venir (ie) to come
la **venta** sale
ventaja advantage
la **ventana** window
ver to see
el **verano** summer
el **verbo** verb
verdad true; la — truth
verdadero, -a real, truthful
verde green
la **versión** version
el **vestido** dress
vestir (se) (i) to dress; (to get dressed)
veterinario, -a veterinary

vez time, occasion; **cada —** each time; **de — en cuando** every now and then; **en — de** instead of; **otra —** again

la **vía** the way; **— aérea** air mail

viajar to travel

el **viaje** trip

la **víctima** victim

la **victoria** victory

la **vida** life

viejo, -a old

el **viento** wind

viernes Friday; el (los)— on Friday(s)

el **vigor** vigor

el **vinagre** vinegar

el **vino** wine

la **virgen** virgin

la **virtud** virtue

la **visa** visa

la **visita** visit

visitar to visit

la **vista** view, sight

visto, -a seen

las **vitaminas** vitamins

la **vivienda** housing; dwelling

vivir to live

vivo, -a alive, live; bright

el **vocabulario** vocabulary

la **vocal** vowel

volar (ue) to fly

el **volcán** volcano

el **voltaje** voltage

el **volumen** volume

la **voluntad** will

voluntario, -a voluntary

volver (ue) to return; **— a** (+ *inf*) to (*verb*) again

volverse (ue) to become (suddenly)

vosotros, vosotras *fam pl* you

votar to vote

el **voto** vote

la **voz** voice

el **vuelo** flight

vuestro, vuestra, os, as *fam pl* your

Y

y and

ya already

yo I

Z

la **zanahoria** carrot

el **zapato** shoe

la **zapatería** shoe store; shoe repair shop

el **zapatero** shoe maker; shoe repairman

la **zona** zone

Inglés-español

A

a, an **un, una**
abandon **abandonar**
ability **la habilidad**
able: to be **poder (ue)**
abnormal **anormal**
abnormality **la anormalidad**
above **arriba, encima de**
abundance **la abundancia**
academic year el **curso**
accelerate **acelerar**
accent el **acento**
accentuation la **acentuación**
accept **aceptar**
accompany **acompañar**
accomplish **lograr**
account la **cuenta**
accounting la **contabilidad**
ache el **dolor**
achieve, to accomplish **lograr, realizar**
acknowledge **reconocer (zc)**
acquainted (to be) **conocer (zc)**
across from **en frente de**
act el **acto; actuar**
action la **acción**
activity la **actividad**
actress la **actriz**
actually **en realidad**
adapt **adaptar**
add **añadir; sumar**
additional **adicional**
address la **dirección**
adequate **adecuado, -a**
adjective el **adjetivo**
administer **administrar**
admirable **admirable**
admission ticket la **entrada;** el **boleto**
advance **adelantar, avanzar**
advancement el **adelanto**
advantage la **ventaja**
adventure la **aventura**
advice el **consejo**
advise **aconsejar**
affection el **cariño**
affectionate **afectuoso, -a**
affirmative **afirmativo, -a**
afraid (to be) **tener miedo**
after **después (de)**
afternoon la **tarde**
again **otra vez**
age la **edad**
agency la **agencia**

aggression la **agresión**
aggressor **agresor, -a**
agile **ágil**
agree (grammatically) **concordar (ue)**
agreed, agreement **(de) acuerdo**
agriculture la **agricultura**
agronomist el **agrónomo**
ahead **adelante**
air el **aire**
air mail **vía aérea; correo aéreo**
airplane el **avión**
airport el **aeropuerto**
alcohol el **alcohol**
algebra el **álgebra**
alive **vivo, -a**
all **todo, -a**
all right, well **bueno; bien**
almost **casi**
alone **solo, -a**
already **ya**
also **también**
although **aunque**
always **siempre**
ambition la **ambición**
American **americano, -a**
among **entre**
amusing **divertido, -a**
ancestor el **antepasado**
and **y, e** (before **i** and **hi**)
Andean **andino, -a**
angle el **ángulo**
anglo-saxon **anglosajón, -a**
angry **enojado, -a**
animal el **animal**
animated **animado, -a**
anniversary el **aniversario**
announce **anunciar**
announcement el **anuncio**
annual **anual**
answer la **respuesta**
answer (to) **contestar, responder**
antecedent el **antecedente**
apartment el **apartamento,** el **piso** (Spain)
apogee el **apogeo**
appear **aparecer (zc)**
appetite el **apetito**
appetizer el **aperitivo**
applaud **aplaudir**
applause el **aplauso**
apple la **manzana**
appointment la **cita**
approach **acercarse**

appropriate   apropiado, -a
approve   aprobar (ue)
April   abril
architect   el arquitecto
area   el área
Argentinian   argentino, -a
argue   discuter
arid   árido, -a
armament   el armamento
arm (body)   el brazo
arm (weapons)   las armas
army   el ejército
army officer   el oficial
around   alrededor de
arrange   arreglar
arrival   la llegada
arrive   llegar
art   el arte
artesan   el artesano, la artesana
article   el artículo
artist   el, la artista
as   como
as much (many)...as   tanto(s)...como
as soon as   tan pronto como
ask (a question)   preguntar, hacer una pregunta
ask for something   pedir (i)
aspect   el aspecto
athlete   el, la atleta; el, la deportista
Atlantic   el atlántico
attack   el ataque
attack (to)   atacar
attend   asistir a
attendance   la asistencia
attention   la atención
attentively   atentamente
attitude   la actitud
attract   atraer
attractive   atractivo, -a
audience   la audiencia
August   agosto
aunt   la tía
author   el autor, la autora
authorize   autorizar
auto(mobile)   el auto(móvil), el carro, el coche
autonomy   la autonomía
autumn   el otoño
avenue   la avenida
avocado   el aguacate
avoid   evitar

B
babysitter   la niñera
bachelor's party   despedida de soltero
back (human)   la espalda
background   el fondo, el trasfondo

backwardness   el atraso
bacon   el tocino
bad   mal(o), -a
bag   la bolsa
balance   el equilibrio
ball   la pelota
ballpoint pen   el bolígrafo
banana   el plátano
bank   el banco
banquet   el banquete
baptism   el bautismo
baptize   bautizar
barbecue   el churrasco
barrier   la barrera
baseball   el béisbol
base   basar
based   basado, -a
basket   la canasta
basketball   el básquetbol, el baloncesto
basque   vasco, -a; vascuence
bath   el baño
bathe   bañarse
bathing suit   el traje de baño
bathroom   el baño, el cuarto de baño
battle   la lucha, la batalla
bay leaf   el laurel
be   estar (location, condition);   ser (typical; possession; material)
be...years (old)   tener...años (de edad)
beach   la playa
beans   los frijoles
beat   batir
beautiful   hermoso, -a
because; because of   porque; a causa de, por
become angry   enojarse
become ill   enfermarse
become   hacerse
bed   la cama
bedroom   el dormitorio, la alcoba
beef steak   el biftec, bisté
beer   la cerveza
before   antes de, antes de que
begin   empezar (ie), compenzar (ie)
beginning   el comienzo, el principio; at the — al principio, al comienzo
behind   detrás (de)
believe   creer
belong   pertenecer (zc)
below   abajo; debajo
belt   el cinturón
bench   el banco
benefit   el beneficio
besides   además
better   mejor; the best, el mejor
between   entre
big   grande, enorme

bill   la **cuenta**
biographic   **biográfico, -a**
biology   la **biología**
birth   el **nacimiento;** — control,   **control de la natali-**
   dad; — rate   la **natalidad**
birthday   el **cumpleaños;** el **santo**
black   **negro, -a**
blackboard   la **pizarra**
blame   la **culpa;** to — **culpar**
block (city)   la **cuadra;** la **manzana**
blonde   **rubio, -a**
blouse   la **blusa**
blow   el **golpe**
blue   **azul**
board, ruling group   la **junta**
body   el **cuerpo**
bond   el **lazo**
book   el **libro**
bookkeeper   el **tenedor de libros**
bookstore   la **librería**
boots   las **botas**
border   la **frontera**
bored   **aburrido, -a**
born (to be)   **nacer (zc)**
boss   el **jefe,** la **jefa**
both   **ambos, ambas**
bother   **molestar**
bottle   la **botella**
boulevard   el **bulevar**
bowl   **escudilla, plato hondo;** — of soup,   el **plato de**
   sopa
boxing   el **boxeo**
boy   el **muchacho,** el **niño**
boycott   **boicotear**
boyfriend   el **novio** (sweetheart), el **amigo** (friend)
boyscout   el **explorador**
branch office   la **sucursal**
brand   **marcar**
bread   el **pan**
break   **romper**
breakfast   el **desayuno;** to have — **desayunar**
breath   **respirar**
bride   la **novia**
bridge   el **puente**
bring   **traer**
brochure   el **folleto**
brother   el **hermano**
brown   **pardo, -a, marrón**
brunette, dark   **moreno, -a**
bubbling wine   **espumante**
building   el **edificio**
bull   el **toro;** — fighter,   el **torero;** — ring,   la **plaza de**
   toros
bullfight   la **corrida de toros**
burial   el **entierro**
bus   el **autobús,** el **bus,** el **camión (México)**

business   el **negocio,** el **comercio**
businessman   el **hombre de negocios,** el **comerciante**
busy   **ocupado**
but   **pero**
butter   la **mantequilla**
buy   **comprar**
by   **por** (by way of, by means of); — a certain date or time
   para; — the way   **a propósito**
bycicle   la **bicicleta**

C
cab   el **taxi**
cake   la **torta,** el **pastel**
calculate   **calcular**
calendar   el **calendario**
call   la **llamada;** to call (long distance)   **llamar (a larga**
   distancia)
called (to be)   **llamarse**
calm down   **calmarse**
camera   la **cámara**
canal   el **canal**
candidate   el **candidato**
candy   los **dulces**
canoe   la **canoa**
cap   la **gorra**
capable   **capaz**
capacity   la **capacidad**
capital (city)   la **capital**
capitalist   el, la **capitalista**
captivity   el **cautiverio**
capture   **capturar**
car   el **carro,** el **coche**
card   la **tarjeta**
care   **cuidado;** to — **cuidar**
career   la **carrera**
careful   **cuidado, cuidadoso, -a;** to be — **tener cuidado**
carnival   el **carnaval**
carrot   la **zanahoria**
carry   **llevar**
cat   el **gato**
cathedral   la **catedral**
catholic   **católico, -a**
cause   **causa;** to — **causar**
celebrate   **celebrar**
celebration   la **celebración**
center   el **centro**
central   **central**
Central America   **Centroamérica, América Central**
century   el **siglo**
cereal   el **cereal**
certain   **cierto, -a**
chair   la **silla**
chalk   la **tiza**
chalkboard, blackboard   la **pizarra**
change (to)   el **cambio;** — clothes   **mudarse de ropa**

channel   el **canal**
character   el **carácter;** — (in a play)   el **personaje**
charm   el **encanto**
charming   **encantador, -a**
chat   la **charla**
cheap   **barato, -a**
cheese   el **queso**
chemistry   la **química**
chess   el **ajedrez**
chicken   el **pollo**
chill   **enfriar**
choice   la **selección**
choose (to)   **escoger; seleccionar**
chores   los **quehaceres**
Christmas Eve   la **Nochebuena**
Christmas   la **Navidad**
chronicle   **cronica**
church   la **iglesia**
circle   el **círculo**
circumstance   la **circunstancia**
city   la **ciudad**
civilization   la **civilización**
clarify   **aclarar**
class   la **clase**
classic   **clásico, -a**
classmate   el **compañero de clase**, la **compañera...**
clean   **limpio, -a**
clean (to)   **limpiar**
clear   **claro, -a**
clergy   el **clérigo**
client   el, la **cliente**
clinic   la **clínica**
clock   el **reloj**
close   **cerrar (ie)**
closed   **cerrado, -a**
clothing   la **ropa**
clothing size   la **talla**
cloud   la **nube**
club   el **club**
coast   la **costa**
coat   el **abrigo**
cocktail   el **coctel**
cocoa   el **cacao**
coconut   el **coco**
coexist   **coexistir**
coffee   el **café**
coffee pot   la **cafetera**
cognate   **cognado**
cold   **frío, -a;** to be —,   **tener frío; catarro, resfriado** (illness)
collect   **cobrar**
cologne   la **colonia**
colonial   **colonial**
color   el **color**
comb (to)   **peinarse**
combination   la **combinación**

combine   **combinar**
come   **venir;** — back   **volver, regresar;** — in   **entrar**
comedy   la **comedia**
comfort   la **comodidad**
comfortable   **cómodo, -a**
command   el **mandato** (grammar); to —   **mandar, ordenar**
commemorate   **conmemorar**
comment   **comentar**
commerce   el **comercio**
commercial   **comercial**
commitment   el **compromiso**
common   **común**
communicate   **comunicar**
communion   la **comunión**
communist   el, la **comunista**
community   la **comunidad**
companion   el **compañero**
company   la **compañía**, la **firma**, la **empresa**
compare   **comparar**
comparison   la **comparación**
compete   **competir (i)**
competent   **competente, capaz**
competition   la **competición**, la **competencia** (business)
competitor   el **competidor**
complain (about)   **quejarse (de)**
complete   **completar**
complex   **complejo, -a**
compliment   el **piropo**
compose   **componer**
composer   el **compositor**, la **compositora**
composition   la **composición**
comprehension   la **comprensión**
computer   la **computadora** (America);   el **ordenador** (Spain)
computer science   la **computación**
concert   el **concierto**
conclusion   la **conclusión**
condiment   el **condimento**
condition   la **condición**
conduct   la **conducta**
conductor   el **conductor**
conference   la **conferencia**
congratulate (to)   **felicitar**
congratulations   **felicitaciones**
connect   **conectar**
connection   la **conexión**
conquer   **conquistar**
conqueror   el **conquistador**
conquest   la **conquista**
constitution   la **constitución**
construct   **construir (construyo)**
consult   **consultar**
contact   el **contacto**
contemplate   **contemplar**
contemporary   **contemporáneo, -a**

contest   la **competición**
context   el **contexto**
continue   **continuar; seguir (i)**
contrary   **contrario, -a**
contribute   **contribuir (contribuyo)**
control   el **control;** to — **controlar**
converse   **conversar, charlar**
cook   **cocinar**
cookies   las **galletitas dulces**
cool (weather)   **fresco;** it is —, **hace —**
coordinate   **coordinar**
corn   el **maíz**
correct   **revisar; corregir (i)**
correspondence   la **correspondencia**
correspondent   el, la **corresponsal**
cost   **costar (ue)**
cotton   el **algodón**
cough   la **tos;** to — **toser**
count   el **conde**
count (on)   **contar (con);** to — **contar (ue)**
country, nation   el **país**
countryside   el **campo**
coup d'etat   el **golpe de estado**
couple   el **par;** la **pareja** (married couple); el **matrimonio**
course   el **curso;** of — **por supuesto**
courteous   **cortés**
courtesy   la **cortesía**
cousin   el **primo,** la **prima**
cover   **cubrir**
cracker   la **galleta**
crazy   **loco, -a**
create   **crear**
creative, creator   **creador, -a**
cross   la **cruz;** to — **cruzar**
cry   **llorar; gritar**
cultivate   **cultivar**
cultivation   el **cultivo**
culture   la **cultura**
cumin (spice)   el **comino**
cup   la **taza**
cure   la **cura;** to — **curar**
curious   **curioso, -a**
curve   la **curva**
custard   el **flan;** la **natilla**
custom   la **costumbre**
customer   el, la **cliente**
customs   la **aduana**
cut   **cortar**

D

damage   el **daño** to — **dañar**
dance   la **danza,** el **baile;** to — **bailar**
danger   el **peligro**

dare   **atreverse (a)**
dark   **oscuro, -a;** — complected   **moreno, -a**
date   la **fecha;** la **cita** (appointment)
daughter, child   la **hija**
day   **día;** all — long   **todo el día;** every —   **todos los días**
dead   **muerto, -a**
deaf   **sordo, -a**
deal with   **tratarse de**
dear   **querido, -a**
death   la **muerte**
debt   la **deuda**
decadence   la **decadencia**
decaffeinated   **descafeinado, -a**
deceit   el **engaño**
deceive   **engañar**
December   **diciembre**
decide   **decidir (se)**
declare   **declarar**
decline   **decaer**
decorate   **decorar, adornar**
defect   el **defecto**
defend   **defender (ie)**
deform   **deformar**
degree   el **grado**
delay   la **demora;** to — **demorar**
delicious   **delicioso, -a; sabroso, -a**
demand   **exigir (j)**
demanding   **exigente**
denial   la **negación**
denounce   **denunciar**
deny   **negar (ie)**
department   el **departamento**
department store   el **almacén**
depend (on)   **depender (de)**
deplorable   **deplorable**
descend   **bajar**
describe   **describir**
desert   el **desierto**
deserve   **merecer (zc)**
desire   **desear**
desk   el **escritorio;** student's desk   **el pupitre**
dessert   el **postre**
detail   el **detalle**
detain   **detener (ie)**
detective   el **detective,** el **investigador**
determined   **determinado, -a**
develop   **desarrollar**
development   el **desarrollo**
diagram   el **diagrama**
dialog   el **diálogo**
diary   el **diario**
dictator   el **dictador**
dictatorship   la **dictadura**
dictionary   el **diccionario**
die   **morir, morirse (ue)**

diet   la **dieta,** el **régimen**
difference   la **diferencia**
different   **diferente; distinto, -a**
difficult   **difícil**
difficulty   la **dificultad**
dine   **cenar**
dining room   el **comedor**
dinner   la **cena,** la **comida**
direct   **directo, -a**
direction   la **dirección**
directly   **directamente**
director   el **director,** la **directora**
disagreeable   **antipático, -a**
discipline   la **disciplina**
discontent   **descontento, -a**
discord   la **discordia**
discount   el **descuento**
discover   **descubrir;** discovery   el **descubrimiento**
discrepancy   la **discrepancia**
discuss   **discutir;** discussion   la **discusión**
dish   el **plato**
disobedient   **desobediente**
displeasure   el **disgusto**
disrespectful   **irrespetuoso, -a;** to be — **faltar el respeto**
distance   la **distancia**
distinguish (oneself)   **distinguir (se)**
district   el **distrito**
do   **hacer**
doctor   el **doctor,** la **doctora;** el **médico**
document   el **documento**
dog   el **perro**
doll   la **muñeca**
dollar   el **dólar**
dominate   **dominar, controlar**
donate   **donar**
done   **hecho, -a**
door   la **puerta**
dormitory (college)   la **residencia (estudiantil)**
double   **doble**
doubt   la **duda;** to — **dudar**
downtown   el **centro**
dozen   la **docena**
drain   **escurrir**
drawing   el **dibujo**
dream   el **sueño;** to — (about)   **soñar (ue) (con)**
dress   el **vestido;** to — (oneself)   **vestirse (i)**
drink   el **refresco,** la **bebida;** to — **tomar, beber**
drive   **manejar**
drought   la **sequía**
drug   la **droga**
during   **durante**
duty   el **deber,** la **obligación**
dynamic   **dinámico, -a**

E

each   **cada**
ear (inner)   el **oído;** (outer) la **oreja**
early   **temprano**
earn   **ganar**
earthquake   el **terremoto**
east   el **este,** el **oriente**
easy   **fácil**
eat   **comer;** — lunch **almorzar (ue)**
economist   el, la **economista**
economy   la **economía**
educate   **educar; instruir**
educated   **educado, -a; culto, -a**
education   la **educación**
effect   el **efecto**
effect   **efectuar**
efficient   **eficaz, eficiente**
effort   el **esfuerzo**
egg   el **huevo**
eight   **ocho**
eighteen   **dieciocho**
eight hundred   **ochocientos**
eighty   **ochenta**
elderly   el **anciano,** la **anciana**
elect   **elegir (i) (elijo)**
election   la **elección**
elective   **electivo, -a**
electricity   la **electricidad**
elegant   **elegante**
eleven   **once**
eliminate   **eliminar**
embrace   el **abrazo;** to — **abrazar**
emergency   la **emergencia**
eminent   **eminente**
emission   la **emisión**
emphasis   el **énfasis**
employ   **emplear, dar empleo**
employee   el **empleado,** la **empleada**
employment   el **empleo**
empty   **vacío, -a**
enchilada   la **enchilada**
encourage   **animar**
end   el **fin,** (adj) el **final**
energy   la **energía**
engagement   el **compromiso**
engineer   el **ingeniero,** la **ingeniera**
engineering   la **ingeniería**
English   el **inglés,** la **inglesa**
enjoy   **disfrutar**
enormous, huge   **enorme**
enough   **suficiente, bastante**
enter   **entrar**
enterprise   la **empresa**
entertain   **entretener;** entertainment el **entretenimiento**
entity   la **entidad**

entrance   la **entrada**
envelope   el **sobre**
environment   el **ambiente**
epoch   la **época**
equal   **igual**
equator   el **ecuador**
equipment   el **equipo**
equivalent   **equivalente**
err   **errar, equivocarse**
error   el **error**
escape   **escapar (se)**
essay   el **ensayo**
essential   **esencial**
establish   **establecer (zc)**
estimate   **estimar**
ethnic   **étnico, -a**
Europe   **Europa**
European   **europeo, -a**
evening, night   la **noche**
event   el **evento,** el **suceso**
every   **todo, todos, -as**
everyone, everybody   **todo el mundo**
evident   **evidente**
exact   **exacto, -a;** exactly **exactamente**
exaggerate   **exagerar**
exam   el **examen**
example   el **ejemplo**
excellent   **excelente**
exchange   el **cambio,** el **intercambio;** to — **cambiar**
excite (oneself)   **emocionar (se), exitar (se)**
excursion   la **excursión**
excuse   la **excusa;** to — **excusar;** excuse me (sorry)
   perdón; — me (permission) **con permiso**
execution (firing squad)   el **fusilamiento;** la
   ejecución
exercise   el **ejercicio;** to — **hacer ejercicios**
exhaust   **acabarse**
exhibition   la **exhibición**
exist   **existir**
existence   la **existencia**
exit   la **salida**
expense   el **gasto**
expensive   **caro, -a**
experience   la **experiencia**
explain   **explicar**
explanation   la **explicación**
exploit   **explotar**
exploration   la **exploración**
explore   **explorar**
export   **exportar**
exporter   **exportador, -a**
express   **expresar**
expression   la **expresión**
expressive   **expresivo, -a**
extense   **extenso, -a**
extraordinary   **extraordinario, -a**

extreme   **extremo, -a**
eye   el **ojo**

F

face   la **cara;** to — **enfrentarse**
facilitate   **facilitar**
fact   el **hecho**
factory   la **fábrica**
faithful, loyal   **fiel, leal**
fall   la **caída;** to — **caer(se);** — asleep **dormirse**
fame   la **fama**
familiarize (oneself)   **familiarizar (se)**
family   la **familia**
famous   **famoso, -a, notable, célebre, conocido, -a**
fantastic   **fantástico, -a**
fantasy   la **fantasía**
far (from)   **lejos (de)**
farewell   la **despedida**
farewell party   **fiesta de despedida**
farm (small)   el **minifundio**
farmer   el **campesino,** el **agricultor**
fashion   la **moda**
fat   **gordo, -a; grueso, -a**
father   el **padre**
fatherland   la **patria**
favor   **favor;** to — **favorecer (zc)**
favorite   **favorito, -a**
fear   **miedo;** to — **tener miedo, temer**
feature, trait   el **rasgo**
February   **febrero**
feed   **dar de comer**
feel   **sentir (ie);** to feel fine (bad) **sentirse bien (mal)**
feel like   **tener ganas de**
fellowship   la **compadrería**
feminine   **femenino**
fertile   **fértil**
fever   la **fiebre**
few   **pocos**
fifteen   **quince**
fifty   **cincuenta**
figure   la **figura**
file   el **archivo**
file to   **archivar**
fill (out, up)   **llenar**
find   **hallar, encontrar (ue)**
fine, penalty   **la multa;** to — **multar**
fine arts   **bellas artes**
finger   el **dedo**
finish   **terminar; acabar**
fire   el **fuego**
fireplace   el **hogar**
firm (business)   la **firma,** la **empresa**
first   **primero, -a**
fish   el **pescado;** to — **pescar**
five   **cinco**

five hundred **quinientos**
fix **arreglar, reparar**
flame la **llama**
flatterer **lisonjero, -a**
flavor el **sabor**
flee **huir (huyo)**
flight el **vuelo**
flirt **piropear**
floor el **piso**, el **suelo**
flow el **flujo**
flower la **flor**
flu la **gripe**
fly **volar (ue)**
follow **seguir (i);** following **siguiente**
food el **alimento**, la **comida**
foot el **pie**
for **para** (destination, purpose, deadline) **por** (for the sake of, by, in exchange for)
force la **fuerza;** to — **forzar (ue)**
forehead la **frente**
foreign **extranjero, -a**
forget **olvidar**
forgive **perdonar**
fork el **tenedor**
form la **forma;** to — **formar**
formal **formal**
former **antiguo, -a**
formidable **formidable**
fortunate **afortunado, -a**
fortune la **fortuna**
forty **cuarenta**
foster **fomentar**
fountain la **fuente**
four **cuatro**
fourteen **catorce**
fourth **cuarto**
France **Francia**
free **libre**
freedom, liberty la **libertad**
freeze, frost la **helada**
French (language) el **francés**
frequency la **frecuencia**
frequently **frecuentemente**
fresh **fresco, -a**
Friday el **viernes;** on —(s) el **(los) viernes**
friend el **amigo**, la **amiga**
friendly **amable**
friendship la **amistad**
from **de, desde**
front **frente**
fruit la **fruta**
fry, fried **freír (i); frito, -a**
frying pan la **sartén**
fulfill **cumplir**
full (literary) **pleno; lleno, -a**

furniture los **muebles**
future el **futuro**

G

game, set el **juego**
garage el **garage**
garbage la **basura**
garden el **jardín**
garlic el **ajo**
gas station la **gasolinera**
general el **general**
generation la **generación**
generous **generoso, -a**
genteel **gentil**
gentleman el **caballero**
geographic **geográfico, -a**
geography **geografía**
German **alemán, -a;** Germany **Alemania**
get **conseguir (i), obtener;** — married **casarse;** — on, mount **montar;** — tired **cansiarse;** — up **levantarse;** — used to **acostumbrarse**
giant el, la **gigante**
gift el **regalo**
girl la **niña**, la **muchacha**, la **chica**
girlfriend la **novia** (sweetheart), la **amiga** (friend)
give **dar (doy), regalar** (gifts)
glad **contento, -a;** to be — **alegrarse, estar contento**
glad to meet you **mucho gusto**
glass (drinking) el **vaso**
glove el **guante**
go **ir;** — away **irse, marcharse;** — to bed **acostarse (ue);** — up **subir;** — toward **dirigirse a**
God **Dios;** my —! **¡Dios mío!**
gold el **oro**
Golden Age **Siglo de Oro**
good **bueno, -a;** — afternoon **buenas tardes;** — bye **adiós;** — evening **buenas noches;** — looking **guapo, -a** — morning **buenos días;** — night **buenas noches**
govern **governar (ie)**
government el **gobierno**
governor el **gobernador**, la **gobernadora**
grade, note la **nota**
graduate **graduarse (me gradúo)**
graduation la **graduación**
grain el **grano**
grammar la **gramática**
grandfather el **abuelo**
grandmother la **abuela**
grandparents los **abuelos**
grape la **uva**
grapefruit la **toronja**
graphic **gráfico, -a**
grass la **hierba**
grateful **agradecido, -a;** to be — **agradecer (zc)**
grave **grave**

great **estupendo, -a; gran(de)**
green **verde**
greet; to salute **saludar**
grilled meat **carne asada;** la **parrillada (Argentina)**
groceries los **comestibles**
groom el **novio**
grouchy **cascarrabias**
group el **grupo**
guard, to keep — **guardar**
guava (tropical fruit) la **guayaba**
guerrilla la **guerrilla**
guess **adivinar**
guest el **huésped**
guide el, la **guía;** to — **guiar**
guilt la **culpa**
guitar la **guitarra**
gymnasium el **gimnasio**

H

hair el **pelo**
half **medio, -a**
ham el **jamón**
hand la **mano;** to shake hands **dar la mano**
handbag la **bolsa**
hand made **hecho a mano**
handsome **guapo, -a**
happen **pasar; suceder; ocurrir**
happiness la **felicidad; la alegría**
happy **contento, -a, alegre;** to be — **alegrarse**
hard **duro, -a; defícil**
hardly **apenas**
harm **daño;** to — **dañar**
harvest la **cosecha;** to — **cosechar**
hat el **sombrero**
hate **odiar**
hatred el **odio**
have **tener** (possession); **haber** (auxiliary); to — a birth-
    day **cumplir años;** to — a good time **divertirse (i)**
he **él**
head la **cabeza**
headache (el) **dolor de cabeza**
health la **salud**
hear **oír**
heat el **calor**
heat **calentar (ie)**
heaven el **cielo**
heavy **pesado, -a**
helicopter el **helicoptero**
Hello! **¡Hola!; Aló!**
help **ayudar**
hemisphere el **hemisferio**
her(s) *dir. obj.* **la;** *ind. obj.* **le;** *obj. of prep.* **ella;** *poss. adj.*
    su(s); de ella
here **aquí; acá**
hero el **heroe**

heroine la **heroína**
hers **suyo, -a, -os, -as; de ella**
herself **se**
highly **sumamente**
highway la **carretera**
him *dir. obj.* **lo;** *ind. obj.* **le;** *obj. of prep.* **él**
himself **se**
his **su, sus; suyo, -a, -os, -as**
Hispanic **hispánico, -a**
historical **histórico, -a**
history la **historia**
holiday **día de fiesta**
home el **hogar;** at — **en casa**
homework; chore la **tarea**
hope la **esperanza;** to — **esperar**
horror el **horror**
horse el **caballo**
hospital el **hospital**
hot **caliente;** to be — **tener calor** (persons); to be —
    hace calor (weather)
hotel el **hotel**
hour la **hora**
house la **casa**
housewife el **ama de casa (f)**
housing la **vivienda**
How many? **¿Cuántos? ¿Cuántas?**
How much? **¿Cuánto? ¿Cuánta?**
How? **¿Cómo? ¿Qué**
hug **abrazo**
human **humano, -a;** — being **ser humano**
humanities **filosofía y letras**
humanity la **humanidad**
humid **húmedo, -a**
humor **humor**
hundred **cien(to)**
hunger el **hambre** *(f)*
hungry; to be — **tener hambre**
hurricane el **ciclón, el huracán**
hurry **prisa;** to be in a — **tener prisa**
hurry up **darse prisa**
hurt **lástimar;** to ache **tener dolor de —**
husband el **marido, el esposo**
hut **casucha**

J

jacket la **chaqueta**
Jai-Alai **jai-alai** (Basque game similar to handball)
January **enero**
Japan el **Japón;** Japanese **japonés, -a**
job el **trabajo;** el **puesto**
journalism el **periodismo**
jovial **jovial**
joy la **alegría**
judge el **juez**
juice el **jugo**

July **julio**
June **junio**
jungle la **selva**
just **justo, -a**
justice la **justicia**

K

key la **llave**
kilo, kilogram el **kilo,** el **kilogramo**
kilometer el **kilómetro**
kindergarten el **kindergarten,** el **jardín de infancia**
king, monarch el **rey,** el **monarca**
kiss el **beso;** to — **besar**
kitchen la **cocina**
knife el **cuchillo**
know (facts) **saber;** to — how **saber** + *inf;* to be acquainted with **conocer (zc)**
knowledge el **conocimiento**

L

laboratory el **laboratorio**
lack **falta;** to — **hacer falta**
lake el **lago**
lamp la **lámpara**
land la **tierra**
language la **lengua,** el **idioma**
large, big **grande**
last **último, -a;** to — **durar**
last night **anoche;** — week la **semana pasada**
late **tarde**
later **más tarde;** see you — **hasta luego**
latifundio el **latifundio**
Latin **latino, -a;** — American **latinoamericano, -a**
laugh (at) **reírse (de);** to — **reír (i)**
law la **ley,** las **leyes;** study of law el **derecho**
lawn el **césped**
lawyer el **abogado,** la **abogada**
lazy **perezoso, -a**
leader el **líder**
leaf la **hoja**
learn **aprender**
learned **culto, -a, educado, -a**
leave **salir;** — behind **dejar**
left la **izquierda**
leg la **pierna** (human); la **pata** (animal, furniture)
legitimate **legítimo, -a**
lemonade la **limonada**
lend **prestar**
less **menos;** — than **menos de**
lesson la **lección**
let's go! **¡vamos!**
letter la **carta** (correspondence); la **letra** (alphabet)
lettuce la **lechuga**
level el **nivel**
liberate **liberar**

library la **biblioteca**
life la **vida**
lift, to raise **levantar**
light (color) **claro, -a;** light (weight) **ligero, -a**
light; lights la **luz;** las **luces**
like **como**
like, to please **gustar**
likewise **igualmente**
limit el **límite;** to — **limitar**
line la **línea;** la **cola**
lined in a row **enfilado, -a**
listen **escuchar; oír**
literary **literario, -a**
literature la **literatura**
little (amount) **poco, -a**
live **vivir**
lively **animado, -a; alegre**
livestock el **ganado;** — industry la **ganadería**
living room la **sala**
llama la **llama**
local **local**
long **largo, -a**
longed for **suspirado, -a**
look la **mirada;** look (at) **mirar;** — for **buscar;** — like (resemble) **paracerse (zc)**
look carefully for **fijarse**
lose **perder (ie)**
lost **perdido, -a**
lottery la **lotería;** — ticket el **billete de lotería**
love el **amor,** el **cariño;** to — **amar; querer (ie)**
lower **bajar, reducir (zc)**
loyal **leal, fiel**
luck la **suerte**
lucky **dichoso;** to be — **tener suerte**
luggage el **equipaje**
lunch el **almuerzo;** to eat — **almorzar (ue)**

M

machinery la **maquinaria**
made **hecho**
magazine la **revista**
magic la **magia**
magnetic la **cinta magnética**
magnetism el **magnetismo**
mailman el **cartero**
main **principal**
maintain **mantener**
major (in college) la **especialización (universitaria)**
majority la **mayoría**
make **hacer**
male el **varón** (human); **macho** (animal); used also to denote exaggerated masculinity
man el **hombre**
manager el, la **gerente;** el **administrador,** la **administradora**

manner   la **manera**
many   **muchos, muchas;** so — **tantos, -as**
map   el **mapa**
March   **marzo**
maritime   **marítimo, -a**
mark   **marcar**
market   el **mercado**
marmalade   la **mermelada**
married   **casado, -a**
marry (to)   **casarse (con)**
marvelous   **maravilloso, -a**
Marxist   **marxista**
masculine   **masculino, -a**
mathematics   las **matemáticas**
matter (subject)   el **asunto;** to — **importar**
May   **mayo**
maya, mayan   **maya**
me   *dir and ind obj* **me;** *after prep* **mí**
mean   **significar; querer decir**
means   los **medios**
meat   la **carne**
mechanic   el **mecánico**
medieval   **medieval**
meet   **encontrarse (ue), reunirse;** to — **someone** (first time)   **conocer a alguien**
medicine   la **medicina**
mediocre   **mediocre**
member   el **miembro**
memory   la **memoria;** to learn by — **aprender de memoria**
mention   **mencionar**
menu   el **menú,** la **lista**
merchandise   la **mercancía**
merchant   el **comerciante**
message   el **recado,** el **mensaje**
mestizo   **mestizo, -a**
metal   el **metal**
meter   el **metro**
method   el **método**
Mexican   el **mexicano,** la **mexicana**
microwaves   el **horno de micro-ondas**
middle   **medio, -a;** — class   la **clase media**
midnight   la **medianoche**
military   **militar**
milk   la **leche**
million   **millón**
minimum   **mínimo, -a**
mine   la **mina;** to — **minar**
mine   **mío, -a, -os, -as**
mineral   el **mineral**
minority   la **minoría**
minute   el **minuto**
mirror   el **espejo**
miss (emotionally)   **echar de menos, extrañar**
Miss   **señorita**
mistaken; to be —   **equivocarse**

Mister   **señor**
Mrs.   **señora**
mix   **mezclar**
mixed   **mixto, -a**
model   el **modelo**
modern   **moderno, -a**
modernism   el **modernismo**
modify   **modificar**
moment   el **momento**
monarchy   la **monarquía**
Monday   **lunes;** on Monday(s)   el (**los**) **lunes**
money   el **dinero**
monk   el **monje**
month   el **mes**
monument   el **monumento**
moon   la **luna**
Moors   los **moros**
more   **más;** — than + number;   **más de;** — than   **más que**
morning   la **mañana;** in the —   **por la mañana**
mother   la **madre**
motion picture   la **película**
motivate   **motivar**
motive   el **motivo**
motor   el **motor**
mountain   la **montaña**
mouth   la **boca**
move   **mover (ue);** to — away (residence)   **mudarse**
movement   el **movimiento**
movie   la **película;** — theatre   el **cine**
much   **mucho, -a**
multitude   la **multitud**
mural   el **mural;** muralist   el, la **muralista**
museum   el **museo**
music   la **música;** musical   **musical;** musicality   la **musicalidad;** musician   el, la **músico**
mutual   **mutuo, -a**
my   **mi, mis**

N
name   el **nombre**
nap   la **siesta**
napkin   la **servilleta**
narrate   **relatar, narrar, contar (ue)**
narrative   la **narrativa**
narrow   **estrecho, -a, angosto, -a**
nation   la **nación,** el **país**
national   **nacional**
natural   **natural;** naturally   **naturalmente**
nature   la **naturaleza**
near   **cerca (de)**
necessary   **necesario, -a**
necessity   la **necesidad**
need   **necesitar**
negation   la **negación**

negative **negativo, -a**
neighbor **el vecino, la vecina**
neither **tampoco;** — nor **ni...ni**
nephew **el sobrino**
nepotism **el nepotismo**
nervous **nervioso, -a**
never **nunca, jamás**
nevertheless **sin embargo**
new **nuevo, -a**
news **las noticias**
newscast **el noticiero**
newspaper **el periódico**
New Year **el Año Nuevo**
next to **junto a; al lado de**
niece **la sobrina**
nine **nueve**
nine hundred **novecientos**
nineteen **diecinueve**
ninety **noventa**
ninth **noveno, -a**
no, not **no;** *adj* **ningún, ninguno**
nobody, no one **nadie**
noise **el ruido;** noisy **ruidoso, -a**
none **ninguno**
noon **el mediodía**
normal **normal**
north **el norte**
North America **América del Norte;** North American
    norteamericano, -a
Northeast **noreste;** Northwest **noroeste**
nose **la nariz**
note (to) **anotar, apuntar;** notes **los apuntes**
notebook **el cuaderno**
nothing **nada**
notice **notar, fijarse en**
noun **sustantivo**
novel **la novela**
novelist **novelista**
November **noviembre**
now **ahora**
nowadays **hoy día**
nuclear **nuclear**
number **el número**
numerous **numeroso, -a**
nun **la monja**
nurse **la enfermera, el enfermero**
nutrition **la nutrición**

O

obey **obedecer (zc)**
object **el objeto**
obligate **obligar**
observe **observar**
obstacle **el obstáculo**

obtain **obtener, conseguir (i)**
occasion **la ocasión;** (time) **vez**
occupation, trade **el oficio**
occupied **ocupado, -a**
occur **ocurrir**
ocean **el océano**
October **octubre**
of **de**
of course **por supuesto; como no**
offer **ofrecer (zc)**
office **la oficina**
official **oficial**
oil **el aceite**
OK **está bien**
old **viejo, -a;** (former) **antiguo, -a**
older **mayor;** oldest **el, la mayor**
olive oil **el aceite de oliva**
omelet **la tortilla**
on **sobre, en**
on account of **a causa de; por**
one **uno, un, una**
one hundred **cien(to)**
onion **la cebolla**
only **solamente; sólo**
open **abierto, -a;** to — **abrir**
opera **la ópera**
operate **operar**
operation **la operación**
operator **el operador, la operadora**
opinion **la opinión**
opportunity **la oportunidad**
oppose **oponerse a**
opposition **la oposición**
optimist **optimista**
option **la opción**
or **o; u** before **o/ho**
orange **la naranja**
order **el orden:** (orderliness; succession); **pedido, la or-
    den** (for goods); **mandar** (to command)
organize **organizar**
orientation **la orientación**
origin **el origen**
original **original**
ornament **el ornamento**
other, (another) **otro, -a, -os, -as**
ought **deber**
our, ours **nuestro, -a, -os, -as**
outing **la excursión**
outside **afuera; por fuera, fuera (de)**
outstanding **notable; famoso, -a;** to be — **destacarse**
owner **el dueño, la dueña; propietario, -a**

P

package **el paquete**
paid **pagado, -a**

painter el **pintor,** la **pintora;** — of murals el, la **muralista**
painting; paint la **pintura**
palace el **palacio**
pale **pálido, -a**
panorama el **panorama**
pants los **pantalones**
papaya (fruit) la **papaya**
paper el **papel**
paragraph el **párrafo**
paralize **paralizar**
parenthesis el (los) **paréntesis**
parents los **padres**
park el **parque;** to — (a car) **estacionar**
parrot el **loro**
part la **parte**
participate **participar**
particular **particular**
party la **fiesta;** political — el **partido político**
pass **rebasar** (a car); **aprobar (ue)** (a subject); **pasar**
passenger el **pasajero,** la **pasajera**
passport el **pasaporte**
past **pasado, -a**
paternalism el **paternalismo**
patience la **paciencia**
patio el **patio**
patriotic **patriótico, -a**
pay **pagar;** — attention **prestar atención**
peace la **paz**
peach el **melocotón;** el **durazno (México)**
pear la **pera**
peas los **guisantes**
peasant el **campesino,** la **campesina**
peel **pelar**
pen el **bolígrafo**
pencil el **lápiz**
peninsula la **península**
people la **gente**
pepper la **pimienta**
percent **por ciento;** percentage **porcentaje**
perfume el **perfume**
perhaps **tal vez; quizás**
permission el **permiso**
permit el **permiso;** to — **permitir**
person la **persona**
personalism el **personalismo**
personnel el **personal**
perspective la **perspectiva**
persuade **persuadir**
persuasion la **persuación**
petroleum el **petróleo**
pharmaceutical **farmacéutico, -a**
pharmacist el, la **farmacista**
pharmacy la **farmacia**
phenomenon el **fenómeno;** phenomenal **fenomenal**
philosophy la **filosofía;** philosopher el **filósofo**

phone el **teléfono;** to — **llamar por teléfono;** phonebook la **guía de teléfonos**
photo(graph) la **foto(grafía)**
phrase la **frase**
physical **físico, -a**
physician el **médico**
physics la **física**
pianist el, la **pianista**
pick up **recoger (j)**
picture la **película (movie);** la **foto**
pilot el **piloto**
piñata la **piñata**
pine tree el **pino**
pineapple la **piña**
pink **rosado, -a;** color **rosa**
pity **lástima;** what a — **¡qué lástima!**
place el **lugar;** to — **poner, colocar**
plain el **llano;** los **llanos** (flat lands)
plan el **plan;** to — **planear, pensar (ie)** + *inf*
plant la **planta**
plate el **plato**
play **jugar (ue)** (games); **tocar** (an instrument)
player el **jugador,** la **jugadora**
pleasant (person) **simpático, -a**
please **por favor;** to — **gustar, complacer**
pleasure el **placer;** el **gusto**
plumber el **plomero**
plural **plural**
poached **escalfado, -a**
poem el **poema**
poet el **poeta,** la **poetisa**
poetry la **poesía**
point el **punto;** — of view **punto de vista**
police la **policía** (police force); policeman el **policía,** policewoman la **mujer policía**
politics la **política;** politician el **político**
pollutant el **contaminador**
pollute **contaminar;** polluted **contaminado, -a**
pollution la **contaminación**
poor **pobre**
Pope el **Papa**
popular **popular**
population la **población**
pork la **carne de cerdo**
portal el **portal**
position la **posición**
potato la **papa,** la **patata**
pottery la **alfarería**
pound la **libra**
pour **echar, vester (ie)**
poverty la **pobreza**
power el **poder**
practice **practicar**
prayer la **oración**
precise **preciso, -a**
predicament el **apuro**

predominate **predominar**
prefer **preferir (ie)**
preoccupied **preocupado, -a**
prepare (oneself) **preparar(se)**
present (day) **actual**
present el **regalo;** to — **presentar**
presentation la **presentación**
preserve **preservar; conservar**
president el, la **presidente**
prestigious **prestigioso, -a**
preterite el **pretérito**
pretty, lovely **bonito, -a; lindo, -a**
previous **anterior, previo, -a**
price el **precio**
pride el **orgullo**
priest el **cura,** el **sacerdote**
principal el **director,** la **directora** (of a school); **principal** (adj)
priority la **prioridad**
private **privado, -a, particular**
problem el **problema**
procession la **procesión**
prodigious **prodigioso, -a**
produce **producir (zc)**
product el **producto**
production la **producción**
profession la **profesión**
professional **profesional**
professor el **profesor,** la **profesora**
program el **programa**
progress el **progreso;** to — **progresar**
proliferation la **proliferación**
prominent **prominente**
promise la **promesa;** to — **prometer**
promote **ascender (ie)**
pronoun el **pronombre**
pronounce **pronunciar**
pronunciation la **pronunciación**
protect **proteger (j)**
protection la **protección**
protocol el **protocolo**
provided that **con tal que**
prowess la **proeza**
public **público, -a**
publicity la **propaganda comercial**
pudding el **pudín**
Puerto Rican **puertorriqueño, -a**
pull out **arrancar**
punch (drink) el **ponche**
punctual **puntual**
purchase **comprar;** purchases las **compras**
purchasing agent el **agente de compras**
pure **puro, -a**
put **poner;** — in **meter;** — on (clothes) **ponerse;** — up with **soportar**

Q

quality la **calidad**
quarter **cuarto;** — after **y cuarto;** — till **menos cuarto**
queen la **reina**
question la **pregunta;** to — **preguntar, interrogar**
queue (line) la **cola**
quiet **callado, -a;** to be — **callarse**
quite a bit **bastante**

R

race la **raza;** la **carrera** (competition)
radical **radical**
radio el, la **radio**
railroad el **ferrocarril**
rain la **lluvia;** to — **llover (ue);** it rains **llueve;** it's raining **está lloviendo**
raincoat el **impermeable**
rare **raro, -a**
rather (than) **más bien (que)**
ration la **ración;** to — **racionar**
reach **alcanzar**
read **leer**
reader el **lector**
reading la **lectura**
ready **listo, -a**
real **real, verdadero, -a**
realize **darse cuenta de**
realism el **realismo**
realist; realistic **realista**
reality la **realidad**
reason la **razón**
reasonable **razonable**
receipt el **recibo**
receive **recibir**
recent **reciente**
recently **recientemente**
recipe la **receta**
recommend **recomendar**
reconcile **reconciliar**
reconstruction la **reconstrucción**
record el **disco;** to — **grabar**
record player el **tocadiscos**
recorder la **grabadora**
recreation el **recreo**
rectangle el **rectángulo**
red **rojo, -a**
reduce **reducir (zc)**
refer **referir (ie);** to refer to **referirse a**
refined; fine **refinado, -a; fino, -a**
reform la **reforma;** to — **reformar**
region la **región**
register **matricularse** (school); **registrarse** (hotel)
regular **regular**
rehearsal el **ensayo;** rehearse **ensayar**

relation **relación**

relative el **pariente** (family); **relativo, -a**

religion la **religión**; religious **religioso, -a**

remedy el **remedio**; to — **remediar**

remember **recordar (ue)**

remote **remoto, -a**

rent el **alquiler**; to — **alquilar**

repair **reparar; arreglar**

repeat **repetir (i)**

report el **informe**

represent **representar**

representation la **representación**

representative el, la **representante**

repression la **represión**

require **requerir (ie)**; required course **curso obligatorio**

requirement el **requisito**

reservation la **reserva**, la **reservación**

reserved **reservado, -a**

residence la **residencia**

resource el **recurso**

respect el **respeto**; to — **respetar**

respectful **respetuoso**

respective **respectivo, -a**

responsible **responsable**

rest el **resto** (remainder); el **descanso**; to — **descansar**

restaurant el **restaurante**; el **café**

restore **restaurar**

result el **resultado**; to — **resultar**

return **regresar, volver (ue)**; **devolver (ue)** (an article)

review el **repaso**; to — **repasar**

revolution la **revolución**

rhythm el **ritmo**

ribbon la **cinta**

rice el **arroz**

rich **rico, -a**

riddle la **adivinanza**

ride **ir en coche** (car); — on horseback **montar a caballo** — a bicycle **montar en bicicleta**

right la **derecha** (direction); el **derecho** (legal); to be — **tener razón**

ring el **anillo**

risk el **riesgo**; to — **arriesgar**

ritual **ritual**

rival el, la **rival**

river el **río**

road el **camino**

roasted **asado, -a**

roll, list la **lista**

room el **cuarto**; la **habitación**

root la **raíz**

rose, rose color **rosa; rosado, color rosado**

round **redondo, -a**

routine la **rutina**

row la **fila**

royal **real**

ruin la **ruina**; to — **arruinar**

run through **recorrer**

S

sad **triste**

saffron (spice) el **azafrán**

said **dicho**

saint **santo, san, santa**; —'s day el **día del santo**

salad la **ensalada**

salary el **sueldo**, el **salario**

sale la **venta**

sales agent el **vendedor**, el **agente de ventas**

sales manager **gerente de ventas**

sales clerk el, la **dependiente**

sales person el **vendedor**, la **vendedora**

salt la **sal**; salty **salado, -a**

same **mismo, -a**

sand la **arena**

sandals las **sandalias**

sandwich el **sándwich**

sarcastic **sarcástico, -a**

sardine la **sardina**

Saturday **sábado**; on Saturday(s) el (los) **sábado(s)**

sausage la **salchicha**; el **chorizo**

save **ahorrar** (money); **salvar** (a life)

say **decir (i)**

scarce **escaso, -a**

scene la **escena**

schedule el **horario**

school la **escuela**; el **colegio**

science la **ciencia**

scissors las **tijeras**

scotch tape la **cinta de celofán**

scramble **batir, revolver (ue)**

scrambled **revuelto, -a**

scream **gritar**, el **grito**

sea el **mar**

season la **temporada**; (theater, sports . . .) la **estación** (weather)

seat el **asiento**

second **segundo, -a**

secondary **secundario, -a**; — school **escuela secundaria**

secretary el **secretario**, la **secretaria**

section la **sección**

see **ver**; — you later **hasta luego**; — you soon **hasta pronto**; — you tomorrow **hasta mañana**

seem **parecer (zc)**

seen **visto**

sell **vender**

semester el **semestre**

seminar el **seminario**

send **mandar, enviar (envío)**

sensibility la **sensibilidad**

sentence   la **claúsula**, la **frase**
sentimental   **sentimental**
separate   **separar**
separation   la **separación**
September   **septiembre**
series   la **serie**
serious   **serio, -a;** seriously   **en serio**
serve   **servir (i)**
service   el **servicio**
set the table   **poner la mesa**
seven   **siete;** seven hundred   **setecientos**
seventeen   **diecisiete**
seventh   **séptimo, -a**
seventy   **setenta**
several   **varios, -a**
severe   **severo**
sex   el **sexo**
shade, shadow   la **sombra**
share   **compartir**
shave   **afeitarse**
shawl   el **sarape**, el **chal**
she   **ella**
sheet   la **hoja de papel** (paper); bed —   la **sábana**
shellfish   los **mariscos**
ship   el **barco;** to —   **enviar (envío)**
shirt   la **camisa**
shoe   el **zapato;** — store, repair   la **zapatería**
shoemaker   el **zapatero**
shop   **tienda;** to —   **hacer compras**
shopping (to go)   **ir de compras**
shopping center   el **centro comercial**
short   **bajo, -a** (stature); **corto, -a** (length)
short story, tale   el **cuento;** — story writer   el, la, **cuentista**
should, ought   **deber**
shout   **gritar**
show   **mostrar (ue)**
shrimp   el **camarón**
sick   **enfermo, -a**
side   el **lado**
sidewalk   la **acera**
signal   la **señal**
signature   la **firma**
silence   el **silencio**
silver   la **plata;** Silver Wedding Anniversary   las **bodas de plata**
similar   **similar; parecido, -a**
similarity   la **semejanza**
simple   **sencillo, -a**
since   **desde, como**
sincere   **sincero, -a**
sing   **cantar**
singer   **cantante**
single   **soltero, -a**
sister   la **hermana**
sit down   **sentarse (ie)**

situated   **situado, -a**
situation   la **situación**
six   **seis;** six hundred   **seiscientos**
sixteen   **dieciséis**
sixth   **sexto, -a**
sixty   **sesenta**
size   la **talla; tamaño** el **número**
skate   **patinar**
skinny   **flaco, -a, delgado, -a**
skirt   la **falda**
sky   el **cielo**
skyscraper   el **rascacielos**
slave   el **esclavo**, la **esclava**
sleep   **dormir (ue);** to fall asleep   **dormirse**
sleepy, to be —   **tener sueño**
slice   **rebanada**
small   **pequeño**
smell, odor   el **olor;** to —   **oler (ue)**
snack   la **merienda**
snow   la **nieve;** to —   **nevar (ie);** snowfall   la **nevada**
so   **tan** (+ adj or adv); **así** (thus); — that   **con tal que**
soap   el **jabón**
soap opera   la **telenovela**
soccer   el **fútbol**
sociable   **sociable**
social   **social**
social gathering   la **tertulia**
society   la **sociedad**
socks   los **calcetines**
soft   **suave**
soft boiled   **tibio**
soldier   el **soldado**
solution   la **solución**
solve   **solucionar**
some   **unos, unas; algunos, -as** (from a group)
someone   **alguien**
something   **algo**
son, child   el **hijo**
song   la **canción**
songbook   el **cancionero**
soon   **pronto;** as — as   **tan pronto como;** sooner or later   **más tarde o más temprano**
sordid   **sórdido**
sorry (to be)   **sentir (ie);** I am —   **lo siento**
soul   el **alma**
soup   la **sopa;** el **gazpacho** (cold vegetable soup)
south   el **sur**
South America   **América del Sur; Sudamérica**
souvenir   el **recuerdo**
space   el **espacio**
Spain   **España**
Spaniard   el **español**
Spanish   (language) el **español**
speak   **hablar**
special   **especial**
specific   **específico, -a**

specifically   **específicamente**
speed   la **velocidad**
spend (time)   **pasar (tiempo);** to — (money)   **gastar (dinero)**
spices   los **condimentos,** las **especias**
spicy   **picante**
spontaneous   **espontáneo, -a**
spoon   la **cuchara**
sport   el **deporte**
spring   la **primavera**
square   la **plaza**
square   **cuadrado; cuadra** (block)
stability   la **estabilidad**
stair   la **escalera**
stand up   **pararse, levantarse**
state   el **estado;** to — **declarar**
station   la **estación;** train — la **estación de trenes**
stay   **quedarse**
steak   el **bisté;** el **biftec**
step   el **paso**
stereo   el **estéreo**
still   **todavía**
stimulate   **estimular**
stock market   la **bolsa**
stockings   las **medias**
stomach   el **estómago**
stop   **parar (se);** (bus, taxi)   **parada;** (Halt!)   **¡Alto!**
store   la **tienda;** el **almacén** (dept. store)
storm   la **tormenta**
strange   **raro, -a; extraño, -a**
strawberry   la **fresa**
street   la **calle**
strict   **estricto, -a**
strike   la **huelga**
strong   **fuerte**
structure   la **estructura**
struggle   la **lucha;** to — **luchar**
student   el, la **estudiante;** student
study   el **estudio;** to — (for)   **estudiar (para)**
style   el **estilo**
subject (academic)   la **materia;** el **sujeto**
subjunctive   el **subjuntivo**
substantive   **sustantivo**
suburbs   las **afueras**
subway   el **metro**
success   el **éxito**
such   **tal;** — as   **tal como**
sufficient   **suficiente; bastante**
sugar   el **azúcar**
suggest   **sugerir (ie)**
suggestion   la **sugerencia**
suit   el **traje**
suitcase   la **maleta**
summarize   **resumir**
summary   el **resumen**
summer   el **verano**

sun   el **sol;** it is sunny   **hace sol**
Sunday   **domingo;** on — el **domingo**
superior   **superior**
supermarket   el **supermercado**
supervisor   el **supervisor,** la **supervisora**
supper   la **cena**
support   **apoyar** (morally);   **mantener** (financially)
suppose   **suponer**
sure   **seguro, -a**
surname   el **apellido**
surprise   **sorprender;** la **sorpresa**
surround   **rodear**
survey   la **encuesta**
suspect   **sospechar**
suspicious   **sospechoso, -a**
sweater   el **suéter**
sweet   **dulce**
sweetheart   **novio, -a**
swim   **nadar;** swimming   la **natación**
sword   la **espada**
syllable   la **sílaba**
symbol   el **símbolo**
symbolize   **simbolizar**
synonymous   **sinónimo**
system   el **sistema**

T

table   la **mesa**
taco   el **taco**
take   **tomar;** to — away   **quitar;** to — off (clothes)   **quitarse;** — out   **sacar;** to — a trip   **hacer un viaje;** — ride (walk)   **dar un paseo;** — care of   **cuidar;** — a person somewhere   **llevar**
talc   el **talco**
tall   **alto, -a**
taste   el **sabor;** to — **probar (ue);** to — like   **saber a**
tasty   **sabroso, -a; delicioso, -a**
taxes   los **impuestos**
tea   el **té**
teach   **enseñar**
teacher   el **maestro,** la **maestra**
team   el **equipo**
tea spoon   la **cucharita**
technician   el **técnico**
technique   la **técnica**
telephone   el **teléfono;** to — **llamar por teléfono**
television   la **televisión;** TV set   **el televisor**
tell   **decir (i), contar (ue)**
ten   **diez**
tennis   el **tenis**
tenth   **décimo, -a**
territory   el **territorio**
terrorist   el, la **terrorista**
test   el **examen**
thanks   **gracias;** to thank   **dar las gracias**

that **ese, esa** (near you); **aquel, aquella** (over there); neuter *pron* **eso, equello;** — one **ése, aquél**

the **el, la, los, las**

theatre el **teatro**

their **su, sus;** theirs **suyo, -a, -os, -as**

them *dir obj* **los, las;** *ind obj* **les;** *obj of prep* **ellos, ellas**

theme el **tema**

then **entonces; pues, luego**

there **allá, allí;** — is, — are **hay;** — was, — were **había**

therefore **por eso; por lo tanto**

these **estos, estas;** *pron* **éstos, éstas**

they **ellos, ellas**

thin **delgado, -a; flaco, -a** (familiar)

think **pensar (ie);** to think about **pensar en**

third **tercer (o), -a**

thirst la **sed**

thirsty (to be) (very) — **tener (mucha) sed**

thirteen **trece**

thirty **treinta**

this **este, esta;** *pron* **éste, ésta;** *neuter pron* **esto;** —way **así**

those **esos, esas; aquellos, aquellas;** *pron* **ésos, ésas; aquellos, aquellas**

though **aunque**

thought el **pensamiento**

thousand **mil**

three **tres;** — hundred **trescientos**

throat la **garganta**

Thursday **jueves;** on — el **jueves**

thus **así**

ticket el **boleto,** el **billete,** la **entrada**

tie la **corbata**

tight **estrecho**

time el **tiempo,** la **hora;** at times **a veces, algunas veces**

timid **tímido, -a**

tire la **llanta**

tired **cansado, -a;** to become — **cansarse**

title el **título**

to, at **a**

toast (bread) **pan tostado**

toaster la **tostadora**

tobacco el **tabaco**

today **hoy**

toe el **dedo del pie**

together **juntos, juntas**

tomato el **tomate**

tomb la **tumba**

tomorrow **mañana;** — morning (afternoon, evening) **mañana por la mañana, (tarde, noche)**

tongue la **lengua;** el **idioma**

tongue-twister el **trabalenguas**

tonight **esta noche**

too **también;** — much **demasiado, -a;** — many **demasiados, -as**

tooth el **diente**

tornado, twister el **tornado;** el **remolino**

tourism el **turismo**

tourist el, la **turista**

toward **hacia**

towel la **toalla**

town el **pueblo**

trade el **comercio,** el **intercambio;** to — **comerciar**

tradition la **tradición**

traditionally **tradicionalmente**

traffic el **tránsito,** el **tráfico,** — circle la **glorieta**

traffic light el **semáforo**

train el **tren;** to — **entrenar**

training el **entrenamiento**

tranquil **tranquilo, -a**

translate **traducir (zc)**

transportation el **transporte**

trash la **basura**

travel **viajar**

travel agency la **agencia de turismo**

treatment el **tratamiento**

tree el **árbol**

tremendous **tremendo, -a**

triangle el **triángulo**

tribe la **tribu**

tribute el **tributo**

trip el **viaje**

tropical **tropical**

trousers los **pantalones**

truck el **camión**

true **verdadero, -a; cierto, -a**

trust **confianza,** to — (in) **confiar (en)**

try (to) **tratar (de);** — on **probarse (ue)**

T-shirt la **camiseta**

Tuesday **martes;** on Tuesday(s) el (los) **martes**

tuna el **atún**

turn off/out **apagar**

turn on **encender (ie)**

turn el **turno;** to — **doblar** (a corner)

twelve **doce**

twenty **veinte**

twist **torcer (ue) (tuerzo)**

two **dos;** two hundred **doscientos**

type la **clase**

typical **típico**

tyrant el **tirano**

U

ugly **feo, -a**

umbrella el **paraguas**

uncle el **tío;** uncle and aunt los **tíos**

undecided **indeciso**

under **debajo (de)**

underlined **subrayado**

undershirt la **camiseta**

understand **comprender, entender (ie)**
understanding la **comprensión**, el **entendimiento**
unemployment el **desempleo**
unevenness el **desnivel;** la **desigualdad**
uniform el **uniforme**
union el **sindicato** (labor union); la **unión**
unite **unir**
united **unido, -a**
United States **Estados Unidos;** U.S. **E.E.U.U.**
universal **universal**
university la **universidad**
unknown **desconocido**
until **hasta; hasta que**
unworthy **indigno**
upon **en, sobre;** — (doing something) **al** (+ inf); — ar-
    riving **al llegar**
uproot **arrancar**
upstairs **arriba**
urban **urbano, -a**
urgency la **urgencia**
urgent **urgente**
us **nos;** obj of prep **nosotros, nosotras**
use el **uso;** to — **usar**
used **usado, -a**
useful **útil**
useless **inútil**
usual **usual**
utilize **utilizar**

V

vacation las **vacaciones;** to be on — **estar de vaca-
    ciones**
valley el **valle**
variation la **variación**
variety la **variedad**
vegetable(s) la(s) **legumbre(s)**
verb el **verbo**
very **muy;** — much **muchísimo**
very rich **riquísimo**
veterinary **veterinario, -a**
view, sight la **vista**
vigor el **vigor**
vinegar el **vinagre**
virgin la **virgen**
virtue la **virtud**
visit la **visita;** to — **visitar**
vocabulary el **vocabulario**
voice la **voz**
volume el **volumen**
voluntary **voluntario, -a**
vote el **voto;** to — **votar**
vowel la **vocal**

W

wages el **sueldo**
wait (for) **esperar;** waiting room **sala de espera**

waiter el **camarero**
waitress la **camarera**
wake up **despertar(se) (ie)**
walk **caminar; andar**
wall la **pared**
wallet la **cartera**
want **querer (ie), desear**
war la **guerra**
wash **lavar;** wash oneself **lavarse**
waste el **desperdicio;** to — **desperdiciar**
watch el **reloj**
water el **agua** (f)
way la **vía**
we **nosotros, nosotras**
weapon el **arma**
wear **llevar, usar**
weather el **tiempo**
wedding la **boda**
Wednesday **miércoles;** on —(s) el (los) **miércoles**
week la **semana;** last — la **semana pasada;** next — la
    semana próxima
weekend el **fin de semana**
weep, cry **llorar**
weigh **pesar**
weight el **peso** (also monetary unit for several countries)
welcome **bienvenido, -a;** you are — **de nada, no hay
    de que**
well **bien**
west el **oeste**
what? **¿qué?** rel pron **lo que**
wheat el **trigo**
when **cuando**
whenever **siempre que**
where **donde;** where? **¿dónde?; ¿adónde?** (direction)
whether **si**
which **cual (es);** adj **que**
while **mientras (que);** a little — **un rato**
white **blanco, -a**
who? **¿quién(es)?**
whom **aquien(es)**
whose **cuyo, -a, -os, -as;** whose? **¿de quién(es)?**
why **¿por qué?;** that is — **por eso**
wide **ancho, -a**
wife **esposa, mujer, señora**
will la **voluntad**
win **ganar**
wind el **viento**
window la **ventana**
windy (to be) **hacer viento**
wine el **vino;** red — **vino tinto;** bubbling — **espumante**
winner el **ganador**
winter el **invierno**
wisdom la **sabiduría**
wish **deseo;** to — **desear**
with **con;** — me **conmigo;** — you (fam sing) **contigo**
within **dentro de**

without   **sin; sin que**
woman   la **mujer, señora**
wood   la **madera**
wool   la **lana**
word   la **palabra**
work   la **obra** (art);   el **trabajo;** to —   **trabajar; funcionar; andar** (a machine)
worker   el **obrero,** el **trabajador**
world   el **mundo**
worry   **preocuparse (de);** worried   **preocupado, -a**
worse   **peor;** worst   el **peor**
worth, to be   **valer**
worthy   **digno, -a**
write   **escribir**
writer   el **escritor**
wrong, to be   **no tener razón; equivocarse**

Y
year   el **año**
yellow   **amarillo, -a**

yes   **sí**
yesterday   **ayer**
yet   **ya;** not —   **todavía no**
yield   **ceder**
you (fam)   **tú; vosotros, -as;** (formal) **usted, ustedes**
you   *dir obj pron* **te** *(fam),* **lo, la, os, los, las;**   *ind obj pron* **te le, os, les;**   *prep pron* **ti, vosotros, as, Ud., Uds.**
young   **joven,** *(pl)* **jóvenes;** — man   el **joven;** — woman   la **joven**
younger   **menor,** más **joven;** youngest   el, la **menor**
your   **tu(s); vuestro, -a, -os, -as; su(s)**
yours   **tuyo, -a, -os, -as; vuestro, -a, -os, -as; suyo, -a, -os, -as; de Ud.(s)**
youth   la **juventud**

Z
zero   **cero**
zone   la **zona**
zoo   **parque o jardín zoológico**

Índice

Photo credits

ii–iii, Hazel Hankin. 2–3, Hazel Hankin. 4, Peter Menzel. 9, Peter Menzel. 10 (top left), Helena Kolda; (top right), Photo Researchers Inc./ Helena Kolda; (bottom left), Helena Kolda; (bottom right), Photo Researchers Inc./Helena Kolda.
11 (top), Helena Kolda; (center), Beryl Goldberg; (bottom far left), Peter Menzel; (bottom left), Peter Menzel; (bottom center), Hazel Hankin; (bottom right), Peter Menzel; (bottom far right), Peter Menzel. 12 (top), Beryl Goldberg; (center far left), Peter Menzel; (center left), Peter Menzel; (center right), Helena Kolda; (center far right), Photo Researchers Inc./Helena Kolda; (bottom far left), Hazel Hankin; (bottom left), Peter Menzel; (bottom right), Helena Kolda; (bottom far right), Photo Researchers Inc./Helena Kolda. 15 (bottom left), Peter Menzel. 23 (bottom left), Beryl Goldberg; (top right), Photo Researchers Inc./Bernard Pierre Wolff; (bottom right), Oscar Ozete. 32, Beryl Goldberg. 33, Peter Menzel. 34 (top left), Peter Menzel; (right), AP/Wide World Photos; (bottom), AP/Wide World Photos. 35, Monkmeyer Press/Rogers. 50–1, Beryl Goldberg. 52 (top), Peter Menzel; (center), Beryl Goldberg; (bottom), Peter Menzel. 102 (left), Photo Researchers Inc./ Renee Lynn; (right), Oscar Ozete. 122, (top), Beryl Goldberg; (bottom left), Peter Menzel; (right), Beryl Goldberg. 123 (top), Peter Menzel; (bottom left), Peter Menzel; (bottom right), Image Works/Larry Mangino. 124 (left), Image Works/Alan Carey; (right), Beryl Goldberg. 129 (top left), Oscar Ozete; (top center), Beryl Goldberg; (top right), Peter Menzel; (center), Peter Menzel; (bottom left), Peter Menzel; (bottom right), Peter Menzel. 136, Photo Researchers Inc./Carl Frank. 137, Photo Researchers Inc./Carl Frank. 140–1, Peter Menzel. 143, Photo Researchers Inc./Rapho/Nat Norman. 144, Monkmeyer Press/Allyn Baum. 149, Peter Menzel. 177, Peter Menzel. 178, Beryl Goldberg. 226, Beryl Goldberg. 240 (top), Alinari/ Art Resource; (bottom), Museo del Prado. 241 (top and bottom), The Museum of Modern Art, New York. 242 (top, left), Beryl Goldberg; (top right), Courtesy of the Art Institute of Chicago; (bottom), Photo Researchers Inc./Carl Frank. 243 (top left), Metropolitan Opera Press Dept., Lincoln Center; (top right), AP/Wide World Photos; (bottom), Beryl Goldberg. 244 (left), Sygma Photo/Philippe Ledru; (right), UPI/Bettman Archive. 246, Museo del Prado.

Realia credits

29, 86, 104, 197, 228 *Diario las Américas* (Miami); 224, 225 *Excelsior* (Mexico City).